12.95

REPRESENTATIVE GOVERNMENT IN WESTERN EUROPE

REPRESENTATIVE GOVERNMENT IN WESTERN EUROPE

Michael Gallagher

Trinity College
Dublin, Ireland

Michael Laver

University College
Galway, Ireland

Peter Mair

University of Leiden
The Netherlands

McGraw-Hill, Inc.

New York   St. Louis   San Francisco   Auckland   Bogotá
Caracas   Lisbon   London   Madrid   Mexico   Milan
Montreal   New Delhi   Paris   San Juan   Singapore
Sydney   Tokyo   Toronto

REPRESENTATIVE GOVERNMENT IN WESTERN EUROPE

2 3 4 5 6 7 8 9 0 HAL HAL 9 0 9 8 7 6 5 4 3 2

ISBN 0-07-036684-5

This book was set in Galliard by Better Graphics, Inc.
The editors were Bert Lummus and Tom Holton;
the production supervisor was Annette Mayeski.
The cover was designed by Joan E. O'Connor.
The photo editor was Anne Manning.
The photo researcher was Elyse Rieder.
Arcata Graphics/Halliday was printer and binder.

Library of Congress Cataloging-in-Publication Data

Gallagher, Michael, Ph.D.
    Representative government in Western Europe / Michael Gallagher. Michael Laver, Peter Mair.
    p.   cm.
    ISBN 0-07-036684-5
    1. Representative government and representation—Europe—Case studies.   2. Political parties—Europe—Case studies.   3. Europe—Politics and government—1945-   I. Laver, Michael, (date). II. Mair, Peter.   III. Title.
JN94.A91G35   1992
321.8'043'094—dc20   91-15221

ABOUT THE AUTHORS

Michael Gallagher is a Lecturer in the Department of Political Science, Trinity College, University of Dublin. He is author of *The Irish Labour Party in Transition* (Manchester, 1982) and *Political Parties in the Republic of Ireland* (Manchester, 1985), and coeditor of *Candidate Selection in Comparative Perspective: The Secret Garden of Politics* (London and Beverly Hills, 1988) and of *How Ireland Voted 1989* (Galway, 1990).

Michael Laver holds the chair of Political Science and Sociology at University College, Galway, Ireland. He has previously taught at Queens University Belfast and the University of Liverpool and was a Visiting Professor at the University of Texas at Austin and at Harvard University. Recent books include (with Norman Schofield) *Multiparty Government* (Oxford University Press, 1990) and (with W. Ben Hunt), the forthcoming *Policy and Party Competition* (Routledge, New York). He is coeditor of the *European Journal of Political Research* and is currently involved in developing a new approach to the study of party competition and government formation.

Peter Mair is Senior Lecturer in Comparative Politics in the University of Leiden in the Netherlands, and previously held appointments in Ireland, Italy, and Britain. His books include *The Changing Irish Party System* (London, 1987), and, with Stefano Bartolini, *Identity, Competition and Electoral Availability: The Stabilisation of European Electorates, 1885–1985* (Cambridge, 1990), which was awarded the Vth Stein Rokkan Prize for Comparative Social Science Research. Among his recent edited books are *The West European Party System* (Oxford, 1990) and *Understanding Party System Change in Western Europe* (London, 1990). He is currently engaged in a major cross-national research project on party organizational change and adaptation since 1960.

CONTENTS

PREFACE

We set out in this book to discuss contemporary Western European politics from a distinctive point of view. In the first place, we concentrate upon the politics of representation, focusing especially on parties, elections, and governments. In the second place, our approach is wholeheartedly comparative. We organize our discussions around particular important themes in the politics of representation, not around particular important countries. Indeed, our main motivation in writing this book is that there are still far too few authors who discuss European politics in terms of themes rather than countries.

We are convinced that the benefits of our approach far exceed the costs. By restricting ourselves to the politics of representation, we give ourselves the space to take seriously the large body of comparative research and writing on this theme that can be found in the recent literature. By insisting on a comparative rather than country-by-country approach, we give ourselves the opportunity to bring a much larger amount of evidence to bear upon the problem at hand.

We feel strongly that many of the most important features of the politics of representation in Western Europe are overlooked by those who concentrate their attentions upon only a few "important" countries. The smaller European democracies are often the sources of the most suggestive evidence on matters as diverse as the social bases of voting, electoral law, and coalition bargaining. If we want to find out about differences between urban and rural voters, for example, Scandinavia is one of the first places we should start looking. If we want to find out how proportional representation electoral systems work, we do well to begin with the Netherlands. Comparing Ireland and Denmark is a good way to begin to understand what makes some minority governments stable and others not. The list could be extended indefinitely. Confining ourselves to a few big countries is not the way to come to grips with some of the most important and exciting features of the politics of representation in Western Europe.

Our way of doing things does have costs, of course, and it is as well to be aware of them. The most obvious has to do with depth. In a book of a certain size, if we broaden our coverage to look at a wider range of countries, then our treatment of each is inevitably bound to be less detailed. In our view, the benefits of adding more countries to the frame of reference are greater than the benefits of adding more detail on a small number of countries, but others may come to the opposite conclusion about this inevitable trade-off. There are plenty of other books for these people to read, so we need not feel too sorry for them, but we should remember that they do have a point. In taking several steps back to expand our field of view, we may lose sight of important details. But we may also gain a better sense of perspective.

Another potential cost has to do with consistency. We cannot, obviously, discuss every European country in relation to every theme that we select. But if we pick and choose those countries to illustrate particular points, the reader may not get a clear sense of what is going on in *any* particular European country. We have adopted a three-pronged approach to this problem, which we hope allows us to get the best of both worlds. First, we do tend to concentrate in the text on those examples best suited to helping us explore particular themes. We do this to maximize the benefits of our broadly based approach. Second, while some of our information comes from authors who studied only a limited subset of European countries, we do our best in the tables summarizing particular themes to include entries for *every* Western European country. We do this to ensure consistency and completeness at least at the level of basic information.

Finally, we have selected a group of seven countries on which we lavish somewhat greater attention. These are Britain, France, Germany, Italy, the Netherlands, Spain, and Sweden. We selected these countries because between them they provide considerable variation on most of the important dimensions of politics that we wish to consider. They give us a wide geographic spread, from far north to deep south. They include large and small countries; rural and urban countries; Protestant, Catholic, and "mixed" countries; richer and poorer countries; countries with stable governments and countries with unstable governments; new and old democracies; the countries with the most, and the least, proportional electoral systems; and so on. We discuss the party systems of each of these countries in Chapter 2. In subsequent chapters, no matter which examples we have used in the main text, we pause in our discussion at key points to present a short box that summarizes key information for each of the seven countries in our core group. In this way we allow interested readers to follow this core group through our entire discussion and thereby reap many of the benefits of the more restricted country-based approach, while paying none of its costs.

As in all other things, the ultimate proof of the pudding is in the eating. Our experience of teaching courses in Western European politics has led us to become increasingly dissatisfied with the narrow choice of texts organized on a thematic basis. Accordingly, we have produced the text that, as teachers of Western European politics, *we* have been looking for. We have been encouraged by our discovery, in discussions with colleagues and in reading the comments of referees, that we are not alone. Our hope is that we have done at least modest justice to the ambitious goals that we set for ourselves.

We have had another difficult decision to make, which became more apparent as we were writing this book, during 1989 and 1990. This has to do with the rapidly unfolding developments in Eastern Europe. Each one of us has woken up at least once in the dark hours before dawn, wondering whether "Western Europe," as a distinct political entity, still exists, given the rapid spate of contested elections in formerly communist states. We gave serious consideration to including these countries in our discussions, and we will obviously have to keep this matter under continuous review for future editions. But we have decided that the common postwar experience of the Eastern European states has left a legacy that still marks them off as quite distinct from Western European countries.

We have also been forced to make decisions about our coverage of Western Europe's largest state, known for most of the postwar era as the Federal Republic of Germany. Before 1990, this state was familiarly referred to as West Germany, but after the absorption of the former communist-run East German state (the German Democratic Republic), this name ceased to be appropriate. In the following chapters, therefore, we refer to "Germany" when discussing features of the current German state, but we also occasionally use the term "West Germany" when referring to events or patterns that applied to the preunification state. At the time of writing, almost all data available, and cited in tables, referred to preunification Germany.

Another country for which terminology is in some sense ambiguous is the United Kingdom. Formally, the United Kingdom of Great Britain and Northern Ireland includes England, Wales, and Scotland (that is, Great Britain), as well as Northern Ireland. In the tables and boxes that follow, we always use the term "United Kingdom," or "U.K.," for the sake of consistency. In the text, for stylistic reasons, we refer sometimes to "Britain" and sometimes to the "United Kingdom."

This book, therefore, is about the politics of representation in Western Europe, as we have known this since the early 1950s. We begin with a brief introduction to the countries of Western Europe, looking at the main sources of social and economic variation between them. We move on to look at the main constitutional features of a form of government that is very distinctively Western European, namely parliamentary democracy. Some democratic systems, notably the United States, lay a heavy constitutional emphasis on separating the powers of the legislature and the executive. European parliamentary democracies, on the other hand, with the partial exception of France, do not separate these roles nearly so rigidly. The most obvious symptom of this is that the executive is typically formed out of the legislature and is responsible to it. We explore this rule and other rules of the European political game in Chapter 1.

In Chapter 2, we begin our discussion of representative politics, looking at the "party systems" that determine the choices offered to voters at election time. Here we introduce the seven party systems to which we will be paying special attention. In Chapter 3, we look at the "families" of parties that make up the cast of characters in most Western European elections. We look at the families of communist parties, social democratic parties, liberal parties, Christian democratic parties, the far right, and so on. In Chapter 4, we look at the social and economic patterns, or "cleavages," that underpin party choice; we consider how these patterns might be changing and whether party systems themselves are in a state of flux. In Chapter 5, we step inside parties to look at some of their workings—at how they choose leaders and candidates and at how they raise money.

The first five chapters look at the politics of representation at an electoral level, while Chapters 7 and 8 look at politics at the elite level of legislatures and governments. Chapter 6, however, looks at the institution linking the two, the electoral system that turns votes cast into seats won. Many different electoral systems are used throughout Western Europe, which is the world's premier laboratory for all who are interested in the workings of electoral law. Having looked at how European legislatures are produced, we move on in Chapter 7 to look at what they do. The most important thing that they do, as we saw in Chapter 1, is to produce and support a government. Since few European parties win a majority of seats in the legislature, forming a government typically involves forming a coalition. In Chapter 8, we consider whether the formation of governments with different party compositions makes a difference to the policies that eventually emerge. While this is a topic that is only beginning to attract the interest of political scientists, it is clearly one that is vital to our understanding of the democratic process. If governments don't make a difference, after all, it is difficult to see why we should take an interest in the elections, the coalition bargaining, and all the other steps in the political process by which governments are selected.

The final section of the book deals with politics outside the party system. In Chapter 9, we look at the role of interest groups and pressure politics. Many political decisions, after all is said and done, are made by governments without recourse to the legislature—many incomes policies, for example, are forged in this way—and these decisions may well be strongly influenced by those who set out to apply pressure to the government. Finally, in Chapter 10, we look at the politics of the European Community. One of the most important developments in postwar Europe has been the process of European integration. European states, competing in a world dominated by superpowers, have seen the need to act together in many fields, especially in economic affairs. Drawing an analogy with the United States, many politicians have argued that European countries should act as a coordinated bloc rather than as a set of small actors, each with a different set of priorities. The European Community that includes twelve of these states has gone farther down the road to uniting sovereign nations than any previous experiment in voluntary international integration.

Notwithstanding the trend toward European integration, however, Western Europe remains a collection of countries with intriguingly different cultures, traditions, and political styles. There is no such thing as a "typical" European country, which is why it is so important to look at the group of European countries taken as a whole rather than at individual European countries one at a time. When we look at European politics in this way, distinct patterns do emerge. It is the search for such patterns that is the guiding purpose of this book.

ACKNOWLEDGMENTS

A number of colleagues have helped us in the writing of this book, by reading and commenting on chapters or by assisting in the tracking down of obscure pieces of information. In particular we should like to thank W. Ben Hunt, Peter

Humphreys, Patrick Keatinge, Tom Mackie, Michael Marsh, Bríd O Connor, Karin Tilmans and Dermot Scott. The book has also been improved as a result of the careful scrutiny given to earlier drafts by the following publisher's reviewers: John W. Books, University of North Texas; George A. Codding, Jr., University of Colorado–Boulder; Russell Dalton, Florida State University; John T. S. Keeler, University of Washington; Mark J. Kesselman, Columbia University; Kathleen Howard Kinawy, Bowling Green State University; Thomas D. Lancaster, Emory University; Gary Marks, University of North Carolina–Chapel Hill; Frank Myers, SUNY–Stony Brook; W. Phillips Shively, University of Minnesota; and Randy Soderquist, University of Pittsburgh. Michael Laver's work on this project was supported by grants from the National Science Foundation (SES-88-22307 and SES-89-14294). Undergraduate students at University College Galway were subjected to the cruel and unusual punishment of having to use an earlier draft of the book as a course text.

Michael Gallagher
Michael Laver
Peter Mair

REPRESENTATIVE GOVERNMENT IN WESTERN EUROPE

Introduction: Western Europe in Vital Statistics

Even though Western Europe is divided into more than twenty independent countries, it is still quite physically small when compared with North or South America, or with Asia or Africa. However, while the area covered by Western Europe is little more than a third of that covered by the United States, some of the distances involved can still be quite large. On its north-south axis, as Figure 1 shows, Western Europe ranges for about 4000 kilometers, from North Cape 500 kilometers inside the Arctic Circle, at the top of Norway, to the southern coastline of the Greek island of Crete, 200 kilometers south of Tunis, the capital of the North African state of Tunisia. This is about the same distance as that between Winnipeg and Managua, or Minneapolis and Panama. Along the east-west axis, however, the distance from Lisbon, the continent's most western city, to Vienna, one of its most eastern cities, is less than 2500 kilometers—roughly the distance between Salt Lake City and Pittsburgh.

Despite the relatively small area, the population of Western Europe, at about 360 million, is almost half as big again as that of the United States. As Table 1 shows, population density, on average about four times that of the United States, is highest in the Netherlands and northern Germany, a heavily populated region where the concentration of major cities and industrial infrastructure supports a population of more than 350 persons per square kilometer. In the more peripheral areas of Western Europe, by contrast, population density is relatively low; there are fewer than 19 persons per square kilometer in the vast but sparsely populated country of Sweden and 62 persons per square kilometer in the harsh and inhospitable landscape of Basilicata in southern Italy. In the peripheral Irish Republic, for example, a land area of about 70,000 square kilometers supports a population of about 3.5 million; in the more centrally located Netherlands, on the other hand, an area of some 41,000 square kilometers, little more than half that of Ireland, supports a population of almost 15 million, more than four times that of Ireland.

Western Europe is an immensely diverse area, riven by many cultural, religious, and linguistic boundaries. Despite an overwhelmingly Christian culture, for exam-

Figure 1
Western Europe

TABLE 1
General and Demographic Data on Western European Democracies

Country	Capital	Area, 000 km²	Population Total, 000	Population Per km²	Mean Temperatures* High	Mean Temperatures* Low	% Catholic
Austria	Vienna	83.9	7,595	90.5	67	31	85.4
Belgium	Brussels	30.5	9,879	324.0	64	35	96.0
Denmark	Copenhagen	43.1	5,130	119.0	64	32	0.6
Finland	Helsinki	338.0	4,946	14.6	64	21	0.4†
France	Paris	549.0	55,873	101.8	65	37	76.4
Germany(W.)	Bonn	248.6	61,451	247.2	66	34	43.8
United Germany		357.0	76,750	215.0			37.1†
Greece	Athens	132.0	10,010	75.8	82	48	0.4
Iceland	Reykjavik	103.0	250	2.4	52	31	1.0†
Ireland	Dublin	70.3	3,538	50.3	59	40	94.0
Italy	Rome	301.2	57,441	190.7	77	46	83.2
Luxembourg	Luxembourg	2.6	375	144.2	64	33	93.0
Malta	Valletta	0.3	343	1,086.5	79	54	97.3
Netherlands	The Hague	40.8	14,765	361.9	64	36	36.1
Norway	Oslo	324.2	4,211	13.0	63	24	1.0†
Portugal	Lisbon	92.4	9,819	111.5	73	51	94.1
Spain	Madrid	504.8	38,996	77.3	76	41	99.0
Sweden	Stockholm	450.0	8,438	18.8	64	26	1.3
Switzerland	Berne	41.3	6,672	161.6	65	30	47.6
U.K.	London	244.8	57,065	233.1	59	41	8.5
U.S.A.	Washington	9,372.6	246,329	26.3	75	33	30.0

*Temperatures are shown in degrees Fahrenheit. They are the mean temperatures during the hottest and coldest months in the capital city (except in the case of the U.K. where each temperature is a national average).
†Estimate.
Note: Demographic and religious data refer to the mid-1980s.

ple, a marked source of diversity is created by the balance between Roman Catholics and the various Protestant denominations. Table 1 and Figure 2 show that in some places Roman Catholics are an overwhelming majority—for example, in the southern and western parts of Europe, where the proportion of Catholics ranges from 99 percent in Spain to about 75 percent in France. In Greece, the majority adhere to the Greek Orthodox Church, closer in many ways to Catholicism than to Protestantism. Elsewhere, Roman Catholics tend to be very thin on the ground. This is true in northern Europe, particularly in the Scandinavian countries—Denmark, Finland, Iceland, Norway, and Sweden—where the overwhelming proportion of the population is at least nominally affiliated with a variety of Protestant denominations. Indeed, it is only in the central spine of Western Europe—in Germany, the Netherlands, and Switzerland—that we find some sort of even balance between Catholics and Protestants, with Catholics forming a significant minority of the population. Even in these countries, Catholics tend to cluster in areas where they constitute an overwhelming majority—in areas such as Limburg in the south of the Netherlands, for example, or Bavaria in southern Germany. Catholics also constitute a substantial minority in Northern Ireland, which forms part of the United Kingdom, and where a virtual civil war between Catholics and Protestants has now persisted for more than two decades. Note,

Figure 2
Percentage of Catholics in Western Europe

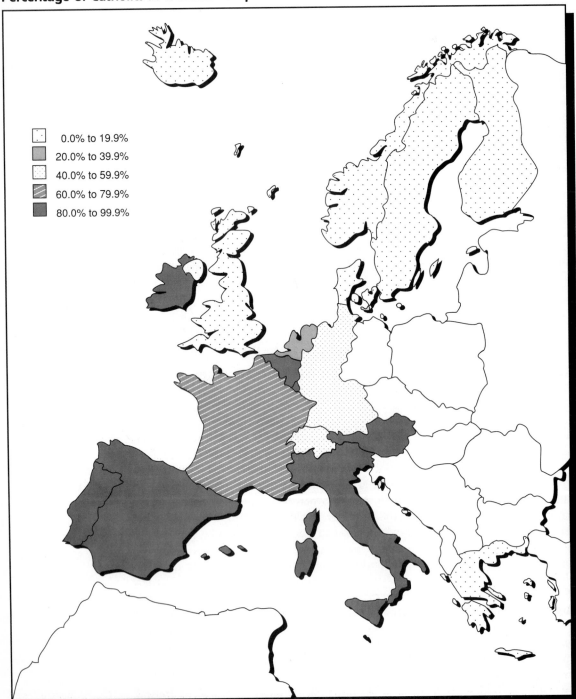

however, that the nominal affiliations listed in Table 1 exaggerate the numbers of active adherents of the various churches—the proportion of nonpracticing Catholics is particularly pronounced in France and southern Europe, for example.

Cultural diversity involves much more than religious differences, of course. Virtually every Western European country has its own language, the only major exceptions being Austria, where almost everyone uses German; Ireland, where almost everyone uses English; Belgium, where 57 percent use Flemish (a variant of Dutch) and 42 percent use French; Luxembourg, where the native language coexists with both French and German; and Switzerland, where 74 percent use German, 20 percent use French, and 5 percent use Italian. In addition, a variety of countries have small linguistic minorities—these include the Basque minority in Spain, the German-speaking minority in northeast Italy, the Swedish minority in Finland, the Welsh in Britain, and Gaelic speakers in both Ireland and Scotland. Across Western Europe as a whole, German is the most widely used native language, being used by roughly one person in every five (21 percent), followed by French (17.5 percent), English (17 percent), Italian (16 percent), Spanish (8.5 percent), and Dutch (6 percent).

Germany also enjoys the strongest economy in Western Europe; even before unification, its gross domestic product (GDP) was more than a quarter again as big as that of France (see Table 2). In general, however, the individual European economies are dwarfed by that of the United States. The combined GDPs of the four largest economies—those of Germany, France, Italy, and the United Kingdom—actually equal no more than 75 percent of that of the United States.

The highest figures for GDP per head of population can be found in the Scandinavian countries and Switzerland, at levels substantially exceeding the equivalent figure for the United States. Before these figures can be used to compare real living standards, however, they must be adjusted to take account of the relative cost of living in each country. Thus Table 2 also lists GDP per capita for European countries at purchasing power parity, that is, adjusted so that a fixed sum buys the same bundle of goods and services in every country. Table 2 and Figure 3 show that when purchasing power is taken into account, the GDP per capita in the United States is almost 17 percent higher than that in Switzerland, the highest in Western Europe. Differences within Western Europe, however, are even more marked. Levels of GDP per capita, taking purchasing power into account, range from highs of $16,700 in Switzerland and $16,322 in Norway to lows of just $6750 in Portugal and $6799 in Greece.

This imbalance of prosperity within Western Europe is clearly related to different levels of economic modernization. With some exceptions, it is an imbalance that also tends to be organized in terms of a geographic division between richer countries in northern and central Western Europe and poorer countries in the Mediterranean south. Indeed, this difference is strikingly evident in terms of regional disparities within the boundaries of a single country, Italy. The very prosperous northern part of the country enjoys one of the highest standards of living in Western Europe, contrasting sharply with the southern part of Italy, one of Western Europe's poorest regions. Lower levels of prosperity also tend to be quite strongly associated with a continuing reliance on agriculture as a major source of employment, as well as with more poorly developed industrial and service sectors.

TABLE 2
Economic Data on Western European Democracies

| Country | Gross Domestic Product at Market Prices | | | Current Government Expenditure as % of GDP |
| | Total, $ billions | Per Capita | | |
		Current Exchange Rates, $	Current PPPs,* $	
Austria	126.7	16,748	12,506	47.4
Belgium	151.4	15,180	12,623	50.6
Denmark	105.3	20,912	13,555	57.3
Finland	114.7	21,266	13,792	35.9
France	948.5	17,002	13,603	49.4
Germany(W.)	1,200.2	19,581	14,161	43.1
Greece	53.8	5,244	6,799	43.9
Iceland	5.2	23,936	16,068	27.6
Ireland	32.7	9,182	8,146	50.0
Italy	864.0	14,430	12,985	46.1
Luxembourg	6.6	17,592	15,558	46.2
Malta†	1.5	3,810	NA	42.0
Netherlands	225.0	15,461	12,832	53.3
Norway	93.1	21,564	16,322	47.6
Portugal	45.2	4,265	6,750	40.4
Spain	376.3	8,722	9,343	36.1
Sweden	189.3	21,546	14,772	57.8
Switzerland	174.4	27,581	16,700	30.4
U.K.	831.6	14,413	13,428	41.2
U.S.A.	5,165.8	19,558	19,558	34.8

*Purchasing power parities (PPPs) are the rates of currency conversion which eliminate differences in price levels between the countries. A given sum of money, when converted into different currencies at these rates, will buy the same basket of goods and services in all countries. This gives a much more realistic picture of the different levels of GDP per capita.
†Estimated figures.
Note: Economic data refer to 1988–1989.

Differences in employment patterns are less marked than once was the case, however. In Western Europe as a whole, as Table 3 and Figure 4 show, only Greece, Iceland, Ireland, Portugal, and Spain still have a level of agricultural employment that exceeds 10 percent of the labor force, while in Belgium, Germany, Luxembourg, Malta, the Netherlands, Sweden, and the U.K. the level has fallen below 5 percent, a level comparable to that of the United States. In all Western European countries without exception, the service sector now constitutes the largest single source of employment.

Table 3 also shows that in almost half of the Western European countries, services account for more than 60 percent of employment, as in the United States. The level falls below 50 percent only in Greece and Portugal. Despite this relative prosperity, as Figure 5 shows, unemployment levels in Western Europe remain quite high, on the average 2 percent higher than in the United States and exceeding 10 percent in Ireland, Italy, and Spain. In those countries with lower levels of unemployment, there are higher levels of female participation in the labor force, suggesting that women find it easier to become economically active where there is a more restricted pool of available labor.

Figure 3
GDP per Capita at PPP

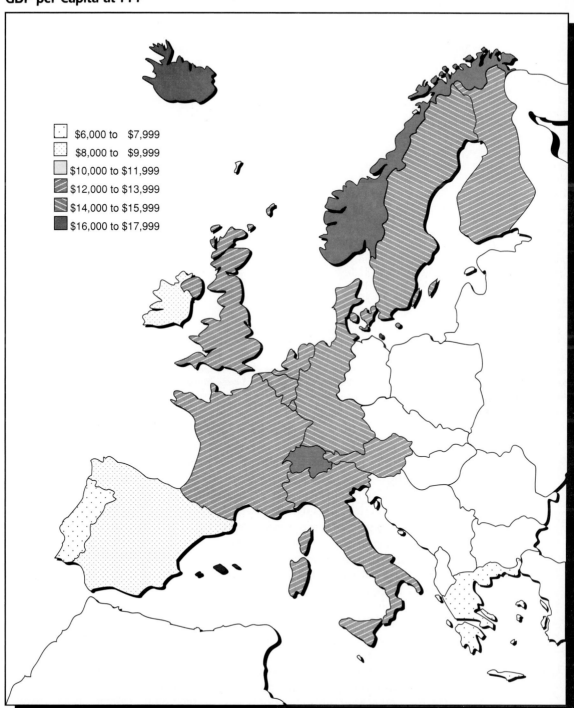

TABLE 3
Labor Force Data on Western European Democracies

Country	% of Labor Force Employed in			% Unemployed	Female Participation*
	Agriculture	Industry	Services		
Austria	8.1	37.4	54.5	3.6	53.7
Belgium	2.7	28.0	69.3	9.0	51.8
Denmark	5.8	27.2	67.1	7.2	78.3
Finland	9.8	30.6	59.6	3.4	73.0
France	6.8	30.3	62.9	9.6	55.7
Germany(W.)	4.0	39.8	56.2	5.5	54.4
Greece	26.6	27.2	46.2	7.7	41.7
Iceland	10.4	31.1	58.5	0.7	NA
Ireland	15.4	27.8	56.8	16.7	37.6
Italy	9.8	32.4	57.8	10.9	43.9
Luxembourg	3.4	31.6	65.0	1.7	47.6
Malta	2.9	35.9	61.2	4.0	NA
Netherlands	4.8	26.4	68.8	8.3	50.6
Norway	6.4	26.4	67.1	4.9	72.8
Portugal	20.7	35.1	44.2	5.7	59.1
Spain	14.4	32.5	53.1	16.9	34.1
Sweden	3.8	29.5	66.7	1.4	80.1
Switzerland	5.7	35.1	59.2	0.6	57.9
U.K.	2.3	29.8	68.0	6.4	63.5
U.S.A.	2.9	26.9	70.2	5.2	66.9

*Female labor force as a percentage of all females aged 15–64.
Sources (Tables 1–3): OECD in Figures, 1990 Edition, OECD, Paris, 1990. *Britannica Book of the Year 1985,* Encyclopaedia Britannica, Chicago, 1985. *Western Europe 1989: A Political and Economic Survey,* Europa Publications, London, 1988.
Note: Labor force data refer to 1988–1989.

Table 2 and Figure 6 highlight the different levels of government expenditure, relative to the GDP, in different European countries. These figures relate to spending on public welfare programs—such as health, education, employment, and housing—as well as public employment in the defense forces, administration, and publicly owned companies. Governments in Denmark and Sweden spend almost 60 percent of the GDP, followed by governments in three countries which spend over 50 percent—the Netherlands (53 percent), Belgium (51 percent), and Ireland (50 percent). Most of the remaining countries fall between 50 percent and 40 percent, with only four countries—Finland (36 percent), Iceland (28 percent), Spain (36 percent) and Switzerland (30 percent)—falling below this level. Thus, of Western European countries, only the Swiss and Icelandic governments spend a smaller proportion of national income than the U.S. government (35 percent).

Taking all of these factors into account, it can be seen that when we talk about Western Europe, we are not talking about a homogeneous group of countries that can be treated as if they were one. We are talking about a collection of places with quite distinctive social and economic profiles. Whether these differences are large or small depends upon your point of view. As we have suggested, to travel within Italy from prosperous north to poor south is to see a quite striking social transition. Yet even the poor southern part of Italy is in no sense whatsoever one of the

Figure 4
Percentage of Labor Force in Agriculture

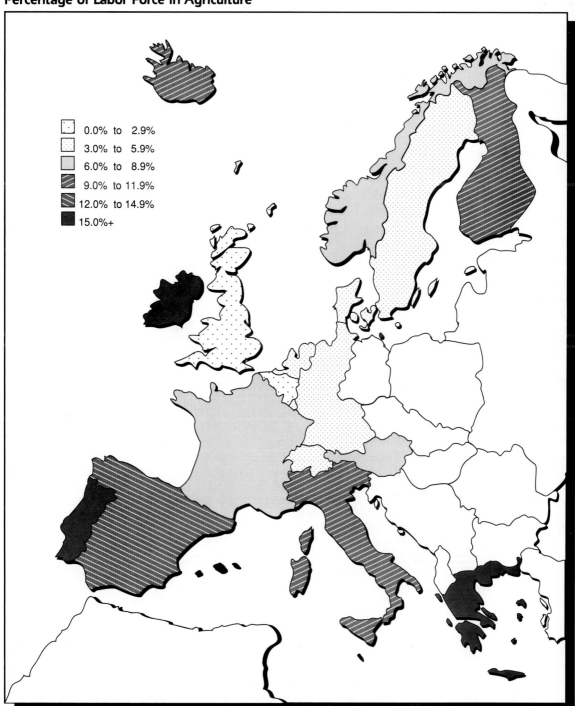

Figure 5
Percentage Unemployed

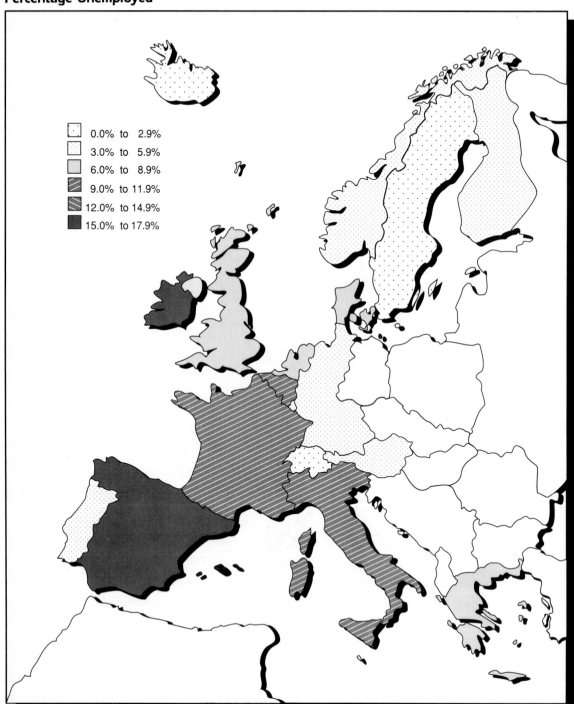

Figure 6
Government Spending as a Percentage of GDP

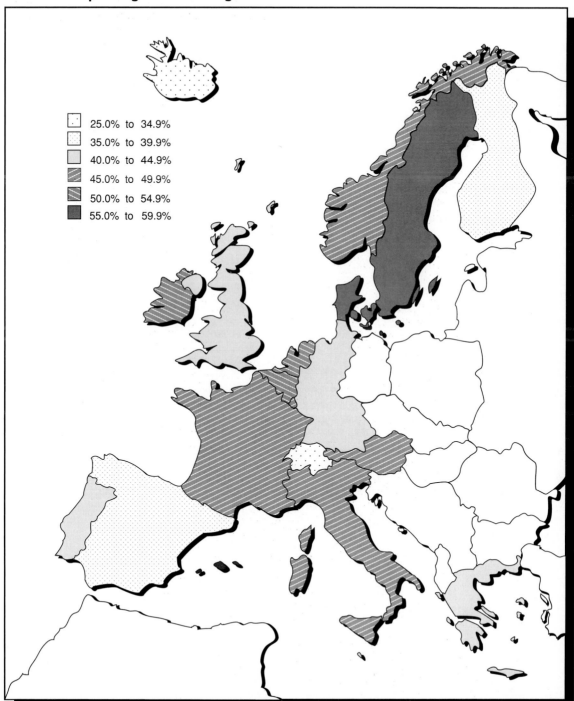

world's poor regions—its level of prosperity is far above that of virtually every third world state, whether we measure this in terms of money, life expectancy, literacy, or indeed any other aspect of the quality of life. People in southern Italy are governed by a democratically elected government in Rome and use a currency, the lira, that is tied firmly, via European Community monetary policy, to the German mark, the French franc, and the British pound.

For all their diversity, therefore, the countries of Western Europe constitute the world's largest collection of wealthy capitalist democracies. Many of them are tied together in a political union, the European Community, which we discuss in detail in Chapter 10. The differences that we have highlighted above must be kept in mind in the comparative discussions that follow—we are, after all, talking about a collection of different countries, and that is one of the things that makes the study of Western European politics so interesting. But these differences must not be exaggerated. This is why it makes sense to analyze politics in the collection of Western European countries in terms of their underlying similarities as well as their distinctive features. This is the main purpose of the chapters that follow.

CHAPTER 1
THE RULES
OF THE
GAME

In this book we describe politics in Western Europe as an arena in which the hopes and fears of citizens are transformed into the public policies that affect their everyday lives. In the chapters that follow, we look first at the political parties laying claim to the allegiance of citizens in each European system. We examine what goes on inside these parties and then turn to the electoral systems that transform the choices of citizens who turn out to vote into a collection of politicians sitting in a legislature. We consider what happens after elections have been held, when a political executive, responsible for making and implementing key policy decisions, must be formed. We look at what these executives actually do once they have taken office. Finally, we assess the representation of interests outside the parliamentary system—the power and role of interest groups, and the impact on the lives of European citizens of international decision making in the European Community.

Before we do any of this, however, we set out the rules by which political games are played in Western European arenas. These rules are quite distinct from those to be found in the United States, for example, something that makes politics in Washington a different business from politics in London, say, or in Paris, Brussels, Stockholm, Rome, or Madrid. Western European states are almost all run according to the principles of "parliamentary government," a set of institutions and behavior patterns that gives a particularly important role to political parties and parliamentary elections. Constitutionally, these principles have to do with the relationship between legislature, executive, and judiciary—that is, between parliament, government, and the courts—and with the role of the head of state. In addition, as we shall see, the successful operation of a system of parliamentary government depends upon the role played by political parties in both the legislature and the electorate. Since this role is, in turn, determined by the constitutional environment in which the parties must operate, we begin with the constitution.

CONSTITUTIONAL FEATURES OF PARLIAMENTARY DEMOCRACY

The Chief Executive and the Head of State

The most distinctive features of Western European parliamentary democracies have to do with the political executive, the "government" that actually runs each country. By far the most important of these features is that the executive in general and the chief executive in particular are not elected directly. Instead, they are chosen, indirectly, from the legislature. Related to this is the fact that the head of state is not, in most cases, the chief executive (France is the exception) but rather a figure who is intended to be "above" day-to-day politics, with a number of significant symbolic, procedural, and diplomatic functions.

Western European countries do not tend to have an effective separation of powers between legislature and executive, in the form to be found in the United States, but there is a clear separation of powers between the political executive and the head of state. This is a historical product of the evolution of many European states from traditional autocratic monarchies to the parliamentary democracies that exist today. Many modern European states, indeed, are still headed by monarchs—the list of "constitutional monarchies" embraces Belgium, Britain, Denmark, the Netherlands, Norway, Spain, and Sweden, while Luxembourg's head of state is a grand duke (see Table 1.1). Furthermore, Europe's republics have tended to evolve

TABLE 1.1
Heads of State in Western Europe, 1991

	Constitutional Status of Head of State	Head of State, January 1991	When Came to Office	How Came to Office
Austria	President	Kurt Waldheim	1986	Direct election
Belgium	Monarch	King Baudouin II	1951	Heredity
Denmark	Monarch	Queen Margrethe II	1972	Heredity
Finland	President	Mauno Koivisto	1982	Direct election
France	President	François Mitterrand	1981	Direct election
Germany	President	Richard von Weizsäcker	1984	Election by legislature
Greece	President	Konstantinos Karamanlis	1990	Election by legislature
Iceland	President	Vigdís Finnbogadóttir	1980	Direct election
Ireland	President	Mary Robinson	1990	Direct election
Italy	President	Francesco Cossiga	1985	Election by legislature
Luxembourg	Grand Duke	Jean	1964	Heredity
Malta	President	Vincent Tabone	1989	Election by legislature
Netherlands	Monarch	Queen Beatrix	1980	Heredity
Norway	Monarch	King Harald V	1991	Heredity
Portugal	President	Mário Soares	1986	Direct election
Spain	Monarch	King Juan Carlos	1975	Heredity*
Sweden	Monarch	King Carl XVI Gustaf	1973	Heredity
Switzerland	President	Favio Cotti	1991	Election by legislature
U.K.	Monarch	Queen Elizabeth II	1952	Heredity

*Spain was a republic from 1931 to 1975. Juan Carlos, the grandson of the king ousted in 1931, was nominated by the dictator General Franco to succeed him as head of state and duly took over this position when Franco died in 1975.

a role for the president, as head of state, that is very much like that of a constitutional monarch. This role is typically that of an elder statesperson above the mundane, albeit important, details of day-to-day politics, fulfilling instead the elevated functions required of any head of state in a constitutional democracy. These functions are symbolic (as a personal embodiment of the nation for all to see and for some to love and respect), procedural (presiding over major state occasions such as the opening of parliament, providing the final ratification of laws, and so on), or diplomatic (the most important of these is greeting other heads of state and visiting dignitaries). The only real European exception to this model is France, with a much less clear-cut separation of powers between parliament and the presidency and, in consequence, a much more "politicized" presidency, along U.S. lines.

The precise powers of the head of state vary from country to country. In contemporary Western Europe, the only head of state with real muscle is the president of France, who appoints the prime minister, chairs cabinet meetings, and can dismiss the prime minister and dissolve parliament. Even so, France does not have a full-fledged presidential system like that of the U.S.A., because the constitution clips the president's wings in a number of ways. In consequence, what operates in France is a unique blend of a parliamentary system as practiced elsewhere in Western Europe and American-style presidentialism; it could be seen as a "semi-presidential" system. For most of the last thirty years, the president's party has had a majority of seats in the National Assembly, and the president's preeminence has not been challenged. But between 1986 and 1988, the Socialist President Mitterrand was confronted by an assembly controlled by the parties of the right, and the

French President François Mitterrand (right) and Prime Minister Jacques Chirac during their uneasy political "cohabitation." (Orban/Sygma)

ambiguities in the office came to the fore. Mitterrand chose the right-wing leader, Jacques Chirac, as prime minister—he had little choice, since any other appointee would have been voted down by the assembly—and there was an uneasy two-year period of "cohabitation" during which both Mitterrand and Chirac felt constrained by the powers possessed by the other. This came to an end when Mitterrand defeated Chirac in the 1988 presidential election; Mitterrand immediately dissolved the assembly, and the Socialists won enough seats at the ensuing elections to be able to form a government with the aid of some centrist deputies (members of parliament). Normal service, including the preeminence of the president, was resumed.

In no other Western European country does the president have such an important position, and the rest of the countries we deal with in this book (with the possible exception of Switzerland, as discussed below) can accurately be described as parliamentary democracies. Even so, European heads of state are not entirely without power. In particular, presidents elected directly by the people might potentially have at least moral authority behind them if they intervene in the political process. Directly elected presidents can be found in six countries; besides France, these are Finland, Austria, Iceland, Ireland, and Portugal. Of these, Finland comes closest to being "semipresidential" in nature. The Finnish constitution gives the president a central role in foreign policy, and in the postwar decades the long-serving President Kekkonen did more than anyone else to establish harmonious relations with Finland's giant neighbor, the U.S.S.R. The Finnish president has been able to wield influence in domestic policy, too, but for the most part the initiative in policy making lies with the government (Arter, pp. 79–161). In Austria, Iceland, Ireland, and Portugal the president exercises certain responsibilities in specified circumstances but in practice does not get involved in day-to-day politics. In the other republics, the president is elected indirectly, usually by members of parliament.

Monarchs might be thought of as anachronisms in the twentieth century, but they can still have an important role to play. In the past, some have succumbed to the temptation to intervene politically, using their power and position to favor some parties over others. This has usually caused widespread resentment and has rebounded on the monarchs. It was the main factor behind referendums leading to the abolition of the monarchy in Greece and Italy, and the Belgian monarchy survived only narrowly in a vote in 1950. Royal houses that have remained aloof from partisan politics have managed to survive, and given the often high degree of public cynicism toward politicians, a king or a queen may command more respect than an elected leader.

The outstanding example of a monarchy playing an important role in society comes from Britain, where the Queen sits at the apex of the social system. Over a century ago, the constitutional authority Walter Bagehot identified the monarchy as a powerful force for preserving the status quo, commenting that the British working classes would never rebel against the established order because to do so would be to rebel against the Queen, to whom they were intensely loyal. For much the same reason, some on the left of British politics today would like to abolish the monarchy, which they see as a symbol of inequality, and make the country a republic. Nonetheless, the British monarchy is so popular with the public that the chance of any drastic change in its role is very slim.

Pomp and ceremony as Queen Elizabeth II presides over the state opening of the United Kingdom Parliament. (Courtesy British Information Services)

No other European monarchy wraps itself in as much pomp and ceremony as the British royal family, but its very existence as a symbol of the nation can be important. King Baudouin of Belgium has described himself as "the only Belgian," a reference to the fact that virtually all others in the linguistically divided country think of themselves first and foremost as either Flemish (if they speak the Flemish language) or Walloon (if they speak French). The monarchy is one of the few symbols with which both language groups can identify. In Spain, too, the monarchy exercised a vital political role in the years after the death of the dictator Franco in 1975. King Juan Carlos played a leading part in the reconstruction of a democratic political system, which has led to his being described as an archetypal "modernising monarch" (Pridham, p. 155), and his intervention was decisive in thwarting an attempted coup in 1981. In other countries, monarchies have deliberately shed themselves of the mystique often assumed to attach itself to royalty; members of the Swedish and Dutch royal families are as likely to be seen riding bicycles in the street as dressed in the regalia of office.

Overall, then, modern Europe's monarchs and presidents cannot be dismissed as mere ciphers. Apart from the explicit powers that some of them have in the area of government formation, which we discuss in Chapter 7, they can play a significant part in legitimizing the entire political system. However, it is true to say that they generally keep out of the risky business of day-to-day politics, and so real executive

Sweden's King Gustav and his wife Silvia enjoy Olympic cycling in Los Angeles. (UPI/Bettmann)

power in today's Western European states is in the hands not of the head of state but of the executive branch of the government.

The political boss of most Western European countries, therefore, is not the titular head of state but a political chief executive, almost always referred to in English translations as the *prime minister*. The prime minister chairs a committee of senior ministers known as a cabinet. The cabinet, comprising in virtually every country a group of prominent elected politicians, is thus the political embodiment of the executive arm of the state. The prime minister, typically the leader of one of the largest legislative parties, is chief executive.

The power of a European prime minister, by virtue of his or her being both chief executive and the head of a powerful legislative party, can be considerable—far greater in his or her own country than that of a U.S. president in his. This is especially true in countries with a tradition of single-party majority governments, such as Britain. The only threats to this power come from inside the governing party, and such threats can usually be dealt with easily. Even in more typical European coalition systems, it is usually the case that the prime minister has gained office by virtue of having a powerful bargaining position in the legislature. Either way, the result is that once the executive decides to act, the legislature usually concurs. When the executive cannot persuade the legislature to do its bidding, it often regards its position as untenable and resigns.

Relations between the Legislature and the Executive

In classical democratic theory, there is a clear separation of the powers of the legislature and the executive: the former makes the laws, and the latter executes them. But in practice there is no effective separation of powers between the

German Prime Minister Helmut Kohl addresses the first meeting of the united German parliament, in the Berlin Reichstag. (Reuters/Bettmann)

legislature and the executive in Western Europe, in contrast to the situation in the United States. The theoretical distinction between making laws and executing them is not so clear in practice (Loewenberg and Patterson, p. 232). Moreover, in most European countries—France and Norway are the main exceptions—members of the government sit in the legislature, so the two bodies are almost fused into one. The executive derives from the legislature and depends for its continued existence on legislative support. As we shall see in Chapter 7, this means that the first and overwhelmingly most important parliamentary business after a legislative election is the formation of a government. The bottom line in all of this has to do with the selection of a senior legislator to be nominated as prime minister and the selection of others to be nominated for cabinet positions. Each cabinet minister, once nominated, acts as the political head of a major government department. The executive so formed is thus an "administration" in its widest sense. It has full political control over major decision making and is also accountable for the enactment and implementation of the decisions.

Once a government has formed, the permanent political question before every European legislature is whether there is an alternative prime minister and cabinet that would be preferred to the incumbents by a majority of the legislature. If there is, and the legislature expresses this formally in a vote, then the government is defeated and the alternative is installed in office. Faced with this prospect, the incumbent government often anticipates the inevitable and resigns anyway. The crucial consequence of this is that in most European states, the legislature can bring down the government at any time by withdrawing its support. (Switzerland is the main exception to this rule, and for this reason, it might well not be regarded as a parliamentary government system.)

Because most European countries use proportional representation electoral systems, which hardly ever give "artificial" parliamentary majorities to parties that win less than a majority of votes, most European governments depend for their existence on legislative coalitions composed of more than one party. This means that if the legislative coalition backing the government should collapse for any reason, an executive can fall quite suddenly. Thus it is quite common in Western European countries for there to be changes in government between elections as a result of developments in legislative politics, changes on which the electorate is not asked to pass judgment. Italy is the classic example of this, but the phenomenon can also be found in such "stable" coalition systems as Germany.

Despite the power that European legislatures have to make or break governments, this does not by any means imply that Western European legislatures hold the whip hand in legislature-executive relations. The very high levels of party discipline in parliament, to which we will be returning below, mean that party oligarchs are powerful people, particularly when they are in government. Assuming that the government controls a majority of seats in parliament—minority governments, which we discuss in Chapter 7, are a slightly different story—party leaders can usually rely on party discipline to push the government program through the legislature, more or less regardless of the views of the opposition.

This, of course, marks one of the key differences between parliamentary and presidential systems of government. The point is spelled out by Richard Rose: in liberal democracies, the American president is "the only government leader likely to have more than half his proposals rejected. A government with a parliamentary system is virtually certain of having at least two-thirds [and usually a markedly higher proportion] of all government proposals enacted as law" (Rose, p. 69). Moreover, not only do government proposals generally get adopted by European parliaments, but the other side of the coin is that proposals not initiated by the government are almost invariably unsuccessful. Members of parliament in Western Europe simply do not see themselves as American-style "legislators" with the role of initiating and piloting through pieces of legislation. Although most parliaments contain provision for a bill to be proposed by a deputy or a group of deputies—this is termed a "private member's bill" in the United Kingdom—such a bill very rarely becomes law unless the government decides to back it.

In terms of the standard categorizations of legislatures, European parliaments are "reactive" rather than "active" (Mezey, p. 36). They are what Polsby describes as "arena" legislatures rather than "transformative" ones; whereas the latter (of which the American Congress is the only real example) possess initiative in making laws, arena legislatures are mainly just "formalized settings for the interplay of significant political forces in the life of a political system" (Polsby, p. 277). A common theme in studies of European politics has been the "decline of parliaments," which have everywhere, it seems, lost to the grasping hands of governments the power they supposedly possessed late in the nineteenth century. By the middle of the twentieth century, it was generally agreed that governments acted while parliaments just talked.

Having said this, we must add that parliaments in Western Europe are not mere rubber stamps, and government is not simply a matter of "cabinet dictatorship." There are two qualifications that need to be made to such a picture. One is that such a high proportion of government legislation is approved by parliament only because the government takes account of the likely reaction of parliament. In discussing this, we can draw on Lijphart's useful distinction between two categories of democratic regimes. The first is the Westminster-type "majoritarian" model; the United Kingdom provides the clearest European example, with Ireland, Luxembourg, Sweden, and Norway also displaying many of the characteristics of political systems in this category (Lijphart, p. 216). In the archetypal majoritarian system, the government of the day has an assured majority among members of parliament and can rely on getting all of its legislation through virtually unscathed, provided it does not embark on a course of action so far removed from traditional party policy (or so unpopular in the country at large) as to alienate a significant number of its own followers, in which case it is likely to make concessions to its dissidents. The majority party or coalition is prepared, if necessary, to railroad all of its legislation through regardless of the feelings of the opposition. The second of Lijphart's categories is the consensual model; the clearest European example here is Switzerland, with Belgium, the Netherlands, and Italy also in this category. The emphasis here is, as the name suggests, on finding a broad consensus in parliament if possible rather than on merely imposing the will of the parliamentary majority; in countries in this category, as in Belgium, cabinets "tend to have a genuine 'give-and-take' relationship with parliament" (Lijphart, p. 25).

The second qualification that needs to be made to the picture of supine parliaments and cabinet dictatorship is that parliaments can sometimes play a significant role through a system of parliamentary committees. In Germany, which (along with Austria) is generally regarded as having one of the strongest committee systems, all legislative proposals coming from government go to a specialist committee, which examines the draft bill carefully and usually suggests amendments. The committees, it is true, are composed on a party basis, but the deputies on a committee are in many cases experts in the committee's area of competence. They approach their task in a serious and relatively nonpartisan spirit, so the amendments they propose to the proposals are often accepted by the government. In Austria, committees are sometimes charged with devising legislation in a particular area, with the full parliament virtually certain to accept their recommendations. Even in countries where committees do not play any real part in the making of policy, they may have a significant oversight role which involves assessing and supervising the implementation of policy by the government. This applies in both consensual and majoritarian models: even in the archetypal majoritarian system practiced at Westminster, the committee structure was expanded greatly in the 1980s and has acquired the potential to be a check on the behavior of the government, at least to the extent of being able to discover and give unwelcome publicity to the adverse consequences of certain government decisions (Drewry).

With all the qualifications, though, power in Western Europe undoubtedly lies far more with governments than with legislatures when it comes to making policy. In addition to this power, which relies upon party discipline, governments in many

European countries have the constitutional authority to dissolve the legislature and force an election whenever they choose. (At least, they, or sometimes specifically the prime minister, typically have the power to recommend the dissolution to a head of state, who almost invariably takes this advice. The main exceptions here are Finland, Norway, and Switzerland.) Governments typically choose to dissolve legislatures when they expect to do well in the subsequent election, a factor that makes the timing of elections an important strategic variable in many European countries. While every European country has a maximum time between elections that is fixed by law (usually four or five years, though three in Sweden), the actual time between elections in most countries is a matter of practical politics and varies considerably. This is obviously in stark contrast to the situation in the U.S.A., for example, where the time between elections is strictly mandated, and barring a revolution in the meantime, the dates of elections to be held several centuries hence are already determined.

Thus the power of the legislature to end the life of a government is balanced, in most Western European countries, by the power of the government to end the life of the legislature. In this sense, the legislature and executive hold a gun to each other's head, though tight party discipline typically puts the executive in the stronger position. This intimate interaction between the legislature and the executive means that there is a single national political arena in a typical European country. The balance of forces in national politics (though often not the real action) can be seen in the legislature, directly elected by the public at large.

Relations between Politicians and the Judiciary

In contrast to the differences that we find in legislature-executive relations, the formal status of the judiciary is rather similar in each of the countries that we are concerned with. Whether we are talking about Western Europe or North America, indeed, most people are proud of the fact that their legal system is "above" politics. What they mean by this, typically, is that it is very difficult for politicians, be they members of the legislature or of the executive, to influence the outcome of particular legal cases. The main exception to this generalization, namely the suspicion of many Italians that politicians can and do interfere in the administration of justice in their country (Spotts and Wieser, pp. 150–162; LaPalombara, pp. 226–228), merely establishes the rule for the rest of Western Europe. Moreover, across Western Europe, even including Italy, politicians cannot easily rid themselves of judges whose views they don't like. Within this basically common framework, though, there are some striking practical variations in the legal systems of different Western European countries, and these differences do have a bearing on the relationship between politicians and the judiciary.

European legal systems can be divided in a straightforward manner into two general types. The smaller group comprises those countries with a common-law tradition, while the more typical group comprises those countries originating within a continental tradition of "Roman" law that has now been transformed into a comprehensive system of legal codes. Common-law systems are confined to Britain and English-speaking former British colonies. In the European context this means Britain and Ireland, and this group also includes most of the United States and Canada, as well as Australia and New Zealand. Codified legal systems of one form or another prevail in all other Western European states; more generally, this group includes many former continental European colonies, including Louisiana, much of Latin America, and parts of Canada.

The essential feature of a codified legal system is that the ultimate foundation of the law is a comprehensive and authoritative legal code. Upon this foundation is built a superstructure of statutes enacted by the legislature. Every legal decision, in principle, can be deduced from the legal code and subsequent enacted statutes. No reference need be made to any existing body of case law. The code, when it is introduced, wipes the legal slate clean and starts afresh. Given this, it is not surprising that the first and most influential of the modern legal codes is the Napoleonic Code, the *Code Napoléon*, which emerged as a part of the new order after the French Revolution. The five basic codes upon which all of French law still rests are the Civil Code (1804), the Code of Civil Procedure (1806), the Code of Commerce (1808), the Code of Criminal Procedure (1811), and the Penal Code (1811). Subsequent legislation has built extensively on these, though changes have often been incorporated as amendments to the original codes.

The role of French as a *lingua franca* at the time of the French Revolution, together with the fact that so many continental European states went through fundamental constitutional revisions during the nineteenth century, meant that the Napoleonic Code was widely adopted as a starting point for legal codes elsewhere. "This code was attractive in form; it was written in French; it was, or seemed to be, easy to understand; it claimed to be catholic, in the true sense; it was secular without being irreligious, and democratic without being revolutionary; in short according to the creed of nineteenth-century liberalism, it set out in chapter and verse the fundamental articles of the social contract" (Lawson, Anton, and Neville Brown, p. 5). As a consequence, the influence of the *Code Napoléon* can be clearly seen in the legal systems of Belgium, Luxembourg, the Netherlands, Italy, Spain, and Portugal.

The second major source of codified European law is the German Civil Code of 1896. Besides Germany, the five Scandinavian countries—Norway, Sweden, Denmark, Finland, and Iceland—are usually identified, for historical and cultural reasons, with this tradition. Differences between the German and French traditions are minor, however, compared with the difference between all codified continental traditions on the one hand and the Anglo-American system of common law on the other. "A French lawyer will analyse a problem and will give a 'consultation' in a manner and in a language which a German, a Japanese, a Spaniard or a Brazilian will readily understand, whereas all alike will not improbably be disconcerted by the reasoning of the Englishman or the American. And the converse is equally true" (Lawson et al., p. 5).

The reason for this fundamental difference is that the common-law systems rely very much less on "laws," seen as acts of parliament, and very much more on "the law," seen as the accumulated weight of precedent set by the decisions, definitions, and interpretations made by judges. Many key legal principles and rules are thus established, not in statutes made by the legislature but in judgments made by the judiciary. In a French court, an *avocat* will cite an important precedent in order to persuade a judge about a particular argument, but the judge is not obliged to follow this; the judge deduces the final judgment from the legal code. In a British, Irish, or U.S. court, the same precedent, if it applies to the case in question, *is* the law.

These distinctions have an important bearing upon two interrelated matters that concern us here. The first has to do with the role of the legislator, and the second has to do with the separation of powers between the legislature and the judiciary. Obviously, legislation is vital in both types of systems: laws enacted by parliament override legal precedent both in common-law systems and in codified-law systems. The superior status of enacted statute law in the codified legal systems, however, does have a bearing on the work of legislators. In France, for example, and in many other continental European systems, parliamentary debates, committee reports, and other public pronouncements that are related to the passing of the legislation—the *travaux préparatoires* (preparatory works), as they are usually called—may be used as sources of a legal opinion as to what parliament had in mind when it passed a law. This is typically ruled out in a common-law system such as that of Britain, in which the sum total of the work of the legislature is the text of the laws that it enacts.

In most European countries, then, the job of a judge is to apply the law, not to make it. In a common-law system, a judge's job is also to make law. While it is a fundamental principle in all European countries that politicians should not interfere with the workings of the courts, especially with regard to the outcome of individual cases, the potential for conflict between the legislature and the judiciary is obviously greater in a common-law system. This is because individual cases provide one of the most important vehicles by which the law is moved forward in a common-law system. And the law that is made by judges, of course, can conflict with the judgments of legislators.

To take one recent example, Irish law on the extradition of prisoners alleged to have committed "political" offenses in Britain or Northern Ireland has two sources—the relevant statutes and the judgments of the Supreme Court in leading cases. Despite the legislation, however, politically important decisions on extradition have been made, as often as not, by the Supreme Court. In a key judgment (on the McGlinchy case), alleged crimes such as murder were found, contrary to precedent, not to be amenable to the defense against extradition that if they had been committed, the motivation had been political. Judgments such as these, with direct political overtones, have the potential to cause resentment among politicians and have, on occasion, led to quite strong criticism of the judiciary. An obvious U.S. parallel can be found in the politics of abortion, the legal basis for which rests heavily on a Supreme Court decision (*Roe* v. *Wade*). If this decision is reversed or seriously undermined, then U.S. abortion policy will effectively be transformed without recourse to the legislature. In continental European systems in which judges see themselves less as lawmakers and more as expert legal technicians, the separation of the legislature and the judiciary is likely to be less controversial. This is because decisions on individual cases can have little impact on the law. This distinction between common-law and codified-law systems over the political role of the judiciary is probably, for our purposes at least, the most striking difference between them.

Besides having the potential in certain countries to "make" the law, the judiciary may also have a role to play in assessing the validity of laws passed by the legislature. Legislation has to be compatible with the constitution if it is to find its way onto the statute books, and in some countries it is the courts that have the responsibility of determining the constitutionality of acts of parliament. Judicial review is a feature of the common-law rather than the civil-law tradition, and in no Western European state do the courts have as much power as their American counterparts when it comes to interpreting the constitution. Of the two common-law countries, Britain has no written constitution; even here, it is true, the courts have the power to prevent ministers from exercising power beyond their legal authority (*ultra vires*), though there is nothing to prevent parliament from then changing the laws to confer the desired power on the ministers. The Irish courts have and exercise the power of judicial review, but to nothing like the same extent as the courts in the U.S.A.

In civil-law countries, the role assigned to the judiciary, that of deciding the precise meaning of the words of a law but not of adding to this meaning, generally precludes active consideration of the validity of the laws themselves, although in some of the Scandinavian countries the courts are prepared in a very limited way to adjudicate on the constitutionality of laws. In some civil-law countries, however, a special constitutional court exists to fulfill this function; of these courts, the German constitutional court is perhaps the best known and the most influential (Conradt, pp. 192–195; Smith, pp. 204–210). Some of its decisions have a major bearing on the political process: in the 1950s it banned a communist party and a neonazi party; in the 1970s it struck down abortion legislation passed by the left-center majority in parliament; and in 1983 it insisted on major changes to the population census forms. In September 1990, it complicated the process of German reunification by declaring unconstitutional the electoral system originally proposed for the first all-German elections in December of that year. In addition, it arbitrates in disputes over the jurisdiction of various organs of government and has several times given judgments that have protected the rights of the *Land* (provincial) governments and parliaments against threatened encroachment by their central (federal) counterparts. In a few other countries, too, including Italy and Austria, special constitutional courts exist to pronounce on the constitutionality of legislation. In both Italy and Austria, most members of the constitutional courts are political appointees and may be receptive to the views of their party when considering a particular case (Spotts and Wieser, p. 153; Steiner, p. 403).

In France, too, the constitutionality or otherwise of legislation is determined by a body that is as much political as judicial, the Constitutional Council (see Safran, pp. 178–181). The council has nine members, all appointed for nine-year terms. Three are chosen by the president, three by the speaker of the lower house, and three by the speaker of the upper house. Certain categories of measures passed by parliament need clearance from this body before they become legislation. Because of the slow turnover of its members, the council can act as a brake on government, especially when a new government is confronted by a council appointed primarily by supporters of the old regime, as happened when the Socialist government came into office in 1981 and the council compelled it to moderate its program of taking some companies into public ownership.

The Legislature, the Executive, and the Bureaucracy

As we saw above, a typical Western European government comprises a cabinet that is chaired by a prime minister and made up of senior party politicians, most of whom are also the political heads of important government departments. (In some countries—for example, Italy—it is customary for some members of the cabinet to be "ministers without portfolio," which means that they have a seat at the cabinet table and a vote but do not control a government department.) Two important doctrines govern the behavior of ministers in most European countries—these are the doctrine of collective cabinet responsibility and the doctrine of individual ministerial responsibility.

The doctrine of collective cabinet responsibility means that once the cabinet has made a decision on some matter, it is collectively bound by the decision; those who opposed the decision in private cabinet meetings, for example, are expected not to criticize it subsequently in public. Every minister is equally responsible for every decision made by the cabinet, regardless of whether he or she argued for or against it at the time. A minister who cannot accept responsibility for a cabinet decision should resign. In coalition cabinets, where internal cabinet divisions may well cut along party lines, this doctrine is much more difficult to enforce than in one-party cabinets, where the normal instruments of party discipline (see below) will suffice. Nonetheless, even in a coalition system, an individual minister cannot go too far in criticizing the collective decisions of the cabinet without being expected to resign.

For our current purposes, however, it is the doctrine of individual ministerial responsibility that is more pertinent. This doctrine implies that each minister is individually responsible to the cabinet, and thereby indirectly to the legislature, for all decisions made within the department of which he or she is the political head. The buck stops with the minister concerned for all administrative mistakes and misjudgments. If the mistake is bad enough, the minister must resign, even if he or she had no direct involvement in it. This, in theory, gives ministers a strong incentive to police the department for which they are personally responsible. And, constitutionally, it is one of the main mechanisms by which the operation of the civil service can be held publicly accountable.

The extent to which a European cabinet minister is in practice able to police the bureaucracy in his or her particular area of jurisdiction has long been a topic of heated debate. The formal position is that the civil service is no more than an efficient but unfeeling administrative machine, a neutral policy-implementation system that merely puts into practice decisions made elsewhere, provides information to facilitate future decisions, and has no opinions about any of this. According to this ideal, policing the bureaucracy is simply a technical administrative problem of designing the appropriate monitoring systems, since the interests of politicians and bureaucrats will never conflict.

In practice, two important factors affect the relationship between minister and civil service department. The first concerns the nature of the civil service itself, in particular its patterns of recruitment and training. The second concerns the role of the group of close political advisers that most ministers now maintain. Political advisers are becoming increasingly important buffers between governments and bureaucracies.

Considering first the nature of the civil service, we find that, as with legal systems, European bureaucracies can rather easily be divided into two broad types. On the one hand, there is a "generalist" style of civil service in the British mold. This type of bureaucracy is characterized by a heavy reliance on general administrators, as opposed to specialists, and by a heavy emphasis on socialization into a particular decision-making culture, as opposed to technical training in particular administrative skills. The archetypal case is the British civil service. The generalist style was also inherited by the Irish civil service, while strong tendencies in this direction can be seen in Italy, Spain, and Portugal. On the other hand, there is a more "technocratic" style of civil service. This type of bureaucracy is characterized by a much greater reliance both on technical specialists and on technical training, either in administrative skills or in specialized roles (for example, statistician, economist, and engineer). Very typical cases are France, with its elite civil service school, the *École Nationale d'Administration*, and Germany, the Netherlands, and Scandinavia, in which most recruits to the civil service are law graduates with comprehensive training in public and administative law.

While much is made of such differences by those whose primary intellectual concern is with the internal workings of the bureaucracy, their impact upon the interface between the partisan political system and the civil service may not be as great as some suggest. It is more or less the received wisdom these days, both among more traditional institutional theorists in the tradition of Wildavsky, for example, and among economic modelers in the tradition of Niskanen, that bureaucracies can be seen as groups of people concerned about advancing their own interests (Niskanen; Wildavsky). This results in a general tendency, other things being equal, for bureaucracies to expand rather than contract and for them to resist political change that runs counter to bureaucratic interests. For our purposes, the importance of this is that it suggests that control of the bureaucracy is a political as well as technical administrative problem.

Turning to the second factor, the political advisers that mediate between political "master" and bureaucratic "servant," we find that it is the need for political as well as administrative control of the bureaucracy that explains the steady growth in the number of ministers who have recourse to teams of personal advisers. This group of advisers typically consists of up-and-coming young civil servants (chosen because they are sympathetic to the minister's own ideas), as well as outside consultants and senior party research staff. This system is probably most highly developed in France, where the head of the team of advisers may be endowed with the authority of the minister (Page, p. 240). Even in Britain, where the number of "political" civil service jobs has traditionally been very small, the practice is growing fast. This growth accelerated in the period 1979–1990, as a result of the Thatcher administration's increased use of personal advisers, fueled by suspicions that career civil servants were not going to be the most enthusiastic allies in carrying out a program of drastic cuts in the public sector, including the civil service itself.

Notwithstanding these developments, the notion that the bureaucracy is politically accountable as a result of the legislative accountability of its political masters is more of a cozy fiction than a hard political reality. In Europe, as elsewhere, only the very greatest scandals and administrative blunders are likely to lead to the dismissal or resignation of a minister. Only when civil servants fear that their behavior could have consequences that attract wide publicity are they likely to be deterred by the threat of ministerial fury.

For the rest of the public administration, the accountability of Western European bureaucracies depends upon a burgeoning system of administrative law. Typically, in the codified legal systems of continental Europe (see above), control over the administration is exercised by a system of administrative courts. These might deal, for example, with matters of taxation, with appeals against planning decisions, or with any of the other decision-making powers of the bureaucracy. These courts operate side by side with the courts that decide matters of civil and criminal private law; their decisions have equal standing. Administrative courts are typically operated by judges and advocates who are trained lawyers who have chosen to specialize in public and administrative law, and who are as much a part of an independent judiciary as their colleagues who specialize in private law.

Administrative law still exists, of course, in common-law systems, even in Britain, which has no written constitution. It operates in the first instance via a system of tribunals, boards, and other institutions (some of which look rather like courts, others of which look more like informal board meetings) that is far less coherently organized. The final recourse in these cases, however, is the ordinary system of civil courts, in which important matters of administrative law may be decided. The increasing complexity of the activities of the bureaucracy, as well as the impetus given by the entry of Britain and Ireland into the European Community (see Chapter 10), has meant that administrative law has increasingly been treated as a subject in its own right. More and more specialist administrative lawyers are emerging—experts in challenging land-use planning decisions, for example, or in the area of corporate tax assessments. Albeit in an ad hoc manner, there is thus an increasing tendency for interested parties to be able to contest bureaucratic decisions, even in the common-law systems.

Putting the Institutions Together

The institutional theory of parliamentary government concentrates the political accountability of the entire governmental process on the legislative vote of confidence in the executive. Parliamentary government can be said to be representative government because the legislature is held to represent the population as a whole (a matter to which we return in Chapter 6) and because the government is responsible to, and can be dismissed by, the legislature (Chapter 7). The administration of government is conducted by a civil service, overseen by ministerial masters who are themselves responsible to the cabinet and thus to the legislature.

In theory, of course, the legislature itself can legislate—it can pass laws that implement policy decisions. But control by the government over both the legislative agenda and the civil service (vital in the planning and drafting of effective legislation) greatly undermines the practical political effect of this theoretical legislative role. What the legislature can do, and what legislatures regularly *do* do, is eject the government from office. The fact that Western European governments must be able to survive in the legislature is, when all is really said and done, what makes Western European politics democratic.

BEHAVIORAL FEATURES OF WESTERN EUROPEAN PARLIAMENTARY DEMOCRACIES

While formal institutions define many of the essential characteristics of parliamentary democracy, they are not the whole story. Several key aspects of political behavior in Western Europe interact with the institutions to create the distinctive features of a typical European parliamentary system. Perhaps the most important of these features is that political parties are powerful and generally well-disciplined. Virtually all parliamentarians in Western Europe belong to some political party or another. This means that when we talk about "the legislature," we are not really talking about the interaction of a large number of legislators. We are as often as not talking about the interaction of a small number of political parties. While in Chapter 5 we will look in detail at the internal politics of political parties, it is obvious even at a cursory glance that the leaders of these parties are far more important people, politically, than the typical rank-and-file members of parliament.

Given the vital role of the legislative vote of confidence in the executive, discussed above, the existence of large and disciplined voting blocs is central to the practice of European parliamentary democracy. The coherence of European parties when compared, for example, with their U.S. counterparts depends upon two basic and related behavioral phenomena. The first is that voters tend to vote for parties rather than for individual candidates. The second is that party leaders have a number of methods by which they are able to enforce party discipline. While we will return to political parties several times in our subsequent discussions, we must explore these particular points now, in order to be able to provide a comprehensive picture of European parliamentary democracy.

Voters Vote for Parties

Notwithstanding some of the folk myths that are still handed down in British, French, and Irish politics, most European voters, when they vote in a parliamentary election, are voting first and foremost for a party rather than for a person. Even in those few countries where the myth that voters choose people rather than parties is still cherished, prominent and colorful individuals who eschew parties and fight elections as independents usually come to a sticky end—often at the hands of faceless opponents wielding nothing but a party label. Most European parliamentarians have achieved their status by being members of political parties rather than by being particularly outstanding individuals in their own right.

European voters tend to vote for parties rather than people in legislative elections precisely because when they vote, they feel that they are helping to choose a government. Since it is the government rather than the parliament that decides public policy, voters' main concern is with which party or parties will control the government rather than with the personal qualities of individual candidates. They therefore have strong incentives to look for a clear-cut choice between alternative governments or, at the very least, between party blocs powerful enough to change the complexion of governments during the process of coalition bargaining. Except in very finely poised situations, a legislator who is not a member of a political party is not likely to have much of an impact on government formation and maintenance, the single most important job of European legislatures.

The fact that it is parties rather than individual candidates that are ultimately important in European elections means that European legislators get a far smaller "personal vote" than their U.S. counterparts. (The personal vote is the vote won by a candidate because of his or her perceived merits rather than because of the party he or she represents.) This is a direct consequence of the system of parliamentary government and has a number of political effects. Three are of direct relevance here.

First, because the size of a politician's personal vote is so much smaller in Europe than it is in the United States, the fate of European candidates is determined much more by national political forces than it is by what particular people have done for particular local constituencies. European politicians who want to advance their careers face incentives to concentrate on national politics rather than on the provision of goodies for their local constituents.

A second, related matter is that incumbent candidates have much less of a built-in advantage in Europe than they do in the United States. In the United States, the incumbent is the one who brings home the bacon, thereby building a personal vote that provides a strong insulation from winds of political change at the national level. Many local incumbents in the United States are able to survive what appear to be national landslides against their party, and the result has been an average reelection rate for incumbents of over 90 percent in House elections since the war. In Europe, in contrast, being an incumbent gives little inherent advantage when it comes to the next election. In Britain, the benefits of incumbency have been estimated at around 500 votes for a long-serving MP, or about 1 percent of the total votes cast (Upton, p. 68). The difference between Britain (and virtually every other European country) and the U.S.A. is that individual MPs can do far less for their constituents than their American equivalents: "the mainstays of the US Congressman's particularistic usefulness to his constituents" were all largely shut off from the influence of the backbench MP from the middle of the nineteenth century onward (Cox, pp. 133–134). Because the personal vote is so much smaller in Europe, when the political tide turns against a particular party its candidates tend to lose their seats, no matter who they are or what they have done for their constituency. It is true that some list systems of proportional representation can insulate senior party figures by placing them high on party lists (see Chapter 6) and that under other electoral systems, which pit candidates of the same party against each other, there is such a thing as a personal vote for individuals within the party fold. Even so, prominent politicians can nonetheless disappear abruptly from the scene, through no fault of their own, simply because their party is doing badly.

The third, and probably the most important, consequence of the fact that European voters vote for parties rather than for people is that party labels are valuable commodities in Europe. This makes party legislators unwilling to defy the party line in the legislature, for fear of what will happen to them in the next election if they are expelled from the party and/or not picked as party candidates for the election, a subject to which we return in Chapter 5. And this, of course, is one of the main reasons why European legislative parties are so highly disciplined. The battlefields of European politics are littered with the corpses of those who have defied the party line.

Party Leaders Exercise Disciplinary Power

Party discipline is thus the product of a system of incentives that motivates parliamentarians. We have already seen that one such incentive is fear of losing the party label in the next election, given that voters choose parties rather than people and do so because it is parties rather than people that can influence the shape of governments. Party leaders have power over rank-and-file members of parliament because the latter know that if they become habitually disloyal to the party line in parliament, the candidate selectors (usually a group of local party activists) may well deny them access to the party label in the next election and thereby cast all but the most resilient out into the political wilderness.

A second source of power for party oligarchs is that if they are not already senior government members, then they are the people who will be senior government members when the party next gets into government. This means that European party leaders are the gatekeepers to political office; they can use this position to reward those who are loyal to the party and punish those who are not. In Britain's House of Commons, the most closely studied European parliament, there is clear evidence that the increase in party cohesion in parliamentary voting around the end of the nineteenth century was strongly linked to an increase in the number of MPs seeking ministerial posts and concluding that the best way of gaining preferment was to remain loyal at all times to the party leadership, a process that led to voters developing a strong party rather than personal orientation in elections (Cox, pp. 75–79). This system of incentives for parliamentarians now applies in virtually every European parliament. Thus, party discipline is made much stronger by the system of parliamentary government. Since the legislature is the main recruiting ground for members of the executive, those who aspire to executive office must behave themselves in the legislature. If they do not, they will displease those with the power to promote them.

PARTIES AND INSTITUTIONS IN WESTERN EUROPEAN PARLIAMENTARY DEMOCRACIES

The relatively tight discipline of political parties in Western Europe, combined with the institutions of parliamentary government, has led some to label the typical European system as one of "party government." Many examples can be found of cases where the prime minister of a country has been changed, without reference to the electorate, as a result of internal party politics, one of the most spectacular being the ousting of three-time election winner Margaret Thatcher as leader of the British Conservative party and prime minister in November 1990, due to discontent among Conservative MPs. Many more examples can be found of cases where the entire government of a country has changed, without reference to the electorate, as a result of bargaining between party leaders. Yet, while the conduct of elections is typically constrained by a complex panoply of lofty laws and constitutional provisions, the conduct of internal party politics and the selection of party leaders are usually regarded as purely the private concerns of each party.

It is difficult to overestimate the importance of party discipline in setting the whole tone of politics in a typical European country. The system of parliamentary government simply would not work without it. This is because the party oligarchs who constitute the political executive would never know when they would be able to retain the support of the legislature. Governments would thus be liable to fall unpredictably and would have no guarantee of being able to implement their legislative program. This scenario reads very much like a description of the political chaos that beset the European system in which party discipline was at its lowest— the French Fourth Republic. Here, discipline was almost as weak as it typically is in the United States, and the result, in a parliamentary government system, was chronic political instability. In only thirteen years, the Fourth Republic experienced twenty-four changes of government and fifteen prime ministers, the last six governments surviving just 6, 18, 28, 22, 36, and 27 days, respectively. The situation was brought to an end in 1958, with the establishment of the Fifth Republic. This entailed adopting a constitution that moved France significantly away from parliamentary government toward the more American, presidential system that we have already outlined. This entire episode is one of the very strongest pieces of evidence in favor of the argument that parliamentary government cannot exist without party discipline. Above all, it explains why political parties, the subject of the next series of chapters, feature so prominently in our account of representative government in Western Europe.

References

Arter, David: *Politics and Policy-Making in Finland*, St. Martin's Press, New York, and Wheatsheaf, Brighton, 1987.

Conradt, David P.: *The German Polity*, 4th ed., Longmans, New York and London, 1989.

Cox, Gary W.: *The Efficient Secret: The Cabinet and the Development of Political Parties in Victorian England*, Cambridge University Press, Cambridge, England, 1987.

Drewry, Gavin (ed.): *The New Select Committees: A Study of the 1979 Reforms*, Clarendon, Oxford, 1985.

LaPalombara, Joseph: *Democracy Italian Style*, Yale University Press, New Haven and London, 1987.

Lawson, F. H., A. E. Anton, and L. Neville Brown: *Amos and Walton's Introduction to French Law: Third Edition*, Clarendon Press, Oxford, 1967.

Lijphart, Arend: *Democracies: Patterns of Majoritarian and Consensus Government in Twenty-one Countries*, Yale University Press, New Haven and London, 1984.

Loewenberg, Gerhard, and Samuel C. Patterson: *Comparing Legislatures*, Little, Brown, Boston, 1979.

Mezey, Michael L.: *Comparative Legislatures*, Duke University Press, Durham, N.C., 1979.

Niskanen, W.: *Bureaucracy and Representative Government*, Aldine-Atherton, Chicago, 1971.

Page, E. C.: "Comparing Bureaucracies," in J.-E. Lane (ed.), *Bureaucracy and Public Choice*, Sage, London, 1987, pp. 230–254.

Polsby, Nelson W.: "Legislatures," in Fred I. Greenstein and Nelson W. Polsby (eds), *Handbook of Political Science*, vol. 5: *Governmental Institutions and Processes*, Addison-Wesley, Reading, Mass., 1975, pp. 257–319.

Pridham, Geoffrey: "Southern European Socialists and the State: Consolidation of Party Rule or Consolidation of Democracy?" in Tom Gallagher and Allan M. Williams (eds.), *Southern European Socialism: Parties, Elections, and the Challenge of Government*, Manchester University Press, Manchester, England, 1989, pp. 132–162.

Rose, Richard: *Understanding Big Government: The Programme Approach*, Sage, London and Beverly Hills, 1984.

Safran, William: *The French Polity*, 2d ed., Longmans, New York and London, 1985.

Smith, Gordon: *Democracy in Western Germany: Parties and Politics in the Federal Republic*, 3d ed., Gower, Aldershot, 1986.

Spotts, Frederic, and Theodor Wieser: *Italy: A Difficult Democracy*, Cambridge University Press, Cambridge, England, and New York, 1986.

Steiner, Kurt: *Politics in Austria*, Little, Brown, Boston, 1972.

Upton, Graham J. G.: "The Components of Voting Change in England 1983-1987," *Electoral Studies*, vol. 8, no. 1, 1989, pp. 59-74.

Wildavsky, A.: *The Politics of the Budgetary Process*, Little, Brown, Boston, 1964.

CHAPTER 2
PATTERNS IN PARTY POLITICS

This book is about the politics of representation in Western Europe. Much of it, in some way or another, is about party politics. We therefore begin by looking at the political parties that lay claim to representing the interests of European voters. Most of these parties can be classified as belonging to one or another of a small number of party "families"—the family of Christian democratic parties, for example, or of secular liberal parties. We look in detail at these party families in the following chapter. In this chapter we look at the way in which the character of political competition in any given country is conditioned by a particular constellation of competing parties, each described in terms of its relative strength and the set of policies with which it is associated. As we shall see, while every country has a distinctive blend of party families, which we might think of as its "party system," there are also striking similarities between party systems in different countries. This means that we can classify party systems into a limited number of general types. As a general introduction to the key themes that we will be discussing, therefore, we look in this chapter at the party systems of seven European countries.

The countries that we have chosen to look at below, and to return to systematically at points throughout the text, have not been chosen at random; together they capture key variations in the core themes that we discuss. They include all the "big" countries (Britain, France, Germany, Italy, and Spain), as well as two of the most interesting smaller democracies (the Netherlands and Sweden). They include very old democracies (Britain and France), as well as a very new democracy (Spain); party systems dominated by two large parties (Britain and, to a lesser extent, Germany); and systems with many parties (Italy and the Netherlands). They include systems dominated by socialist parties (Spain and Sweden), by Christian democratic parties (Germany and Italy), and by conservative parties (Britain). Finally, they include systems in which elections are conducted under a plurality voting system (Britain and France), as well as those which employ different forms of proportional representation (Germany, Italy, the Netherlands, Spain, and Sweden); and they include systems which invariably produce a single-party government (such as Britain), those which invariably produce a coalition government (Germany, Italy, and the Netherlands), and those which alternate between a single-party and coalition government (Sweden).

As we argued in the Preface, we in no sense claim that the countries we have selected are "typical"—it should already be clear that there is no such thing as a typical Western European country. We have chosen the seven party systems described below because, between them, they include most of the types of variation that we must use if we are to be able to describe the complex mosaic of Western European party systems.

SEVEN WESTERN EUROPEAN PARTY SYSTEMS

Party Politics in Britain

On the face of it, the British party system appears to be one of the most clear-cut in Western Europe. Two large and more or less evenly matched parties confront one another. On one side is the Labour party, a self-consciously socialist party which initially mobilized in order to promote and defend the interests of the working class. The party has always enjoyed a close relationship with the trade union movement and has traditionally seen itself as the political wing of a wider labor movement. Despite this, Labour governments have sometimes found themselves in bitter confrontation with the trade unions over attempts to impose national income policies, notably during the long 1978–1979 "winter of discontent" that led to Labour's defeat in the 1979 general election and ushered in the era of Conservative governments, led by Margaret Thatcher until 1990, and then by John Major.

The Conservative party is Labour's main opponent. The major aims of the Conservatives are to defend the rights of private property, to encourage market forces, and to resist the encroachment of the state into spheres of (especially economic) activity seen as being properly the realm of unregulated private individuals. For most of its history, however, the party has defended the traditional moral order, even if this has meant state involvement in regulating personal morality. The Conservatives have also been advocates of tough law-and-order policies and nationalist foreign policy stances based upon a strong military profile. This has often led the party to advocate high levels of public spending on policing and national defense. In contrast to the support for Labour, the Conservatives' strongest support comes from middle-class voters and the most privileged sectors of British society.

As Table 2.1 shows, the Conservatives won a majority of seats in the U.K. parliament in elections in 1979, 1983, and 1987, thanks in part to a disproportional first-past-the-post electoral system (see Chapter 6). They thus governed Britain throughout the 1980s. During that period they sought to weaken the power of the trade unions, to reduce the size of the state sector, and to sell off many public enterprises to the private sector (see Chapter 8). Throughout the same period

TABLE 2.1
Elections in Britain since 1979

Party	1979		1983		1987	
	% Votes	No. of Seats	% Votes	No. of Seats	% Votes	No. of Seats
Conservatives	43.9	339	42.4	397	42.0	376
Labour	36.9	269	27.6	209	30.7	229
Liberal party*	13.8	11	13.7	17	12.8	17
Social Democrats*	—	—	11.6	6	9.7	5
Scottish National party	1.6	2	1.1	2	1.4	3
Welsh nationalists	0.4	2	0.4	2	0.4	3
Irish nationalists	0.6	2	0.8	2	0.8	4
Ulster unionists	1.3	10	1.4	15	1.2	13
Others	1.4	—	0.8	—	1.1	—
Total	100.0	635	100.0	650†	100.0	650

Party composition of government:
Conservatives, 1979, 1983, 1987

*Formed an electoral pact in 1983 and 1987.
†The number of seats in the House of Commons was increased in 1983.

Labour offered consistent opposition to this program, resisting attacks on public spending, opposing encroachments on trade union rights, and defending existing levels of public provision of a range of goods and services.

The opposition between these starkly contrasted partisan views is clearly of major importance to the people of Britain. Deciding which view is to prevail has fundamental implications for the basic concerns of almost every individual citizen. This important ideological decision is sharply defined for voters, since only the two major parties have a realistic chance of winning an overall legislative majority. Voters are therefore in effect choosing between two alternative governments with clearly distinctive policy profiles. The party that wins an election with a working majority has every opportunity to implement its policy program. In 1979, for example, the Conservatives held an overall majority of 43 seats in the 635-seat House of Commons; in 1983, when reelected, they enjoyed a majority of 144 seats in the newly enlarged 650-seat House; in 1987, they enjoyed a majority of 102 seats. Given such clear majorities, the Conservative governments of the 1980s had little fear of defeat and hence experienced few real difficulties in pushing through their strongly partisan program.

This image of clear-cut confrontation between two sharply distinguished parties, each hoping to form a majority government on its own, is, of course, something of a simplification. There are, for example, several small regionally based nationalist—and antinationalist—parties. There is the Scottish National party, as well as a Welsh nationalist party (Plaid Cymru). In Northern Ireland, which remains an integral part of the United Kingdom, there are two parties which advocate breaking away from the United Kingdom and favor unity with the Irish Republic: the Social Democratic and Labour party (SDLP) and Sinn Fein. There are also two unionist parties which fight to preserve Northern Ireland as part of the

United Kingdom: the Ulster Unionist party and the Democratic Unionist party. But while often winning substantial support in their own local areas and taking some seats in the House of Commons, these parties hardly impinge at all on the British party system taken as a whole. In 1987, for example, the total number of seats won by regional parties in the House of Commons was only 23, fewer than one-fifteenth of the Conservative total and just about one-tenth of the number of seats won by Labour!

Of greater potential importance as a deviation from pure two-party politics in Britain is the presence of a "center" party or parties. Traditionally represented by the long-established Liberal party, this center group promotes policies which fall between the more radical alternatives of Labour and the Conservatives, and it wins some support from both major social classes. The center received a major electoral boost in the early 1980s when the Social Democratic party, a moderate faction of the Labour party, split off as a result of what it saw as the unwelcome growth of the Labour left. Together, the Liberals and Social Democrats formed an alliance of the center and posed perhaps the greatest postwar challenge to the dominance of two-party politics. In 1987 they won almost 23 percent of the vote, just 8 percent less than Labour. Indeed, in the southern part of England, this alliance actually displaced Labour as the major challenger to the Conservatives.

In the event, however, even this development had little real impact. Despite the electoral popularity of the Liberal–Social Democratic alliance, the bias against third parties in the British simple-plurality voting system (see Chapter 6) left the two center parties with only 17 out of 650 seats for their 23 percent of the vote. When the chips were down, the alliance did little to disturb the traditional British two-party system—at least at the parliamentary level—and the parties involved in it, despite merging formally in an attempt to improve their fortunes, subsequently went into serious electoral decline, with the majority of members of the SDP eventually joining the Liberals in a new, but still electorally weak, Liberal Democrat party. (On the British party system, see Drucker and also Finer; for a more limited but more contemporary assessment, see Seldon.)

Party Politics in Sweden

In Sweden, as in Britain, there is a major socialist party which initially mobilized in order to promote and defend the interests of the working class and forged strong links with the trade union movement. There is also a Swedish conservative party, now known as the Moderates, which sets out to defend the interests of the middle class and the more privileged sectors of the population. In this sense, Sweden is no different from Britain, with the representation of class interests taking the form of a partisan conflict between left and right. But it is here that the parallels end, for as Table 2.2 shows, the actual balance of forces on both the left and the right in Sweden differs sharply from that in the United Kingdom.

The Swedish Social Democrats have been much more successful than the British Labour party, holding governmental power in Sweden almost without interruption from the early 1930s through the mid-1970s. Indeed, the Social Democrats in Sweden have been the most successful socialist party in Western Europe and have used this success to establish one of Western Europe's strongest and most egalitarian welfare states (see Castles and also Stephens).

TABLE 2.2
Elections in Sweden since 1979

Party	1979		1982		1985		1988	
	% Votes	No. of Seats	% Votes	No. of Seats	% Votes	No. of Seats	% Votes	No. of Seats
Social Democrats	43.2	154	45.6	166	44.7	159	43.6	156
Communist party	5.6	20	5.6	20	5.4	19	5.9	21
Ecology party	—	—	1.7	—	1.5	—	5.5	20
Liberal party	10.6	38	5.9	21	14.2	51	12.2	44
Center party	18.1	64	15.5	56	9.9*	43	11.4	42
Christian Democrats	1.4	—	1.9	—	2.5*	1	3.0	—
Moderates	20.3	73	23.6	86	21.3	76	18.3	66
Others	0.8	—	0.3	—	0.5	—	0.1	—
Total	100.0	349	100.0	349	100.0	349	100.0	349

Party composition of government:
Coalition of Center party, Liberals, and Moderates, 1979–1981
Coalition of Center party and Liberals, 1981–1982
Social Democrats, with external Communist party support, 1982–

*Formed an electoral pact in 1985.

The second point of contrast between Sweden and Britain is that despite their success, the Swedish Social Democrats have never monopolized the representation of the left. They have always been challenged by a small but persistent Communist party, which usually wins about 5 percent of the popular vote. Given Sweden's proportional electoral system, this usually translates into about 5 percent of parliamentary seats. The challenge posed to the Social Democrats by the Swedish Communist party is nevertheless a reasonably amicable one, and the smaller party has often supported its larger rival in parliament, enabling the Social Democrats to take control of the government even when they do not command a majority of seats, as has been the case since 1982. In 1989, in the wake of the collapse of the communist regimes in Eastern and Central Europe, the Swedish Communist party changed its name to the Left party.

A third point of contrast with Britain is that unlike the British Conservatives, the Swedish Moderates fall very considerably short of monopolizing the non-socialist opposition in parliament. On the contrary, the Swedish center and right are quite severely fragmented. In addition to the Moderates, there is a small Liberal party, which commanded some 10 percent of parliamentary seats during the 1980s and draws support primarily from middle-class voters who are reluctant to endorse the more conservative Moderates. There is also a Center party, which initially grew as an agrarian party seeking to represent the interests of Swedish farmers and now draws support from across the social spectrum; it won around 12 percent of parliamentary seats in the 1980s. The Moderates, which polled an average of 20 percent of the votes in the 1980s, are thus just one of three nonsocialist parties competing on the center-right of the Swedish party system. It is this fragmentation of the right that has allowed the Social Democratic party to dominate Swedish politics for much of this century.

Even so, the Social Democrats have not had it all their own way. The three parties of the center-right cooperated to form a series of antisocialist coalitions in the late 1970s and early 1980s, and the overall pattern of votes in Sweden tends to be finely balanced between the left and center-right blocs. The combined support for the Communists and the Social Democrats on one side almost exactly matches the combined vote won by the Moderates, the Liberals, and the Center party on the other. This "two-bloc" competition thus has some similarities with the two-party competition that characterized British politics in the postwar period. (On the Swedish party system, as well as Scandinavian party politics in general, see Berglund and Lindstrom, Sainsbury, and Einhorn and Logue.)

Party Politics in Germany

On the face of it, at least for most of the postwar period, the West German party system has appeared very similar to that of Britain. Here, too, there are two main protagonists: the Social Democrats (SPD), the traditional party of the working class, and the Christian Democrats (CDU/CSU), the main representative of conservative interests. Between these two parties, with a small but enduring presence, lies a liberal party, the Free Democrats (FDP). Although the Free Democrats poll fewer votes than their British counterpart, they have always won quite a substantial representation in the Bundestag, the lower house of the German parliament, since the electoral system ensures that all parties polling 5 percent or more of the vote are represented in proportion to their electoral support (see Chapter 6).

Despite superficial similarities between the British and German systems, however, there are also some striking contrasts. In the first place, the relatively strong parliamentary presence of the Free Democrats has ensured that neither of the two major parties is able single-handedly to command a majority of seats in the Bundestag (see Table 2.3). In Germany, therefore, in contrast to Britain, coalition government has been the norm. Indeed, the last occasion on which a single party secured an overall majority in the Bundestag was in 1957, when the Christian Democrats, under their powerful and popular leader Konrad Adenauer, won just over 50 percent of the votes and 54 percent of the seats. Even then, however, a coalition government was formed, with the CDU being joined in government by the now defunct German party, which then held 17 seats in the Bundestag. Since then, the FDP has provided the necessary coalition support for each of the major parties, and (with one exception during the "grand coalition" between the CDU and the SPD in 1966–1969) it has been a junior partner in every government since 1961. The FDP cooperated with the CDU from 1961 to 1966 and resumed support in 1982, and it cooperated with the SPD from 1969 through 1982.

In addition to its powerful governmental role, the FDP can be distinguished from the British Liberals in two other respects. First, it promotes an emphatically conservative liberalism. It emphasizes individual as opposed to collective rights and lays a greater emphasis than even the CDU on the need to roll back the state and maximize private freedoms. Second, the FDP's roots can be found in secular opposition to Catholic politics rather than in liberal opposition to secular conservatism. Despite its brokerage role in government formation, the FDP can therefore be seen as being substantially to the right of the British center parties.

The second major point of contrast with Britain concerns the CDU. As its name implies, the CDU is not simply a conservative party; it is also a Christian party, a party that has traditionally placed substantial weight on the defense of religious values against the secularism of both the SPD and the FDP. Heir to the primarily Catholic Center party of Weimar Germany, which was the major representative of

TABLE 2.3
Elections in West Germany since 1980

Party	1980		1983		1987	
	% Votes	No. of Seats	% Votes	No. of Seats	% Votes	No. of Seats
Christian Democrats (CDU/CSU)	44.5	226	48.8	244	44.3	223
Social Democrats	42.9	218	38.2	193	37.0	186
Free Democrats	10.6	53	7.0	34	9.1	46
Greens	1.5	0	5.6	27	8.3	42
Others	0.5	0	0.4	0	1.3	0
Total	100.0	497	100.0	498	100.0	497

Party composition of government:
Coalition of Social Democrats and Free Democrats, 1980–1982
Coalition of Christian Democrats and Free Democrats, 1982–

the moderate right in the period prior to the mobilization of nazism, the postwar Christian Democrats have since broadened their support base through an explicit appeal to Protestant voters. This new pan-Christian strategy was facilitated by the fact that a large proportion of the Protestant electorate in Germany resided in what was to become the German Democratic Republic, thus undermining the potential for the emergence in West Germany of distinctively Protestant parties such as those which proved so crucial in Dutch politics (see below). Second, the "Christian Democrats" are effectively two parties, the CDU proper and its permanent political ally, the Bavarian Christian Social Union (CSU). Unlike the CDU, the CSU is distinctively Catholic and, to the extent that it operates autonomously, is generally regarded as the most conservative party in West Germany.

The third, albeit less marked, contrast with Britain is to be found in the character of the socialist party, the SPD. From its origins in the late nineteenth century as the most radical and powerful socialist party in Europe, when the SPD leadership included some of the foremost Marxist intellectuals in the international socialist movement, the party has developed into one of the most moderate and centrist social democratic organizations in Western Europe. The SPD was effectively excluded from office in the early years of postwar West Germany, and it suffered from the reaction against political extremism which flowed in the wake of both nazism and the communist takeover of East Germany. In 1959, in an effort to acquire a legitimate role in the new state, the party adopted what became known as the Bad Godesberg program, accepting the principle of the free market economy and a commitment to NATO, and effectively endorsing the policies then being pursued by the incumbent Christian Democratic government. This transformation was finally completed in 1966, when, as noted above, the party joined in a grand coalition with the Christian Democrats. Since then, the degree of ideological conflict between the two major parties has been quite insignificant, and the contemporary West German party system is now among the most consensual in Western Europe (e.g., see Klingemann).

The combination of alignments based on class (SPD versus CDU and FDP) and religion (CDU versus SPD and FDP) has led Pappi (pp. 12–14) to view the German party system as being characterized by a "triangular" rather than "unidimensional" pattern of competition. According to this view, various alliances can and do prove possible. Thus the moderate socialism of the SPD and the residual Catholic emphases of the CDU can find common ground in a defense of the welfare state and of consensual rather than confrontational policy making. The SPD and FDP, in turn, can find common ground in rejecting the incorporation of Catholic values into public policy (on issues such as abortion and divorce, for example). And the CDU and FDP can—and most often do—find common ground in their defense of the interests of private property and capital.

Over the past decade, two factors have emerged that may undermine this particular balance. In the first place, in 1983 and in 1987 the new, radical Green party managed to win sufficient electoral support to push it past the 5 percent threshold imposed by the German electoral system and gained strong representation in the Bundestag. If the Greens are able to maintain this level of support in future elections, even though they once again fell below the 5 percent threshold within the West German areas of the all-German elections of 1990 (see below), party competition could well develop into a confrontation between two rival blocs, with the SPD and Greens confronting the CDU and FDP. To be sure, there would be much difficult negotiation and internal party conflict before the SPD and Greens agreed on a common program for government. Nevertheless, the presence of the Greens does have the potential to destroy the pivotal role of the FDP in German politics and create a two-bloc pattern quite similar to that which, for example, characterizes party competition in Sweden.

The second, and incomparably the more important, recent development has been the collapse of East Germany and the unification of the two German states. Greater Germany must now accommodate more than 12 million new voters who have yet to be socialized into stable partisan identities and whose political behavior may therefore prove quite volatile for some time to come. In the first democratic elections in East Germany, in March 1990, these new electors voted over-whelmingly for the Christian Democrats (which won 47 percent of the poll), with the Social Democrats winning just 22 percent and the reformed Communist party winning 16 percent.

The Christian Democratic successes were confirmed more recently in the first Bundestag elections of the newly unified state, which were held on December 2, 1990. These were the first all-German elections since Hitler seized power in 1933 and once again left the coalition of the Christian Democrats and the liberal FDP with a clear overall majority, in which they now hold a total of 398 seats in the newly enlarged Bundestag, as against 264 seats for the combined opposition parties. Indeed, the FDP success was even more marked than that of the CDU, and the party polled a substantially larger share of the vote in the eastern part of the country than it did in the west (see Table 2.4).

TABLE 2.4
Results of All-German Election of December 2, 1990

Party	% Votes	No. of Seats	% Votes in West Germany	% Votes in East Germany
Christian Democrats (CDU/ CSU)	43.8	319	44.1	43.4
Social Democrats	33.5	239	35.9	23.6
Free Democrats	11.0	79	10.6	13.4
Greens (West)	3.9	—	4.7	—
Bündnis '90/ Greens (East)	1.2	8	—	5.9
Democratic Socialism (PDS)	2.4	17	0.3	9.9
Republicans	2.1	—	2.3	1.3
Others	2.1	—	2.1	2.5
Total	100.0	662	100.0	100.0

Source: Süddeutsche Zeitung, 4 December 1990.

A number of other aspects of these crucial elections should also be underlined. In the first place, and as part of the transitional arrangements prior to complete unification, the rule whereby parties require a national minimum of 5 percent of the vote in order to win representation in the Bundestag (see Chapter 6) was modified for the purposes of these first all-German elections. Rather than treating the threshold as applying to Germany as a whole, it was agreed that a party would need 5 percent in *either* the area that was formerly West Germany *or* in the area that was formerly East Germany. Thus, while the former East German Communist party, now reorganized as the Party of Democratic Socialism (PDS), won only 2.4 percent in terms of the nation as a whole, it won some 10 percent of the vote in the former East Germany, which was double the threshold and sufficient to win the party 17 seats.

Second, what was perhaps even more striking about the 1990 results was the poor showing of the Greens, which failed to reach the threshold in the west (they polled only 4.7 percent), and which have continued to be represented in the Bundestag only under the auspices of the *Bündnis '90*, the alliance of East German citizens' movements that includes New Forum, the popular movement that had spearheaded the 1989 protests and revolution. The western Greens had suffered as a result of their own internal divisions and from their opposition to unification, and had also been damaged by the increased salience of economic issues and by the rival SPD's adoption of many of the environmental policy priorities.

Third, and despite the success of the incumbent coalition, the German party system is now more fragmented than at any point in the past thirty years, with five parties represented in the Bundestag, ranging from the *Bündnis '90* to the reformed East German Communist party, the PDS. Moreover, since Germany will probably revert in its next elections to a nationwide 5 percent threshold, and since the "new" East German voters have yet to be integrated into a system of stable partisan loyalties, future all-German elections could prove quite volatile, with a substantial proportion of votes shifting from one party to another in response to quite short-term factors. Either way, the relatively stable and cozy balance that has characterized the West German party system over the past two decades is unlikely to persist. (On the West German party system in general, see Padgett and Burkett, Pappi, Smith, and Dalton.)

Party Politics in the Netherlands

Like politics in Sweden and unlike politics in Britain and West Germany, Dutch politics is highly fragmented. Many parties compete for electoral and parliamentary support. Like West Germany and unlike Sweden and Britain, however, the Netherlands does not have competition between two clearly distinguished parties or blocs. Rather, three large parties, none in a position to win a working majority on its own, provide the major alternatives before voters. The various maneuverings of these parties create a shifting system of coalitions and alliances.

The first of these parties is a socialist party, the Labor party (PvdA), which usually wins roughly a third of the vote. Given the exceptionally proportional Dutch electoral system, this guarantees the Labor party roughly a third of the parliamentary seats (see Table 2.5). Both programmatically and in terms of its electoral support, the party stands as the effective equivalent of the Swedish and

TABLE 2.5
Elections in the Netherlands since 1981

Party	1981 % Votes	1981 No. of Seats	1982 % Votes	1982 No. of Seats	1986 % Votes	1986 No. of Seats	1989 % Votes	1989 No. of Seats
Communist party	2.1	3	1.8	3	0.6	—	—	—
Pacifist Socialists	2.1	3	2.3	3	1.2	1	—	—
Radical Political party	2.0	3	0.7	2	1.3	2	—	—
Green Left*	—	—	—	—	—	—	4.1	6
Labor party	28.3	44	30.4	47	33.3	52	31.9	49
Democrats '66	11.1	17	4.3	6	6.1	9	7.9	12
Liberals	17.3	26	23.1	36	17.4	27	14.6	22
Center party	0.1	—	0.8	1	0.4	—	0.9	1
Evangelical People's party'	0.5	—	0.7	1	0.2	—		
Christian Democrats	30.8	48	29.4	45	34.6	54	35.3	54
Reformed Political League	0.8	1	0.8	1	1.0	1	1.2	2
Political Reformed party	2.0	3	1.9	3	1.7	3	1.9	3
Reformed Political Federation	1.2	2	1.5	2	0.9	1	1.0	1
Others	1.8	—	1.4	—	1.4	—	1.2	—
Total	100.0	150	100.0	150	100.0	150	100.0	150

Party composition of governments:
Coalition of Christian Democrats, Labor party, and Democrats 66, 1981–1982
Coalition of Christian Democrats and Liberals, 1982–1989
Coalition of Christian Democrats and Labor party 1989–

*An electoral pact formed by the Communist party, the Pacifist Socialists, the Radicals, and the Evangelical People's party.

British socialist parties. It bases itself primarily in the traditional working class and promotes both the role of the welfare state and a more egalitarian distribution of social and economic resources. Given its relatively small size, however, it has little hope of forming a government of its own and is obliged to forge alliances with parties to its right.

The first of these is the Christian Democratic Appeal (CDA), which wins more or less the same level of support as the Labor party. As its name implies, however, and like the major nonsocialist party in Germany, the Dutch CDA is not simply a conservative party. It also seeks to represent the views of Christian voters, both Protestant and Roman Catholic. Religious divisions, reflecting conflicts both between the different Christian denominations and between those who are generally proclerical and those who are anticlerical, have always been important in Dutch politics. For much of the postwar period, indeed, Protestant and Catholic voters were represented by two separate Protestant parties and one Catholic party. Since 1977, however, and partly as a result of the general weakening of religious ties and the decreasing political salience of interdenominational divisions, these three parties have united behind one pan-Christian party, the CDA. Over and above its defense of religious values, the CDA maintains a moderate conservative position in relation to social and economic policies, drawing electoral support from all major social classes.

The third major party in the Netherlands is the Liberal party (VVD). This usually wins less than 20 percent of the vote and is a much more distinctively middle-class party than the CDA. The Liberals represent the main secular opposition to the Labor party and are far less willing than the CDA to compromise in the direction of Labor's social and economic concerns. At the same time, however, the VVD is also hostile to the representation of religious values in politics. In this respect it sometimes finds common ground with the Labor party in opposition to the CDA. Indeed, the Liberal party first mobilized in Dutch politics primarily as middle-class opposition to the growing appeal of religious parties. (This links the Dutch Liberals to the German FDP and sets them apart from the British and Swedish Liberals, both of which originated as moderate middle-class alternatives to secular conservative opponents, and both of which are still oriented toward more centrist policies.)

Thus, when it comes to class issues and an economic program emphasizing the need for a minimum of state intervention and a maximum reliance on market forces, the Dutch Liberals identify more strongly with the CDA than with Labor. In terms of the religious-secular divide, however, the Liberals find themselves on the same side as Labor. At the same time, because the CDA's conservative appeal is more moderate than that of the Liberals, the CDA sometimes seeks alliances with Labor rather than with the other right-wing party.

The result, as might be expected, is a shifting pattern of coalition government. In 1981, for example, the CDA formed a short-lived government coalition with Labor, a government which was displaced by a CDA-Liberal alliance in 1982. This government survived until 1989, when it was displaced by a CDA-Labor coalition. At center stage in Dutch party politics, therefore, are three key actors which go in and out of government in a shifting series of alliances. This pattern is complicated by the presence of a number of smaller parties, left-wing and right-wing, secular and religious. None of these, however, is nearly as central to the government formation process as the three main parties. (On the Dutch party system, see Daalder, 1987; Wolinetz; and Daalder and Irwin.)

Party Politics in Italy

At first sight, the differences between party politics in Italy and party politics in Britain, Sweden, West Germany, or the Netherlands may not appear very great. In Italy, as in each of the other countries, a left-right opposition lies at the heart of party competition, reflecting the confrontation between parties promoting working-class interests and those promoting the interests of better-off social groups. As in Britain and Sweden, the traditional left, represented in Italy by both a communist and a socialist party, usually wins about 40 percent of the vote. And as in West Germany and the Netherlands, there is also a religious-secular divide, although in Italy proclerical forces are exclusively Catholic.

The distinguishing feature of the Italian party system is not so much the particular interests which are represented but rather the depth of the divisions between the competing parties. The major party on the traditional left has been the Italian Communist party (PCI), which, in early 1991, after much agonizing, and in reaction to the collapse of the communist regimes in Eastern and Central Europe, changed its name to the Democratic Party of the Left (Partito Democratico de

TABLE 2.6
Elections in Italy since 1979

Party	1979		1983		1987	
	% Votes	No. of Seats	% Votes	No. of Seats	% Votes	No. of Seats
Communist party	30.4	201	29.9	198	26.6	177
Proletarian Democracy	0.8	—	1.5	7	1.7	8
Socialist party	9.8	62	11.4	73	14.3	94
Radical party	3.5	18	2.2	11	2.6	13
Greens	—	—	—	—	2.5	13
Social Democrats	3.8	20	4.1	23	3.0	17
Republican party	3.0	16	5.1	29	2.1	21
Liberal party	1.9	9	2.9	16	2.1	11
Christian Democrats	38.3	262	32.9	225	34.3	234
Italian Social Movement	5.3	30	6.8	42	5.9	35
South Tyrol Peoples party	0.6	4	0.5	3	0.5	3
Sardinian Action party	0.1	—	0.2	1	0.4	2
Val d'Aosta Union	0.1	1	0.1	1	0.1	1
Lombard League	—	—	—	—	0.5	1
Others	2.3	7	1.9	1	1.7	—
Total	100.0	630	100.0	630	100.0	630

Party composition of government:
Coalition of Socialists, Social Democrats, Republicans, Liberals, and Christian Democrats, 1979–*

*While this so-called *pentapartito* cabinet has frequently resigned and been reconstituted in this period, the party composition has remained unchanged.

Sinistra—PDS). This has long been the strongest communist party in Western Europe and averaged 29 percent of the votes during the 1980s (Table 2.6). For most of the postwar era, the PCI retained the aura of a far-left opposition, and the strength of PCI support thus marked the Italian party system off from many other European democracies. At the opposite end of the left-right ideological spectrum in Italy is the neofascist Italian Social Movement (MSI), which usually polls about 6 percent of the vote.

Ranged between these extremes are five more central parties. The biggest of these is the Christian Democratic party (DC), which usually polls about 30 percent of the popular vote. Like the Dutch CDA, this party combines a moderately conservative economic appeal with the promotion of religious values.

Two other parties mobilize on the center-right in Italy—the Liberals and the Republicans between them average about 7 percent of the vote. While the tiny Liberal party is the more right-wing of the two and has an ideological position similar to that of its Dutch and German counterparts, the Republicans reflect the more centrist politics characteristic of the liberal parties in both Sweden and the United Kingdom. Both are largely middle-class parties that endorse many of the conservative economic appeals of the DC while rejecting its emphasis on religious values.

On the center-left of the system lies the small Social Democratic party (PSDI), which usually polls about 4 percent of the vote. More influential on the left is the Socialist party (PSI), which usually polls about 12 percent of the vote and shares many of the concerns of the major socialist parties in Britain, Sweden, the Netherlands, and West Germany.

The Italian party system, therefore, comprises both a more fragmented and a more polarized set of alternatives than can be found in the other countries we have considered. As a consequence, it is impossible for a clear-cut left- or right-wing bloc to present itself to voters as a realistic governing option. On the left, the combined support of the PCI, PSI, and PSDI, together with that of the smaller radical parties, might appear sufficient to form a government coalition. Yet because of the perceived extremism of the PCI, this option seemed impossible to realize, at least through the end of the 1980s. There might also seem to be a potential parliamentary majority on the right, but this option also proves impossible to realize given the far-right position of the MSI—suggestions by the Christian Democrats that they might deal with the MSI have proved very unpopular with voters. The consequent exclusion of both ends of the political spectrum from government has often left the remaining parties searching for a parliamentary majority through the creation of persistent—if unstable—governments of the center, much like the pattern that prevailed in the French Fourth Republic (see below). The participants typically ranged from the socialists to the Christian democrats to the liberals, who combined into a five-party (*pentapartito*) coalition stradding the center-left and the center-right. (On the Italian party system, see Di Palma, Farneti, and Donovan.)

Party Politics in France

The current French constitution dates from 1958, which marked the beginning of the French Fifth Republic. Before this, France was governed under the constitution of the Fourth Republic, dating from 1945. During the Fourth Republic the French party system bore many similarities to that of Italy. Politics on the left was dominated by a large pro-Stalinist Communist party (PCF), which polled an average of about 27 percent of the vote. There was also a steadily weakening Socialist party, which averaged less than 19 percent of the vote. The center was occupied by a Radical party, which won an average of 12 percent, and by the Catholic Popular Republican Movement (MRP), which polled over 25 percent in the 1940s but which then fell back to just 12 percent in the 1950s. On the right, a secular conservative party persisted throughout the period, with around 13 percent of the vote. In the 1950s, however, the conservatives were marginalized by two rivals on the right, the Gaullists (winning 22 percent of the vote in 1951) and the Poujadists (winning 12 percent in 1956), both reflecting a far-right opposition to the constitutional arrangements of the Fourth Republic. Faced with anticonstitutional opposition from both left and right, which proved both more extremist and more powerful than in Italy, the center was unable to hold and the result, as we have seen, was chronic political instability.

Three key changes have occurred in the party system of the Fifth French Republic (Bartolini, pp. 104–115). First is the disappearance of the extreme right as a result of the institutionalization of Gaullism (now known as Rally for the Republic—RPR) under the new regime. This trend was partially reversed in the late 1980s as a result of the emergence of the xenophobic and extremely right-wing National Front (see Table 2.7). The second major change is the emergence of a much more clearly defined bipolar pattern of competition, much like the two-bloc

TABLE 2.7
Legislative Elections* in France since 1981

Party	1981		1986		1988	
	% Votes	No. of Seats	% Votes	No. of Seats	% Votes	No. of Seats
Communist party	16.1	43	9.8	35	11.3	27
Socialist party/ Left Radicals	37.8	281	31.4	211	37.6	280
Other Left	1.3	0	3.0	5	0.4	0
Union for French Democracy	19.3	63	41.0†	277	18.5	129
Rally for the Republic	20.8	80			19.2	128
Other Right	2.7	6	3.8	14	2.9	12
National Front	—	—	9.7	35	9.6	1
Ecologists	1.1	0	1.2	0	0.4	0
Others	0.9	1	0.1	1	0.1	0
Total	100.0	474	100.0	577	100.0	577

Party composition of government:
Coalition of Socialists/Left Radicals, and Communist party, 1981–1984
Socialists/Left Radicals, 1984–1986
Coalition of UDF and RPR, 1986–1988
Socialists/Left Radicals, 1988–

*Voting percentages refer to first-ballot results.
†Electoral alliance between UDF and RPR.

model in the Swedish case, in which the left, represented by the Socialist party (PS) and the Communist party, competes against the right, represented by the new Gaullist party (RPR) and the coalition of forces which organizes under the label Union for French Democracy (UDF). The emergence of this bipolar pattern was facilitated by the abandonment of the proportional electoral formula which had been used in the Fourth Republic and its replacement by a double-ballot majority system, which encourages competition between just two candidates in each constituency in the second round of voting (see Chapter 6). It was also encouraged by the introduction of a directly elected presidency in 1962, which also involves just two candidates competing in the second round of voting (see Table 2.8).

The third change which has occurred during the Fifth Republic is a shift in the balance of forces within both the left and the right. For a variety of reasons, both ideological and institutional (Bartolini), the PCF has been increasingly marginalized in recent years, and the left is now dominated by the Socialist party. The PS, together with its electoral allies among the left radicals (MRG), now commands the largest share of the vote in France. The PCF has fallen to just 10 percent of the poll and plays at most a supporting role for the PS. Indeed, in 1981, for the first time ever, the PS emerged with an overall majority of seats in the lower house of the French parliament (the *Assemblée Nationale*), although it initially chose to govern in coalition with the PCF. In the same year, with its candidate François Mitterrand, the party won the presidency for the first time ever, albeit with PCF support.

There has also been a substantial shift in the balance of forces on the right, with the disappearance of the MRP and, more recently, a relative decline in support for the Gaullists relative to support for the UDF. [The latter, like the center-right electoral alliances in Spain (see below), combines liberal, Christian, and conservative forces.] In the presidential elections of 1974, for example, the Gaullist candidate Chaban Delmas ran a poor third in the first ballot, with the election eventually being won by Giscard d'Estaing, one of the key figures behind the formation of the UDF.

TABLE 2.8
Presidential Elections in France since 1981

	1981		1988	
	% Votes		% Votes	
Party	1st Ballot	2d Ballot	1st Ballot	2d Ballot
Communist party	15.3	—	6.8	—
Socialist party	25.8	51.8	34.1	54.0
Union for French Democracy	28.3	48.2	16.5	—
Rally for the Republic	18.0	—	19.9	46.0
Other Left	5.6	—	4.5	—
Other Right	3.0	—	—	—
National Front	—	—	14.4	—
Ecologist	3.9	—	3.8	—
Total	100.0	100.0	100.0	100.0

Recent party competition in France, therefore, not only has taken the form of a much better defined confrontation between left and right, but also has, at least until recently, been increasingly dominated by the more moderate of the forces within each bloc.

The Socialists have played the dominant role in French government for most of the 1980s. Mitterrand was reelected to the presidency for a second seven-year term of office in 1988, and the PS also maintained control of the Cabinet from 1981 to 1986, a control which it regained in 1988. Initially elected on quite a radical program of social and economic reform, which included a commitment to the widespread nationalization of private-sector services, the PS has since become more centrist and, as Machin (p. 68) has observed, has now developed a more "modernizing, moderate and managerial image."

Despite the consolidation of the French party system during the Fifth Republic, the growth in support for the National Front has placed immense strains on the capacity of the center-right to maintain a cohesive alternative. In an effort to stave off this new competition, the Gaullists have tended to move toward the right, with the result that French politics now bears many of the characteristics of a system such as that in Italy, and it may well be that future stability will be ensured only through alliances of the center against the extremes of both the left and the right. (On the modern French party system in general, see Bartolini; Wilson, 1982; and Machin.)

Party Politics in Spain

Before the collapse of Communist rule in Eastern Europe in 1989 and 1990, Spain was one of Europe's youngest democracies. The elections held in Spain in 1977, two years after the death of the right-wing dictator General Franco, were the first since Franco had seized power after the defeat of the democratic Republican forces in the 1936–1939 Civil War. As in the early years of many other new democracies, the first period of Spanish democracy was characterized by the creation of many new parties and by great electoral volatility. What is striking about the Spanish case, however, is that this situation of flux has continued, particularly on the center-right of the political spectrum.

The early stages of the transition to democracy in Spain were dominated by the Union of the Democratic Center (UCD), a broad coalition of various center-right and center-left groups under the leadership of Adolfo Suarez, a former minister in Franco's cabinet and the first prime minister of democratic Spain. This coalition of forces, while electorally successful in 1977 and 1979, was also inherently very fragile and collapsed dramatically in 1982, when its share of the vote fell from 35 percent to less than 7 percent (see Table 2.9). Suarez himself had resigned as prime minister and had abandoned the party in 1981, setting up a new party, the Social and Democratic Center, in 1982, which has since remained a marginal force.

With the collapse of the UCD, the key role in the Spanish party system passed to the Socialist party (PSOE), which polled almost half the votes in 1982 and almost 40 percent in 1989. With the help of the bias shown toward larger parties in the Spanish electoral system, this level of support has guaranteed Socialist party government in Spain since 1982.

TABLE 2.9
Elections in Spain since 1979

Party	1979 % Votes	1979 No. of Seats	1982 % Votes	1982 No. of Seats	1986 % Votes	1986 No. of Seats	1989 % Votes	1989 No. of Seats
Communist party	10.8	23	4.1	4	—	—	—	—
United Left	—	—	—	—	4.6	7	9.1	17
Socialist party	30.5	121	46.5	202	44.3	184	39.6	176
Union of the Democratic Center	35.0	168	6.7	12	—	—	—	—
Social and Democratic Center	—	—	2.8	2	9.2	19	7.9	14
Peoples Coalition/ Peoples Alliance/ Peoples party	6.5	10	25.8	106	26.1	105	25.8	106
Catalan Convergence and Union	2.7	8	3.9	12	5.0	18	5.0	18
Extreme Right	2.1	1	—	—	—	—	—	—
Basque Nationalists	1.7	7	1.9	8	1.4	6	1.2	5
Basque Left	0.5	1	0.5	1	0.5	2	0.5	2
Herri Batasuna	1.0	3	1.0	2	1.2	5	1.1	4
Andalusian Socialists	1.8	5	0.4	0	0.4	0	1.0	2
Others	7.4	3	6.4	1	7.3	4	8.8	6
Total	100.0	350	100.0	350	100.0	350	100.0	350

Party composition of governments:
Union of Democratic Center, 1979–1982
Socialist party, 1982–

Socialist dominance in Spain has also been facilitated by the fragmentation of the center-right opposition; indeed, in its second decade of democracy, Spain remained among the most fragmented of the European party systems. The vacuum on the center-right left by the failure of the UCD remained unfilled. The largest single party on the right is the Peoples party (PP), formerly known as the Peoples Alliance, which forms the dominant group within the sporadically cohesive Peoples Coalition (CP), a federation of diverse parties which embraces liberal, Christian democratic, and conservative factions. Other opposition forces on the center-right include the Catalan Convergence and Union, also a loose alliance of conservative, Christian, and liberal elements, united in their support for greater regional autonomy for Catalonia as well as in their opposition to socialist policies.

Opposition to the left of the political spectrum is focused primarily in the Spanish Communist party (PCE), which was one of the major parties in the ill-fated Second Spanish Republic (1931–1936) and which had also constituted one of the most powerful clandestine oppositions to Francoism during the period of the dictatorship. The PCE and its leader, Santiago Carrillo, were also at the forefront of the shift toward Eurocommunism in Western Europe in the late 1970s, when a number of leading communist parties sought to distance themselves from Moscow and attempted to forge a new, more consciously democratic strategy for reform (e.g., Lange and Vanicelli). But despite some early speculation that the PCE might emerge as the leading party of the left and thus occupy a position similar to that of the PCI in Italy, the party has, in fact, remained quite marginal. It was only through the recent formation of an electoral cartel—the United Left—with a number of other small parties of the left that the PCE could be seen as a serious political force.

The fragmentation of the Spanish party system has also been compounded by the emergence of a plethora of regional political forces. In addition to the Catalan coalition which was mentioned above, parties representing the local interests of Andalusia, Galicia, Aragon, Valencia, and the Canary Islands have also won representation in the *Cortes*, the Spanish parliament. Regionalism is strongest in the Basque country in northern Spain, supporting three parties, the Basque Nationalist party (PNV), a proindependence conservative party; the Basque Left (EE), a moderate nationalist party of the left; and Herri Batasuna (Popular Unity), a radical left-wing nationalist party, which also endorses ETA, a Basque paramilitary organization engaging in an armed struggle against the Spanish state. The Basque region is one of the most distinctive and industrially prosperous in Spain, with a population of over two million and with its own language and culture. Two-thirds of Basque voters now support one or another of the Basque national parties, and the region has been plagued by a level of political dissension and violence comparable to that in Northern Ireland.

The overall picture is thus of a fragmented and as yet largely unstructured party system in which conflicts between the left and the right overlay and intersect conflicts between the center and the periphery and between church and state. Indeed, it is sometimes difficult to conceive of Spain as having a single "party system" in the sense in which this concept applies to the more established Western

European democracies. The parties themselves are, in the main, loosely organized coalitions of different interests and different leaders which, with the notable exception of the powerful and governing Socialist party, drift in and out of transitory electoral cartels. (On the Spanish case in general, see Bar, Bell, Gunther et al., Preston, and Gallagher and Williams.)

UNIFORMITY AND DIVERSITY

Each of the party systems that we have considered has at its core a basic confrontation between the left and the right, reflecting the polarization of class interests. Each contains one or more parties that we might think of as being at the center. Beyond this, however, differences between systems appear to be more striking than similarities.

Thus in Sweden and the United Kingdom, liberal parties are to be found between the left and the right, and they reflect a more moderate class alternative than that promoted by conservative parties. In the Netherlands, Germany, and Italy, on the other hand, traditional liberalism has its roots in a secular conservatism—and the liberal parties are to be found on the right. In Sweden and the United Kingdom, class confrontations define the only major dimension in politics, although in Sweden the pattern is more complex, given the role of agrarian interests. In Italy, the Netherlands, and Germany, on the other hand, religion provides a second dimension of party competition. Differences also extend to the pattern of government formation. In France, Spain, Germany, Sweden, and the United Kingdom the left can hope to govern alone. In the Netherlands the left has for long been too weak, and in Italy too divided, to do so; in each case the left has been obliged to forge coalitions with parties on the center and right. Finally, while Germany, the Netherlands, Sweden, and Britain have strongly structured party systems, Spain and, to a lesser extent, France have systems which include loose and often fragmented alliances which lack the cohesion and discipline normally associated with European political parties.

Given such diversity, to speak of a "typical" Western European party system is clearly unrealistic. Nonetheless, the countries in certain groups do seem quite similar to one another. The Swedish party system, for example, has been compared with the party systems in Denmark and Norway by observers who speak of a typical "Scandinavian" party system (Berglund and Lindstrom; Einhorn and Logue). The Netherlands has been compared with Belgium and Switzerland in an extensive literature that treats them as "consociational democracies" responding to very deep-seated social and ethnic cleavages (Lijphart, 1977). The deep ideological divisions in the Italian party system have been compared with those in France between 1946 and 1958 and with those in Finland, as examples of "polarised pluralism" (Sartori). The new southern European democracies of Greece, Spain, and Portugal have also been extensively compared in a literature that highlights the common problems experienced in recent processes of democratization (Pridham; Gallagher and Williams). In short, while it may be far too simplistic to speak of Western European politics as a set of variations on a single theme, it is reasonable to think of Western European politics as reflecting variations on a limited set of themes.

Conflict between the Right and the Left

One theme that recurs in almost all Western European countries concerns the role of the left-right dimension in structuring politics. The terms "left" and "right" have always been widely accepted as part of the common political currency of Western Europe. To be on the left has traditionally meant supporting a communist or socialist party claiming to represent the interests of the organized working class. Every Western European country, without exception, has such a party. This, more than anything else, is the common theme in the politics of representation in Western Europe, and it also, incidentally, marks off the Western European experience from that in the United States.

To be on the center and right has meant supporting those who stand against the communist or socialist parties. On the center-right, however, there are few features common to all the Western European countries. In some countries, parties of the right have a distinctly religious basis; in others, they are secular. In other countries again, parties of the right traditionally have reflected rural or farming interests; in still others, they have represented a particular cultural or linguistic subculture.

One of the most striking features of Western European party politics is thus that while the left has been reasonably homogeneous and has normally been represented by at most two parties, the right has been more fragmented, including religious, secular, agrarian, nationalist, and other parties under the same broad umbrella.

Describing the right and the left in terms of the class interests which were traditionally represented by particular parties is only part of the story. There is also clearly a separate ideological sense in which we can speak of such parties as having programs that are on the left or right of the political spectrum. The problem here is that while it is easy to identify parties which mobilized in defense of particular social interests, it is less easy to specify who is on the left or the right in purely ideological terms.

The problem is compounded by the actual behavior of parties. In the 1970s and early 1980s, for example, the major socialist parties in Britain, Denmark, and the Netherlands experienced splits which led to more right-wing elements within these parties setting up alternative organizations—Democratic Socialists '70 in the Netherlands, the Center Democrats in Denmark, and the Social Democratic party in Britain. In terms of traditional interest representation, all three of these new parties might be regarded as being on the left in that all derived from the historic political alignment forged by the working class. In ideological terms, however, these parties were far from being on the left and often empathized with the traditional parties of the center-right of their respective party systems.

A similar problem arises in relation to the traditional right. In Italy, for example, a split from the traditionally right-wing Liberal party in the mid-1950s led to the formation of the Radical party. While spurning alliances with the Socialist and Communist parties, the Radical party quickly developed ideologically into one of the most left-wing of Italian parties. A similar split occurred in the Dutch Liberal party in the mid-1960s. The new party that formed as a result, Democrats '66, clearly aligned itself on the ideological left. In all of these cases, the "sociological" or "organizational" alignment of the new parties ran counter to their developing "ideological" positions.

The final confusion is of more recent origin and concerns the mobilization of environmentalist, or "green," parties in Western Europe. This is a new but increasingly relevant and pervasive phenomenon which has emerged from the organizational traditions of neither the left nor the right. Indeed, these parties are sometimes described as reflecting a wholly "new" politics which, in terms of both social support and organizational form, represents a genuine challenge to traditional alignments. Increasingly, however, these new parties are seen as moving toward the ideological left of the political spectrum, particularly when they demand both radical economic change and new forms of social justice. Here, too, therefore, organizational and social definitions of the left and the right fit uneasily with more strictly ideological criteria.

Conflict within the Right and the Left

When a country has two or more parties on the traditional left—a socialist and a communist party, for example—we might expect them to act in concert in an attempt to realize shared goals. In practice, however, this is often not the case. In Italy, as we have seen, the Socialist party has typically cast its lot with the Christian Democratic party and smaller parties of the right and has refused to consider an alliance with its Communist ideological neighbor. Even though the combined vote of the Italian left has sometimes exceeded 40 percent, Italian voters have never been offered the prospect of a left-wing coalition government. Relations between Communists and Socialists have often been very strained in France also. Here, however, an eventual alliance of the two parties did lead to a left-wing victory in the presidential elections of 1981, the first time that the left had come to power under the constitutional arrangements of the Fifth French Republic. Prior to this historic breakthrough, the French Socialists had often despaired of finding common ground with their Communist neighbors and had opted instead to chase alliances on the center and right of the party system.

A similar pattern can be seen on the right. Far-right parties, such as the neofascists in Italy, the National Front in France, or the newly emerging Republicans in Germany, may share many concerns with their more moderate neighbors of the right. Their sheer extremism, however, makes it difficult for them to form alliances. In party systems which are ideologically polarized, indeed, it is usually easier for parties of the center-right to find common ground with parties of the center-left than it is for either to find common ground with fellow left- or right-wing parties.

Other Dimensions of Party Politics

While the division between right and left is by far the most salient dimension structuring party politics in most Western European countries, other dimensions are also important. There are many discussions of these, but a useful summary is provided by Lijphart (1981). He identifies among others a religious dimension (salient in Austria, Belgium, France, Germany, Italy, the Netherlands, Norway, and Switzerland); a "cultural-ethnic" dimension (reflected by language divisions in Belgium and Finland); an urban-rural dimension (salient in Scandinavia); and a "post-materialist" dimension (identified by Lijphart in 1981 as being salient in the Netherlands, Norway, and Sweden).

Laver and Hunt (1991), in a recent survey of political scientists working on particular countries, found a willingness to distinguish a number of component parts of the traditional left-right dimension, of which the two most commonly cited were economic policy and a social policy dimension reflecting stands on issues such as abortion and homosexual law reform. Going beyond the components of the left and the right, Laver and Hunt found that the most commonly cited dimension of politics for Western European systems, by the end of the 1980s, was an environmental, or "green," dimension. Attitudes on matters such as abortion and homosexuality are clearly related to religious values. By the late 1980s, however, political scientists rarely cited urban-rural divisions or foreign policy as being among the most important factors structuring party politics.

It should be clear from the preceding discussion that while the terms "left" and "right" might seem to provide a convenient shorthand for describing party politics in different countries using broadly similar terms, superficial similarities can be deceptive. Given the range of variation that can be found in the different party systems of Western Europe, an alternative response might be to claim that since every country is different, we should simply look at the countries one at a time (accepting that, in reality, we will probably have time for only the big ones). Yet, as we have suggested, while each of the countries considered at the beginning of this chapter is clearly distinctive, each does represent something of a pattern, with elements that can be found elsewhere.

One of the most convenient ways of providing an overview of the combination of uniformity and diversity that characterizes the Western European party mosaic is to speak of "party families." Thus, while there are differences between "Christian democratic parties" in different countries, there are also striking similarities that go far beyond mere name and religious affiliation. Such parties tend to be located on the center-right of the system, to be flanked by both social democratic and other right-wing parties, to be commonly found at the heart of government coalitions, and so on. Accordingly, we move our discussion forward by looking in the next chapter at several party "families" in Western Europe. Our intention in doing this is to highlight the point that while no two parties are exactly alike, the parties in particular groups do bear striking resemblances to each other.

References

Bar, Antonio: "The Emerging Spanish Party System: Is There a Model?" in Bartolini and Mair, pp. 128–155.

Bartolini, Stefano: "Institutional Constraints and Party Competition in the French Party System," in Bartolini and Mair, pp. 103–127.

—— and Peter Mair (eds.): *Party Politics in Contemporary Western Europe*, Cass, London, 1984.

Bell, David (ed.): *Democratic Politics in Spain*, Frances Pinter, London, 1983.

Berglund, Sten, and Ulf Lindstrom: *The Scandinavian Party System(s)*, Studentlitteratur, Lund, 1978.

Castles, Francis C.: *The Social-Democratic Image of Society*, Routledge and Kegan Paul, London, 1979.

Daalder, Hans: "In Search of the Center of West European Party Systems," *American Political Science Review*, vol. 78, no. 1, 1984, pp. 92–109.

——: "The Dutch Party System: From Segmentation to Polarization—And Then?" in Hans Daalder (ed.), *Party Systems in Denmark, Austria, Switzerland, the Netherlands, and Belgium*, Frances Pinter, London, 1987, pp. 193-284.

—— and Galen A. Irwin (eds.): *Politics in the Netherlands: How Much Change?* Cass, London, 1989.

Dalton, R. J.: *Politics in West Germany*, Scott, Foresman, Glenview, Ill., 1989.

Di Palma, Giuseppe: *Surviving without Governing: The*

Italian Parties in Parliament, University of California Press, Los Angeles, 1976.

Donovan, Mark: "Party Strategy and Centre Domination in Italy," in Mair and Smith, pp. 114–128.

Drucker, H. M. (ed.): *Multi-Party Britain*, Macmillan, London, 1979.

Einhorn, Eric S., and John Logue: "Continuity and Change in the Scandinavian Party Systems," in Wolinetz (ed.), pp. 159–202.

Farneti, Paolo: *The Italian Party System (1945–1980)*, Frances Pinter, London, 1985.

Finer, S. E.: *The Changing British Party System, 1945–79*, American Enterprise Institute, Washington, D.C., 1980.

Gallagher, Tom, and Allan M. Williams (eds.): *Southern European Socialism: Parties, Elections and the Challenge of Government*, Manchester University Press, Manchester, 1989.

Gunther, Richard, Giacomo Sani, and Goldi Shabad: *Spain after Franco: The Making of a Competitive Party System*, University of California Press, Berkeley, 1986.

Katzenstein, Peter J.: *Small States in World Markets: Industrial Policy in Europe*, Cornell University Press, Ithaca, N.Y., 1985.

Klingemann, Hans-Dieter: "Electoral Programmes in West Germany," in Ian Budge, David Robertson, and Derek Hearl (eds.), *Ideology, Strategy and Party Change*, Cambridge University Press, Cambridge, England, 1987, pp. 294–323.

Lange, Peter, and M. Vanicelli (eds.): *The Communist Parties of Italy, France and Spain*, Allen & Unwin, London, 1981.

Laver, Michael, and W. Ben Hunt: *Policy and Party Competition*, Routledge, New York, 1991.

Lijphart, Arend: *Democracy in Plural Societies*, Yale University Press, New Haven, 1977.

———: "Political Parties: Ideologies and Programs," in David Butler, Howard Penniman, and Austin Ranney (eds.), *Democracy at the Polls: A Comparative Study of Competitive National Elections*, American Enterprise Institute, Washington, D.C., 1981.

———: *Democracies: Patterns of Majoritarian and Consensus Government in Twenty-one Countries*, Yale University Press, New Haven, 1984.

Machin, Howard: "Stages and Dynamics in the Evolution of the French Party System," in Mair and Smith, pp. 59–81.

Mair, Peter, and Gordon Smith (eds.): *Understanding Party System Change in Western Europe*, Cass, London, 1990.

Padgett, Stephen, and Tony Burkett: *Political Parties and Elections in West Germany: The Search for a New Stability* Hurst, London, 1986.

Pappi, Franz Urban: "The West German Party System," in Bartolini and Mair, pp. 7–26.

Preston, Paul: *The Challenge of Democracy in Spain*, Methuen, London, 1986.

Pridham, Geoffrey (ed.): *The New Mediterranean Democracies: Regime Transition in Spain, Greece and Portugal*, Cass, London, 1984.

Sainsbury, Diane: "Scandinavian Party Politics Re-examined: Social Democracy in Decline?" in Bartolini and Mair, pp. 67–102.

Sartori, Giovanni: *Parties and Party Systems*, Cambridge University Press, Cambridge, England, 1976.

Seldon, Anthony (ed.): *UK Political Parties since 1945*, Philip Allen, London, 1990.

Smith, Gordon: *Democracy in West Germany: Parties and Politics in the Federal Republic*, 3d ed., Gower, Aldershot, 1986.

Stephens, John D.: *The Transition from Capitalism to Socialism*, Macmillan, London, 1979.

Wilson, Frank L.: *French Political Parties under the Fifth Republic*, Praeger, New York, 1982.

———: "When Parties Refuse to Fail: The Case of France," in Kay Lawson and Peter Merkl, (eds.), *When Parties Fail: Emerging Alternative Organizations*, Princeton University Press, Princeton, 1988, pp. 503–532.

Wolinetz, Steven B.: "The Netherlands: Continuity and Change in a Fragmented Party System," in Wolinetz (ed.), pp. 130–158.

——— (ed.): *Parties and Party Systems in Liberal Democracies*, Routledge, London, 1988.

CHAPTER 3
PARTY FAMILIES

As we argued in the previous chapter, while no two political parties are quite the same, the parties in particular groups share considerable family resemblances. Three characteristics can be used to define different party families in Western Europe.

First, parties can be grouped according to some shared "genetic" origin— parties which mobilized in similar historical circumstances, or with the intention of representing similar interests, can be treated as having a distinct family resemblance. On these grounds all socialist or social democratic parties, for example, can be considered as belonging to the same family, as can all agrarian parties.

The second set of family resemblances is defined by the parties themselves, in terms of the way in which they forge links across national frontiers. Such links may take the form of transnational federations, such as that established by various liberal parties. It may also take the form of a membership of institutionalized multinational political groups, such as those to be found in the European Parliament (see Chapter 10), and while this involves only the twelve member states of the European Community (Belgium, Denmark, France, Germany, Greece, Ireland, Italy, Luxembourg, the Netherlands, Portugal, Spain, and the United Kingdom), it nevertheless offers a clear guide to the extent of cross-national partisan collegiality in Western Europe.

The final way in which party families can be identified has to do with the extent to which the policies pursued by one party in a country are similar to those pursued by another party in another country. There are some problems with this, since the "same" policy may mean quite different things in the practical politics of two different countries, but to ignore professed policies altogether when looking for similarities between parties would clearly be to stick our heads in the sand.

While no single one of these criteria provides a clear-cut classification, a judicious balance of the three suggests that we think in terms of about ten different party families in Western Europe. In this chapter we present a brief description of each of these families. We chart changes in their electoral strength over time; we contrast the support they enjoy in different countries; and we offer a brief account of the key issues with which each family is concerned.

Despite problems of definition, we have divided these different families of parties into three broad groups—families of the left, which include social democrats, communists, the new left, and the green parties; families of the center and right, which include Christian democrats, secular conservatives, liberals, farmers' parties, and the far right; and "other" families, including regionalist and nationalist parties, as well as others that cannot easily be classified into a distinct group. We report the electoral fortunes of the different families in each Western European country, in terms of the average electoral support in each of the four postwar decades, concentrating on those countries that have had an uninterrupted history of democratic politics in this period (thus largely excluding Greece, Portugal, and Spain). Finally, where data are available, we report the issue priorities of each party family, measured in terms of the commitments made in election platforms in the 1970s and 1980s.

After discussing the different party families, we consider in the rest of the chapter how different families fit together to make up different party systems. While, as we have said, there is no single composite, or "typical," Western European party system, it is quite clearly the case that once we describe party systems in these broad terms, there are only a few broad types of party system that are different from each other in really important respects.

FAMILIES OF THE LEFT

There are four basic party families to be found on the left-hand side of Western European party systems. Social democratic parties are the strongest and most enduring of Western Europe's political families, not only on the left but also in European politics taken as a whole. Communist parties are a very clear-cut group, comprising those parties which began as pro-Soviet splits from social democratic parties in the wake of the Russian Revolution of 1917. The third and fourth families on the left are the "new left" and the greens, which represent more varied collections of more recently formed parties, often grouped together under the general label "left-libertarian parties" (Kitschelt). While all four families can be seen as representing the contemporary left in Western European politics, they clearly incorporate between them some huge variations both of ideology and of interest representation.

The Social Democratic Family

Organized social democracy is one of the oldest surviving political forces in Western Europe. Even in the 1980s, the social democrats remained the single most important group in contemporary politics. The majority of the social democratic parties first entered electoral politics in the last quarter of the nineteenth century and were initially mobilized to represent the political interests of the growing working class, often acting in concert with the trade union movement. In some cases, as in Britain, a social democratic party was actually created by the trade unions in order to represent their interests in parliament. In other cases, as in the Netherlands, a political party was formed first in its own right and later established links with the trade unions.

As the franchise was extended to include more and more working-class voters, the social democratic parties grew in support. In the majority of European countries they gained their first experience of government in the years immediately following World War I. By the late 1940s, the position of the social democrats in European politics was well established. It was largely as a result of their intervention that most Western European welfare states were expanded during the 1950s and 1960s (Flora).

As Table 3.1 shows, the strongest social democratic presence in contemporary Western Europe can be found in Austria, France, Germany, Norway, and Sweden, where in each case the average social democratic share of the vote was at or above 35 percent during the 1980s. Social democracy has also proved to be the strongest single political force in Greece, Portugal, and Spain, where democracy was re-established in the 1970s following periods of authoritarian rule. In a second group of countries—Belgium, Denmark, Finland, Luxembourg, the Netherlands, Switzerland, and the United Kingdom—the social democratic share of the vote is somewhat smaller yet still exceeded 20 percent throughout the 1980s. Finally, there is a group of countries in which the social democrats are notably weak. In Iceland and Italy the social democratic share of the vote throughout the 1980s was

TABLE 3.1
Social Democrats: Electoral Performance, % of Vote

	1950s	1960s	1970s	1980s	Parties Competing in 1980s
Austria	43.3	45.0	50.0	45.4	Socialist party
Belgium	35.9	31.0	26.6	28.0	Socialist party (PS + SP)
Denmark	40.2	39.1	33.6	31.9	Social Democrats
Finland	25.9	26.9	25.1	25.4	Social Democrats
France	25.9	18.6	22.1	35.0	Socialist party, Left Radicals
Germany	30.3	39.4	44.2	39.4	Social Democrats
Iceland	19.5	15.0	14.8	17.1	Social Democrats, Social Democratic Federation
Ireland	10.9	14.8	12.7	8.9	Labour party
Italy	18.0	19.4	14.4	16.4	Socialist party, Social Democrats
Luxembourg	37.1	35.0	35.4	32.3	Socialist Workers party, Independent Socialist party*
Netherlands	30.7	25.8	31.9	31.0	Labor party
Norway	47.5	45.4	38.8	37.4	Labor party
Sweden	45.6	48.4	43.7	44.5	Social Democrats
Switzerland	26.0	26.0	25.7	21.2	Social Democrats, Autonomous Socialist party
United Kingdom	46.3	46.1	39.1	29.2	Labour party
Mean	32.2	31.7	30.5	29.5	

*The party has not contested all elections in the 1980s.

less than 20 percent. In the Italian case, the socialist vote has long been divided between two parties, with the Social Democrats being both smaller and more centrist. Social democrats poll less than 10 percent of the vote in Ireland, where the Labour party has long been the Cinderella of European social democracy.

In general, as can be seen from Table 3.1, the electoral position of social democracy declined during the postwar period in Western Europe, from an average of more than 32 percent in the 1950s to less than 30 percent in the 1980s. This decline was most marked in Denmark, Norway, and particularly the United Kingdom, where social democratic parties at one time polled more than 40 percent of the vote, ranking with the Austrian and Swedish parties as the most powerful of the European socialist parties. A sharp decline is also evident in Belgium, where the socialist alternative has lost a fifth of its support. But the electoral decline of social democracy is not pervasive—in no other country has there been anything like the massive erosion of support which occurred in Britain during the 1980s. Indeed, in France by the late 1980s, the Socialist party polled a higher share of the vote than at any comparable period in the postwar era, while in West Germany, the Social Democrats won more support by the end of the 1980s than during the 1950s. Elsewhere, socialist support remained fairly stable during postwar decades.

Now that European welfare states have been established for such a long period, it is easy to forget the radicalism which was once an integral part of social democracy in Western Europe. In many cases, the social democratic parties adopted an explicitly Marxist philosophy and ultimately envisaged the replacement of capitalism by a genuinely socialist order. During the period in which the franchise was being expanded to include the working class, social democratic parties sought the full extension of political rights and the introduction of social policies designed to protect the interests of workers and the unemployed.

With time, however, the initial radical impulse of social democracy began to wane. As Michels argued, electoral imperatives implied more professional organizational techniques, and this did much to blunt the parties' political purism. A further push toward moderation occurred when the Russian Revolution of 1917 precipitated splits in the socialist movement. The consequent creation of communist parties drew away many of the more radical members from the social democratic parties. The moderation of the views of the social democratic parties was also, in part, a product of their very success. The experience of participating in government, particularly in the wake of World War II, increased pressures toward ideological compromise and firmly ensconced social democratic parties at the heart of the political order they initially sought to overthrow. Finally, much of the early radicalism of the social democrats was dissipated as a result of the successful implementation of their short-term policies: full political rights were won, and welfare states grew quickly in most European countries. As a consequence of all this, the social democrats came to settle for a political role based on managing a mixed economy. They steadily dropped what Kirchheimer described as their "ideological baggage" and extended their electoral appeal to the middle class, particularly the middle class working in the rapidly expanding state sector, thus becoming catchall parties.

Table 3.2 shows the results of an analysis of the policy emphases in social democratic election manifestos in a wide range of European countries (Budge,

TABLE 3.2
Social Democrats (No. of Party Programs = 52): Issue Priorities*

1. Expansion of social services (10.78)
2. Social justice (6.47)
3. Specific economic goals (4.97)
4. Democracy (4.58)
5. Noneconomic groups (4.49)
6. Technology/infrastructure (4.00)
7. Controlled economy (3.93)
8. Environmental protection (3.90)
9. Planning (2.23)
10. Decentralization (2.22)

*Each figure in parentheses indicates the mean percentage of the election programs devoted to the relevant theme.

Robertson, and Hearl). The policy emphases of contemporary social democratic parties retain a commitment to welfarism and egalitarianism but place less emphasis on the need to control and regulate economic life. Social democratic party manifestos no longer present a direct ideological challenge to the capitalist order in Western Europe. What remains of their traditional radicalism has passed either to increasingly marginalized communist parties or to "new left" and green parties which grew in the 1960s and 1970s. (On social democracy in general, see Paterson and Thomas, 1977, 1986.)

The Communist Family

Significant communist parties can be found in fewer countries than their social democratic rivals and, in the main, are less successful at winning votes. In contemporary Western Europe, as can be seen from Table 3.3, communist parties command a substantial proportion of the vote only in Italy and, to a lesser extent, in

TABLE 3.3
Communist Parties: Electoral Performance, % of Vote

	1950s	1960s	1970s	1980s	Parties Competing in 1980s
Austria	4.3	1.7	1.2	0.7	Communist party
Belgium	3.4	3.7	2.9	1.4	Communist party (KPB + PCB)
Denmark	4.5	1.0	3.0	0.9	Communist party
Finland	22.1	21.6	17.6	13.9	People's Democratic Union, Democratic Alternative*
France	23.9	21.4	21.0	12.4	Communist party
Germany	1.1	—	—	—	NA
Iceland	(16.4)	(16.3)	(23.7)	(15.3)†	People's Alliance
Italy	22.7	26.1	30.7	28.3	Communist party
Luxembourg	11.6	14.0	8.2	5.1	Communist party
Netherlands	4.4	3.2	3.4	1.1	Communist party*
Norway	4.3	1.8	1.0	0.9	Communist party
Sweden	4.2	4.2	5.1	5.6	Communist party
Switzerland	2.7	2.6	2.4	0.9	Communist party
Mean‡	8.4	7.8	8.0	5.8	

*The party has not contested all elections in the 1980s.
†Figures in parentheses indicate that the classification of the party concerned was ambiguous.
‡Here, as elsewhere, this is the all-country mean (n = 15).

Finland, France, and Iceland. Explicit communist parties are effectively nonexistent in Ireland and the United Kingdom and have now become marginalized in Austria, Belgium, Denmark, the Netherlands, Norway, and Switzerland. While they have proved more serious contenders for votes in the new southern European democracies—Greece, Portugal, and Spain—there has recently been some slippage in their vote in these countries too. In general, across the whole postwar period, average electoral support for communist parties has fallen from more than 8 percent in the 1950s to less than 6 percent in the 1980s. Moreover, the recent changes in Eastern Europe and the USSR are now likely to undermine even further the support for and legitimacy of these parties. In Finland, Italy, and Sweden, for example, the communist parties have already changed their names, abandoning the communist label.

Yet even these relatively modest voting figures tend to exaggerate the importance of communist parties in those countries where they might appear on the face of things to count as a relevant political force. In Italy, for example, which hosts the strongest of the Western European communist parties, the 1980s witnessed a major erosion of the distinctively communist element in both party ideology and party organization. Most commentators now regard the modern Italian Communist party (PCI) as being effectively social democratic. Indeed, the PCI itself is now oriented quite explicitly toward social democracy and has changed its name to the Democratic Party of the Left (PDS). In France, on the other hand, the distinctively communist identity of the French Communist party (PCF) has been jealously guarded, at substantial electoral cost. The 1980s witnessed a major electoral decline of the PCF, to the benefit of its more moderate and increasingly successful socialist rival. In Iceland, the People's Alliance (PA) has largely shied away from promoting a distinctive communist identity. As its name suggests, it actually is an alliance which includes quite a substantial social democratic component. Finally, the communist party in Finland, known as the Finnish People's Democratic Union (FPDL), banned prior to World War II, enjoys a peculiar status owing to the country's close geographic and cultural links with the Soviet Union. Even here, however, the FPDL is an alliance that includes a social democratic component. The strains in this eventually led to a split between more moderate and extreme elements in 1985 and to the creation of the more orthodox Democratic Alternative.

The European communist parties were almost all formed in the immediate wake of the Russian Revolution of 1917, espousing Leninist principles and advocating the revolutionary road to socialism. They thereby established themselves as a radical alternative to the parliamentarism of social democracy. These parties were formally aligned with, and took their lead from, the Soviet Communist party. This leadership was organized initially through Comintern, the Communist (or Third) International, which lasted from 1919 to 1943. It was later organized through the less formal Cominform network, which lasted from 1947 to 1956. This alliance with Moscow, together with the evident radicalism of the communist parties, ensured that they were typically regarded as antisystem oppositions, and as such, they often polarized the party systems in which they operated.

Inevitably, they had little experience with government office, although, in the immediate wake of World War II, bolstered by the credibility that they had achieved as a result of their crucial role in the antifascist resistance, several communist parties were to enjoy brief periods as partners in the widely based coalition governments which sought to reestablish democratic politics in countries such as Austria, Belgium, Denmark, Finland, France, and Italy. Since then, communist parties have been involved in government only in Iceland, Finland, and, in the early 1980s, France. Beyond this, however, they have sometimes offered the parliamentary support necessary to sustain other parties in office, while not formally joining the cabinet. In Italy, for example, the PCI acted to sustain the Christian Democrats in office in the late 1970s, while in Sweden, the small but remarkably persistent Communist party, now renamed the Left party, has regularly provided the parliamentary support necessary to maintain the Social Democrats in office.

In part as a response to electoral decline or stagnation, in part as a means of ending their political isolation, many Western European communist parties began to distance themselves from Moscow during the postwar period. This shift heralded the emergence of "Eurocommunism" in the 1970s, in which the Italian, French, and Spanish parties, in particular, sought to elaborate a distinctively non-Soviet strategy for achieving political power. However, this strategy of legitimation did not reap the hoped-for political rewards, and the 1980s witnessed further electoral decline.

Partly as a result of the Eurocommunist strategy, the policy emphases of communist parties did not differ markedly, by the mid-1980s, from those of their social democratic rivals. As can be seen from Table 3.4, communist parties also emphasize questions of welfare, social justice, and the need for democratic decision making. Where they do differ from the social democrats is in their emphasis on state involvement in the economy and in their opposition to the free market. They emphasize the need for a controlled economy as well as the need for public ownership or nationalization. They are also much more explicit in their claim to represent the specific interests of the traditional working class and trade unions, in contrast to the more catchall electoral appeal of social democracy. (For a recent assessment of the Western European communist parties, see Waller and Fennema.)

The New Left

The third party family on the left is usually described as the "new" left. As can be seen from Table 3.5, patterns of popular support for the new left make it easier to understand the general decline of social democratic and communist voting. The trend in support for the new left runs counter to that for the traditional left, having

TABLE 3.4
Communist Parties (No. = 17): Issue Priorities*

1. Controlled economy (7.20)	6. Environmental protection (3.62)
2. Labor groups (6.05)	7. Nationalization (3.45)
3. Social justice (6.00)	8. Specific economic goals (3.05)
4. Expansion of social services (5.50)	9. Noneconomic groups (2.57)
5. Democracy (4.26)	10. Productivity and growth (1.76)

*Each figure in parentheses indicates the mean percentage of the election programs devoted to the relevant theme.

TABLE 3.5
New Left Parties: Electoral Performance, % of Vote

	1950s	1960s	1970s	1980s	Parties Competing in 1980s
Denmark	—	7.7	8.3	14.4	Socialist People's party, Left Socialists
Iceland	—	—	—	7.8	Women's Alliance
Ireland	—	—	1.4	3.9	Workers' party, Democratic Socialist party
Italy	—	2.2	3.3	4.0	Radicals, Proletarian Democracy
Netherlands	0.6	3.0	4.0	3.7	Pacifist Socialist party,* Radical Political party,* Green Left*
Norway	—	4.0	6.9	6.8	Socialist Left party
Switzerland	—	—	0.9	3.5	Progressive Organizations/ Alternative Greens
Mean	0.0	1.1	1.7	2.9	

*The party has not contested all elections in the 1980s.

risen from just 1 percent in the 1960s in Western Europe as a whole to almost 3 percent in the 1980s. This suggests a reshuffling rather than a decline of the left.

The new left family is very heterogeneous. It ranges from Marxist parties in Denmark, Ireland, Italy, and Norway to "postmaterialist" and left-libertarian parties in the Netherlands and Switzerland, as well as the Italian Radicals; and it includes the explicitly feminist Women's Alliance in Iceland.

The first new left parties emerged in the 1960s. These tended more toward an orthodox Marxist position, having often emerged as a result of divisions within the established communist parties. The later new left parties, on the other hand, tended to be stimulated by the wave of student radicalism of the late 1960s, and they have also been spurred on by the growing ecology movement. Indeed, it is often difficult to distinguish these new left parties from more orthodox green parties (see below), and since the emergence of the latter, the two groups have frequently worked in concert. (See also Kitschelt, who groups both types of parties under the label "left-libertarian.")

As Table 3.5 shows, new left parties have established themselves in only a scattering of the Western European polities. There is no new left party of relevance in Austria, Belgium, Finland, France, Germany, Sweden, or the United Kingdom, nor in any of the new southern European democracies. Even where new left parties do exist, they often remain quite marginal. It is only in Denmark, where two new left parties compete, that the new left vote exceeds 10 percent.

Not the least as a result of their diverse origins, the policy emphases of new left parties reflect a wide-ranging set of concerns (Table 3.6). On one hand the new left parties echo traditional communist parties in their opposition to market forces and their concern for public ownership and a controlled economy. Again like traditional communist parties, and quite unlike their green allies, they emphasize an explicit appeal to the traditional working class. And while they emphasize a commitment to the welfare state, social justice, and environmental protection, in

TABLE 3.6
New Left Parties (No. = 17): Issue Priorities*

1. Labour groups (6.79)	6. Specific economic goals (3.38)
2. Social justice (6.57)	7. Environmental protection (2.79)
3. Expansion of social services (5.29)	8. Noneconomic groups (2.62)
4. Freedom (4.74)	9. Controlled economy (2.58)
5. Democracy (4.58)	10. Nationalization (2.16)

*Each figure in parentheses indicates the mean percentage of the election programs devoted to the relevant theme.

common with all left parties, they also promote a more libertarian emphasis on freedom and democracy.

Green Parties

Radical left politics can be seen as having developed in four distinct phases. As we have seen, the first, most important, and most enduring of these phases was the emergence of social democratic parties in the late nineteenth century. The second phase involved the split in social democracy in the wake of the Russian Revolution and the consequent emergence of the communist alternative. Here, too, the new parties proved reasonably enduring and, in certain limited instances, grew to a majority position on the left. The third phase was the mobilization of the new left in the 1960s and 1970s, a movement that managed to establish itself in mainstream politics in only a handful of countries, and in these largely at the expense of the traditional communist parties. Finally, in the late 1970s and 1980s came the fourth phase—the emergence of "Green," or ecology, parties. Green parties tend to poll only a small percentage of the total vote. Nevertheless, their recent growth and pervasiveness have generated substantial interest among students of the Western European party mosaic. As we saw in the previous chapter, political scientists polled in 1989 by Laver and Hunt frequently nominated the environmental dimension as an important feature of party politics in a range of European countries.

Table 3.7 shows that Green parties had, by the late 1980s, gained parliamentary representation or at least a respectable level of electoral support in the vast majority of Western European countries. To be sure, the Green alternative remains essentially marginal and on the average accounts for little more than 2 percent of the vote in Western Europe. But the Greens represent a new and growing phenomenon, and average figures mask the increase in Green support that has occurred in the most recent elections. They also mask substantial variations between countries. In Belgium, Germany, and Luxembourg, for example, the Green share of the vote averaged more than 5 percent in the 1980s—it exceeded 8 percent by the end of the decade in the latter two countries, though the German Greens suffered a setback in the first all-German elections held in December 1990 (see Chapter 2).

In contrast to this, there is as yet no Green representation in Iceland, the Netherlands, Norway, or the United Kingdom. Yet even in these countries, some qualifications are necessary. In Iceland, for example, while there is no Green party, the "new left" Women's Alliance might be regarded as a functional equivalent. The

TABLE 3.7
Green Parties: Electoral Performance, % of Vote

	1980s	Parties Competing
Austria	4.1	Greens (separate lists)
Belgium	6.1	Greens (Agalev + Ecolo)
Denmark	0.7	Greens*
Finland	2.7	Greens
France	0.9	Ecologists
Germany	5.1	Greens
Ireland	0.4	Green party*
Italy	1.2	Greens*
Luxembourg	6.8	Greens (various lists)
Sweden	2.9	Ecology party
Switzerland	3.9	Greens (various lists)
Mean	2.3	

*The party has not contested all elections in the 1980s.
Note: Because of the recent origin of the green parties, only figures for the 1980s are relevant here.

same is true for the two new left parties in the Netherlands: the Pacifist Socialist party and the Radical Political party. In the most recent Dutch election, these forged a joint electoral list with the declining communist party and the unrepresented greens, an alliance that billed itself as the "Green left." In the United Kingdom, where the British Green party has yet to make an impact on national elections, it polled almost 15 percent of the vote in the 1989 British direct elections to the European Parliament. This was the largest national vote share ever won by a green party, but given the British electoral system (see Chapter 6), it yielded not a single seat. Finally, green politics began in the late 1980s to make an impact in the new democracies of southern Europe, with the election of a Green MP in the November 1989 election in Greece and of a Green MP as part of the broad United Democratic Coalition in Portugal in 1987.

The policy emphases of Green parties, as might be expected, give pride of place to the need to protect the environment. This involves promoting policies that would curb economic growth and require substantial regulation of industrial and commercial activity. Green manifestos also emphasize the need for international peace and disarmament and urge an increase in the level of development aid provided for third world countries. They emphasize social justice, particularly with regard to the need for equal treatment of women, as well as of ethnic and racial minorities. Green parties also emphasize participatory democracy and even attempt to structure their own organizations in such a way as to allow maximum grass-roots involvement.

Bearing in mind the rapidly rising salience of the issues emphasized by the Green parties, we should probably judge their success less in terms of electoral support and more in terms of the extent to which environmental protection can be seen to rank high on the policy agendas of all political parties on the left, as well as of both agrarian parties and liberal parties. (On Green parties in general, see Mueller-Rommel.)

BOX 3.1
The Left

FRANCE

The most notable development within the left in France has been the eclipse of the traditionally powerful and strongly pro-Soviet Communist party (PCF) and the corresponding rise of the Socialists (PS) under François Mitterrand. The left as a whole has been stronger in France in the 1980s than at any other period since the 1950s, and the PS, as the dominant group within the left, now controls both the presidency and the cabinet. Neither the new left nor the greens have managed to make much of an impact, the latter never polling more than about 4 percent of the vote in national elections, although they did exceed 10 percent in the 1989 elections to the European Parliament.

GERMANY

It is in Germany that the green movement has mounted its most severe challenge to the traditional left in Western Europe. The Social Democrats (SPD) had long enjoyed an effective monopoly of the left, helped largely by the fears of extreme politics in the wake of nazism and by the long-term constitutional ban on the Communist party. Now that monopoly has been broken by the successful mobilization of a green vote, and the position of the SPD is likely to be further weakened by the incorporation of a large conservative electorate within the newly reunified German state.

ITALY

Italy now has the largest Communist party in Western Europe (the PCI), recently renamed the Democratic Party of the Left, and given the demise of the communist regimes in Eastern Europe, it may soon be one of the largest communist parties in the world. The left has always been strategically divided in Italy, with the PCI persistently excluded from government and the Socialists (PSI), together with the more centrist Social Democrats (PSDI), forming an essential part of frequent Christian Democrat–led five-party coalitions. The left in Italy has been further fractured by the successful mobilization of a green party, as well as by the persistent presence of small, radical new left parties, most notably Pro-letarian Democracy and the Radical party. In an effort to meet the challenge from both its right and its left, the party is now in the process of abandoning the communist label and transforming itself into a modern European social democratic party. Despite these changes, however, the overall left vote in Italy has remained quite stable.

THE NETHERLANDS

The Dutch left has often been excluded from government, since the Christian Democrats (CDA) and Liberals (VVD) have, between them, usually managed to win a majority of seats. In fact, between 1958 and 1989, when it finally managed to dislodge the Liberals and replace them as the partner of the CDA in government, the Labour party (PvdA) had been in government on only three occasions, totaling less than seven years. Electoral support for the PvdA has tended to grow in recent years, but the party has always faced a challenge from the left. This came initially from a small Communist party and more recently from two new left parties, the Pacifist Socialists and the Radicals, all three of which have now joined forces as a new Green Left party.

SPAIN

The Socialist party (PSOE) is now the most successful of the parties in Spain; it formed a single-party-majority government following each of the three elections preceding 1990, a pattern quite similar to that in Greece in the wake of democratization. The PSOE is one of the most moderate of Europe's socialist parties, a factor which has done much to hamper the mobilization of a successful opposition on the center-right. Despite its initial hopes following the transition to democracy, the Communist party (PCE) has failed to make a major impact in politics and has recently joined forces with other left-wing critics of the PSOE in a loose alliance called the United Left. Like Greece and Portugal, Spain has never really witnessed the emergence of a new left or green party, but other left-wing forces are represented within the various nationalist and regionalist groups.

(Continued on next page)

SWEDEN

Sweden, often seen as the model for radical social democracy, maintains what is perhaps the most successful Social Democratic party (the SAP) in Western Europe. This party has dominated government for more than forty years and has built up and maintained the most advanced welfare state in Europe, as well as what is arguably the most regulated society. However, while successful in both electoral and policy terms—it held government continuously from 1932 until 1976—the SAP is by no means free from challenges on the left and is now particularly concerned by the sudden growth of the new Ecology party. The Communist party, now known as the Left party, which has also enjoyed a persistent if relatively small electoral following, tends to cooperate with rather than oppose its larger Social Democratic neighbor.

UNITED KINGDOM

Though the Labour party spent the entire 1980s in opposition, Britain is unique in the extent to which a single party has monopolized the left. While a number of leading Communists gained prominence inside the trade union movement, the Communist party has never been successful in elections, its high point being in 1945, when it won just over 100,000 votes and elected two MPs. Nor has any new left party emerged in recent British elections. Despite poor showings in Westminster elections, however, the British Green party scored a notable success in the elections to the European Parliament in 1989, polling 14 percent of the vote, but because of the electoral system, it failed to return even one MEP.

FAMILIES OF THE CENTER AND RIGHT

The party families of the right are more heterogeneous than those of the left. There is the Christian democratic family, made up of parties that temper mainstream conservatism with a defense of religious values. There are the secular conservative parties, distinguished from the Christian democrats by a more strident antisocialist rhetoric as well as by the absence of traditional links with organized religion. There is a family of liberal parties, a heterogeneous group that includes centrist parties such as the British Liberals and quite right-wing parties such as the Dutch Liberals. Notwithstanding this heterogeneity, however, these parties have forged quite strong transnational links. There is a group of agrarian parties that mobilized in defense of farming interests in a variety of Western European countries. Finally, there is a family of parties composed of neofascist, racist, and/or xenophobic parties of the extreme right.

The Christian Democrats

The largest single family on the center-right of Western European politics is made up of the Christian democratic parties. This family has a base in most established Western European democracies, the main exceptions being Iceland and the United Kingdom. It has also emerged as at least a marginally relevant political force in both Portugal and Spain.

The Christian democratic family contains a number of distinct strands. The first is primarily Roman Catholic in origin and includes Christian parties that began to mobilize in the mid- to late-nineteenth century and are now among the strongest in

Western Europe. This strand is made up of Christian democratic parties in Austria, Belgium, Italy, Luxembourg, and Switzerland, although the Swiss party now wins some support from Protestant voters.

The second strand in Christian democracy comprises two parties that draw substantial support from both Catholics and Protestants. The German Christian Democratic Union (CDU) and its Bavarian sister party, the Christian Social Union (CSU), were both formed in 1945 in the period of immediate postwar reconstruction. They built on the legacy of the former Catholic Center party, one of the dominant parties in Germany before the Nazi regime. In 1945, however, in a deliberate effort to erode the divisions that had been so evident in the prewar period, the new CDU sought the support of both Catholics and Protestants. The second biconfessional Christian democratic party is the Dutch Christian Democratic Appeal (CDA), which was originally divided into three separate parties, the Catholic People's party and two smaller but persistent Protestant parties, the Anti-Revolutionary party (ARP) and the Christian Historical Union (CHU). These formed a federation in 1975 and then fused into a single party in 1980. Both the CDU/CSU and the CDA, with their substantial Protestant components, can be differentiated from the essentially Catholic parties in the first strand of Christian democracy. In all other respects, however, not the least in their inheritance of a long tradition of confessional politics and in the dominant bargaining positions they now enjoy in their respective party systems, these two strands of Christian democracy fill rather similar roles in party politics.

The third strand is largely Protestant and is of more recent origin—the parties involved often first contested elections only after World War II. It is also far more marginal in electoral terms. It comprises the Christian Democrats of Denmark, Norway, and Sweden, together with the minor evangelical and reformed Protestant parties in the Netherlands and Switzerland.

Over and above these cases of quite explicit Christian parties, a Christian democratic element can also be identified in France and Ireland. The French case is the more interesting of the two, since a substantial Catholic party, the Popular Republican Movement, was among the most influential in the French Fourth Republic (1946–1958). With the shifting center-right alliances that have characterized French politics since 1958, however, the distinct Christian alternative has all but disappeared. Much of its more conservative support was eventually captured by the Gaullists, while the more moderate elements operate under the Center Social Democrat label within the loose alliance called the Union for French Democracy. In Ireland, where the population is still more than 90 percent Catholic and rates of church attendance are by far the highest in Europe, there is no tradition of organized Christian democracy. In recent years one of the leading parties of the center-right, Fine Gael, has affiliated with the transnational federations of Christian democratic parties—the European People's party and the European Union of Christian Democrats—and the party is also affiliated with the Christian democratic group in the European Parliament in Strasbourg. Hence, while historically outside the Christian democratic tradition, Fine Gael has proved willing to adopt this transnational organizational identity.

As Table 3.8 shows, and notwithstanding the more recent emergence of the Protestant evangelical parties, Christian democracy as a whole has experienced an

TABLE 3.8
Christian Democrats: Electoral Performance, % of Vote

	1950s	1960s	1970s	1980s	Parties Competing in 1980s
Austria	43.8	46.9	43.2	42.2	People's party
Belgium	45.4	36.3	33.7	27.8	Christian party (CVP + PSC)
Denmark	—	—	3.9	2.4	Christian People's party
Finland	—	0.6	2.9	2.8	Christian League
France	NA	NA	NA	NA	(Center Social Democrats) [UDF]
Germany	47.7	46.3	46.0	45.9	Christian Democratic Union, Christian Social Union
Ireland	(28.1)	(33.4)	(32.8)	(33.9)*	(Fine Gael)
Italy	41.3	38.6	38.5	33.6	Christian Democrats
Luxembourg	37.5	34.3	31.2	33.3	Christian Social party
Netherlands	53.2	49.8	37.8	36.6	Christian Democratic Appeal, Reformed Political League, Political Reformed party, Reformed Political Federation, Evangelical People's party†
Norway	10.3	9.0	11.9	8.7	Christian People's party
Sweden	—	1.1	1.6	2.4	Christian Democrats
Switzerland	24.2	24.4	23.2	22.2	Christian Democrats, Protestant People's party
Mean	22.1	21.4	20.4	19.5	
Mean‡	23.3	22.1	21.1	20.0	

*Figures in parentheses indicate that the classification of the party concerned was ambiguous.
†The party has not contested all elections in the 1980s.
‡Excluding France and Ireland.

erosion of electoral support over the postwar era. Even if we exclude the awkward cases of France and Ireland, average support for Christian democratic parties has fallen from more than 23 percent in the 1950s to just 20 percent in the 1980s. This decline has been most marked in Belgium, where the Catholic party has lost two-fifths of its support. In the Netherlands, the confessional vote has declined by about a third, a fall which proved so dramatic that it precipitated the pan-Christian CDA merger. In Italy, the Christian democratic vote has fallen by about one-fifth. Elsewhere, particularly in Austria, Germany, Luxembourg, and Switzerland, the Christian vote is more or less stable. What is striking, however, is that with the single exception of the small Protestant party in Sweden, no country has experienced a sustained increase in Christian democratic support over the postwar period.

The dominant strand in Western European Christian democracy is clearly represented by the Catholic parties. Even in the case of the biconfessional parties, the Catholic heritage has been well to the fore. This particular heritage dates back to the nineteenth century, when Catholic mobilization took place in response to secularizing and anticlerical impulses from both conservatives and liberals. Since then, however, the issues that first generated these conflicts between church and state have largely been settled, and the parties themselves have developed into mainstream components of the center-right. Their religious emphases surface only in response to the appearance on the political agenda of moral issues such as abortion, euthanasia, and divorce, on which the established Christian churches have strong views. The smaller Protestant parties share these positions but add a concern for reversing what they see as the general trend toward permissiveness and ungodliness. The Norwegian and Swedish parties, for example, have campaigned strongly against both alcohol and pornography.

Christian parties can easily be distinguished from secular conservative parties (see below) because their popular base, their social concerns, and their reluctance to promote policies which might lead to social conflict have always inclined them (the Catholic parties in particular) toward a more centrist, prowelfare program. Indeed, the impetus behind the development of welfare states in postwar Europe derived almost as much from Catholic pressure as it did from social democracy. This was particularly true in countries such as Belgium, the Netherlands, and Italy, where social democracy has always remained relatively weak (see Wilensky). In short, Christian democratic parties tend to be state-oriented parties, sharing common ground with the social democrats in their opposition to neoliberal, libertarian, and individualistic policies.

As Table 3.9 shows more systematically, the primary policy emphases of the Christian parties have been a commitment to welfarism and a defense of traditional values. These parties have also laid much stress on freedom, democracy, and private enterprise, a pattern of concerns which allows them to forge links with the secular right. (On Christian democracy, see Fogarty; Irving, 1979a, 1979b; Madeley, 1977, 1982; and Whyte.)

The Secular Conservatives

Across Western Europe in general, secular conservative parties poll only slightly less than the Christian democrats, with an average of just over 18 percent. They actually outpoll the Christian parties if the new democracies of Greece, Portugal, and Spain are included in the equation, given the appeal of secular conservatism for right-wing voters in these systems. What is most striking about the secular conservative vote in Western Europe in the 1980s is that even this high level of average support is depressed by the fact that conservative parties do not exist at all in a number of countries. Where they do exist, conservative parties do very well, with a vote share that never falls below 20 percent (Table 3.10). If we look only at countries with a conservative presence (Denmark, Finland, Iceland, Ireland, Norway, Sweden, and the United Kingdom—the alliance pattern in France makes it a

TABLE 3.9
Christian Democrats (No. = 33): Issue Priorities*

1. Expansion of the social services (10.25)	6. Social justice (3.81)
2. Defense of traditional morality (6.40)	7. Democracy (3.70)
3. Noneconomic groups (5.08)	8. Arts and leisure (3.44)
4. Private enterprise (4.99)	9. Freedom (2.91)
5. Technology/infrastructure (4.46)	10. Specific economic goals (2.69)

*Each figure in parentheses indicates the mean percentage of the election programs devoted to the relevant theme.

TABLE 3.10
Secular Conservatives: Electoral Performance, % of Vote

	1950s	1960s	1970s	1980s	Parties Competing in 1980s
Denmark	18.4	21.3	21.5	26.0	Conservatives, Progress party
Finland	14.2	14.2	19.6	22.9	National Coalition, Constitutional party
France*	(44.2)	(55.6)	(50.3)	(42.7)†	Gaullists (RPR),‡ Union for French Democracy,‡ (Republican party)
Iceland	41.3	39.5	36.8	38.4	Independence party, Citizen's party‡
Ireland	46.0	45.7	49.1	45.9	Fianna Fáil, Independent Fianna Fáil
Norway	18.7	20.2	24.6	35.1	Conservatives, Progress party
Sweden	17.0	14.4	15.4	21.1	Moderates
United Kingdom	47.6	42.7	41.0	42.2	Conservative party
Mean	16.5	16.9	17.2	18.3	
Mean§	14.5	14.1	14.9	16.6	

*Composite vote including Liberals, Christian Democrats, and Conservatives.
†Figures in parentheses indicate that the classification of the party concerned was ambiguous.
‡The party has not contested all elections in the 1980s as an independent party.
§Excluding France.

problem case), the average vote share of secular conservative parties is a remarkably high 33 percent.

As with liberal and Christian families, there are several strands within secular conservatism in Western Europe. One strand includes what we might think of as "national" parties, which marry a conservative socioeconomic appeal with an emphasis on the pursuit of national interests. This strand includes the Independence party in Iceland, Fianna Fáil in Ireland, the French Gaullists, and the British Conservatives. All four parties stress the importance of national shibboleths, and all decry the "antinational" character of sectional or class politics. A second distinctive strand within European secular conservatism is exemplified by the Progress parties of Denmark and Norway, which began to mobilize in the mid-1970s. These "antitax" parties concentrate on opposing high levels of state spending and what they perceive to be excessive levels of taxation. The third strand is made up of traditional conservative parties in Denmark, Finland, Norway, and Sweden. These parties are characterized by a more moderate opposition to state intervention, married to a commitment to a consensual approach to policy making.

While the secular conservatives are more clearly on the right than the Christian democrats, the two families can in many ways be viewed as functional equivalents. Both represent the major alternative to the appeal of social democracy, and the two families rarely flourish within the same party system. Where secular conservatism is strong, Christian democracy tends to be weak or nonexistent (in the Scandinavian countries, the United Kingdom, Greece, and Spain). Where Christian democracy is strong, secular conservatism tends to be weak or nonexistent (in Austria, Belgium, Germany, Italy, and the Netherlands).

In general, Table 3.10 shows that electoral support for European secular conservatism has grown during the postwar period, increasing from an average of less than 17 percent in the 1950s to more than 18 percent in the 1980s, or from less

TABLE 3.11
Secular Conservatives (No. = 35): Issue Priorities*

1. Private enterprise (10.62)	6. Productivity and growth (3.06)
2. Economic orthodoxy (7.57)	7. Freedom (2.97)
3. Expansion of social services (7.44)	8. Noneconomic groups (2.94)
4. Government efficiency (4.71)	9. Technology/infrastructure (2.91)
5. Social justice (3.40)	10. Law and order (2.89)

*Each figure in parentheses indicates the mean percentage of the election programs devoted to the relevant theme.

than 15 percent to almost 17 percent if we exclude the French case (where the Gaullists and the UDF competed as an electoral alliance). This growth has been largely a product of the increased conservative vote in Scandinavia. In Denmark and Norway, for example, the success of the Progress parties has contributed to a substantial increase in the conservative vote. In Finland and Sweden, conservative support has also increased substantially. Elsewhere, the picture is one of stability, with the United Kingdom being the only country in which secular conservatism has shown a noticeable decline in vote share over the postwar era taken as a whole.

The policy priorities of the secular conservative family are quite distinctive. While the secular conservatives share an emphasis on welfarism with all other party families, this ranks lower in conservative party programs than in the programs of other parties on the right (see Table 3.11). Rather, conservative parties emphasize the need to support private enterprise and to encourage fiscal austerity. They also emphasize government efficiency, as well as law and order. Given the degree of consensus that exists among most of the other Western European party families, therefore, the policy agenda of the secular conservatives is quite distinctive. (On conservative parties in general, see Morgan and Silvestri, Layton-Henry, and Girvin.)

The Liberals

Electoral support for liberal parties in Western Europe has increased in the postwar period and now stands at an average of more than 11 percent of the total vote. The liberal presence is also pervasive. Iceland is the only established European democracy that does not have a relevant liberal party, while liberal parties, broadly defined, have emerged in both Portugal and Spain. Ireland has also witnessed the emergence of a liberal party in the 1980s, the Progressive Democrats. This polled more than 11 percent of the vote in its first electoral outing in 1987, and while its vote declined in 1989, the party did succeed in entering a government coalition with Fianna Fáil. Although a strong liberal tradition exists in France, the present liberal tendency has been largely subsumed within the loose, wide-ranging alliance of the Union for French Democracy.

As Table 3.12 shows, despite the fact that the liberal parties are present in almost all European countries, there is substantial variation in liberal strength. During the 1980s, for example, the liberals won an average of more than 20 percent of the vote in Belgium, the Netherlands, Switzerland, and the United

TABLE 3.12
Liberal Parties: Electoral Performance, % of Vote

	1950s	1960s	1970s	1980s	Parties Competing in 1980s
Austria	8.4	6.2	5.6	7.4	Freedom party
Belgium	11.5	18.3	15.4	21.1	Liberal party (PVV + PRL)
Denmark	8.1	9.3	8.3	5.6	Social Liberal party
Finland	7.1	9.7	5.4	0.9	Liberal People's party
France	NA	NA	NA	NA	(Radical party) [UDF]
Germany	8.6	9.4	8.2	8.9	Free Democratic party
Ireland	—	—	—	3.5	Progressive Democrats*
Italy	4.8	8.1	5.4	6.9	Liberal party, Republican party
Luxembourg	12.6	13.6	21.8	17.5	Democratic party
Netherlands	9.9	12.8	19.7	25.5	Liberal party, Democrats '66
Norway	9.8	9.5	5.8	3.4	Liberal party
Sweden	22.1	16.3	11.8	10.8	Liberal party
Switzerland	31.4	32.9	31.1	30.1	Radical Democrats, Liberal party, Independents party
United Kingdom	5.1	9.9	14.7	23.9	Liberal party, Social Democratic party
Mean	9.3	10.4	10.2	11.0	
Mean†	10.0	11.1	10.9	11.9	

*The party has not contested all elections in the 1980s.
†Excluding France.

Kingdom. They won more than 10 percent in Luxembourg and Sweden. Yet even in countries such as Denmark, Germany, Italy, and Norway, where liberal support falls below 10 percent, the parties concerned often exert a political influence far exceeding that suggested by their low legislative weight. Their position close to the center of the party system often allows them to take on a crucial role as junior partners in coalition governments of the center-right. Indeed, liberal parties are governing parties par excellence—though ironically in the United Kingdom, where the liberal vote has at times exceeded that in virtually every other European country, they have been permanently excluded from office.

While the liberal political family is often seen to represent a "center" group in Western European politics, these parties in practice represent a diverse range of ideological concerns. Historically, liberal parties have been associated with the impulse to extend the franchise, to promote individual rights, and to resist clerical influences in political life. Liberal parties thus constituted the presocial democratic opposition to conservatism and the right. Some of these concerns have survived and are more or less common to all European liberal parties—an emphasis on individual rights and a residual (though increasingly less relevant) anticlericalism. Over time, however, other liberal concerns have mutated, and two clear strands of European liberalism can now be identified.

Within the first strand, an emphasis on individual rights has led to a concern for fiscal rectitude and opposition to all but minimal state intervention in the economy. This right-wing strand of liberalism has been particularly important in Austria (which contains the most rightist of European liberal parties), Belgium,

Germany, Italy, Luxembourg, the Netherlands, and Switzerland. It is also the position toward which the Progressive Democrats in Ireland have gravitated. Thus this brand of liberalism has tended to emerge in countries that are also characterized by strong Christian democratic parties and hence where the anticlerical component of liberalism was once important. Indeed, anticlericalism in these countries has two distinct forms, being represented on the left by socialist and/or communist parties and on the right by secular liberal parties.

The second strand of European liberalism reflects a more centrist, if not left-leaning, position in which a concern for individual rights and progressive politics has engendered an emphasis on social justice and egalitarianism. This is the strand that has tended to emerge in countries where the main right-wing group is a secular conservative party that has taken over the more anti-interventionist liberal tendency and where the anticlerical component in liberalism has proved less relevant. This strand is evident in Denmark, Norway, Sweden, and Britain and is also represented by Democrats '66 in the Netherlands, as well as by the Republicans in Italy.

Those parties which reflect the more libertarian strand of liberalism have experienced greater electoral success in recent years, increasing their share of the vote in Belgium and the Netherlands in particular. In contrast, the more centrist welfare-oriented liberal parties, particularly those in Scandinavia, have experienced a general erosion of support. The exception is Britain, where two centrist parties, both left-leaning, experienced a major increase in support during the 1980s, largely at the expense of the Labour party.

Above all, however, European liberal parties have demonstrated a strong appetite for participation in government, and the policies implied by the different ideological strands of liberalism have not been allowed to get in the way of this. In Belgium and the Netherlands, for example, governments tend to alternate between coalitions of the center-left (Christians and social democrats) and of the center-right (Christians and liberals). In Germany and Austria, on the other hand, notwithstanding their philosophy, the liberals play the role of center parties in government formation negotiations, switching support from time to time between social democrats and Christian democrats. In Scandinavia, yet another pattern is apparent: the dominance of the social democrats encourages liberals, as well as agrarians, to join forces with the other bourgeois parties to construct a "broad-right" antisocialist coalition. In each case, however, the liberals are regular participants in the politics of government formation.

The presence of two major strands of liberal ideology and the diversity of liberal party strategies suggest that an aggregate list of liberal party policy concerns such as that in Table 3.13 may be misleading. While the left-leaning British, Norwegian, and Swedish liberals all place a major emphasis on the need for a controlled economy, this emphasis is absent from the programs of the Austrian, Dutch, and Italian liberals. In common with most other parties, however, all liberal parties emphasize a commitment to welfarism, and, in common with the left and the agrarian parties, they also emphasize the need for environmental protection.

What can also be taken as reasonably characteristic of all liberal parties is an emphasis on freedom, democracy, decentralization, and social justice, reflecting a continuing and pervasive concern for individual rights and freedoms, as well as a

TABLE 3.13
Liberal Parties (No. = 46): Issue Priorities*

1. Expansion of social services (8.48)	6. Noneconomic groups (4.37)
2. Private enterprise (5.23)	7. Freedom (3.80)
3. Democracy (4.84)	8. Specific economic goals (3.28)
4. Environmental protection (4.48)	9. Decentralization (2.66)
5. Social justice (4.39)	10. Controlled economy (2.53)

*Each figure in parentheses indicates the mean percentage of the election programs devoted to the relevant theme.

reluctance to tolerate more authoritarian styles of governing. In a curious way, therefore, liberal parties now reflect a set of political appeals that echoes elements of both the new left and the traditional right. This may well stem from the shared contemporary orientation of all three groups toward an essentially middle-class electoral constituency. (On liberal parties in general, see Kirchner.)

The Agrarians

As can be seen from Table 3.14, while agrarian parties do not exist at all in many countries, where they do exist, they tend to be quite large. Although such parties have sometimes contested elections in both Ireland and the Netherlands, agrarian parties are essentially a Scandinavian phenomenon, with a strong presence in Denmark, Finland, Iceland, Norway, and Sweden. Outside the Nordic area, an agrarian party persists only in Switzerland. Even so, the Swiss "agrarian" party is actually an alliance between a peasant party and two quite different parties and is only marginally compatible with other members of the agrarian political family.

As their name suggests, agrarian parties were primarily special-interest parties. They were initially mobilized in the late nineteenth and early twentieth centuries to represent the specific concerns of farmers and the agricultural sector. With the

TABLE 3.14
Agrarian Parties: Electoral Performance, % of Vote

	1950s	1960s	1970s	1980s	Parties Competing in 1980s
Denmark	22.9	20.0	15.1	11.4	Liberal party
Finland	23.6	23.7	24.1	25.2	Center party, Finnish Rural party
Iceland	22.6	28.2	23.0	20.0	Progressive party, National party,* Association for Equality and Justice*
Ireland	2.8	0.5	—	—	NA
Netherlands	—	3.5	1.3	—	NA
Norway	9.5	9.9	9.8	6.6	Center party
Sweden	11.0	14.2	21.8	12.2	Center party
Switzerland	12.1	11.2	10.8	11.1	Peoples party
Mean	7.0	7.4	7.1	5.8	

*The party has not contested all elections in the 1980s.

economic and demographic decline in this sector over time, agrarian parties have attempted to extend their appeal to middle-class urban voters. This shift was most clearly signaled by a change of name to Center party in Finland, Norway, and Sweden (in 1965, 1959, and 1957, respectively). The strategy proved at least temporarily successful in Sweden, where support for the party grew to almost 22 percent of the vote in the 1970s.

One result of this process of adaptation is the curious amalgam of agrarian party policy emphases that can be seen in Table 3.15. Despite their move away from a distinctively rural base, agrarian parties continue to emphasize the interests of agriculture and farmers and are the only party family to do so. Two other emphases also reflect their particular heritage. There is an emphasis on decentralization, which harks back to their essentially peripheral roots; and there is an emphasis on environmental protection that, in its anti-industrial bias, is also characteristic of such parties. At the same time, however, agrarian parties also emphasize welfare provision, social justice, and the need for a controlled economy, which suggests a leftist orientation; and they favor both private enterprise and the maintenance of traditional moral values, which suggests quite a conservative impulse.

While this mix of policy concerns allows agrarian parties to appeal to both the right and the left, their earlier positions in Scandinavian party systems suggested a quite close alignment with the social democrats. In both Norway and Sweden in the 1930s, for example, some of the most important welfare legislation was passed by social democratic governments supported by agrarian parties—a powerful "red-green" alliance that helped to lay the basis for the present advanced welfare states in these countries. Nowadays, however, agrarian parties attempt to play the role of genuine center parties, bridging the gap between the social democrats and a fragmented bourgeois opposition. In this sense they can now be difficult to distinguish from more orthodox liberal parties (see above). Indeed, the similarities among these groups are highlighted by the fact that the strongest agrarian parties have emerged in systems where liberalism is weak or nonexistent (Finland and Iceland), while the strongest liberal parties tend to be found in countries where there is no agrarian presence (see also Steed and Humphreys).

In general, however, agrarian parties can be regarded as having drifted from the left toward the right over time. On the infrequent occasions when they win government office, they now tend to be the moderate allies of bourgeois coalition partners. (On the emergence of agrarian parties, see Urwin, 1980, and Elder and Gooderham.)

TABLE 3.15
Agrarian Parties (No. = 15): Issue Priorities*

1. Expansion of the social services (11.01)	6. Social justice (4.49)
2. Decentralization (7.77)	7. Controlled economy (3.72)
3. Environmental protection (6.71)	8. Agriculture/farmers (3.45)
4. Private enterprise (6.64)	9. Democracy (3.08)
5. Economic orthodoxy (5.51)	10. Defense of traditional morality (3.03)

*Each figure in parentheses indicates the mean percentage of the election programs devoted to the relevant theme.

The Far Right

Parties of the far right currently compete in only a handful of Western European democracies. The principal protagonists include the National Front (FN) in France, the Italian Social Movement (MSI) in Italy, and National Action in Switzerland (Table 3.16). Though the Republican party in West Germany is not yet a relevant political actor at the national level, a historical legacy and increasing success at the local level suggest its inclusion in this category. There is also the marginally successful Democratic Union for Respect of Work (RAD/UDRT) in Belgium and the even more marginal Center party in the Netherlands.

By and large, parties of the far right are small parties, although in both France and Italy they have proved sufficiently popular to have an impact on the direction and pattern of party competition at the national level, sometimes being in a position to deny a legislative majority to the parties of the center-right.

Extremely conservative and often highly xenophobic (the Italian MSI is the only real exception in this latter regard), these parties are the heirs of the fascist and antisystem right-wing movements that rose to prominence in interwar Europe. These parties have sometimes taken up more contemporary issues, however, building a heterogeneous range of policy concerns that confounds easy understanding. The Swiss National Action, for example, places a high priority on environmental protection, while activists in the Italian MSI are reportedly sympathetic to certain postmaterialist concerns (e.g., Ignazi).

There is some evidence that these parties are gaining in popularity. While the neofascist MSI in Italy has remained at a more or less stable level of support since the 1960s, Swiss National Action only began to mobilize in the 1970s, while the French National Front, building on the short-lived successes of the Poujadist movement in the 1950s, first entered the electoral fray in the 1980s. The far-right party in Belgium is also of recent origin, while the West German Republicans first began their intervention in local elections in 1986. As in France, however, there was an earlier postwar mobilization of the far right in Germany, with the neofascist National Democratic party (NPD) gaining 2 and 4 percent of the vote in the national elections of 1965 and 1969, respectively. (On the extreme right in general, see von Beyme, which, however, also surprisingly includes an analysis of the secular conservatives in Spain.)

TABLE 3.16
Extreme Right: Electoral Performance, % of Vote

	1950s	1960s	1970s	1980s	Parties Competing in 1980s
Belgium	—	—	—	1.3	RAD/UDRT
France	4.3	—	—	6.5	National Front
Germany	1.1	2.1	—	—	NA
Italy	11.1	6.3	6.7	6.4	Italian Social Movement
Netherlands	—	—	—	0.6	Center party
Switzerland	—	—	4.8	3.2	National Action
Mean	1.1	0.6	0.7	1.2	

BOX 3.2
The Center and Right

FRANCE

The 1980s have witnessed increasing divisions and fluctuations within the French center and right. The traditional dominance of the Gaullists (RPR) has been challenged by the growth in the more centrist liberal-Christian-conservative alliance of the UDF, led by Giscard d'Estaing. The problem for the Gaullists has been further compounded by the recent electoral successes of Jean Marie Le Pen's National Front, an extreme right-wing party which campaigns against the immigration of North Africans into France. In 1981, for the first time in the history of the Fifth Republic, the center-right lost the presidency to the socialist candidate, François Mitterrand.

GERMANY

The center-right dominated governments in Germany during the 1980s. In 1982, the small and quite conservative Liberal party (FDP) withdrew from its thirteen-year coalition with the Social Democrats and joined forces with the Christian Democrats (CDU/CSU) under Helmut Kohl. This coalition has been in government ever since, and the CDU in particular has recently gained substantial electoral kudos for its management of the German reunification process.

ITALY

The center-right has been the dominant political force in Italy throughout the postwar period, and the Christian Democrats (DC) have played the dominant role in every government, being the party which has provided the prime minister in all but four of the forty-nine governments which have held office since 1945. Yet while powerful, the DC is dependent upon the support of other, smaller parties, including the two secular center parties, the Liberals and the Republicans, and, more recently, the center-left Socialist party. There is also a very right-wing traditional neofascist party in Italy, the Social Movement (MSI), and more recently, a number of extremely right-wing and xenophobic regional parties have emerged in northern Italy. Like the French National Front, these base their electoral appeal on opposing immigration.

THE NETHERLANDS

The center-right Christian Democratic Appeal (CDA), the largest party in the Netherlands, is also quite a young party, formally dating from 1980, when the Catholic People's party (KVP) merged with two smaller Protestant parties (the ARP and the CHU). The CDA has been in government continually since then, most often in coalition with the relatively conservative Liberal party (VVD) and, since 1989, with the Labor party (PvdA). The traditional patterns of Dutch politics have recently been changed by the relative success of Democrats '66, a left-leaning liberal party formed in 1966 that has joined both the PvdA (in 1973–1977) and the CDA (in 1981–1982) in coalition governments.

SPAIN

Since the initial short-lived success of the Union of the Democratic Center (UCD), the center-right in Spain has been both weak and fragmented. The dominant force is now the People's party (PP), which emerged from a difficult history fraught with alliance and schism and which contains conservative, liberal, and Christian factions. In practice, the very centrist strategy pursued by the dominant socialist party, the PSOE, has left little room for opposition from the center or the right.

SWEDEN

The dominant party on the divided center-right in Sweden is the relatively conservative Moderate Unity party. Like the other center-right parties in Sweden, it has rarely enjoyed government office, although it did join in government with two other center-right parties, the Center party and the Liberal party, in 1976–1978 and again in 1979–1981. In 1978–1979 the Liberals alone remained as a minority government, and in 1981–1982 they shared power with the Center party, again as a minority. Even though the Liberals and the Center party, which originated as a farmers' party, tend to be more inclined than the Moderates to accept the policies of the dominant Social Democrats, the consensual approach which all three parties

(Continued on next page)

adopted in government did little to undermine the long-established social democratic ethos in Sweden.

UNITED KINGDOM

The center and right are far from friendly toward one another in Britain. The Conservative party held government throughout the 1980s, then under the rightwing leadership of Margaret Thatcher (replaced in 1990 by John Major). The result was that many supporters of the center parties found increasingly common ground with Labour in their opposition to Conservative policies. At the beginning of the 1980s it seemed that the center, in the form of the old Liberal party and the newly formed Social Democratic party, was going to become a major force in British politics. However, votes failed to be translated into parliamentary seats, given the electoral system, and the challenge fizzled out. The Social Democrats then disbanded their new party, and the majority of the members merged with the Liberals to form the new Liberal Democratic party.

OTHER PARTIES

Irredentist and Regionalist Parties

While most European countries are presented as being "nation-states," in which the boundaries of nation and state coincide, many incorporate important local minorities of distinct national, linguistic, and ethnic groups. These groups are often represented by parties that have their basis in local ethnic or regional identities, with demands that range from greater regional autonomy to full-fledged irredentist separatism. These parties, while held together as a family by their strong regional or ethnic concerns, vary immensely in their other policy positions and in their general positioning on the left-right scale. They span the entire range of options, from the far-left position of Herri Batasuna in the Basque province in Spain to the far-right position of the Lombard League in Italy. Given the strength of their primary ethnic and regional concerns, however, it is clearly more appropriate to think of these parties as making up a distinct family in their own right rather than as being members of other ideological families.

Regionalist parties can be found in one form or another in almost all Western European states. But despite what are often quite high levels of electoral support in local power bases, these parties are relevant at the national level in only a handful of countries. Belgium, given its deep ethnic and linguistic divisions, provides the most striking examples, including various Flemish (Dutch-speaking) and Walloon (French-speaking) regional parties. Also of some significance are the Swedish People's party, the political voice of the Swedish-speaking minority in Finland; the extremely nationalist Sinn Fein party, which is the political wing of the Irish Republican Army and mobilizes both in the Irish Republic and, within the United Kingdom, in Northern Ireland; the Lega Nord in Italy, a recently formed group of various regional parties promoting the interests of South Tyrol, Sardinia, Val d'Aosta, Venice, and Lombardy (the latter seeks to curtail immigration into Lombardy from southern Italy and won 19 percent of the vote in the 1990 local

TABLE 3.17
Subnational and Regional Parties: Electoral Performance, % of Vote

	1950s	1960s	1970s	1980s	Parties Competing in 1980s
Belgium	1.4	9.0	19.4	12.3	Volksunie, Vlaams Blok, Francophone Democratic Front, Walloon Rally
Finland	7.1	6.2	5.2	5.3	Swedish People's party
Ireland	1.7	1.0	—	1.3	Sinn Fein*
Italy	0.6	0.6	0.7	1.7	South Tyrol People's party, Sardinian Action party, Val d'Aosta Union, Venetian League, Lombard League
United Kingdom	1.6	2.1	4.3	3.7	Scottish National party, Plaid Cymru, Ulster Unionists, Sinn Fein, Social Democratic and Labour party
Mean	0.8	1.3	2.0	1.6	

*The party has not contested all elections in the 1980s.

elections in Lombardy); various Basque separatist parties in northern Spain, including Herri Batasuna, which supports the armed struggle of Basque paramilitary organizations; and, in the United Kingdom, the Scottish and Welsh nationalists, together with constitutional nationalists and unionists in Northern Ireland (see Table 3.17).

In general, the strongest support for these parties is to be found in Belgium, Spain, and the United Kingdom. While these parties remain a tiny electoral minority within most of Western Europe, the early postwar decades did witness a growth in their electoral support, which, in Western Europe as a whole, peaked in the 1970s. Notwithstanding their low overall vote levels, it is important to remember that these movements do command substantial support in their local areas. Roughly two Basque voters in three support Basque nationalist parties, for example. In Northern Ireland virtually all of the vote is won by nationalist or regional (including unionist) parties. Until very recently, none of the mainland British parties was even willing to nominate candidates for elections in the province. When the British Conservative party tested the waters in Northern Ireland in a by-election in 1990, it was utterly trounced by local parties. (On nationalist and regionalist parties in general, see Esman; Rokkan and Urwin; and Urwin, 1983.)

"Others"

As with any other attempt at systematic classification, there are bound to be some cases that defy categorization. There are, as we might expect, parties that just do not seem to be members of any of the cross-national families that we have been discussing. These include a number of small Danish parties, including the long-standing Justice party and the Center Democrats, founded in 1973 by a former senior social democratic politician. Pensioners' parties have recently emerged in

Finland, Italy, and Luxembourg. Europe's first "antigreen" party, the Automobile party, was founded in Switzerland in 1985. It is also important to note that independent candidates and loose, ill-defined alliances can from time to time be significant in a variety of countries—most notably in France, Ireland, and the United Kingdom, where electoral systems place few obstacles in the way of independent candidatures.

It is in Portugal and Spain, however, where "other" parties have been most important. As new party systems emerged in the wake of the transition to democracy in the late 1970s, a number of temporary and shifting alliances appeared, often involving protagonists who shared little other than a desire to ensure the consolidation of democratic practices. These alliances were oriented toward particular domestic problems of democratic transition, bearing little relationship to the interests and programs of parties in the established democracies. In Portugal, for example, a group known as the Democratic Alliance polled more than 48 percent of the vote in 1980 and then fell apart into various factions and units. Two elections later, in 1985, the Democratic Renewal party was created; it won more than 18 percent of the vote before falling back to 5 percent in 1987. The number and size of these loose electoral alliances in Portugal and, to a lesser extent, in Spain indicate that these party systems are still in the process of consolidation. It is this factor more than anything else that undermines comparisons between these party systems and those of the rest of Western Europe.

OVERVIEW: PATTERNS IN THE PARTY SYSTEM

Despite the diversity to be found both between and within the ten party families that we have identified, some clear patterns can also be seen. Thus strong social democratic parties rarely coincide with strong communist parties; agrarian parties do not usually find themselves pitted against major liberal parties; conservatives and Christian democrats rarely meet head-on within the same national party system. Moreover, while the range of party families is extensive, a few key families lie at the heart of party politics in most countries. These are the social democrats, the liberals, the Christian democrats, and the secular conservatives. Each of these families averages more than 10 percent of the vote across the whole of contemporary Western Europe.

These general patterns of contemporary political divisions are summarized in Table 3.18, which also includes the relative strength of party families in Greece, Portugal, and Spain. Taking all eighteen democracies together, we can easily see the key position of the leading party families. The socialists clearly emerge as the most powerful political family, polling an average of 31 percent of the vote. They are followed by the conservatives (19 percent), the Christian democrats (17 percent), and the liberals (11 percent). The next biggest families are the communists, with less than 7 percent, and the remarkably persistent agrarian parties, with less than 5 percent.

Another striking feature of the six largest families is their age. Most were well-established by the turn of the century, while the communists are the youngest,

TABLE 3.18

The Party Families in the 1980s: Mean Electoral Support, by Country, % of Vote

	Communists	New Left	Socialists	Greens	Agrarians	Liberals	Christian Democrats	Conservatives	Extreme Right	Nationalist and Regionalist	Other*
Austria	0.7	—	45.4	4.1	—	7.4	42.2	—	—	—	—
Belgium	1.4	—	28.0	6.1	—	21.1	27.8	—	1.3	12.3	—
Denmark	0.9	14.4	31.9	0.7	11.4	5.6	2.4	26.0	—	—	6.5
Finland	13.9	—	25.4	2.7	25.2	0.9	2.8	22.9	—	5.3	0.6
France	12.4	—	35.0	0.9	—	—	42.7 †	—	6.5	—	—
Germany	—	—	39.4	5.1	—	8.9	45.9	—	—	—	—
Iceland	15.3	7.8	17.1	—	20.0	—	—	38.4	—	—	—
Ireland	—	3.9	8.9	0.4	—	3.5	(33.9)‡	45.9	—	1.3	—
Italy	28.3	4.0	16.4	1.2	—	6.9	33.6	—	6.4	1.7	0.7
Luxembourg	5.1	—	32.3	6.8	—	17.5	33.3	—	—	—	5.8
Netherlands	1.1	3.7	31.0	—	—	25.5	36.6	—	0.6	—	—
Norway	0.9	6.8	37.4	—	6.6	3.4	8.7	35.1	—	—	—
Sweden	5.6	—	44.5	2.9	12.2	10.8	2.4	21.1	—	—	—
Switzerland	0.9	3.5	21.2	3.9	11.1	30.1	22.2	—	3.2	—	2.2
United Kingdom	—	—	29.2	—	—	23.9	—	42.4	—	3.7	—
Greece	12.1	—	43.5	0.2	—	—	—	41.8	—	—	—
Portugal	16.0	—	28.7	—	—	(27.3)‡	6.9	—	—	—	19.1
Spain	6.1	—	43.5	—	—	4.6	2.2	25.9	—	5.2	6.6
Mean (all countries)	**6.7**	**2.5**	**31.0**	**1.9**	**4.8**	**11.0**	**16.7**	**19.0**	**1.0**	**1.6**	**2.3**
Mean (excluding Greece, Portugal, Spain)	**5.8**	**2.9**	**29.5**	**2.3**	**5.8**	**11.0**	**19.5**	**18.3**	**1.2**	**1.6**	**1.1**

*The criterion for inclusion is that the party must win at least 1 percent of the vote or one parliamentary seat.
†Includes liberals, Christian democrats, and secular conservatives.
‡Figures in parentheses indicate that the classification of the party concerned was ambiguous.

85

despite being first mobilized as long ago as the 1920s. While it has become fashionable to assert that Western European politics is being transformed beyond recognition (Dalton et al.; Lawson and Merkl), the deep historical roots of most of the key contestants in European party competition should not go unnoticed (we discuss persistence and change in contemporary European politics in the following chapter; see also Bartolini and Mair).

We can use the relative strengths of each of the six key political families in each country to attempt to identify groups of countries whose party systems have important similarities. This suggests that the single most important factor separating one group of countries from another is whether the major party of the right is a Christian democratic party or a secular conservative party.

Within the group of countries characterized as having a strong Christian democratic party, there is a further important distinction between countries in which the traditional left is relatively strong and the right relatively united (Austria and Germany) and countries in which the left is relatively weak and the right relatively divided (Belgium, Luxembourg, the Netherlands, and Switzerland). Italy, the final country in this "Christian democratic" group, is not easily classified in these terms. While the Italian left is strong, it is also divided between communists and socialists.

Distinctions can also be drawn within the group of countries characterized as having a strong secular conservative party. In Finland, Iceland, and, to a large extent, France, there is both a divided left (note the presence of strong communist parties) and a divided right. There is a subgroup of countries—Denmark, Norway, and Sweden—where the right is divided but where the left is unified behind a major social democratic party. Finally, there is the United Kingdom, which has strong and united parties of both the right and the left.

Overall, while there is no single "typical" Western European party system, there are no more than a few different types of party systems, if we choose to classify these in terms of the relative strengths of the various party families that are involved in electoral competition. There are, of course, alternative ways of classifying party systems—in terms of the structure of coalition bargaining, for example—but the method we have chosen in this particular context emphasizes the character of the partisan appeals made by the key actors. By emphasizing in a comparative manner the interests on behalf of which the various party families were mobilized, as well as the broad ideological distinctions among them, this method of describing party competition encourages us to explore the relationship between party competition and patterns of cleavage in the social structure, the matter to which we now turn.

References

Bartolini, Stefano, and Peter Mair: *Identity, Competition and Electoral Availability: The Stabilisation of European Electorates 1885–1985*, Cambridge University Press, Cambridge, England, 1990.

Beyme, Klaus von (ed.): *Right-Wing Extremism in Western Europe*, Cass, London, 1988.

Budge, Ian, David Robertson, and Derek Hearl (eds.): *Ideology, Strategy and Party Movement: A Comparative Analysis of Party Programs in Nineteen Democracies*, Cambridge University Press, Cambridge, England, 1987.

Dalton, Russell J., Scott C. Flanagan, and Paul Allen Beck (eds.): *Electoral Change in Advanced Industrial Democracies: Realignment or Dealignment?* Princeton University Press, Princeton, 1984.

Elder, Neil, and R. Gooderham: "The Centre Parties of Norway and Sweden," *Government and Opposition*, vol. 13, no. 2, 1978, pp. 218–235.

Esman, Milton (ed.): *Ethnic Conflict in the Western World*, Cornell University Press, Ithaca, N.Y., 1977.

Flora, Peter: "Introduction," in Peter Flora (ed.), *Growth to Limits: The West European Welfare States since World War II*, vol. 1: *Sweden, Norway, Finland, Denmark*, de Gruyter, Berlin, 1986, pp. v–xxxvi.

Fogarty, Michael P.: *Christian Democracy in Western Europe, 1820–1953*, Routledge and Kegan Paul, London, 1957.

Girvin, Brian (ed.): *The Transformation of Contemporary Conservatism*, Sage, Beverly Hills, 1988.

Ignazi, Piero: "La Cultura Politica del Movimento Sociale Italiano," *Rivista Italiana di Scienza Politica*, vol. 19, no. 3, 1989, pp. 431–466.

Irving, R. E. M.: *The Christian Democratic Parties of Western Europe*, Allen and Unwin, London, 1979a.

_____: "Christian Democracy in Post-War Europe: Conservatism Writ Large or Distinctive Political Phenomenon?" *West European Politics*, vol. 2, no. 1, 1979b, pp. 53–68.

Kirchheimer, Otto: "The Transformation of the West European Party Systems," in Joseph LaPalombara and Myron Weiner (eds.), *Political Parties and Political Development*, Princeton University Press, Princeton, 1966, pp. 177–200.

Kirchner, Emil J. (ed.): *Liberal Parties in Western Europe*, Cambridge University Press, Cambridge, England, 1988.

Kitschelt, Herbert P.: "Left-Libertarian Parties: Explaining Innovation in Competitive Party Systems," *World Politics*, vol. 40, no. 2, 1988, pp. 194–234.

Laver, Michael, and W. Ben Hunt: *Policy and Party Competition*, Routledge, New York, 1991.

Lawson, Kay, and Peter Merkl (eds.): *When Parties Fail: Emerging Alternative Organizations*, Princeton University Press, Princeton, 1988.

Layton-Henry, Zig (ed.): *Conservative Politics in Western Europe*, Macmillan, London, 1982.

Lipset, S. M., and Stein Rokkan: "Cleavage Structures, Party Systems and Voter Alignments: An Introduction," in S. M. Lipset and Stein Rokkan (eds.), *Party Systems and Voter Alignments*, The Free Press, New York, 1967.

Madeley, John: "Scandinavian Christian Democracy: Throwback or Portent," *European Journal of Political Research*, vol. 5, no. 3, 1977, pp. 267–286.

_____: "Politics and the Pulpit: The Case of Protestant Europe," in Suzanne Berger (ed.), *Religion in West European Politics*, Cass, London, 1982, pp. 149–171.

Michels, Robert: *Political Parties: A Sociological Study of the Oligarchical Tendencies of Modern Democracy*, The Free Press, New York, 1911, 1962.

Morgan, Roger, and S. Silvestri (eds.): *Moderates and Conservatives in Western Europe*, Heinemann, London, 1982.

Mueller-Rommel, Ferdinand (ed.): *New Politics in Western Europe: The Rise and Success of Green Parties*, Westview Press, Boulder, Colo., 1989.

Paterson, William E., and Alastair H. Thomas (eds.): *Social Democratic Parties in Western Europe*, Croom Helm, London, 1977.

_____: *The Future of Social Democracy*, Oxford University Press, Oxford, 1986.

Rokkan, Stein: *Citizens, Elections, Parties*, Universitetsforlaget, Oslo, 1970.

_____ and Derek W. Urwin (eds.): *The Politics of Territorial Identity*, Sage, Beverly Hills, 1983.

Steed, Michael, and Peter Humphreys: "Identifying Liberal Parties," in Kirchner.

Urwin, Derek W.: *From Ploughshare to Ballotbox: The Politics of Agrarian Defence in Europe*, Universitetsforlaget, Oslo, 1980.

_____: "Harbinger, Fossil or Fleabite? 'Regionalism' and the West European Party Mosaic," in Hans Daalder and Peter Mair (eds.), *Western European Party Systems: Continuity and Change*, Sage, Beverly Hills, 1983, pp. 221–256.

Waller, Michael, and Meindert Fennema (eds.): *Communist Parties in Western Europe: Decline or Adaptation?* Blackwell, Oxford, 1988.

Whyte, J. H.: *Catholics in Western Democracies: A Study in Political Behaviour*, Gill and Macmillan, Dublin, 1981.

Wilensky, Harold L.: "Leftism, Catholicism and Democratic Corporatism: The Role of Political Parties in Recent Welfare State Development," in Peter Flora and Arnold Heidenheimer (eds.), *The Development of Welfare States in Europe and America*, Transaction Books, London, 1981, pp. 345–382.

CHAPTER 4
VOTING PATTERNS AND SOCIAL CLEAVAGES

Enormous historical legacies underpin the appeals of political parties to the citizens of Western Europe. The same factors help to determine the response of citizens to political parties. Indeed, Lipset and Rokkan (1967), in one of the most cogent and influential accounts of the development of modern Western European politics, begin with events that took place more than four centuries ago, at a time when the very idea of mass political parties, let alone that of mass democracy, was unthinkable. Those events, and subsequent developments over the succeeding centuries, continue to provide the parameters of contemporary politics in Western Europe.

To take a very clear-cut example, we saw in the previous chapter that one of the most important distinctions between European party systems concerns whether the major party of the right is a Christian democratic or secular conservative party. We also saw that when there is a major Christian party, it typically depends upon a substantial Catholic vote, the presence or absence of which in turn derives from a history of religious division which dates back to 1517, when Martin Luther pinned his 95 theses on the door of a church in Wittenberg, thus initiating the Protestant revolt against the church of Rome and marking the beginning of what we now know as the Reformation.

The ensuing clash between traditional Catholic Europe and reforming Protestant Europe constituted the first serious division in what had previously been a unifying Christian culture. The continent was effectively fractured in two, and the boundary between the two parts can be seen on a map of Europe by drawing a line between the Dutch city of Rotterdam in the northwest and the Italian city of Venice in the southeast. To the south and west of this line lie the countries that remained loyal to Rome and that remain largely Catholic today: France, Spain, Belgium, Luxembourg, Italy, and Austria, as well as the southern part of the Netherlands and southern Germany. To the north and east of this line lies Protestant Europe: the Scandinavian countries in particular, as well as northern Germany and the northern part of the Netherlands. Britain was also to form part of the Protestant north, while Ireland remained Catholic. In most but not all of the Catholic countries, as we have seen, the major party of the center-right has been or still remains an essentially Catholic Christian Democratic party. In all of the Protestant countries, the major party of the center-right is a secular conservative party. In the Netherlands, the continental fissure also split the nation, leading, as we have seen, to the creation of both Catholic and Protestant Christian parties. What is clear beyond any shadow of a doubt, however, is that the religious history of the previous four centuries still overhangs the development of party politics in contemporary Western Europe. Given this, it is hardly surprising that the broad outline of Western European party systems has proved so enduring.

In this chapter, therefore, we describe the traditional structures of social cleavage that underpin contemporary Western European politics and explore potential new bases of social and political division.

THE MEANING OF CLEAVAGE

Before we consider the actual substance of the social divisions that underpin contemporary Western European politics, it is important to be clear about precisely what we mean by the notion of a cleavage, which implies much more than a mere division, more even than an outright conflict, between two sets of people. In the 1980s, for example, there was a sharp division in a number of countries between those who favored the continued deployment of nuclear missiles and those who favored nuclear disarmament. This division cut deep and often led to violent conflict, in the form of protests and street demonstrations. It was also pervasive, being an important item on the political agenda in countries as diverse as the United Kingdom, Italy, West Germany, and the Netherlands. But the nuclear missile issue, while acute, pervasive, divisive, and conflictual, did not constitute a fundamental cleavage in the sense identified by Lipset and Rokkan, for whom a cleavage has three quite specific connotations (Bartolini and Mair, 1990, pp. 212–249).

First, a cleavage involves a *social division* that separates people who can be distinguished from one another in terms of key social characteristics such as occupation, status, religion, or ethnicity. Thus a cleavage may separate workers from employers, or Catholics from Protestants, or those who speak French from those who speak Dutch, and so on. A cleavage cannot be defined at the political level alone (as with the division over nuclear disarmament, for example).

Second, the groups involved in the division must be *conscious of their collective identity*—as workers or employers, for example—and be willing to act on this basis. This sense of collective identity is of crucial importance in the emergence and maintenance of cleavages. Without it, no "objective" social division will be transformed into a salient sociopolitical cleavage. For example, while the gender division between men and women is one of the most significant social divisions in any society, it has not until recently generated the sense of collective gender identity that provides the potential for turning gender into a salient basis for sociopolitical cleavage (and many argue that it has still not done so).

Third, a cleavage must be expressed in *organizational* terms. This is typically achieved as a result of the activities of a trade union, a church, a political party, or some other organization that gives formal institutional expression to the interests of those on one side of the division. In Britain, for example, while an objective social reality of distinctive national groups has always existed in Scotland and Wales, and while there has also been a clear collective sense of national identity within these groups, Welsh and Scottish nationalist politics have only sporadically achieved organizational expression. Hence the nationalist cleavage in Britain has often been dormant.

It is important to maintain an emphasis on each of the three components of a cleavage, since this helps us to understand how cleavages can persist or decay. A change in the cleavage structure of a society can occur as a result of changes in the social divisions that underpin cleavages, as a result of changes in the sense of collective identity that allows cleavages to be perceived by those involved, or as a result of changes in the organizational structure that gives political expression to cleavages. As we shall see below, those who suggest that there has recently been a fundamental transformation of traditional politics in Western Europe argue that there is evidence of change in all three components.

THE STRUCTURE OF CLEAVAGES IN WESTERN EUROPE

In their seminal analysis of the political development of Western Europe, Lipset and Rokkan suggest that the historical parameters that continue to determine contemporary political alignments result from the interaction of four major cleavages. First, there is the cleavage that divides the dominant culture (in the center of the political arena) from subject cultures (in the periphery). Second, there is the cleavage that divides church from state. Third, there is the cleavage that divides those involved in the primary economy (typically in the countryside) from those in the secondary economy (typically in the town). Fourth, there is the cleavage that divides employers from workers (Lipset and Rokkan, 1967, pp. 13–26, and also in Mair, 1990, pp. 99–111; see also Rokkan, 1970, Chapter 3).

The Center-Periphery Cleavage

Lipset and Rokkan refer to the cleavage between the "subject culture" and the "dominant culture," now more commonly described as the cleavage between a country's sociopolitical "center" and its "periphery." This cleavage derives from the era during which both the boundaries and the political authority of modern European states were being forged. When these modern states were being built, an inevitable clash emerged. On one side were those, typically at the center of the political system, who sought to standardize the laws, markets, and cultures that lay within state boundaries. On the other side were those, normally in the periphery of the new states, who sought to preserve their independence and autonomy.

The desire for autonomy was rooted in a variety of factors. In some cases linguistic or minority national groups resisted the encroachment of what they regarded as essentially foreign government. In other cases religious groups resisted the new codes, customs, and values which were imposed from the center. Either way, pockets of resistance to centralization persisted in many of the developing nation-states. In some cases this resistance led eventually to secession, as when Ireland left the United Kingdom. In some cases it led to the granting of substantial local autonomy within the larger state, as with the separate Dutch-speaking (Fleming) and French-speaking (Walloon) communities in Belgium. In some cases it ended with effective absorption, as with the Breton minority in northwest France. The most common outcome, however, of this conflict between nation builders and subject populations was a diffuse but persistent tension between the two. This created a center-periphery cleavage in many Western European countries which remains visible to this day. It manifests itself in patterns of political attitude and voting behavior, as well as in the persistence of small linguistic or other cultural minorities. [One recent estimate suggests that 37 million citizens of the European Community, 9 percent of the total EC population spread across 35 different regions, speak minority languages, such as Basque, Catalan, Breton, Welsh, Scottish Gaelic, and Irish Gaelic (see Griffiths).] The center-periphery cleavage is salient even among some of the "smaller" democracies in which the geographic, as opposed to the sociopolitical, distance between the center and the periphery is not very large.

The Church-State Cleavage

The process of state building created a second cleavage, at once more sharply defined and more critical. This involved the conflict between state builders and the church, a conflict epitomized by the secular challenge posed by the French Revolution more than two hundred years ago. This was, and remains, a conflict about rights and privileges. It had to do with whether policies on crucial questions of public morality and, above all, education would be determined by the state or by the church.

The church-state cleavage developed in very different ways in Protestant and Catholic societies. The newly formed Protestant churches were essentially national churches that had largely become "agents of the state" (Lipset and Rokkan, 1967, p. 15). They thus had little incentive to challenge the policies of the state. Indeed, it was often only as a result of an alliance with the state that these churches had been able to establish themselves as legal entities. (This was not always the case. In the Netherlands, for example, the more fundamentalist Protestant adherents of the Dutch Reformed Church also opposed the secular ideas of the French Revolution in 1789, prompting the creation of the Anti-Revolutionary party, a party that remained a significant independent electoral force until the end of the 1970s.)

In the case of the Catholic church, the potential for conflict with the state was enormous. First, the Catholic church saw itself as being "above" the state, owing its allegiance to a supranational religious organization based in the Vatican. Second, the Catholic church persistently sought to insulate its adherents from secularizing tendencies, creating an autonomous cultural environment that proved resistant to state penetration. Thus Catholics sought to maintain their own independent schools and rejected state provision of secular education. They also sought to ensure that state laws on issues of public morality, such as divorce and censorship, would reflect Catholic values. Conflict between church and state was thus almost inevitable. This was obviously true in those countries where Catholics constituted a substantial religious minority, as in the Netherlands and Germany. It was also true, however, in countries such as France and Italy. In both countries, while the population was nominally all Catholic, the French Revolution had prompted a major secularist impetus which found expression in the anticlericalism of the early Liberal and Radical parties. In the case of Ireland, almost uniquely, the vast majority of the population remained practicing Catholics, secularism failed to take root, and state policy actually enshrined the Catholic belief system.

Thus the practical impact of the church-state cleavage was very unevenly distributed, proving a major source of political mobilization only in those countries with a substantial Catholic minority. In those countries, as we have seen, Christian Democratic parties now constitute a powerful electoral force. In the Protestant north and east of Europe, on the other hand, an accommodation between church and state was reached without too much difficulty. No substantial religious cleavage emerged, and so room was left for the mobilization of alternative cleavages.

The Rural-Urban Cleavage

The third cleavage identified by Lipset and Rokkan concerns the conflict between the traditionally dominant rural interests and the new commercial and industrial classes of the cities. This conflict was already apparent in the medieval period but became particularly acute with the beginning of the industrial revolution. While acute, however, the rural-urban cleavage was not always persistent. In Britain and Germany, in particular, but also in most of the rest of continental Western Europe, divisions between the two groups did not form an enduring partisan conflict. In Scandinavia, on the other hand, as well as in parts of Eastern Europe, urban interests proved much more dominant, and sustained rural opposition to the urban elites resulted in the creation of powerful agrarian parties which persisted to the present century.

But while the rural-urban cleavage may now be largely dormant in relation to conflicts between traditional landed and urban interests, there is also a sense in which the cleavage may now be acquiring a new, "postindustrial" relevance. Two factors are involved here. First, like the United States, many European countries now face severe problems in balancing the interests of city and country, problems that often derive from the concentrations of urban poverty and racial tension in inner cities, the remedies for which are seen to demand increasing government intervention and expenditure. At the same time, many more wealthy citizens flee inner cities in search of suburban and/or rural comforts, eroding the tax base of cities while continuing to take advantage of their services and thus generating a new clash of interests between city and country. Second, at least within the countries of the European Community (see Chapter 10), a new and sometimes violent conflict has arisen as a result of the drive to free the movement of agricultural produce between countries, while at the same time reducing subsidies to farmers. City folk clearly favor the cheaper food produced by both strategies, but farmers are increasingly discontented with the threatened slump in their standard of living. Farmers now make up a very small proportion of the work force in most Western European countries, and so it is unlikely that they could generate and sustain new agrarian political movements. But (for example, in France and Germany) there are often enough of them to tip the balance between the existing parties, and they can therefore pose a threat to their traditional representatives on the center-right.

The Class Cleavage

By far the most important cleavage to emerge from the industrial revolution was the conflict between the owners of capital together with their allies among the established elites, on the one hand, and the newly emerging working class, on the other. The process of industrialization meant that throughout nineteenth-century Europe, workers became increasingly concentrated in an essentially urban factory system. This provided a social environment in which they began to develop organizations, both trade unions and political parties, which sought to improve their conditions of work and to enhance their life chances. The increasing concentration of production enabled the organizations of the emerging working class to compensate for their lack of economic resources by mobilizing large groups of workers in collective action.

However, while the class cleavage is present in all Western European countries, its organizational expression shows two contrasting patterns. In all countries during the industrial revolution, and in the majority of countries thereafter, the political demands of workers were expressed by a Socialist party. In the wake of the Russian Revolution of 1917, as we have seen, more radical workers shifted toward a Communist alternative, and in a number of countries, support for such parties equaled and even surpassed that of the Socialist party. According to Lipset and Rokkan (1967, pp. 21–23), much of the explanation for the relative success of Communist parties lies in how bourgeois elites first responded to the workers' demands. Where they were more accommodating and pragmatic, as in Scandinavia and Britain, workers eschewed radical alternatives and became integrated into national politics. Where the bourgeois response was more repressive and the extension of political and social rights to the working class was resisted most adamantly—as in France, Germany, Italy, and Spain—workers adopted a more radical agenda, preparing the ground for the later acceptance of Communist parties. Thus, while the class cleavage is characteristic of all the Western European democracies, the political expression of working-class interests has in some countries been divided between a Socialist party and a Communist party, though this political division between socialists and communists does not itself have the properties of an independent sociopolitical cleavage, as we outlined these above.

The Interaction of Different Cleavages

History has left a complex mosaic of social divisions in Western Europe. While the cleavage between workers and employers has found expression in each Western European country, cleavages relating to center-periphery or rural-urban divisions, or to church-state relations, emerged in ways that were specific to particular countries. Thus, while the major similarities between Western European political systems derive from the class cleavage, the major differences between them can be explained to a large extent by the idiosyncratic development of other, often preindustrial social cleavages.

One way to distinguish Western European countries is in terms of the interaction between the various cleavages that are present in the system. As the class cleavage emerged in Austria, for example, it overlapped the important church-state cleavage. This resulted in a Christian Democratic party, which represents both "owners" and the church, and a Socialist party, which represents both workers and anticlericals. The two key cleavages cut along the same lines.

In the United Kingdom, in contrast, a single social cleavage has come to dominate politics. Church-state tensions were largely resolved through the creation of a national church during the Reformation, while the rural-urban cleavage was resolved when the landed aristocracy and the emerging industrial capitalists made common cause during the nineteenth century. Center-periphery tensions largely evaporated in 1921, with the secession of Ireland from the United Kingdom, a radical break that also helped to solve lingering problems of church-state relations reflected in opposition between the overwhelmingly Catholic Ireland and largely Protestant Britain. Nothing remained to interact with the class cleavage, and the result has been the emergence of two large political blocs distinguished from one another almost exclusively on the basis of their traditional class appeals.

In other cases, important cleavages cut across one another. In the Netherlands, as we have seen, the church-state cleavage first resulted in the creation of three different forces, representing Catholics, Protestants, and anticlericals. When the class cleavage emerged, however, it cut across the church-state cleavage. This implied the formation of a new party, the Labour party (PvdA), which opposed both the bourgeois religious parties and the bourgeois anticlerical Liberal party. In France, too, the church-state cleavage cuts across the class cleavage. The Catholic Popular Republican Movement (MRP) opposed the secular socialists and the communists, on the one hand, and the secular bourgeois liberals and radicals, on the other, finding reasonably common ground with the more religiously inclined conservative Gaullist movement. In terms of social and economic policy, however, the MRP looked left and found itself making common cause with the workers' parties against the liberals, radicals, and Gaullists.

Overall, therefore, what we might think of as the "cleavage structure" of a particular society has two distinct features. The first has to do with the particular cleavages which have survived historically as important lines of social and political division. The second has to do with the extent to which these important lines of division cut across one another. Thus a religious cleavage and a class cleavage may both cut along the same lines (if all workers are Catholic, for example, and all owners are Protestant), or they may cut across one another (if whether or not someone is a worker has no bearing on whether he or she is Protestant or Catholic). It is this pattern of interaction between cleavages that underpins the structure of party competition in most Western European states.

BOX 4.1
Traditional Cleavage Structures

FRANCE
Three crosscutting cleavages remain of substantial relevance in contemporary France: a class cleavage, separating the right from the left; a religious cleavage, separating the Gaullists, the National Front, and Catholic groups within the UDF from the Socialists, the Communists, and the liberal and conservative elements within the UDF; and a center-periphery tension, which pervades all parties and which reflects the inevitable and persistent response to the domination of Paris.

GERMANY
For much of the postwar period, the class cleavage has been the dominant cleavage in Germany, crosscut by a formerly much stronger church-state cleavage. Rural-urban tensions, which proved important in the nineteenth century, have now effectively disappeared. Given the reunification of east and west, however, Germany could witness the reemergence of a version of the center-periphery cleavage, as well as increased church-state divisions, with the interests of the relatively poorer and more secular east potentially conflicting with those of the richer and more Catholic west. It is interesting to note that one of the last obstacles to German reunification was the harmonization of the law on abortion, which was more permissive in East Germany.

ITALY
Much like France, Italy also experiences the three separate but crosscutting cleavages of class, religion, and center-periphery. Growing secularization has undermined the salience of the religious divide and has led Italy to adopt legislation permitting both divorce and abortion. The class cleavage has also waned, but there is evidence to suggest that center-periphery tensions are acquiring a new and more powerful resonance. This is not only reflected in the emergence of regional parties, particularly in northern Italy, but also exacerbated by the persistent inequalities between the richer north and the poorer south.

THE NETHERLANDS
Cleavages of class and religion are also the dominant cleavages in Dutch politics, although increased secularization and a blurring of class boundaries have tended to erode the strongly "pillarized" subcultures on which the traditional cleavage structure in the Netherlands rested. While there are few if any remaining center-periphery tensions in the Netherlands—the country is too small for them—local regional identities prove remarkably strong and continue to be sustained by the very uneven geographic distribution of the different religious groups.

SPAIN
Two cleavages clearly dominate Spanish politics —the class cleavage and the center-periphery cleavage. While the strength of the Socialist party might suggest that class is substantially more important, no other Western European country contains such a range or variety of regionalist and subnationalist parties. At the same time, however, the class cleavage also operates within the subnational and regional party systems, with left-right divisions cutting across local solidarities. Despite a long tradition of church-state conflict, religion has had a surprisingly marginal impact on politics since the transition to democracy.

SWEDEN
The rural-urban cleavage has been particularly important in Swedish politics, as in Scandinavian politics more generally. Since the strongly rural Agrarian party changed its name to the Center party in 1957 and began to appeal to a wider section of the Swedish electorate, however, the relevance of this cleavage has clearly waned. While a minor religious cleavage is reflected in the small electoral following of the Christian Democrats, a Protestant party that campaigns against permissiveness and alcohol consumption, the dominant cleavage in Sweden is clearly the class cleavage.

UNITED KINGDOM
Britain has perhaps the simplest cleavage structure in Western Europe. Class is by far the dominant cleavage, with the less significant religious and rural-urban divisions having waned in the nineteenth century. A small center-periphery cleavage does persist, however, reflecting the multinational character of the U.K. state and pitting Scottish, Welsh, and Irish nationalists against the English center.

THE PERSISTENCE OF CLEAVAGES AND THE FREEZING OF PARTY SYSTEMS

Since the work of Lipset and Rokkan (1967), it has become common to speak of the "freezing" of Western European party systems at about the time of the 1920s, as a result of the remarkable persistence of the social cleavages that underpin party politics. Cleavages persist for four main reasons. First, they persist when the interests with which the cleavage is concerned remain relevant and the groups which are polarized retain a sense of collective identity. Second, major new political identities are likely to be mobilized only when substantial bodies of new votes are incorporated into mass politics, and no such large-scale incorporation has occurred since the granting of universal suffrage. Third, the rules of the game are such that they favor the persistence of those parties which devised the rules in the first place. Fourth, parties can attempt to isolate their supporters from competitors and thereby "narrow" the electoral market.

The first reason why cleavages persist is that they concern people who are divided from one another on the basis of real and enduring issues. As long as workers continue to feel that they have a common interest that is distinct from the interests of employers, or farmers, or Catholics, or those who speak French, for example, and as long as this remains relevant at the level of politics and government, the cleavage around which workers are aligned is likely to persist. Conversely, if the social distinctiveness of being a worker becomes blurred, or if it is no longer seen to be relevant politically, the class cleavage might become dormant. (This is precisely the argument of those who emphasize the changing character of contemporary Western European politics.)

The second reason why cleavages persist is that European electorates are now fully mobilized (Rokkan, 1970; Lipset and Rokkan, 1967). This helps to explain why the "freezing" of many European party systems is typically said to have occurred around the 1920s. Lipset and Rokkan argued that the political alignments forged when a group of voters is newly enfranchised are strong and enduring. They thus emphasized the importance of the 1920s, the period when universal suffrage was generally introduced. This is not, of course, to suggest that the cleavages that were relevant in the 1920s will always remain salient. Rather, it implies that subsequent political realignments involve winning the support of voters who are already aligned in terms of a particular cleavage structure, a more difficult task than attracting voters with no established alignments.

The third explanation for the persistence of cleavages has to do with the laws that govern the conduct of elections. As we shall see in Chapter 6, the first-past-the-post electoral system that operates in Britain (and the United States) is often said to favor the development of a two-party system. The proportional representation (PR) systems that operate in the majority of Western European states are more conducive to multiparty politics. It might be argued that by not penalizing minority parties, PR electoral systems help to maintain minor cleavages. Conversely, first-past-the-post systems, by squeezing out small parties, may eliminate minor cleavages and allow the most salient cleavage to dominate the system as a whole. As Lipset and Rokkan forcefully remind us, however, the rules of the game do not emerge out of thin air; they are legislated by political parties. They will therefore tend to protect established interests (Lipset and Rokkan, 1967, p. 30; see also Sartori, 1987).

In a separate analysis of electoral systems, Rokkan (1970, pp. 147–168) argued that the adoption of PR resulted from, rather than led to, multiparty politics. PR electoral systems were adopted in countries where there were distinct cultural or linguistic minorities. When the mass working class was enfranchised in countries where other cleavages were already present, the rules of the game were often modified so as to ensure the continued representation of the existing smaller parties. This, of course, facilitated the persistence of the cleavages along which they aligned.

A fourth factor which encourages the persistence of cleavages has to do with party organization (see Chapter 5). In a desire to insulate party supporters from the competing appeals of their opponents, many European parties have involved themselves in a host of social activities. They have attempted to establish a presence in many different areas of their individual supporters' lives, organizing social clubs, welfare services, recreational facilities, and the like, thus offering adherents a range of services to sustain them from the cradle to the grave. Although such behavior was mainly a characteristic of working-class Socialist parties (the best account is in Roth), this process of "encapsulation" was also attempted by some of the Christian parties, notably the Catholic People's party in the Netherlands (Bakvis) and the People's party in Austria (Diamant). This process of integrating and encapsulating supporters thus characterized many of the new mass parties that challenged the most elitist traditional "cadre" parties in the era of popular enfranchisement (Duverger; Neumann, 1956a; Panebianco). These mass parties thereby helped to create and sustain specific political subcultures in which they hoped that party voters would express a more permanent sense of "belonging" rather than make a more instrumental, and changeable, policy-oriented voting decision. These mass parties attempted to corner the electoral market by building long-term voter attachments. To the extent that they succeeded, they stablized cleavage structures and the party systems upon which these were based.

The persistence of cleavages and party systems is the major thrust of Lipset and Rokkan's work, which has since become the benchmark for many subsequent analyses of Western European party systems. Writing from the perspective of the late 1960s and noting that the last new cleavage which had emerged had been the class cleavage, solidified some forty years before, Lipset and Rokkan (1967, p. 50) rounded off their analysis with the conclusion that "the party systems of the late 1960s reflect, with few but significant exceptions, the cleavage structures of the 1920s. . . . The party alternatives, and in remarkably many cases the party organizations, are older than the majorities of the national electorates." This was to become known as the "freezing hypothesis"—that party systems in Western Europe had "frozen" into place in the 1920s, with any subsequent changes either marginal or temporary.

The freezing hypothesis offered an influential theoretical and historical explanation for the stability of European electoral behavior in the 1950s and 1960s. This was the period in which the potentially vulnerable new West German party system had stabilized, given the success of Konrad Adenauer's Christian Democrats and the abandonment of radical policies by the Social Democrats in 1959. It was the period in which the policies of the Labour party in Britain had become almost indistinguishable from those of the centrist Conservative government in a process of convergence which became popularly kown as "Butskellism," a neologism derived from the names of R. A. Butler, then Conservative treasury minister, and Hugh Gaitskell, then leader of the Labour party. It was the period in which the polarized party system of Italy seemed set to stabilize under the center-right control of the Christian Democrats and in which the unstable French Fourth Republic had been replaced by the stable presidential system of the Fifth Republic. It was the period of unchanging social democratic hegemony in Scandinavia. In more general terms, it was a period described by some observers as one in which there was a "waning of opposition" (Kirchheimer, 1957) and an "end of ideology" (Bell).

This seemingly pervasive political consensus, together with the marked increase in mass prosperity that characterized Western Europe in the first postwar decades, clearly enhanced the prospects for democratic stability in the continent. It also seemed to be accounted for rather neatly by the processes of inertia suggested by Lipset and Rokkan. When Rose and Urwin set out to test the freezing hypothesis, they found that "whatever index of change is used . . . the picture is the same: the electoral strength of most parties in Western nations since the war has changed very little from election to election, from decade to decade, or within the lifespan of a generation . . . the first priority of social scientists concerned with the development of parties and party sytems since 1945 is to explain the absence of change in a far from static period in political history" (Rose and Urwin, 1970, p. 295).

FROM PERSISTENCE TO CHANGE?

Thus political scientists became convinced during the late 1960s that European party politics had settled down into a very stable pattern. However, while Lipset, Rokkan, and others were putting the finishing touches to their various analyses of persistence, the image of tranquillity was rudely shattered. Signs of change had actually been apparent in 1968, when student protests and violent street demonstrations raged throughout Western Europe and the United States. There were also signs of a challenge to the consensus within more mainstream politics, however.

The stability of Norwegian politics, for example, was fractured in the early 1970s as a referendum on Norway's entry into the European Community re-awakened the dormant center-periphery conflict and provoked major splits in the traditional parties. In the United Kingdom in 1974, nationalist parties from Scotland and Wales won a record share of the vote, while in Northern Ireland the political violence that had erupted in 1968 continued unabated, claiming almost 500 lives in 1972 alone. In Belgium, the rise of Flemish and Walloon nationalist movements provoked major splits in all three traditional parties, while in the Netherlands, the major Catholic party and its two traditional Protestant opponents were forced into an electoral alliance in order to stave off their severe electoral losses. Meanwhile, in Italy in 1976, the Communist party won its highest share ever of the vote and came within 5 percent of overtaking the ruling Christian Democrats. In France in 1974, a candidate supported by both the Socialists and the Communists came within 1 percent of finally snatching the presidency from the center-right. In short, it now seemed to be the case that "a week is a long time in politics," as former British Labour leader Harold Wilson once observed. While "stability" was the catchword of the 1950s and the 1960s, "change" became the catchword of the 1970s.

Nowhere were the changes of the 1970s better illustrated than in Denmark, for a long time "one of the most dull countries to deal with for a student of voting behaviour" (Pedersen, 1968), where "hardly anyone raises his voice and the rhetoric of revolution finds few admirers" (Dahl, p. 4).[1] This image was utterly transformed by the election of December 1973. The number of parties in the Danish parliament (*Folketing*) suddenly doubled from five to ten. The combined vote share of the four parties which had traditionally dominated Danish politics—Social Democrats, Social Liberals, Liberals, and Conservatives—fell from 84 percent to just 58 percent. A new radical conservative antitax party, the Progress party, suddenly emerged as the second largest party. These dramatic changes occurred during a period of only 27 months since the previous Danish election and are summarized in Table 4.1.

Table 4.1 shows big changes in the vote shares of the parties. The Progress party gained almost 16 percent of the vote. Other gains were made by the Center Democrats (+7.8), Communists (+2.2), Christians (+2.0), and Justice party (+1.2). The Social Democrats lost 11.7 percent of the vote. Other losses were suffered by the Conservatives (−7.5), Liberals (−3.3), Social Liberals (−3.2), and Socialist People's party (−3.1). If we measure electoral volatility as the sum of the vote shares gained by all winning parties (or the sum of the vote shares lost by

---

[1] Both quotes are cited in Pedersen (1987, pp. 1–2), which offers a succinct and insightful account of the Danish party system. For a more recent analysis, see Bille.

TABLE 4.1
Denmark's "Earthquake" Election of 1973

	1971		1973	
	% of Votes	Seats	% of Votes	Seats
Social Democrats	37.3	70	25.6	46
Conservatives	16.7	31	9.2	16
Liberals	15.6	30	12.3	22
Social Liberals	14.4	27	11.2	20
Socialist People's	9.1	17	6.0	11
Christian People's	2.0	0	4.0	7
Justice party	1.7	0	2.9	5
Left Socialists	1.6	0	1.5	0
Communists	1.4	0	3.6	6
Progress party	—	—	15.9	28
Center Democrats	—	—	7.8	14
Others	0.2	0	—	—
Total	100.0	175	100.0	175

all losing parties), electoral volatility in Denmark between 1971 and 1973 was 29.1 percent, a very high figure indeed.[2]

The first comprehensive analysis of increasing electoral volatility in Western Europe came, appropriately enough, from a Danish researcher, Mogens Pedersen (1979, 1983), whose work was stimulated by the extraordinary level of change in his own country. Pedersen documented the change that was also evident in Norway and the Netherlands and, to a lesser extent, in Switzerland, the United Kingdom, Finland, and Sweden. He concluded that there was a significant "unfreezing" of European party systems. A similar conclusion was reached by Maguire, who replicated and updated Rose and Urwin's analysis at the end of the 1970s. Just one decade later, using identical statistical techniques, Maguire found much greater instability and argued that Western European party systems "cannot now be regarded as inherently stable structures" (p. 92). Thus, while the priority at the end of the 1960s had been to explain stability, by the end of the 1970s the priority had become to explain why many party systems seemed to be subject to sudden change.

CHANGE IN EUROPEAN PARTY SYSTEMS?

The argument that party systems in Western Europe have been through a period of sudden and pervasive change is by now a received wisdom (Crewe and Denver; Dalton et al.; Shamir; Wolinetz, 1979, 1988). Explanations for this include the impact of changes in three main areas: the social structure of European countries; patterns of individual behavior; and the behavior of political parties together with the issues which concern them. More generally, and in direct opposition to the freezing hypothesis, recent analyses suggest that there has been a decline in the hold of traditional cleavages and a rise in the political impact of new cleavages.

Change in the Social Structure

In Western Europe in 1950, according to one recent estimate, an average of 26 percent of the working population was engaged in agriculture; 38 percent was engaged in industry and 36 percent in the service sector. Thirty years later, in 1980, the proportion engaged in agriculture had fallen to just 7 percent, while that in the service sector had increased to 53 percent, with some 40 percent still engaged in industrial work (Ambrosius and Hubbard, pp. 58–59). These socioeconomic changes have had profound implications.

First, the vast majority of Western European citizens are now employees rather than self-employed. Flora (p. xxix) estimates that the proportion of blue- and white-collar employees rose from roughly two-thirds of the Western European

---

[2] Calculations of levels of aggregate volatility must be treated very carefully, however, since the figures may be artificially raised as a result of one-off party splits and mergers. In the Danish example, for instance, the Center Democrats were not a wholly new party but rather a split from the Social Democrats. A more realistic index of volatility would therefore measure change in 1973 by comparing the combined vote share of the divided parties (25.6% + 7.8% = 33.4%) with the previous vote share of the Social Democrats (37.3%) in order to produce a figure of 3.9% for the net party change and a figure of 21.2% for the election as a whole (see Bartolini and Mair, 1990, pp. 311–312). Subsequent calculations of levels of electoral volatility will follow this latter rule.

population in 1950 to more than four-fifths in 1980. Second, this change has involved massive growth in urbanization. Across Europe as a whole in 1950, according to Ambrosius and Hubbard (p. 40), in only seven countries did more than a quarter of the population live in large cities. By 1980 all but three countries had reached this level of urbanization. (The exceptions were Ireland—which has since passed this threshold—Czechoslovakia, and Albania.)

Third, technological changes in both the industrial and service sectors have led to the erosion of traditional class boundaries. As the population has become more educated and more prosperous, life-styles have begun to converge. Previous lines of division between different sectors of the population have tended to become blurred, while the number of people in the traditional blue-collar working class has declined quite sharply. Manual workers in Britain accounted for 47 percent of the British electorate in 1964, for example, but by 1983 they accounted for just 34 percent (Heath et al., 1985). Similar trends are apparent elsewhere in Western Europe. In Norway, for example, 60 percent of survey respondents identified themselves in 1969 as belonging to the working class; by 1981, this figure had fallen to just 45 percent (Sainsbury, 1984, p. 84). The pattern is confirmed by a more recent general survey of eight Western European countries—Austria, Denmark, Germany, the Netherlands, Norway, Sweden, Switzerland, and the United Kingdom. This showed that while an average of 70 percent of the labor force could be categorized as manual working class around 1950, by 1980 this figure had fallen to just 48 percent. There were particularly dramatic declines in Denmark—from 70 to 42 percent—and the Netherlands—from 69 to 41 percent (Visser, p. 50). As Ambrosius and Hubbard (pp. 76, 78) put it, a "socio-historical watershed was crossed in the Europe of the 1960s." Changes in economic and industrial structures, together with a major growth in welfare states, broke down traditional barriers and effected a general "democratization" of affluence.

The Decline of Class Voting?

In addition to these dramatic demographic changes in the social structure of many European countries, there is evidence that the sense of identification between particular groups and the political parties that formerly represented their interests is also waning. For example, Table 4.2 shows that in Britain, the traditionally

TABLE 4.2
Party Preferences and Social Class in Britain*

	1951		1979		1983	
	Nonmanual Workers	Manual Workers	Nonmanual Workers	Manual Workers	Nonmanual Workers	Manual Workers
Conservative	75	34	60	35	55	35
Liberal	3	3	17	15	28	22
Labour	22	63	23	50	17	42
Total	100	100	100	100	100	100

*The numbers are percentages.
Source: Heath et al., 1985, p. 30.

strong association between manual workers and the Labour party, on one hand, and between nonmanual workers and the Conservative party, on the other, is gradually diminishing. The Labour lead over the Conservatives among manual workers was 29 percent in 1951. It had fallen to just 15 percent in 1979 and to just 7 percent in 1983. The Conservative lead over Labour among nonmanual workers declined from 53 percent in 1951 to 38 percent in 1983.

Survey data from other Western European countries also illustrate a convergence of the partisan preferences of traditional social classes. The "Alford index" provides a simple measure of the extent to which socialist voting within the working class is greater than that within the middle class, with higher values reflecting more cohesive class voting (Alford). In Britain, for example, the Alford index for 1951 was a relatively high 41 percent (the percentage of Labour support among manual workers, 63, less the percentage of Labour support among nonmanual classes, 22). It fell to just 25 percent in 1983. Table 4.3 shows that values of the Alford index in West Germany have fallen from 37 percent in 1957 to just 9 percent in 1987, reflecting a substantial convergence of the party preferences of social classes. A smaller decline in class voting was evident in Sweden, with the values of the Alford index falling from 53 percent in 1956 to 38 percent in 1979.

To be sure, the Alford index is crude, and there are problems with its comparability across countries, given different ways of categorizing social classes. In Sweden, for example, the decline in class voting seems much less pronounced when lower nonmanual workers are classified as middle class rather than working class (Sainsbury, 1987). In Britain, the adoption of a five-category classification ranging from "the salariat" to the blue-collar working class also suggests that the decline in class voting has actually been much more muted than might appear from a simple two-category classification (Heath et al., 1985). This suggests a need to refine conceptions of social class, as these are related to voting. Be that as it may, the evidence does suggest that there was a substantial decline, during the 1970s and 1980s, in the distinctiveness of the party preferences of traditional social classes in the different Western European countries. Thus, although workers continue to support parties of the left in greater proportions than does the electorate as a whole (as can be seen from Table 4.4), with the difference being particularly marked in the Scandinavian countries and Austria, the bias is not now as strong as was the case in the early postwar decades. Moreover, since this decline has been accom-

TABLE 4.3

**Trends in Class Voting in Germany and Sweden,
% Voting Socialist in Working Class less % Voting Socialist in Middle Class (Alford Index)**

	1953	1957	1961	1965	1969	1972	1976	1980	1983	1987
West Germany	30	37	28	26	12	17	16	16	10	9

	1956	1960	1964	1968	1970	1973	1976	1979
Sweden	53	55	47	42	40	44	36	38

Sources: Dalton, 1990, p. 110; Sainsbury 1987, p. 515.

TABLE 4.4
Working-Class Support for Parties of the Left

Country	Year	Party	% Overall Support	% Working-Class Support	Difference
Austria	1988	Socialists	32	52	+20
Denmark	1987	Social Democrats	29	43	+14
Finland	1987	Socialists and Communists	38	61	+23
France	1988	Socialists and Communists	41	54	+13
Germany	1987	Social Democrats	37*	53	+16
Ireland	1989	Labour party and Workers' party	11	15	+ 4
Netherlands	1986	Labor party	34	38	+ 4
Norway	1984	Labor party and Socialist Left	46*	64	+18
Sweden	1985	Social Democrats and Communist party	50*	72	+22
United Kingdom	1987	Labour party	31*	43	+12

*Refers to the actual vote won in the election of that year (in Norway, the election of 1985).
Sources: Christian Haerpfer, "Die Sozialstruktur der SPOe" *Österreichische Zeitschrift Für Politikwissenschaft,* no. 4, 1989; Jorgen Goul Andersen, "Denmark: Environmental Conflict and the 'Greening' of the Labour Movement," *Scandinavian Political Studies,* vol. 13, no. 2, 1990; Sten Berglund, "The 1987 Eduskunta Election in Finland," *Scandinavian Political Studies,* vol. 11, no. 1, 1988; Alain Guyomarch and Howard Machin, "François Mitterrand and the French Presidential and Parliamentary Elections of 1988," *West European Politics,* vol. 12, no. 1, 1989; Russell J. Dalton, *Citizen Politics in Western Democracies,* Chatham House, Chatham N.J., 1988; *Irish Political Studies,* vol. 5, 1990; Dutch Election Study, 1986; Diane Sainsbury, "Party Strategies and the Electoral Trade-Off of Class-Based Parties," *European Journal of Political Research,* vol. 18, no. 1, 1990; Martin Harrop, "Voting and the Electorate," in Henry Drucker et al. (eds.), *Developments in British Politics 2, rev. ed.,* Macmillan, London, 1989.

panied by a major *demographic* contraction of the traditional working class, it implies that the traditional social basis of the class cleavage is being undermined.

The Decline of Religious Voting?

A similar pattern is evident in the relationship between religion and party voting, although the implications of this are less far-reaching, since religious divisions have been relevant to contemporary politics only in certain countries. We should not underestimate the importance of religion in patterns of party preference, however, since the evidence suggests that religious differences exert a much more pervasive impact than the presence of explicitly religious parties might indicate. Religious differences may also help to determine party choice in situations where the parties concerned are all ostensibly secular.

In France, for example, the decline of the Catholic party (MRP), in the early 1960s, does not imply the wholesale decline of religion as a factor in voting behavior. According to a 1978 survey, more than 50 percent of regular church-goers supported parties of the center-right, as against just over 20 percent of those who never attended church. This contrast led to the conclusion that about 20 percent of the variation in partisan choice between supposedly "secular" parties was actually explained by patterns of church attendance (Lewis-Beck, pp. 438–439). Overall, survey results in the 1960s indicated that religious divisions, when they were salient, actually had a stronger impact on party choice than social class (Rose and Urwin, 1969; Lijphart).

There is strong evidence to suggest that religion nowadays tends to have a much lower impact on voting behavior. First, there is evidence of growing secularization.

In Italy in the twenty years between 1956 and 1976, for example, regular church attendance among Catholics fell from 69 percent to 37 percent (Amyot, p. 44). Only 25 percent of the electorate regularly attended church in West Germany in 1987, as against 40 percent in the 1950s—with the church attendance among Catholics alone dropping from over 50 percent to just 30 percent in the same period (Dalton, 1990, p. 103). An even sharper decline is evident in the Netherlands, where the proportion of Catholics attending church on a weekly basis has fallen from some 93 percent in 1946 to just 26 percent in 1986, although here regular church attendance within the different Protestant denominations has tended to remain fairly stable (Irwin and Holsteyn, p. 36).

Second, there are signs of declining cohesion in the political preferences of those who do attend church on a regular basis. In Austria, for example, the Catholic People's party (ÖVP) had enjoyed the support of 84 percent of "active" Catholics in the 1950s and 80 percent in the 1960s. By the 1970s, however, the mean support for the party among these active Catholics had fallen to 71 percent (Houska, p. 120). A similar trend is evident in the Netherlands. In the 1950s, not only was the Catholic church larger and more actively involved in the daily lives of its adherents (see Bakvis), but the vast majority of practicing Catholics supported the Catholic People's party (KVP). Indeed, according to a 1956 survey, the KVP, which was then the second largest party in the Netherlands, enjoyed the support of an astonishing 95 percent of practicing Catholics! By 1977, the date of the last election before the merger of the KVP and the two major Protestant parties to form the Christian Democratic Appeal (CDA), the party's support among practicing Catholics had fallen to 67 percent (Irwin and Holsteyn, p. 39).

The contraction of both the traditional working class and the church-going public in contemporary Western Europe, together with their declining political distinctiveness, has inevitably undermined the potential role of traditional social cleavages. This has resulted in the erosion of two of the most important subcultures in modern Europe, creating conditions in which individual preferences may replace collective identification as a basis for party choice.

Other forces also appear to be pushing European electorates in this direction. Dalton (1984; 1988, pp. 18–24), for example, suggests that Europe is experiencing the emergence of a more politically sophisticated electorate. This electorate is characterized by high levels of education and has access, particularly through television, to a huge amount of information about politics. Dalton argues that this leads voters to absorb information and relate to politics on an individual rather than a subcultural basis. This trend may be compounded by a shift toward the privatization of consumption—of housing, health care, education, car ownership, and so on—to promote individualistic and fragmented political responses, which some suggest will push patterns of partisan preference in Western Europe much closer to those in the United States, with the Netherlands offering perhaps the most clear-cut signs of such a development (Irwin and Holsteyn; Irwin and Dittrich).

Let us try to knit these various strands together. A cleavage, it will be recalled, is sustained by three separate elements: a dictinct social base, a sense of collective identity, and a clearly defined organizational expression. In its most extreme form, a cleavage is therefore sustained through the creation of distinctive subcultures within which voting is an expression of social identity rather than a reflection of instrumental choice. In short, voters belong. As Richard Rose once put it, at a time when this sense of belonging was particularly pronounced, "to speak of the majority of voters at a given election as choosing a party is nearly as misleading as speaking of a worshipper on a Sunday 'choosing' to go to an Anglican rather than a Baptist or a Catholic church" (Rose, p. 100). There is now, however, ample evidence to suggest that these traditional demarcation lines are being blurred in contemporary Western Europe. Class divisions are becoming less pronounced, while widespread secularization has reduced the impact of religious divisions. Even within what remains of the traditional social groups, behavior is tending to become less collective, and the traditional variations in political preference between groups are tending to wane. Finally, in what seems to be a response to these changes, political parties are loosening their bonds with specific groups of voters and have begun to appeal to the electorate at large. In short, the evidence suggests a consistent trend toward a much less structured electorate and toward the fragmentation and individualization of political preferences.

CHANGE TOWARD WHAT?

In a recent discussion of electoral change in advanced industrial democracies, Russell Dalton and his colleagues (Dalton et al.; Flanagan and Dalton) have put forward two general models that seek both to explain the nature of the changes occurring in Western European politics and to predict their potential consequences. Their first explanation is based on the role of cleavages. It suggests that as traditional cleavages wane in importance and new cleavages emerge, voters go through a process of "realignment." Their second explanation concentrates on the declining role of political parties. It suggests that almost regardless of the new issues and concerns arising in postindustrial societies, political parties as such will become less and less relevant to the representation of interests. Citizens will turn increasingly toward interest groups and other social movements in order to press their demands, producing a widespread process of "dealignment." While both explanations emphasize the declining political relevance of factors such as class and religion, the realignment thesis emphasizes the growth of postmaterialist concerns, whereas the dealignment thesis suggests that electorates will become ever more unstructured. In reality, as we shall now see, neither thesis is wholly convincing, and the evidence for continuity, as opposed to change, remains compelling.

Toward Realignment?

Despite Lipset and Rokkan's emphasis on the "freezing" of party systems, it has been argued that the new issues that arise in postindustrial societies reflect the emergence of a wholly new cleavage, one that, like more traditional cleavages, is characterized by a social base, a collective identity, and an organizational expression (Alber). In the first place, this new politics is associated with a distinct social base within the new middle class, particularly among younger voters and those with a university education. Second, the values of the new politics are also distinctive, laying particular stress on environmental protection, feminism, and the extension of democratic and social rights (Inglehart, 1977). Third, this new politics is increasingly and pervasively reflected in the emergence of a distinct organizational expression, most clearly represented in the rise of Green parties in most parts of Western Europe, as well as in the earlier "new left" parties, which are increasingly seen as part of the wider new politics constituency (see, for example, Kitschelt). It is in this sense that what has become known as "postmaterialism" can be seen to constitute a new cleavage, the mobilization of which implies a potential realignment of party politics (see also Inglehart, 1984).

There are two reasons to suggest that this scenario may be exaggerated, however. First, despite the evident resonance of some of the issues associated with the new politics, and despite the pervasiveness of the new parties, these parties remain an essentially marginal electoral force. As we saw in Table 3.7, Green parties polled an average of less than 3 percent of the vote in Western Europe in the 1980s. To be sure, this low average figure may underestimate the full extent of support for these parties—it ignores support for new left parties (which Table 3.5 shows to have averaged about another 3 percent in the 1980s), and it fails to take account of the fact that the Green parties achieved their greatest successes only at the end of the 1980s. But even if we take only the most recent elections in each country and consider only Green parties that won at least 1 percent of the vote, then the average Green vote in the ten relevant cases still comes to less than 5 percent of the total. When we add the support for new left parties, the mean vote for parties associated with the new politics remains substantially below 10 percent.

The second reason why it may be precipitate to speak of realignment is that despite their own initial claims, parties associated with the new politics are not really so very different from more traditional parties. There is a sense in which they need not be seen to represent a new dimension in mass politics, cutting across the left and the right; rather, they can be regarded as a new variation within the traditional left. From their formation, Green parties consciously refused to apply terms such as "left" or "right" to their own politics. As Jonathon Porritt, a leading member of the British Green party, put it, "We profoundly disagree with the politics of the right and its underlying ideology of capitalism; we profoundly disagree with the politics of the left and its adherence, in varying degrees, to the ideology of communism. That leaves us little choice but to disagree, perhaps less profoundly, with the politics of the center and its ideological potpourri of socialized capitalism" (Porritt, 1984, p. 43). More recently, however, the capacity to maintain this distinctive approach has been undermined. As Green parties have begun to win seats in local assemblies and national parliaments, they have been obliged to come to terms with mainstream politics, and like their long-established competitors, they find it difficult to stand aloof from day-to-day political bargaining. Even more important, in such situations the Green parties have become increasingly associated with other parties of the left.

Thus, in both Belgium and Germany, Green parties have forged local alliances with established left-wing parties, while in the Netherlands, the tiny Green party actually joined with the Communist party and two small new left parties to form an electoral cartel, the Green Left. Indeed, Porritt's own emphasis had changed by the late 1980s. No longer rejecting notions of left and right, he argued that a crucial issue was the extent to which "today's Green parties [should] identify themselves specifically as parties of the left" (Porritt, 1989, p. 8). A similar drift of the new politics toward the broad left bloc is also evident in the attitudes of postmaterialist voters. In a study charting the changing party preferences of materialist and postmaterialist voters between 1970 and 1985, Inglehart noted that "in 1970, 40 percent of postmaterialists supported parties of the right and center; in 1982–85, only 25 percent did so; 75 percent were voting for the left" (Inglehart, 1987, p. 1299).

In sum, if postmaterialist concerns do signify a potential for change within Western European party systems, this is likely to be a limited realignment which changes some of the terms of reference of the left-right divide while leaving its essential basis intact. Moreover, such change is by no means novel. As we saw in Chapter 3, the terms of reference of the left-right divide have often been in flux. On the left, the initial monopoly of the social democratic parties was challenged fundamentally by the mobilization of communist parties in the wake of the Russian Revolution of 1917 and again by the new left parties of the late 1960s and 1970s. The Green challenge of the late 1980s and the 1990s, to the extent that this challenge is contained within the broad left, may simply be another step in a long and continuing process of adaptation. On the right, despite overall long-term continuity, the political terms of reference have also changed continually, most recently through the decline of Christian democracy and the growth of secular conservative parties, as well as through the rise of xenophobic right-wing parties in such countries as France, West Germany, and Italy.

Table 4.5 summarizes changes in the levels of electoral support for the different party families reported in Chapter 3 and shows the stability of the division *between* the left and the right, as well as the shifting balance *within* both the left and the right, the most striking feature of political change in postwar Western Europe. If realignment is taken to mean the replacement by an alternative cleavage of the

TABLE 4.5
The Left and the Right in Western Europe: Electoral Trends over Time, % of Vote

	1950s	1960s	1970s	1980s
Left:				
Communists	8.4	7.8	8.0	5.8
New left	—	1.1	1.7	2.9
Social Democrats	32.2	31.7	30.5	29.5
Greens	—	—	—	2.3
Total left	40.6	40.6	40.2	40.5
Center and right:				
Agrarians	7.0	7.4	7.1	5.8
Liberals	9.3	10.4	10.2	11.0
Christian Democrats	22.1	21.4	20.4	19.5
Secular Conservatives	16.5	16.9	17.2	18.3
Extreme right	1.1	0.6	0.8	1.2
Total center and right	56.0	56.7	55.7	55.8

fundamental division between the right and the left, then the evidence in favor of realignment is far from convincing. If it is taken to mean a significant shift in party fortunes *within* both the left and the right, then realignment may well be taking place, but it is nothing particularly new.

Toward Dealignment?

The argument that there has been a "dealignment" of Western European party systems rests on three types of evidence: first, a decline in the extent to which voters identify with political parties; second, the emergence of new political parties and the growth in party system fragmentation; third, the general increase in levels of electoral volatility. Evidence for all three factors suggests that the hold of parties in Western Europe is being undermined, but, as we shall see, even these data are not completely persuasive.

Party Identification. One of the clearest symptoms of the process of dealignment in Western Europe can be seen in the declining levels of party identification, the psychological attachment which is alleged to tie voters to parties. At first sight, the evidence of such decline seems quite compelling. In West Germany, for example, the proportion of voters claiming a "strong" or "very strong" sense of identification with a party has fallen from 55 percent in 1972 to just 41 percent in 1987, while the proportion with a "weak" or nonexistent identification has risen from 40 percent to 56 percent (Dalton, 1990, p. 117). In the British case, the proportion claiming a "very strong" identification has fallen from 44 percent in 1964 to just 19 percent in 1987, while the proportion who identify only weakly or not at all has increased from 18 percent to 39 percent in the same period (Heath et al., 1988). More generally, analyzing regular Eurobarometer surveys within the European Community as a whole, Schmitt (p. 125) concluded that the proportion of EC citizens more or less attached to a political party declined by about 10 percent during the 1980s, while the proportion not aligned with any party increased to about 40 percent (see also Mair, 1984, pp. 176–179).

In practice, we must be careful not to read too much into such figures. In the first place, information on party identification is based on survey data, and the cross-national use of survey data is notoriously fraught with problems. Questions must be translated into different languages, and anyway the same questions tend to mean rather different things in different countries, often leading to contradictory results. In addition to these methodological problems, there have been conceptual problems in applying what is essentially a U.S. notion of party identification in the European context. U.S. voters, for a range of institutional reasons (the voter registration process, the holding of primaries, the holding of separate presidential and parliamentary elections), may be able to distinguish between identifying with a party, on the one hand, and voting for that party, on the other. European voters, in contrast, often change their party identification at the same time that they change their vote. Thus, while party identification can remain quite stable in the United States, notwithstanding some electoral volatility, it does not tend to have the same degree of independent stability in Europe (Thomassen).

A second reason to be cautious when interpreting data on the dealignment of party identification in Europe is that many European voters tend to identify primarily with social groups and only indirectly with political parties. Sections of the Italian electorate, for example, may identify with the Christian Democrats only to the extent that they also identify with the Catholic church, which is associated with the DC. In the same way, sections of the British electorate may identify with the Labour party only to the extent that they have a working-class identification, which then translates into a sense of belonging to the Labour party as the party of the working class. In other words, precisely because European parties are cleavage-based, the primary loyalty of a voter may be to the class or social group that defines a cleavage rather than to the party that represents it.

Perhaps the most serious problem with applying the notion of party identification in the European context is that there is evidence that voters in more fragmented party systems can identify with more than one party at the same time (van der Eijk and Niemoeller). Voters on the left, for example, may identify with both a socialist party and a communist party, maintaining a stable sense of belonging to the left bloc as a whole, while shifting their preferences from one party to another according to the particular circumstances of a given election.

Thus, while the evidence of declining party identification in Western Europe seems quite strong, interpreting this evidence is quite difficult. Rather than showing that European party systems are becoming "dealigned," patterns in these data may be a product of applying an inappropriate concept to European multiparty parliamentary democracies.

The Fragmentation of European Party Systems. The second obvious symptom of partisan dealignment is a trend toward the increasing fragmentation of party systems. As political responses to the parties have become more individualized, and as the links between parties and voters have become more attenuated, the space for the creation of new parties has increased. In some cases, as with the environmental or Green parties, new parties reflect the emergence of new issues. In other cases, however, new parties are simply the results of splits in old parties. In Britain, Denmark, and the Netherlands in the 1970s and 1980s, for example, as we saw in Chapter 3, key figures abandoned mainstream socialist parties and formed new parties of the center-left. In Belgium, the politicization of the linguistic divide in the 1970s led not only to the creation of new parties but also to splits in each of the main traditional parties.

As can be seen from Table 4.6, the number of parties contesting individual elections in Western Europe rose from an average of just over six per country in the 1950s to almost eight in the 1980s. This upward trend was particularly pronounced in Belgium and the United Kingdom, where the number of parties doubled, as well as in Denmark and Finland, where it has increased by about 50 percent. Indeed, the only country which has experienced an actual decline in the number of parties in competition was West Germany, where the immediate postwar years witnessed an explosion of minor parties that later disappeared from the political scene.

However, while party systems have become increasingly fragmented and a host of new parties are now in competition, many of these have achieved only marginal electoral success. Some, including the British Social Democrats and the Dutch DS '70, have since ceased to exist. Indeed, a survey of the electoral fortunes of some

TABLE 4.6
Mean Number of Parties* in Competition, 1950–1990

	1950s	1960s	1970s	1980s
Austria	4.0	4.5	4.0	4.5
Belgium	5.7	6.0	9.3	12.3
Denmark	6.5	7.8	10.6	10.5
Finland	6.3	8.0	9.3	9.5
France	7.0	7.3	7.5	7.3
Germany	7.5	4.7	3.0	4.0
Iceland	5.3	5.0	5.0	7.5
Ireland	5.3	4.3	4.0	5.3
Italy	8.5	8.0	8.7	10.0
Luxembourg	4.3	4.5	6.5	6.0
Netherlands	7.7	9.5	11.7	8.5
Norway	6.0	7.0	8.0	7.0
Sweden	5.0	6.3	6.0	7.0
Switzerland	9.0	9.0	10.3	10.0
United Kingdom	3.0	3.0	4.8	6.0
Mean (by country)	6.1	6.3	7.2	7.7

*Includes only those parties polling at least 1 percent.
Sources: Mackie and Rose; Jacobs; Keesings Contemporary Archives.

sixty parties formed since 1960 in Western Europe showed that more than two-thirds of these polled an average of less than 3 percent of the vote in their respective systems and that only about one-sixth polled an average of more than 5 percent (Shaddick). In general, therefore, the trend toward increased fragmentation may tell us more about the willingness of the elite to form new parties than about the mass appeal of these parties once they have been formed.

Electoral Volatility. The third collection of evidence in favor of the dealignment thesis concerns increased electoral volatility (Pedersen, 1979). This increase in volatility is not pervasive throughout Western Europe as a whole, however, Pedersen's own evidence from the 1970s, for example, pointed to an actual decline in volatility in France and West Germany and, albeit less marked, in Italy. In each of these countries, the party system was restructured in the early postwar years, following the reestablishment of the democratic process, and each party system was soon to be stabilized by a strong center-right party. In many other Western European countries, however, the 1970s saw an erosion of the "steady-state" politics of the 1950s and 1960s and an increase in electoral volatility.

Table 4.7, while confirming Pedersen's findings on trends in electoral volatility through the 1970s, shows that these trends did not persist into the 1980s. Indeed, in Western Europe as a whole, as can be seen from the bottom line of Table 4.7, the 1980s witnessed a marginal *decline* in volatility. This decline was particularly marked in Denmark, the Netherlands, Norway, and the United Kingdom. The only country with a consistent increase in aggregate electoral instability across all four decades is Finland, with volatility in Sweden increasing consistently since the 1960s. In France, Germany, and Italy, on the other hand, as well as in Austria and Ireland, a trend of declining volatility was reversed in the 1980s.

TABLE 4.7
Mean Aggregate Electoral Volatility in Western Europe, 1950–1990

	1950s	1960s	1970s	1980s
Austria	4.1	3.3	2.7	5.5
Belgium	7.6	10.2	5.3	10.1
Denmark	5.5	8.7	15.5	9.7
Finland	4.4	7.0	7.9	8.7
France	22.3	11.5	8.8	10.6
Germany	15.2	8.4	5.0	6.3
Ireland	10.3	7.0	5.7	8.1
Italy	9.7	8.2	6.6	8.7
Netherlands	5.1	7.9	12.3	8.5
Norway	3.4	5.3	15.3	10.5
Sweden	4.8	4.0	6.3	7.6
Switzerland	2.6	3.8	6.4	6.3
United Kingdom	4.3	5.2	8.2	3.4
Mean (by country)	7.6	7.0	8.2	8.0

*Refers to net aggregate vote shifts in votes between pairs of consecutive elections, and is equivalent to the sum of the aggregate gains of all winning parties, or the sum of the aggregate losses of all losing parties (see Pedersen 1979).
Source: Updated from Bartolini and Mair, 1990.

Two conclusions can be drawn from these data. First, there is no pervasive trend toward increased electoral volatility in Western Europe. Second, and less obviously, aggregate electoral volatility in Western Europe is actually quite low. Volatility levels can, in practice, exceed 20 percent, as happened in France during the 1950s; the highest levels reached in the 1980s are actually not much more than 10 percent, in Belgium, France, and Norway. (For a fuller discussion, see Bartolini and Mair, 1990, pp. 68–124.)

This general pattern of stability is emphasized when we break down electoral volatility into two component parts: changes in the balance of votes *between* major party blocs, on the one hand, and changes *within* blocks, on the other. In the case of Denmark, for example (see Table 4.1), the losses of the Social Democrats (−11.7), Socialist Peoples (−3.1), and Left Socialists (−0.1) were almost balanced within the socialist bloc by the successes of the Center Democrats (+7.8) and the Communists (+2.2). Within the bourgeois bloc, the gains of the Christians (+2.0), the Justice party (+1.2), and the Progress party (+15.9) were almost balanced by the losses of the Conservatives (−7.5), Liberals (−3.3), and Social Liberals (−3.2). The Danish case is far from exceptional. Throughout postwar Western Europe, the volatility between the main class alignments was much less than the volatility within the class blocs (Bartolini and Mair, 1990). At least as far as the class cleavage is concerned, a much greater proportion of electoral instability is a result of switching votes been friends rather than between enemies, a trend which is also compatible with the notion that European voters may identify with more than one party at the same time.

Despite a surge in the 1970s, therefore, electoral volatility in Western Europe has not continued to rise. Despite the occasional incidence of "earthquake" elections in particular countries, actual levels of volatility remain quite low. The bulk of the volatility in the European multiparty systems seems to be contained within blocs of generally like-minded parties and does not appear to involve volatility across major lines of social cleavage.

BOX 4.2
Trends in Electoral Volatility

FRANCE
Largely owing to its relatively unstructured party system and to shifting patterns of alliance and schism between the different political leaders, France has always had one of the most volatile electorates in Western Europe. More recently, however, as the party system has tended to consolidate under the Fifth Republic, volatility has tended to decline, with the net shift of votes between elections being sometimes less than 10 percent.

GERMANY
Germany was traditionally characterized by an extremely volatile electorate, particularly during the interwar and early postwar years. Throughout the 1950s and 1960s, however, as the West German party system became consolidated, volatility tended to decline. While the emergence of the Greens led to a more unsettled situation in the 1980s, the level of volatility has nevertheless not grown substantially. The highest level recorded in recent elections was a net shift of just over 8 percent of the votes in 1983. However, the reunification of Germany in 1990 and the consequent incorporation of a large body of "new" voters into the electorate are likely to mean a more unsettled period in the future.

ITALY
Despite immensely unstable governments, Italy has been characterized by a surprisingly stable pattern of electoral alignments over the postwar period as a whole. In recent years, however, the emergence of the Radicals and the Greens, as well as the shifting balance of fortunes between Socialists and Communists, has tended to result in a marginal increase in volatility, the highest level for some time being recorded in 1987: a net shift of some 9 percent of the votes.

THE NETHERLANDS
The Netherlands, along with Denmark and Norway, was one of the classic examples of increasing electoral volatility during the late 1960s and the 1970s. Since then, however, volatility has tended to decline, and the party system has tended to stabilize around the new pattern that began to emerge in the late 1960s. In the election of 1989, for example, the net shift in votes was a little over 5 percent, less than half the levels recorded in the early 1970s.

SPAIN
Although Spain, as a new party system, appears to have a relatively unstable electorate, the high mean level of volatility disguises a pattern that is actually quite difficult to characterize. While mean volatility since 1977 has been over 12 percent, as against an average of just 8 percent in the same period in the "older" party systems of Western Europe, this high figure derives entirely from the very exceptional election of 1982, when support for the Union of the Democratic Center fell from 35 percent to less than 7 percent, and when the vote for the Socialist party rose from 31 percent to 47 percent. Overall volatility in that election reached a remarkably high level of over 36 percent. In the previous and subsequent elections, however, average volatility was less than 5 percent, well below the Western European norm.

(Continued on next page)

SWEDEN

Having gone through a prolonged period of electoral stability, Sweden, like its Scandinavian neighbors, experienced an upsurge in electoral volatility in the late 1960s and the 1970s. In Sweden, however, the change was not as marked as that which occurred in Denmark or Norway, and since 1970 the net shift of votes has never exceeded 9 percent. Volatility levels remain quite erratic even now, however, exacerbated by the shifting fortunes of the conservative Moderates, as well as by the recent successes of the Ecology party, although the overall balance between the right and the left has remained remarkably stable.

UNITED KINGDOM

Notwithstanding the temporary and radical electoral flux created by the emergence of the Social Democrats as a split from Labour, electoral volatility has tended to decline in recent British elections. The most volatile election was in February 1974, when both the Scottish and Welsh Nationalists, as well as the Liberals, experienced a major surge in their fortunes, and when the overall electoral support won by the Conservatives and Labour fell to a postwar low.

CONCLUSION

Studies of Western European politics which set out to chart and explain change often conclude with the observation that change is neither so extensive nor so pervasive as was first imagined. "Even if change is widespread," concludes one recent account, "it is important not to overstate its extent. Although few party systems have been as constant as they once appeared to be, all exhibit substantial elements of continuity" (Wolinetz, 1988, p. 296). Taking all the evidence presented in this chapter together, we can see that contemporary Western European politics is characterized at least as much by continuity as it is by change. To be sure, the image of transformation is seductive; but the shock of the new can blind us to the persistence of the old.

The continuities can be easily summarized. The overall balance between the broad left bloc and the broad right bloc is remarkably constant. There is a very low level of aggregate vote redistribution across cleavage boundaries, particularly across the class-cleavage boundary. The principal political protagonists, most notably the social democrats and the Christian democrats, have proved very resilient. New parties, despite their pervasiveness, continually fail to command a major share of the vote.

The changes, however limited, are also evident. There is a growing individualization of political preferences and a weakening of collective identities. There is a decline in the distinctiveness of the social bases of party support. There have been changes in the terms of reference of the division between the left and the right. The balance of support for parties within each bloc has changed in certain cases. And a "postmaterialist" or "new politics" dimension has emerged, albeit without substantial electoral weight, in many of the more established Western European democracies.

The overall picture, then, is one of "peripheral" change, with the "core" of the party systems remaining intact (Smith). European voters are less tied to parties than before and have shown themselves more willing to shift their preferences from one party to another. But they do so cautiously. On the left, voters may shift from a communist party to a socialist party, or from a socialist party to a new left or Green party, but they tend to remain on the left. Voters on the right may shift from a Christian party to a secular party, or from a liberal party to a more conservative party, but they tend also to stay on the right. Ties to individual parties may have weakened, but ties to the broader identities of the left and the right appear to have been maintained. In this important sense, the notion that European party systems are "frozen" continues to look quite plausible.

References

Alber, Jens: "Modernization, Changing Cleavage Structures, and the Rise of the Green Party in West Germany," in Ferdinand Mueller-Rommel (ed.), *New Politics in Western Europe: The Rise and Success of the Green Parties and Alternative Lists*, Westview Press, Boulder, Colo., 1989.

Alford, Robert R.: *Party and Society: The Anglo-American Democracies*, Rand McNally, Chicago, 1963.

Ambrosius, Gerold, and William H. Hubbard: *A Social and Economic History of Twentieth-Century Europe*, Harvard University Press, Cambridge, Mass., 1989.

Amyot, G. Grant: "Italy: The Long Twilight of the DC Regime," in Wolinetz, 1988, pp. 12–30.

Bakvis, Herman: *Catholic Power in the Netherlands*, McGill-Queens University Press, Kingston and Montreal, 1981.

Bartolini, Stefano, and Peter Mair: *Identity, Competition, and Electoral Availability: The Stabilization of European Electorates, 1885–1985*, Cambridge University Press, Cambridge, England, 1990.

———— and ———— (eds.): *Party Politics in Contemporary Western Europe*, Cass, London, 1984.

Bell, Daniel: *The End of Ideology*, The Free Press, New York, 1960.

Bille, Lars: "Denmark: The Oscillating Party System," in Mair and Smith, pp. 28–41.

Crewe, Ivor, and David Denver (eds.): *Electoral Change in Western Democracies: Patterns and Sources of Electoral Volatility*, Croom Helm, London, 1985.

Daalder, Hans, and Peter Mair (eds.): *Western European Party Systems: Continuity and Change*, Sage, London, 1983.

Dahl, Robert A.: *After the Revolution*, Yale University Press, New Haven, 1970.

Dalton, Russell J.: "Cognitive Mobilization and Partisan Dealignment in Advanced Industrial Democracies," *Journal of Politics*, vol. 46, no. 2, 1984, pp. 264–284.

————: *Citizen Politics in Western Democracies: Public Opinion and Political Parties in the United States, Great Britain, West Germany, and France*, Chatham House, Chatham, N.J., 1988.

————: "The German Voter," in Gordon Smith, William E. Paterson, and Peter H. Merkl (eds.), *Developments in West German Politics*, Macmillan, London, 1990, pp. 99–121.

————, Scott C. Flanagan, and Paul Allen Beck (eds.): *Electoral Change in Advanced Industrial Democracies: Realignment or Dealignment?* Princeton University Press, Princeton, 1984.

Diamant, Alfred: "The Group Basis of Austrian Politics," *Journal of Central European Affairs*, vol. 18, no. 2, 1958, pp. 134–155.

Duverger, Maurice: *Political Parties*, Methuen, London, 1954.

Einhorn, Eric S., and John Logue: "Continuity and Change in the Scandinavian Party Systems," in Wolinetz, 1988, pp. 159–202.

Epstein, Leon D.: *Political Parties in Western Democracies*, Praeger, New York, 1967.

Finer, S. E.: *Comparative Government*, Allen Lane, London, 1970.

Flanagan, Scott C., and Russell J. Dalton: "Parties under Stress: Realignment and Dealignment in Advanced Industrial Societies," *West European Politics*, vol. 7, no. 1, 1984, pp. 7–23.

Flora, Peter: "Introduction," in Peter Flora (ed.), *Growth to Limits: The Western European Welfare States since World War II*, vol. 1: *Sweden, Norway, Finland, Denmark*, de Gruyter, Berlin, 1986, pp. v–xxxvi.

Garvin, Tom: "Political Cleavages, Party Politics and Urbanisation in Ireland: The Case of the Periphery-Dominated Centre," *European Journal of Political Research*, vol. 2, no. 4, 1974, pp. 307–327.

Griffiths, Sian: "Survival by Another Name," *Times Higher Education Supplement*, June 15, 1990.

Grofman, Bernard, and Arend Lijphart (eds.): *Electoral Laws and Their Political Consequences*, Agathon Press, New York, 1987.

Heath, Anthony, Roger Jowell, and John Curtice: *How Britain Votes*, Pergamon, Oxford, 1985.

———, ———, and ———: "Partisan Dealignment Revisited," paper presented to the Annual Conference of the Political Studies Association, Plymouth Polytechnic, Plymouth, England, 1988.

Houska, Joseph J.: *Influencing Mass Political Behavior: Elites and Political Subcultures in the Netherlands and Austria*, University of California at Berkeley, Institute of International Affairs, 1985.

Inglehart, Ronald: *The Silent Revolution: Changing Values and Political Styles among Western Mass Publics*, Princeton University Press, Princeton, 1977.

———: "The Changing Structure of Political Cleavages in Western Society," in Dalton et al., pp. 25–69.

———: "Value Change in Industrial Societies," *American Political Science Review*, vol. 81, no. 4, 1987, pp. 1289–1303.

Irwin, Galen A., and Karl Dittrich: "And the Walls Came Tumbling Down: Party Dealignment in the Netherlands," in Dalton et al., pp. 267–297.

——— and J. J. M. van Holsteyn: "Decline of the Structured Model of Electoral Competition," in Hans Daalder and Galen A. Irwin (eds.), *Politics in the Netherlands: How Much Change?* Cass, London, 1989, pp. 21–41.

Jacobs, Francis (ed.): *Western European Political Parties*, Longman, Harlow, 1989.

Katz, Richard S.: "Measuring Party Identification with Eurobarometer Data," *West European Politics*, vol. 8, no. 1, 1985, pp. 104–108.

Kirchheimer, Otto: "The Waning of Opposition in Parliamentary Regimes," *Social Research*, vol. 24, no. 2, 1957, pp. 127–156.

———: "The Transformation of the Western European Party Systems," in Joseph LaPalombara and Myron Weiner (eds.), *Political Parties and Political Development*, Princeton University Press, Princeton, 1966, pp. 177–200.

Kitschelt, Herbert P.: "Left-Libertarian Parties: Explaining Innovation in Competitive Party Systems," *World Politics*, vol. 40, no. 2, 1988, pp. 194–234.

LaPalombara, Joseph: *Democracy Italian Style*, Yale University Press, New Haven, 1987.

Lewis-Beck, Michael: "France: The Stalled Electorate," in Dalton et al., pp. 425–448.

Lijphart, Arend: "Religious vs Linguistic vs Class Voting," *American Political Science Review*, vol. 73, no. 2, 1979, pp. 442–458.

Lipset, S. M.: *Political Man*, Doubleday, New York, 1960.

——— and Stein Rokkan: "Cleavage Structures, Party Systems and Voter Alignments: An Introduction," in S. M. Lipset and Stein Rokkan (eds.), *Party Systems and Voter Alignments*, The Free Press, New York, 1967, pp. 1–64.

Lovenduski, Joni: *Women and European Politics: Contemporary Feminism and Public Policy*, Wheatsheaf, Brighton, 1986.

Mackie, T. T., and Richard Rose: *The International Almanac of Electoral History*, 2d ed., Macmillan, London, 1982.

Maguire, Maria: "Is There Still Persistence? Electoral Change in Western Europe, 1948–1979," in Daalder and Mair, pp. 67–94.

Mair, Peter: "Party Politics in Contemporary Europe: A Challenge to Party?" in Bartolini and Mair, 1984, pp. 170–184.

———: "Continuity, Change and the Vulnerability of Party," in Mair and Smith, pp. 129–142.

——— (ed.): *The West European Party System*, Oxford University Press, Oxford, 1990.

——— and Gordon Smith (eds.): *Understanding Party System Change in Western Europe*, Cass, London, 1990.

Morlino, Leonardo: "The Changing Relationship between Parties and Society in Italy," in Bartolini and Mair, 1984, pp. 46–66.

Neumann, Sigmund: "Toward a Comparative Study of Political Parties," in Neumann (ed.), pp. 395–421.

——— (ed.): *Modern Political Parties*, University of Chicago Press, Chicago, 1956.

Niemoeller, B. and C. van der Eijk: "Partij en Kiezer: Herwaardering van een Relatie," in *Documentatiecentrum Nederlandse Politieke Partijen, Jaarbook 1989*, 1990, pp. 144–162.

Panebianco, Angelo: *Political Parties: Organization and Power*, Cambridge University Press, Cambridge, England, 1988.

Pedersen, Mogens N.: "Current Electoral Research in Denmark," *Scandinavian Political Studies*, vol. 3, 1968, pp. 253–256.

———: "The Dynamics of European Party Systems: Changing Patterns of Electoral Volatility," *European Journal of Political Research*, vol. 7, no. 1, 1979, pp. 1–26.

———: "Changing Patterns of Electoral Volatility: Explorations in Explanation," in Daalder and Mair, pp. 29–66.

———: "The Danish 'Working Multiparty System': Breakdown or Adaptation?" in Hans Daalder (ed.), *Party Systems in Denmark, Austria, Switzerland, the*

Netherlands and Belgium, Frances Pinter, London, 1987, pp. 1–60.

Pizzorno, Allesandro: "Interests and Parties in Pluralism," in Suzanne Berger (ed.), *Organizing Interests in Western Europe: Pluralism, Corporatism, and the Transformation of Politics*, Cambridge University Press, Cambridge, England, 1981, pp. 249–284.

Porritt, Jonathon: *Seeing Green: The Politics of Ecology Explained*, Blackwell, Oxford, 1984.

———: "Foreword," in Sara Parkin, *Green Parties: An International Guide*, Heretic Books, London, 1989, pp. 7–9.

Rokkan, Stein: "Norway: Numerical Democracy and Corporate Pluralism," in Robert A. Dahl (ed.), *Political Oppositions in Western Democracies*, Yale University Press, New Haven, 1966, pp. 70–115.

———: *Citizens, Elections, Parties*, Universitetsforlaget, Oslo, 1970.

Rose, Richard: *The Problem of Party Government*, Macmillan, London, 1974.

——— and Derek Urwin: "Social Cohesion, Political Parties, and Strains in Regimes," *Comparative Political Studies*, vol. 2, no. 1, 1969, pp. 7–67.

——— and ———: "Persistence and Change in Western Party Systems since 1945," *Political Studies*, vol. 18, no. 3, 1970, pp. 287–319.

Roth, Guenther: *The Social Democrats in Imperial Germany: A Study in Working-Class Isolation and National Integration*, Bedminster Press, Totowa, N.J., 1963.

Rustow, Dankwart A.: "Scandinavia: Working Multi-Party Systems," in Neumann (ed.), pp. 169–193.

Sainsbury, Diane: "Scandinavian Party Politics Re-examined: Social Democracy in Decline?" in Bartolini and Mair, 1984, pp. 67–102.

———: "Class Voting and Left Voting in Scandinavia," *European Journal of Political Research*, vol. 15, no. 5, 1987, pp. 507–526.

Sartori, Giovanni: "Political Development and Political Engineering," *Public Policy*, vol. 17, 1968a, pp. 261–298.

———: "The Sociology of Parties: A Critical Review," in Otto Stammer (ed.), *Party Systems, Party Organisation and the Politics of the New Masses*, Institut für Politische Wissenschaft an der Freie Universität), Berlin, 1968b, pp. 1–25.

———: "The Influence of Electoral Laws: Faulty Laws of Faulty Method?" in Grofman and Lijphart, 1987, pp. 43–68.

Schmitt, Hermann: "On Party Attachment in Western Europe and the Utility of Eurobarometer Data," *West European Politics*, vol. 12, no. 2, 1989, pp. 122–139.

Shaddick, Matthew: "New Political Parties in West European Party Systems," unpublished paper, University of Manchester, 1990.

Shamir, Michal: "Are Western European Party Systems 'Frozen'?" *Comparative Political Studies*, vol. 17, no. 1, 1984, pp. 35–79.

Smith, Gordon: "Core Persistence: System Change and the 'People's Party,'" in Mair and Smith, 1990, pp. 157–168.

Therborn, Goran: "The Rule of Capital and the Rise of Democracy," *New Left Review*, vol. 103, 1977, pp. 3–42.

Thomassen, J. J. A.: "Party Identification as a Cross-Cultural Concept: Its Meaning in the Netherlands," in Ian Budge, Ivor Crewe, and Dennis Farlie (eds.), *Party Identification and Beyond*, Wiley, London, 1976, pp. 63–80.

Van der Eijk, C., and B. Niemoeller: *Electoral Change in the Netherlands*, C. T. Press, Amsterdam, 1983.

Visser, Jelle: "In Search of Inclusive Unionism: A Comparative Analysis," Ph. D. thesis, University of Amsterdam, 1987.

Weber, Eugene: *Peasants into Frenchmen: The Modernization of Rural France, 1870–1914*, Stanford University Press, Stanford, 1976.

Wolinetz, Steven B.: "The Transformation of Western European Party Systems Revisited," *West European Politics*, vol. 2, no. 1, 1979, pp. 4–28.

——— (ed.): *Parties and Party Systems in Liberal Democracies*, Routledge, London, 1988.

CHAPTER 5
INSIDE WESTERN EUROPEAN POLITICAL PARTIES

As the last three chapters have made clear, political parties play a vital role in the politics of Western Europe. In many other parts of the world, parties are often peripheral bodies. They may be built around a single leader and cease to exist when this leader disappears from the scene, as has occurred in some third world countries. They may play a secondary role in what are essentially candidate-centered politics, as in the U.S.A. In Western Europe, however, parties really matter. We have seen in earlier chapters that some European parties have a long history, surviving world wars and fundamental changes of regime. We saw in Chapter 1 that the institutions of European parliamentary democracy mean that it is party, rather than candidate, that Europeans vote for at election time. On the whole, government in Western Europe is party government, although other organizations, such as interest groups, are challenging this, as we shall see in Chapter 9. In this chapter, therefore, we move inside parties and ask what sort of bodies they are. We consider how well they are organized; whether they make decisions in a democratic manner; where they get their resources; and how they are adjusting to important social changes, such as the increasing role of the mass media in politics.

BASIC PARTY ORGANIZATION

While there are obviously important differences between parties, the basic elements of party organization are very similar. Members of parties belong to a local unit based on a geographic area, usually known as the "branch." Ideally, the party will aim to establish branches all over the country in order to maintain a presence on the ground and to mobilize potential voters. The branches usually have a role in selecting election candidates, and they are entitled to send delegates to the party's "annual conference," which in many parties is nominally the supreme decision-making body. Delegates at the annual conference usually elect most members of the party's "national executive," which runs the party organization between conferences, adjudicating on internal disputes. This works in conjunction with the party's head office, staffed by the party's own employees, who constitute a "permanent party bureaucracy." The other main element in the party is the "parliamentary group," comprising the party's elected deputies.

In the case of some parties, this basic picture is complicated by the presence of other bodies. A few parties, such as the Italian Christian Democrats and the French Socialists, are highly factionalized. They contain a number of clearly defined groups, often quite institutionalized, with a continuous existence over time; the various factions jostle for power and position within the party. Other parties have interest groups affiliated to them; examples include the Labour parties in Britain and Norway, to which trade unions are affiliated, and the Italian Christian Democrats, who have a variety of groups attached to them, such as the Confederation of Small Farmers and lay Catholic groups.

Western Europe's communist parties have traditionally diverged from this general pattern, with a common and distinctive way of operating based on the principle of "democratic centralism." The idea of this is that the party is run in a democratic manner, with all members being involved in making decisions and electing the central committee. Once a decision has been reached, it is the duty of all members to abide by it without dissent. In practice, however, studies of Western European communist parties show that they tend to be much more "centralist" than "democratic," and the central party bodies, particularly the national executive and the general secretary, usually exercise tight control over the entire party (Waller and Fennema). For example, the annual conference of the French Communist party has been described as not a genuine decision-making occasion but "a celebration of unanimity around the leadership line" (Newman, p. 179). The difficulty of creating genuine debate and discussion within communist parties may have been one of the factors behind the decline in membership in and support for these parties over the last two decades; disgruntled members find that they must either go along with the leadership or leave the party altogether.

Party constitutions usually give the impression that the party is a smoothly functioning organization in which important decisions are reached through a fairly democratic process. The reality, as might be expected, is often rather different. Although some parties do operate reasonably peacefully, others are wracked by constant internal tension. One very common source of conflict concerns the ideological "purity" of party policy. The battle lines are often drawn between party activists, for whom it may be of prime importance that the party adhere to the ideals that led them to join it in the first place, and party legislators, who may well wish to trim ideological sails in order to get into office. Internal conflict along these lines was very prominent, for example, in the British Labour party during most of the 1980s.

PARTY MEMBERSHIP

Belonging to a party in Western Europe is slightly more formal than in some other parts of the world, involving more than just expressing an inclination toward the party in question. Usually, to become a party member one has to pay an annual membership fee and indicate (by signing some kind of pledge) that one accepts the basic principles of the party. One is also expected, at least in theory, to attend regular local branch meetings.

Not surprisingly, most people who vote for a party do not go to the trouble and expense of actually joining it. Party members make up only a minority of party supporters as a whole. Just how large or small this minority is varies a lot, from country to country and from party to party within countries. Indeed, it can be difficult to pin down exactly how many people really do belong to parties, as von Beyme (pp. 159–253) discovered when he attempted to compare data from different countries. Outsiders are often surprised to discover that some parties are simply not sufficiently centralized for anyone in a party to know how many members it has. In Switzerland, for example, the most decentralized country in Europe, party headquarters may have little knowledge of the position in the various cantons around the country. Similarly, most of the Green parties that began to emerge as a significant political force in the 1980s have, on principle, shunned the formal organizational structure of the established parties. It has been written of the Austrian Greens that "they claim not to have a clear idea of the size of their own membership. Their own 1987 constitution claims that they do not wish to be a party organisation in the traditional sense" (Jacobs, p. 496). The same applies to most other Green parties. Other parties may have a good idea of their membership but may be reluctant to disclose the information publicly.

Even when we do manage to get membership figures for a particular party, we sometimes need to treat these skeptically. Parties have an obvious incentive to claim more members than they really have. For example, in the mid-1980s the French Communist party claimed 700,000 members, but analysts suspected that it had more like a third of this figure (Courtois and Peschanski, p. 52; Criddle, p. 154). In addition, the figures passed on to the head office by the local organizational units around the country may not be reliable; the number of delegates each branch can send to the annual conference may depend on how many members it has, so the larger it claims to be, the more delegates it can send. Local members may even pay membership dues for "ghost" members in order to increase their representation. Another problem is the relatively subjective definition of membership in some cases. There may be people in some parties who invariably help the party campaign during elections but who never actually join and thus are not formally considered members, for example. Other parties might still count as members people who, in fact, drifted away years ago but never explicitly resigned. In most parties, furthermore, only a small proportion of members, perhaps 10 percent in many cases, can really be considered activists, that is, regular attenders at local branch meetings and participants in the party's internal affairs.

A further complication in getting a full picture of party membership is that some parties, as we have mentioned, have links with affiliated organizations whose members are deemed automatically to be members of the party. The best-known case is the British Labour party, which has only about a third of a million "direct" members, but roughly five million members of affiliated trade unions are also regarded as party members, even though many of them do not even vote Labour at election time. Indirect membership also occurs in a few other parties, such as the major left-wing parties in Norway and Sweden and the Christian Democratic parties in Austria, Belgium, and Italy. The "real" number of members these parties have is thus particularly difficult to gauge.

TABLE 5.1
Membership of Political Parties in Western Europe

	Percentage of Voters Who Belong to a Political Party	Trends in Membership in Recent Decades
Austria	33	Generally stable, 1950–1980
Belgium	10	Increase from 8% in 1950
Denmark	8	Decline from 23% in 1953
Finland	25	Increase since 1960s
France	4	Decline since 1950s
Germany	5	Virtually doubled since 1960s
Greece	4	Rise since late 1970s
Iceland	34	No information
Ireland	7	Modest increase since mid-1970s
Italy	12	Stable overall since early 1960s
Luxembourg	12	No information
Malta	27	Increase since late 1970s
Netherlands	3	Fallen by half since 1950
Norway	15	Little change since 1960s
Portugal	5	No information
Spain	2	Postwar democratic politics began in 1970s
Sweden	13*	Increase from 1950s to 1980s
Switzerland	24	No information
United Kingdom	5	Decrease 1950s–1970s; modest revival in 1980s
Average	13	—

*Swedish figure excludes the Social Democrats; their members number 1,200,000, or 52 percent of their voters, but most of these members are affiliated through trade unions. No figures are available for direct members. If all 1,200,000 members are counted, the overall figure for Swedish party membership rises to 30 percent.

Note: The figures refer to the membership of those parties for which membership figures are available (practically all apart from Green parties) and are percentages of the votes cast for those parties at the most recent election.

Sources: Austria—Gerlich (p. 82); Belgium—Dewachter (pp. 314–315); Denmark—Pedersen (p. 35), Sundberg (p. 19); Finland—Jacobs (pp. 523–541); France—Criddle (pp. 151–155), Brechon, Derville, and Lecomte (p. 594); Germany—Paterson (pp. 161–165); Greece—Featherstone and Katsoudas (pp. 108, 121, 166); Iceland—Jacobs (pp. 552–564); Ireland—Mair (pp. 103–105); Italy—Hine (1987, p. 81); Luxembourg—Jacobs (pp. 235–247); Malta—Jacobs (pp. 576–582); Netherlands—Daalder (1987b, pp. 234–235); Norway—Valen (p. 214), Urwin (pp. 187–188); Portugal—Jacobs (pp. 288–303); Spain—del Castillo (p. 187); Sweden—Jacobs (pp. 623–634); Sundberg (p. 19); Switzerland—Jacobs (pp. 643–673); United Kingdom—Byrd (p. 210).

Still, when all the qualifications are made, we can come up with at least some reasonably hard facts on party membership in individual countries. The pattern for each country is summed up above (see Table 5.1). It can be seen that in most countries, only 10 percent or fewer of those who vote for a party are sufficiently committed to join it, and, as we have already noted, only a minority of this minority can be considered active in the party. The overall average for our nineteen countries is 13 percent. There are a few countries where a fifth or more of voters join a party: Iceland, Austria, Malta, Finland, and Switzerland. The way in which the parties in Austria saturate society is well documented; about a third of all Austrians belong to a political party, and the parties permeate many aspects of ordinary life by providing social outlets together with a patronage system so extensive that even the most menial public-sector job can be hard to obtain unless one belongs to the party in whose gift it lies. One survey found that over 70 percent of Austrians believed that the prospect of advancing in a career or obtaining housing more easily was an important factor in explaining why people joined a political party (Luther, p. 380).

Despite frequent suggestions that party organizations are declining in Western Europe, no clear trend emerges from Table 5.1. It is true that party membership has fallen quite dramatically in some countries. In Denmark there has been a steady decline in membership over the last thirty years. In 1961, about 600,000 Danes, representing just over a fifth of all registered voters at the time, belonged to a party, but by the early 1980s, this had dropped to fewer than 300,000, representing only 8 percent of registered voters (Pedersen, p. 35). In the Netherlands there has also been a sharp decline, with only about half as many party members in 1985 as in 1950 (Daalder, 1987b, p. 234). In Britain, too, membership fell for about twenty years before picking up somewhat in the 1980s.

In other countries, such as Austria, Italy, and Norway, in contrast, there seems to have been no dramatic overall change, although the membership of individual parties has changed in some cases. In Italy, for example, the Communist party (PCI) has lost members, but the Christian Democrats (DC) have grown in size. And there are still other countries where parties seem to have been picking up members: Belgium, Finland, Germany, Ireland, and Malta. In West Germany, membership in the SPD rose from 732,000 in 1968 to 1,022,000 in 1976, though it then fell back slightly before being boosted by the impact of German unity in 1990, while membership in the CDU/CSU rose from about 400,000 in the late 1960s to 895,000 in 1987 (Paterson, pp. 162–163).

Trying to get a reliable picture of the types of people who join parties in Europe is very difficult (the fullest attempt is made by von Beyme, pp. 212–223). It appears that the working class is less well represented among party members than among party voters in left-wing parties, especially allowing for the fact that these parties often make exaggerated claims about the number of workers they actually have among their membership. Moreover, the proportion of working-class members appears to be in decline in most social democratic parties (Hine, 1986, pp. 269–275). In the governing left-wing parties in southern Europe in the 1980s, a high proportion of members (about a half in the case of the Spanish Socialists) were employees of the state, the beneficiaries of what was termed "socialist clientelism," the practice of putting party members on the public payroll in some capacity (Pridham, 1989, p. 149). Another clear pattern is that women are usually outnumbered by men, particularly in the upper echelons of parties. But since most parties do not possess reliable information on their members' backgrounds, let alone reveal it, it would be unwise to generalize further.

What do party members do? In many parties nowadays, members tend to be most active at election time, playing an important role in campaigning at the grass roots level. They may not be particularly successful when it comes to trying to

BOX 5.1
Membership of Political Parties

FRANCE

Reliable figures on party membership in France are hard to come by, but all reliable estimates concur on figures that represent a low proportion of voters. The Gaullists (RPR) may well have more members than any other party, but even so, their membership numbers less than 10 percent of their voters. The second main right-wing party, the UDF, is a conglomeration of a number of smaller groups and parties, which together do not have as many members as the RPR. The Socialist party, which was the best supported at the polls during the 1980s, has even fewer members than the UDF. According to its own claims, the Communist party has as many members as the above three parties combined, but given its record of electoral decline over the last decade, few analysts attach much credence to the party's figures. Members in all parties, with the occasional exception of the Socialists, have a reputation for being deferential toward their leaders.

GERMANY

Party membership in postwar Germany has fluctuated somewhat but has been consistently low by general Western European standards. The Social Democrats (SPD) have always had the largest number of members. This number declined from the 1950s to the late 1960s but then began to rise dramatically with an influx of young members. Membership rose from 732,000 in 1968 to over a million by 1976. Among the party's new members in 1976, only 21 percent were manual workers, compared with a figure of 55 percent for manual workers among those joining in 1958. The main right-wing party, the CDU/CSU, traditionally attached low priority to the recruitment of members, but after losing office in 1969 it set about strengthening its organization so as to challenge the dominance of the SPD on the ground. Its membership more than doubled during its 13-year period in opposition, but it still had fewer members than the SPD. The FDP has fewer than 100,000 members, and the Greens are smaller still. With the collapse of the East German state during 1990, all the West German parties sought to extend their membership there.

ITALY

The Italian parties publish regular and detailed figures on their membership, in contrast to many parties elsewhere in Europe. The Communist party, the PCI, has generally had more members than its right-wing rivals, the Christian Democrats (DC), but the gap has narrowed greatly since the early 1950s, when the PCI had more than twice as many members as the DC; its lead is now very marginal. In addition, it is accepted that activism and participation have declined among Communist members. Whereas the PCI is strongest in the northern industrial areas of the country, the highest concentration of DC members is to be found in the poorer southern half of the mainland and in Sardinia and Sicily. The DC is a highly factionalised party, and many of its members are recruited by local or national factional "barons" more to bolster their position against other barons than to assist the DC in competing with other parties. The fact that the DC has been in government ever since 1946 gives its faction leaders powerful patronage resources with which to attract followers.

NETHERLANDS

Over the last forty years, the membership of the Dutch parties has declined from a level that was never particularly high by general European standards. The drop has been most pronounced among the religious parties (now combined in the CDA); membership fell from about half a million in 1950 to 130,000 in the late 1980s. In contrast, the VVD (Liberals) actually increased their membership over the same period, while the membership of the Socialist PvdA has remained relatively steady. In most parties, the activity of sections like youth movements and women's groups has declined.

SPAIN

The Spanish parties have exceptionally small memberships; nowhere else in Western Europe

(Continued on next page)

does such a small proportion of voters belong to a political party. In the 1986 election the Socialist party (PSOE) won nearly nine million votes, but it had only about 200,000 members, and the other parties have a similar ratio of voters to members. The legacy of dictatorship is sometimes suggested as an explanation for the phenomenon, as it led to a political culture that did not encourage active participation in politics.

SWEDEN
Swedish party membership, like Swedish politics generally, is dominated by the Social Democrats. Of the 1.6 million Swedes who belonged to a party in the late 1980s, three-quarters belonged to the Social Democrats. However, this figure of 1.2 million Social Democrat members included indirect members, who, as in Britain, were deemed to be party members because of their membership in trade unions affiliated with the party. Like their British Labour counterparts, the Swedish Social Democrats decided in the second half of the 1980s to review their practice in this regard and to move toward phasing out the notion of indirect membership. Among the other parties, the Center party has the most members as a proportion of voters (around 20 percent), a feature it shares

with its counterparts in Finland and Norway. Membership in all the Swedish parties together rose from just over a million in 1948 to 1.6 million by the late 1980s.

UNITED KINGDOM
Party membership in the United Kingdom is low, at around 5 percent of the 33 million votes cast in the most recent election. The Conservatives have the largest number of members, estimated at something over a million, a figure that represents a decline since the 1950s. These members have a reputation for being more right-wing than Conservative MPs and are noted for their consistent calls at annual conferences for the restoration of capital punishment. Labour has only about a third as many direct members as the Conservatives. Members of trade unions that donate money to the Labour party are considered members of the party, but it is clear that many of these trade unionists are not in any sense party supporters. The traditionally close relationship between Labour and the unions has weakened in recent years, and the entrenched position of the unions within Labour's decision-making structures is coming under close and critical scrutiny. The membership of all the other British parties is small.

persuade the floating voters to come off the fence, let alone trying to convert the supporters of other parties. But they have a part to play in mobilizing the faithful: going from house to house and knocking on doors to rekindle dormant loyalties and to show that the party has a local presence. Between elections, undoubtedly, many party branches are not especially active. The more committed members attend branch meetings regularly, to discuss ways of expanding the organization at the local level or to decide their stance on issues due to arise at the next annual conference. Even so, the general impression is that party organizations are merely "ticking over" except during election campaigns.

It was not always like this. As we mentioned in the previous chapter, belonging to a party in the early years of the century could mean living within what was almost a separate subculture within society. This was especially true of left-wing parties with a mass membership, such as the German SPD. Belonging to the SPD was almost a way of life. The party had its own newspaper, which members bought, read, and discussed with each other, and its branch offices all over Germany were centers of social activity for members, running stamp-collecting clubs and sports teams, organizing outings, and so on. It ran its own health service, paid for by members through a health insurance scheme, and sought to look after members and their families from the cradle to the grave. In 1906 it founded a training school in Berlin for the political education of members, grooming the most committed to take up places in the ranks of its full-time employees. Given that many members worked in factories alongside fellow party members and belonged to trade unions associated with the party, they were virtually cocooned from contact with the rest of German society.

But even in the heyday of mass parties, in the first half of the twentieth century, few European parties managed to achieve this degree of penetration of their members' lives, which has in any case declined over the last thirty years or so. Although the number of party members has not necessarily diminished, as we have seen, the commitment of the members may well have waned. The modern welfare state has taken over many of the functions that party insurance schemes once performed. A rise in living standards, a huge increase in leisure outlets, and the advent of television have all combined to reduce the appeal of spending evenings playing table tennis in the local party hall. The Austrian Socialist party (SPÖ), which was claimed by its general secretary as recently as 1982 to be a "second home" for members because of the range of activities it organized for them, including rambling, music, stamp collecting, sports, and gymnastics (Sully, p. 165), is now very much an exception.

Television has undermined much of the rationale for party newspapers, so few European parties nowadays run their own papers, and when they do, these often make a loss. The dedicated party activist, spending much of his or her free time debating and propagating the party's policy and ideology, is becoming a creature of the past. Even in parties with a participatory ethos, such as the German Greens, most members are inactive between elections (Paterson, p. 174).

But this does not mean that ordinary members no longer play a role within European parties. On the contrary, they are important in giving these parties a character quite distinct from that of their American counterparts. The role of European party members in certain key areas gives parties a reasonable degree of coherence, as we shall now see when we look at power within parties.

POWER WITHIN PARTIES

Various attempts have been made to identify different "types" of party organization that might be distinct from each other in a number of ways. The best-known of these schemes was devised in the early 1950s by the French writer Maurice Duverger, who sought to distinguish two types: cadre parties and mass parties. Cadre parties consisted mainly of local notables, "influential persons" whose "name, prestige or connections" would win votes for the candidate locally and would also attract financiers to bankroll the local campaign. Cadre parties did not seek fresh members; indeed, they did not really have members, in the sense of people who paid a subscription and signed a party pledge (Duverger, p. 64). In contrast, mass parties had a large fee-paying membership. Cadre parties, according to Duverger, tended to be right-wing parties in which power rested with the parliamentary group, whereas mass parties were usually ideologically committed left-wing parties, with a sizable permanent bureaucracy working in the head office and with members who tried to keep the parliamentarians on a fairly tight leash.

Of course, very few parties in Europe even then, and even fewer now, could be pigeonholed neatly into one or another of his categories. The German SPD, which was an archetypal mass party early in the twentieth century, now has an organization that differs very little from that of its right-wing rival, the CDU. In Britain, the right-wing Conservative party has many more individual members than the "mass-based" Labour party. The mix of parties existing in Western Europe today is much broader than Duverger's scheme would imply.

What we can say is that most Western European parties operate internally by a mixture of conflict and consensus. We would be unduly gullible if we believed party leaders' frequent claims that reports of internal dissent are just figments of the mass media's imagination—but, at the same time, it would be equally erroneous to visualize European political parties as being in a permanent state of civil war. The various elements in the party organization—the leader, deputies, rank-and-file members, and so on—all jostle for position, but there is rarely open warfare between them. After all, they all belong to the same party and can be assumed to have a broadly similar political outlook. They are bound to disagree on details, but the leader and deputies usually have some freedom of maneuver, provided that they stay within the broad parameters of what is acceptable to the membership.

Consequently, we must resist the temptation to approach the question of where power lies within a party in the spirit of a detective trying to identify a murderer. Power, unlike the hand that slipped the poison into the Napoleon brandy, is divisible. It is just not the case that all power lies in one place and every other part of the party is powerless. Usually, the internal affairs of parties are characterized by a continuous process of accommodation and mutual adjustment. When it comes to the crunch, after all, most party members at every level would rather keep the party together as an effective body than precipitate a destructive split. That said, of course, internal differences are sometimes so great that a split does take place, and a new party is formed. More commonly, however, there is a constant process of give and take, and the party remains together precisely because a balance of power is respected and no one element tries to achieve complete control.

This accommodation is especially noticeable in highly factionalized parties. In some of these parties, such as the Italian Christian Democrats, factions are a permanent feature. Some factions are based primarily on allegiance to individual senior politicians within the party and may or may not have a distinctive position on policies, while others represent some specific interest, such as small farmers, workers, or Catholic lay groups. Although the presence of so many factions hampers the efficiency of the party's organization, it does not pose a threat to the continued existence of the party itself. The factions do not try to take over the entire party and drive their rivals out. Rather, they have reached a modus vivendi under which they share out the "spoils"—government positions, parliamentary nominations, and so on—in approximate proportion to the number of members each faction has in the party. In the French Socialist party, factions tend to be based on support for individual politicians rather than social interests. One study concludes that those factions headed by serious contenders for the French presidency were the most successful, whereas others tended to decline (Cole). Factions in the Flemish Christian Popular party (CVP) in Belgium, in contrast, are based almost entirely on social interests, principally those of farmers, employers, and workers. Even though highly factionalized parties are in some ways divergent from the

European mainstream, they still stand in contrast to the pattern in the U.S.A., where aspiring presidential candidates must construct their own base of electoral support and raise their own funds. Even in the most factionalised Western European parties, aspirants for political positions know that they must establish a base within a party's organization to have any chance of making progress. Going it alone and trying to bypass the party membership is virtually guaranteed to lead nowhere.

There are several important areas of activity where conflict can arise within a party. One such area is the drafting of policy documents, the most significant of which are the party manifesto, the formal declaration in which a party tells the voters what it will do if it gets into government, and the party program, the statement of the party's aims and aspirations, which is generally updated every few years. Party members often differ among themselves as to what should be put in the program and the manifesto, partly because their own values are not identical and partly because some are more concerned than others with winning votes as opposed to maintaining ideological purity. Arguments about the party's policies often surface at annual conferences, where tension is sometimes apparent between parliamentarians and rank-and-file members. The rank and file, especially in left-wing parties, is inclined to suspect the deputies of being seduced by the clublike atmosphere of parliament, of forgetting their roots, of being willing to betray the party's principles to get into the well-padded seats of power. The deputies, in turn, may view some members as being unworldly zealots, unaware that compromises and bargaining are necessary in order to achieve at least part of what the party stands for and hooked on policies that have no hope of ever being acceptable to the wider electorate.

But although party activists often fight over every semicolon in the party's manifesto, this is probably not the most important arena of intraparty conflict. After all, most voters don't even bother to read manifestos. And although a manifesto is in theory a commitment by the party to do certain things if it gets into government, in practice it would be naive to believe that a party, once in government, feels bound to do everything mentioned in its manifesto and to do nothing that is not mentioned there. As we shall see in Chapter 8, even academics who have spent a lot of time on the question find it difficult to reach firm conclusions about the extent to which parties actually do what they promised to do.

A second important area of conflict is the election of the party leader. Most European parties, unlike their American counterparts, have one person who can be clearly identified as the leader, even though there may on paper be several "top jobs," such as party chairperson, party president, parliamentary leader, and general secretary. Generally, the parliamentary leader—the person who would become prime minister if the party formed a government on its own or who stands to receive the senior government post given to the party in a coalition government— is the "real" leader. He (or, more rarely, she) is chosen by the party's deputies. Of course, there are exceptions. In communist parties, the general secretary (who is elected by the membership, though in practice is usually selected by the ruling group) tends to be the most powerful individual. In the Netherlands, the leader of a party's parliamentary group is not necessarily its potential prime minister; the "real" leader is the person who heads the party's list of candidates at election time, a matter decided by the wider party organization. Some leaders are so dominant within their parties that it hardly makes sense to think of anyone having the power to elect or oust them—examples include the Greek PASOK, led by Andreas Papandreou, and many parties in France. In other cases, even when the party leader is also the leader of the parliamentary caucus, this person is chosen from a wider group than deputies alone. For example, a decade of tension within the British Labour party culminated in 1981 in the adoption of a complicated procedure under which the leader was chosen by an electoral college in which the trade unions were given 40 percent of the votes and local constituency organizations 30 percent, while the votes of Labour MPs, who used to be the only selectors, were reduced to just 30 percent.

Important as the selection of the party leader undoubtedly is, it is not the most important decision that is made within political parties. Since each party's parliamentary deputies play a major role in its life and are often the only people with any real say in choosing the party leader and/or deciding party policy, it is obviously important to know who picks the deputies. While in one sense, of course, it is voters who choose deputies, they can choose only between the alternatives they are offered by the parties in the first place. Party deputies must all come out of the pool of people selected as the party's parliamentary candidates. Indeed, many writers have seen the selection of these candidates as perhaps the most important thing that political parties do. To decide who can stand as a major party candidate is to have a big say in who will be in the new parliament. Moreover, since government ministers in most countries are drawn from the ranks of members of parliament, candidate selectors also play a decisive role in determining who sits in the seats of real power. After the 1987 election in the United Kingdom, for example, 605 of the 650 MPs elected represented either the Conservative party or the Labour party. Each of these parties nominated 633 candidates, one in each mainland British constituency. The people who selected these 1266 Conservative and Labour candidates, therefore, exercised an enormous power over who could and who could not get into the House of Commons and, beyond that, into government.

Aspiring politicians who do not meet with the approval of these powerful gatekeepers, the major parties' candidate selectors, find that their political career is dead in the water. Candidate selection is thus a crucial step in the political recruitment process. For this reason, it is also a key area of internal party activity. If one section of a party, such as the party leader or the national executive, has control over the selection process, then this section can almost be said to control the party. Candidate selection is thus a vital matter in every individual European political party; it is also important—indeed, it is one of the key factors—in making European political parties very different from American parties. For this reason, we shall now look rather closely at the way European parties pick their parliamentary candidates.

Candidate Selection

Two points in particular characterize European practice in the area of candidate selection. First, the way in which parties run their affairs, including how they pick their candidates, is a matter for the law in only three countries. In Finland, parties are legally obliged to open up the process of candidate selection to a direct vote of all their members. In Germany, the law stipulates that candidates are to be selected by the local party organization, with the national executive having no power to overturn its decisions. And in Norway, a law outlines a method for selecting candidates that places the process entirely under local control and in return commits the state to underwrite the costs the parties incur in the process. Norwegian parties do not have to follow the prescriptions of the law (though in practice they do), but in that case they must pay their own selection expenses. In every other country, parties can make whatever arrangements they wish when they pick parliamentary candidates.

Second, in all Western European countries, candidate selection is a matter for political parties and their paid-up members, not for ordinary party voters. U.S.-style primaries are not a part of the European political scene. For parties in Europe, the idea of throwing open such a vital part of their activities to ordinary voters, who have no proven commitment to the party, would be anathema. Keeping candidate selection within the party helps to retain the loyalty of ordinary party members. Deciding who will be allowed to use the party's name and resources in the election campaign is often the only real power members have, so allowing them to do this increases the party leaders' ability to retain a substantial body of cooperative members. European parties keep candidate selection firmly under their own control; what varies between parties is exactly what part of the party organization exercises this control. There are many variations across Western Europe, summarized in Table 5.2.

The furthest any party goes down the road toward opening up its selection process to all and sundry is to allow each of its paid-up members a direct say in the choice of parliamentary candidates. Even this is relatively unusual; it is a method employed only in Belgium, Britain (by Labour and some of the minor parties), Finland (where it is obligatory under law), Iceland (by the Social Democrats), and the Netherlands (by one minor party). Most parties consider candidate selection to be too important in its consequences to be left to the unconstrained choice of the party membership at large.

The most common selection method is the convention system: party members in each constituency choose delegates to attend a local nominating convention, also known as a selection conference, which picks the candidates. Just how many members are directly involved varies from party to party. The proportion is rarely more than a third of all members involved and is sometimes as small as 1 or 2 percent. In Ireland, membership participation is very high. The largest party, Fianna Fáil, has rules under which each branch can send three delegates to the convention. Since average branch membership is only about twelve, roughly a quarter of Fianna Fáil members are directly involved in candidate selection (M. Gallagher, p. 121). In contrast, there is little active participation in Italy, where less than 1 percent of the total membership of the main parties is effectively involved in the process (Wertman, p. 160). In some parties, the choice is made by a local party committee, with the convention only giving formal ratification to the committee's choice.

In other parties, the process is more centralized, and all candidates are picked by the national executive, whose size will usually be in the range of 20 to 100. In most parties, the national executive has the formal right to veto people picked at the local level but exercises it only on the very rare occasions when a local convention picks

TABLE 5.2
Candidate Selection in Western Europe

	Most Important Party Body in Selection	Other Important Actors
Austria	Local conventions	National executives
Belgium	Local conventions	—
Denmark	Local conventions	—
Finland	Local members	—
France	National executives	Local conventions
Germany	Local conventions	—
Greece	Party leaders	—
Iceland	Local conventions	—
Ireland	Local conventions	National executives
Italy	National executives	Local conventions, factions
Malta	National executives	—
Netherlands	Local conventions	National executives
Norway	Local conventions	—
Portugal	National executives	Local branches
Spain	Leadership group	Local organization
Sweden	Local conventions	—
Switzerland	Local conventions	—
United Kingdom	Local conventions	—

Sources: Iceland and Malta—Jacobs; Portugal—Bruneau and MacLeod (p. 32), T. Gallagher (p. 17); Spain—de Esteban and López Guerra (pp. 60–72), Tusell Gómez (pp. 119–120); other countries—Gallagher and Marsh.
Note: The table refers to the general pattern within each country; in some countries, there is some variation between parties.

someone it deems totally unsuitable. But there are a few parties where the national executive is the most active body in picking candidates. In the main right-wing parties in France, small groups set up by the national executives arrange many of the candidacies. In Ireland and Italy, the national executives of the main parties sometimes add candidates to the list of those selected locally. In Britain, the head office of the Conservative party plays an important role in screening aspirants for candidacies. It vets all aspirants for candidacies, weeding out many of them for one reason or another, and draws up a list of about 500 names of suitable people who are not already MPs. When local conventions make a selection for their own constituency, they almost invariably pick someone from this approved list (Denver, p. 51). In Europe's communist parties, too, the national executive is usually decisive, given the centralized nature of these parties.

The least open way of all to pick candidates is to leave the choice to the party leader alone. This is feasible only in leader-dominated parties, of which there are now very few in Europe. One of the few clear examples left is the left-wing Greek party PASOK, whose leader, Andreas Papandreou, virtually handpicks the party's candidates. In several parties in the other newly established southern European democracies of Portugal and Spain, too, the party leader or the leadership group has a dominant role in candidate selection.

If we look at candidate selection across Western Europe as a whole, it is easy to brand the process as essentially undemocratic when compared with what happens

BOX 5.2
Selection of Parliamentary Candidates

FRANCE

Parties in France tend to be dominated by a small number of prominent individuals, and this manifests itself in the candidate selection process. The two main right-wing parties, the RPR and UDF, usually fight elections in tandem, so they come to an arrangement as to which of them should contest each constituency. The central authorities of the parties, especially the national executives, play a decisive role in this and are also important in picking the candidates. Communist party candidates are chosen by the national executive. Local members have rather more say in the Socialist party, although here, too, some central involvement is necessitated by the factionalized nature of the party; the factions are required to come to some overall arrangement on sharing the candidacies in order to preserve party unity. In contrast to the position in Britain, local roots are very important; most parliamentary deputies are simultaneously councillors (usually mayors) of their town or village, and resentment is created when candidates are "parachuted" by the central party authorities into a constituency with which they have no links.

GERMANY

Candidate selection is regulated by law, which ensures that the central authorities of the parties have very little power. Selection is carried out by local conventions consisting of delegates from party branches within the constituency. Once these local bodies have made their choice, the central bodies cannot enforce changes. There is very little variation between the parties. Although the German electoral system provides two routes to parliament (see Chapter 6), the parties do not look for different qualities in the candidates they nominate for the list seats and for the constituency seats; indeed, there is considerable overlap between the two sets of candidates.

ITALY

The factionalized nature of the Christian Democratic party makes its candidate selection process more complicated than that of any other party in Europe. Many actors have a say in the process: local party members, regional party organizations, interest groups affiliated with the party (such as lay Catholic groups and the Confederation of Small Farmers), and the factions. The final decisions are made by the national executive, which is in virtually permanent session in the week before the deadline, but the national executive is really just the arena where agreements among the various faction leaders are reached. In the Communist party, the national executive, though important, does not control the party as thoroughly as is the case in most other Communist parties, and the regional party organizations have some input. In the Socialist party, the regional organizations have the biggest role, with the national executive making few changes to their proposals.

NETHERLANDS

There is some variation among the Dutch parties. The largest two, the CDA and the PvdA, employ very similar procedures. In each, local party members have the main influence on the names to go on the party list; the national executive can hope to influence their decisions but is of only secondary importance. In the liberal VVD, the national executive is the most important actor; this party has been affected less than the CDA and PvdA by demands for democratization over the past two decades. A fourth party, Democrats '66, in contrast, places heavy stress on internal democracy and gives a postal vote in the candidate selection process to every paid-up member.

SPAIN

Since Spanish parties are leader-dominated and have very few members, it is not surprising to find that candidate selection is largely controlled by the leadership group. Although the leadership usually feels it wise to pay some regard to the feelings of the local party organization when settling on its lists around the country, it nonetheless retains a fairly free hand in deciding who should carry the party flag. Local activists occasionally

(Continued on next page)

show their displeasure with the centrally made selections by running dissident lists in the election, but these rarely achieve any success.

SWEDEN

As is the case in the other Scandinavian countries, central government and the central party authorities are less powerful in Sweden than across most of Western Europe. Local government is important, and, similarly, the local party branches do not welcome or indeed expect any attempt on the part of party headquarters to dictate to them. Candidate selection in all the Swedish parties is carried out at the constituency level by conventions composed of delegates from the party branches in the constituency and is firmly under the control of the local party organization. This even includes the Left party—Communists, who deviate from the usual communist pattern of central control, a strong testimony to the Swedish concern for local autonomy.

UNITED KINGDOM

All parties adopt a broadly similar method of picking candidates. Local conventions of party members in each constituency select one person from a shortlist drawn up by the committee of the constituency organization. There are two significant differences between the major parties. Candidate selection in the Labour party is complicated by the role of the trade unions in the party's organization: union branches can put forward names and also cast a number of votes at the selection convention. The Conservative party, meanwhile, has moved in recent years toward greater centralization of candidate selection: it maintains a list of about 500 centrally approved aspirant candidates, who have to go through a rigorous screening procedure, and constituency organizations are expected to select from this list. Candidate selection in Britain is unusual in two respects. First, sitting MPs do not have to undergo even a formal process of reselection; they automatically become the party's flagbearers in the next election unless they have aroused so much antagonism among the local membership that the lengthy process that could lead to their "deselection" is embarked upon. Labour embarked upon the idea of mandatory reselection for its MPs in the second half of the 1980s, but this was dropped in the early 1990s, as the party leadership felt that it generated internal tension. While incumbent parliamentarians are almost invariably reselected in all European countries, those outside Britain must at least go through the formalities. Second, whereas parliamentarians in virtually every other country have roots in the constituency they hope to represent, selectors in Britain often pick someone with no connection with the constituency.

in the United States, where primaries allow the electorate at large a decisive say in the selection of party candidates. Since primaries became common early in the present century, and widespread starting in the 1970s, they have come to be seen by many Americans as an integral part of the democratic process. Yet they are not seen as a part of the democratic process in Europe, for two main reasons.

First, voters in several European countries *do* have a degree of choice over which individuals are to represent them in parliament. As we shall see in the following chapter, the electoral systems employed in certain countries allow voters to express preferences between the candidates put forward by their party. The voters' preferences between candidates of the same party are particularly effective in Denmark, Finland, Ireland, Italy, Luxembourg, Malta, and Switzerland. In these countries, the party activists pick, say, eight candidates to represent the party in a particular multimember constituency. The party might win enough votes to entitle it to, say, three seats, and it is the voters, through the preferences they express on the ballot paper, who effectively decide which three of the eight candidates actually take the seats. In a sense, the electoral system allows the primary and the election to take place simultaneously.

Of course, even in these cases European voters do not have as much choice as their American counterparts, because they can pick and choose only from the people already approved by party activists. The control over candidate selection by party activists, however, is an integral part of the party discipline so central to European parliamentary democracy, and this is the second reason why Europeans do not feel deprived by the absence of American-style primaries. Without such party discipline, the stability of parliamentary majorities, and hence of governments, would be permanently in question. Stability is a direct product of the fact that in nearly all European legislatures, the deputies elected on a particular party's ticket almost invariably vote as a bloc, as we pointed out in Chapter 1, and the candidate selection process has a lot to do with this.

This cohesion is not a result of European party leaders ruling their parties with an iron hand and thus ensuring that only compliant individuals are picked as candidates. On the contrary, as we have seen, party leaders, with very few exceptions, do not control the candidate selection process at all. This process is usually in the hands of local members, who may well resent any attempt by the party's top brass to lean on them when they are making their choices. But the effect is much the same. As Leon D. Epstein (pp. 219, 225) has pointed out, local party activists, just like the national leadership, want deputies who are loyal to the party line as defined nationally, so the types of people chosen locally are nearly always perfectly acceptable to the national leadership. It may not matter much *who* within the party chooses its candidates, but it matters a lot that it is *someone* within the party, and not the voters at large, who chooses them.

Once in parliament, deputies know that if they start picking and choosing when to vote with their party and when to defy the party line, there is a good chance that they will be "deselected" in the next election—and that they will have little chance of reelection without the party label. In the U.S.A., self-interest requires politicians to pay careful heed to the views of interest groups, PACs (political action committees), and constituents at large. In Western Europe, it requires them to put the party first, last, and always. Outside the party there is no salvation, or at least no political career prospect.

Although this might seem to lead to "dictatorship of the party," we must remember that deputies have a voice in the party's decisions and that they can always leave it if asked to vote for something they find unacceptable. Voters, too, can turn a party out of office if they feel that its internal affairs are run in too undemocratic a fashion. But in any case, there are many arguments that say there are benefits in deputies having to toe the party line in parliament all the time. It ensures that governments can make unpopular but perhaps necessary decisions without having to placate deputies beholden to local or other interests. It protects deputies from the risk of being picked off one by one and threatened with being targeted at the next election by powerful and well-funded single-issue interest groups. Whatever an interest group might threaten to do to a deputy who doesn't vote as it wants, it is nothing compared with what the party will do if the deputy doesn't vote as *it* wants. In contrast to this picture, some observers of American parties have deplored their inability to control their nominations and, hence, the behavior of their members of Congress. This view is summed up by Walter Dean Burnham, who concludes, "Pure candidate-domination of elections is a recipe for irresponsible, unaccountable performance in office, and is equally a recipe for domination of the political order by the haves at the expense of the have-nots" (Burnham, p. xiii).

So it could be argued that the internal power structure characteristic of European parties has advantages over the two main alternatives: the type of organization or nonorganization that leaves candidates free of any checks from below, as in the U.S.A., or the opposite extreme, which reduces them to ciphers carrying out the wishes of the extraparliamentary organization, as in European communist parties. Most Western European parties have adopted a style of organization that keeps deputies on a fairly long leash held by the ordinary members but does not go so far as to make them mere poodles of unelected activists.

Just how internally democratic parties should be so as to maximize their ability to perform as agents of liberal democracy is one of the big questions of political science, about which entire books have been written (for a discussion of the issues, see Ware, 1987a). In recent years, the topic has been widely debated in southern Europe, where the socialist parties that played important roles in the restoration of democracy in Greece, Portugal, and Spain have been conspicuous for their own lack of internal democracy. Some people are concerned that oligarchic tendencies within these parties do nothing to facilitate the emergence of a more open and democratic political culture, while others feel that the strength of the parties and the degree to which they are embedded in civil society are more important than how internally democratic they are (Gillespie and Gallagher; Pridham, 1990). Whichever view is more valid, there is little dispute that American-style direct primaries are incompatible with strong political parties (Ranney) and that strong political parties are central to European parliamentary democracy.

PARTIES AND MONEY

Because European parties do so much more than U.S. parties, they need more resources. This is not to suggest that there is more money available in European politics than there is in the United States—almost certainly, the reverse is true. But in the U.S.A. most political funds are raised and spent by candidates rather than parties, while in Europe parties are much more central in raising and spending money, as in everything else.

European parties need money for two main reasons. First, they need it to run their organizations: to pay their head office staff and their telephone, postage, and other bills; to hold annual conferences and other meetings; and in some cases to support research institutions linked to the party. Second, they need cash to fight election campaigns, the main item of expenditure for nearly all parties. In most Western European countries parties are not allowed to buy television advertising space, but they find plenty of other ways to spend money at election time: on newspaper and poster advertising; perhaps on a helicopter to whisk the party leader around the country on the campaign trail; on fax machines and mobile phones to keep candidates in touch with party HQ; and on balloons, buttons, and general razzmatazz.

Parties get their money from a variety of sources (general overviews are given in Alexander; Paltiel; and von Beyme, pp. 196–211). Dues paid by members play a role, but nowadays they rarely produce more than a quarter of a party's income. A second source of income is for a party to request, or insist, that its parliamentary deputies and government ministers pay a proportion, perhaps as much as 10 percent, of their official salary into party coffers. Third, parties may engage in fund-raising activities, such as the garden fetes and church hall bazaars for which the British Conservatives are famous, or the range of shops, banks, and trading enterprises often run by communist parties, as in Italy and France. Some parties publish their own newspapers, but these days, as we have already mentioned, they are more often a drain on a party's coffers than a contributor to them.

Besides these three sources arising "internally," that is, from the party's own activities, there are also two important "external" sources of money. First, major interest groups back political parties whose policies they think will help them. In particular, business gives money to right-wing parties, and trade unions give money to left-wing parties. Second, in a growing number of European countries—Austria, Finland, Germany, Italy, Norway, Spain, Sweden—the state gives public money to political parties. Moreover, in almost every country, even if there is no explicit state funding, there are benefits in kind. These include free party broadcasts and mailings during election campaigns and grants to the parliamentary groups to enable them to pay for secretarial and research assistance.

These two external sources of funding, contributions from interest groups and from the state, are linked, because it is concern about the consequences of parties becoming financially dependent on interest groups that has brought about the rise of state financing. Obviously, neither business corporations nor trade unions give money to parties simply out of bigheartedness. At the very least, they hope to help their chosen party get into government and implement policies broadly sympathetic to their own needs. Sponsors may have more tangible benefits in mind, however. A business may give money to a party in the hope (or even on condition) that once in government, it will make a specific decision, perhaps on a tax liability or a request for land-use planning permission, that will repay the investment several times over. This is particularly likely to happen when, as is the case in most European countries, there are no laws, or at most ineffective laws, compelling parties to disclose their financial sources.

The first European country to introduce state funding of its parties was West Germany in 1959. The German scheme has subsequently been expanded and altered several times and now involves huge sums of money. Parties winning more than 0.5 percent of the vote in an election receive 5 deutsche marks for every vote. This adds up to a lot of money, as around 50 million votes are cast at postunification German elections. The result is that the German parties are awash with funds, and even after covering the costs of exceptionally large party bureaucracies and research institutes, they have enough left over to help like-minded parties in the poorer Mediterranean countries. In Germany's case, the past history of dictatorship may create a heightened willingness to spend a lot of money on preserving the institutions of liberal democracy. Other countries have rather more modest schemes, though the principle is the same—parties receive money in approximate proportion to their electoral strength. In some countries all the money is paid by the national government to the parties' national headquarters, while in others, especially in Scandinavia, a significant part of the cash flows from local government to the parties' local organizations.

The pros and cons of taxpayers giving money to political parties have been debated in many European countries. One argument, as we have seen, is that it frees parties from having to dance to the tune of wealthy financial backers and thus reduces corruption in politics generally. It may well have this effect overall, but it certainly does not eliminate the "sleaze factor" entirely. Proof of this came in West Germany when the "Flick scandal" emerged in the mid-1980s. It was discovered that despite all the money they got from the state, the parties still were not satiated; they had been secretly receiving large unreported donations from private companies in return, it was alleged, for massive tax concessions (Paterson, pp. 176–180). Defenders of state financing maintain that there would be even more of this kind of thing if parties were entirely dependent on private sources.

Another argument in favor of state financing is that not all parties can find wealthy interest groups that are keen to give them money. Generally speaking, right-wing parties receive large donations from business, while left-wing parties receive much smaller sums from trade unions. Center parties may get some money from business or, like the British Liberal Democrats, may not receive money from anyone. Parties whose policies appeal to no wealthy interest group—Green parties, for example—may receive only small sums from members and sympathetic individuals. State financing, besides coming without strings attached, is awarded according to a predetermined formula and thus seems to make competition "fairer."

While some people claim that political parties are private bodies and as such have no right to expect money from the public purse, others point out that they fulfill a public function: they are essential to the workings of a democracy and therefore need to be succored. Furthermore, the role of government has expanded greatly in the twentieth century, and government is controlled by a ruling party or parties. Unless parties have the money to explore and expand policy options and to conduct research into the feasibility of their ideas, the country as a whole could suffer from the inadequately thought-out policies they promote.

Certainly, most of the arguments advanced against the provision of state financing for parties don't stand up very well to the evidence. For example, it has been suggested that public funding perpetuates the status quo by bolstering existing parties and making it hard for new ones to break through. However, the West German Greens in the early 1980s, operating within the country that has the most lavish funding for existing parties, proved that if a new party has appealing policies, it will win votes even against well-financed opponents. It has also been argued that if parties are featherbedded by the state, they will lose the incentive to raise money themselves and will no longer try to recruit members. Once again, Germany proves the claim false; despite the comprehensive public financing scheme, party membership has risen significantly over the last two decades (Table 5.1). In fact, it has even been argued that public funding will boost party membership. One comparative study of four Scandinavian countries suggested that a major explanation for the decline in membership in the Danish parties, in contrast to the ability of the parties in Finland, Norway, and Sweden to hold their membership levels, lies in the fact that Denmark, unlike the other three countries, has no state funding of parties.

Consequently, the Danish parties make larger demands on their members, and many former or potential members conclude that the costs of party membership outweigh the possible benefits (Sundberg, pp. 25–26).

Although every European party would no doubt like more money to finance its activities, most parties with reasonable levels of electoral support have sufficient resources to get their message across at elections. Individual party candidates fight elections on a national party platform and thus do not need much money to mount a personal campaign. The need for a personal campaign arises only when a preferential electoral system pits two or more candidates of the same party against each other (see Chapter 6). But even in these cases, a candidate who spends lavishly on a personal campaign rather than fighting as part of the party's team might well incur disapproval, perhaps from voters as well as from party members. Consequently, candidates are not beholden to interest groups and do not need the equivalent of America's PACs to bankroll their campaigns. Once again, we see in Western Europe the dominance of party over candidate, in marked contrast to the situation in the United States.

THE FUTURE OF EUROPEAN PARTIES

Even in the nineteenth century, it was recognized that European and American parties were different from each other. Writers from one side of the Atlantic were prone to praise the parties they knew and lament that those living in the other area were not so fortunate, or, alternatively, they tended to see merit in the transatlantic model and express the hope that their own parties would change in that direction. Some writers, like the Russian émigré Mosei Ostrogorski, lambasted both types of parties for different but apparently equally grave shortcomings.

In the twentieth century, the possibility of convergence has been extensively discussed. One of the first to make a firm prediction was the French writer Maurice Duverger, who maintained that the "mass party," with a large number of fee-paying members, a sizable permanent bureaucracy in the head office, and a clear policy program, was the "new" or "modern" form of party. Starting from the premise that the archetypal mass party was a left-wing party, he used the phrase "contagion from the left" to sum up the argument that other parties had to adopt a similar form in order to compete with the left-wing parties. Consequently, he expected not only European parties but also American ones to gravitate toward this model. He ended his well-known book on parties with this emphatic assertion: "Regrets for the individualistic and decentralised cadre parties of the nineteenth century and imprecations against the vast centralised and disciplined parties of today do not alter the fact that the latter alone suit the structure of contemporary societies" (Duverger, p. 427). This was a characteristically confident assertion, which derived from Duverger's vision of the development of parties toward their apotheosis in the ideal-type mass party.

But others felt that Duverger's "vast centralised" parties were already, even by the time he was writing, dinosaurs ill-equipped to flourish in an environment that was rapidly changing. Leon D. Epstein, writing in the 1960s, was one of the first to put forward such a view. He undertook a careful analysis of all the material he could find on political parties, being more concerned to draw inferences from the available data than to frame theories and look for examples that fitted them. He did not feel that the mass party was "modern"; on the contrary, he thought, mass parties belonged only to particular places and periods. He identified a number of "counter-organisational tendencies" that, he argued, would increasingly undermine the rationale for the existence of large-scale mass political parties (Epstein, pp. 233–260).

First, the increasing use of the mass media, especially television, during election campaigns reduces the need for thousands of ordinary party members to go out knocking on doors to get the message across. Second, in order to pay the higher campaign costs this entails, parties might be inclined to look for big donations from a few corporate backers, either businesses or trade unions, as their members' fees were no longer adequate to cover their costs. Epstein's argument, with his use of the phrase "contagion from the right," was read as implying that he thought European parties would grow more and more like American ones, though he did not explicitly say this.

Certainly, both of these "tendencies" could be expected to lead to a decline in the vitality of party organizations. In the U.S.A., television advertising, opinion polls, and computerized mailing lists were enabling candidates to fight elections with their own professional campaign team and bypass the party organization entirely (Ware, 1987c, p. 120). The growth in the level of financing the parties receive from private interests and, in many countries, from public funds has removed one of the reasons for having a large membership. It has been suggested that the value of a mass local membership is now more symbolic than practical (Urwin, p. 204).

Other reasons could be put forward as to why the "modern" mass party is in reality an endangered species. In the 1960s, Otto Kirchheimer (1966) argued that changes in European society were bringing about changes in the type of party likely to flourish. Class lines were becoming less sharp, and the growth of the welfare state and the mixed economy had cut the ground from under the feet of old-style antisystem socialist parties, dedicated to a radical transformation of society, with members living within a virtual subculture. In addition, middle-class style, with an emphasis on individualism, seemed to be growing at the expense of working-class style, which stressed collective identification and action (Epstein, p. 128). The type of party best suited to these conditions was what Kirchheimer called "the postwar catch-all party," which tried to win votes from nearly all sections of society and which would concentrate on general, bland issues like better health and education services.

From this point of view, a party does not really need a large number of committed members. In the 1980s, Gunnar Sjöblom took this line of thought one step further and argued that members might actually be a handicap to a party, or at least to its parliamentarians. He suggested that various changes in society, such as increased mobility and the growing role of the mass media in conveying political messages, were leading to greater volatility among voters. People were suffering from "information overload"; they were confused by a never-ending stream of reports about proposals, decisions, and speculation and were increasingly likely to vote on the basis of "political paraphernalia"—trivial factors like the style or appearance of the party leader (Sjöblom, p. 385). In this situation, members with a strong commitment to certain principles were a definite liability to the vote-hungry party deputies, who wanted the party to be able to change tack rapidly to take advantage of the shifting winds of public opinion. Party members knocking on doors and trying to drum up support by faithfully plugging a traditional message were even seen as being likely to have a counterproductive effect. Consequently, argued Sjöblom (p. 395), "it may be to the advantage of a party to have few and/or passive members." Indeed, the deputy leader of the Spanish Socialist party said in the 1980s that he would sooner have ten minutes of television broadcasting time than ten thousand members (Gillespie, p. 366).

This argument seems to become even more persuasive when we think about the types of people who might make up the bulk of party members. It has been suggested that there are three main motives that might lead someone to join a party (Clark and Wilson). One is material, the desire to gain some tangible reward; this was important only in old-style American patronage machines and in a very few European countries, such as Austria. The second is solidary, the desire for social contact and a sense of comradeship; with the rise of a wide range of leisure opportunities, the decline in cohesiveness among subcultures and communities, and the advent of a more middle-class style in society generally, which we have already mentioned, this, too, is of declining importance. The third is purposive, a desire to advance certain policy goals. With the first two motives becoming less salient, it is argued, those joining for the third reason form an increasing proportion of members, their ideological commitment no longer diluted by the more pragmatic members who joined for less explicitly political purposes. Even in the days before these trends got under way, there was already a plausible argument, backed up with evidence, to the effect that party members tend to be more "extreme" in their views than either voters or deputies (May). This was expressed colorfully in the 1930s by an observer of the British Labour party, who claimed that its local constituency organizations were "frequently unrepresentative groups of nonentities dominated by fanatics and cranks and extremists" (quoted in McKenzie, p. 194).

All of this might suggest that European parties are on the road to becoming "head without a body" parties like their American counterparts, that is, parties that have deputies in parliament but hardly any real presence on the ground. But this is, in fact, an unlikely scenario. Despite the unappealing picture sometimes painted of European party members, they are not in most cases quite the fanatical ideologues some accounts would lead one to believe. In all probability, most of them are fairly ordinary sober citizens who join a party for a mixture of motives and whose attachment to certain general political principles is accompanied by a desire to see their party do well in elections. For example, a study of British Labour party activists found that while they saw themselves as further to the left than Labour voters, they deliberately selected Labour candidates whose views were more moderate than their own so as not to damage the party's electoral chances (Bochel and Denver, p. 60). In many parties, activists tend to be deferential toward the party leadership and prepared to go along with whatever it wants or does, provided, as we said earlier, that it remains within the broad parameters of what is acceptable.

Besides, even on the most self-interested calculus, parliamentarians are aware that members have their uses. As we saw earlier in the chapter, members play an important role in campaigning at election times by going from house to house to canvass voters, thereby encouraging party supporters to turn out and vote on polling day. Since it is party that is the main voting cue in Western Europe, candidates must sell themselves as representatives of their party rather than purely on their own merits. Consequently, local party members promoting the cause, street by street and house by house, are far more valuable than a high-powered PR exercise staffed by advertising executives from outside the area. Although television is the main political arena during election campaigns, it is an addition to rather than a replacement for the work done by the local organization. And although this local organization is naturally likely to be most active during an election campaign, it is important that it maintain a presence between elections as well. It has been argued that the West German CDU suffered electorally in the 1970s from having a much weaker local organization than its rival, the SPD; this created a "spiral of silence," for its voice was hardly raised in informal social interactions in many areas. Only when the CDU put this right by expanding its membership to assert an active and vigorous presence on the ground did it regain its traditional dominant position (Noelle-Neumann).

So the future may not be so bleak after all for Western European parties. Despite the "counter-organisational tendencies" Epstein spoke of, there are pressing reasons why organization is still needed. In a subsequent addendum to his 1967 book, Epstein stated explicitly that he did not believe European parties would come to resemble American ones (Epstein, pp. 380-381). Alan Ware, in assessing the future of parties, noted that there are some trends that could weaken them and others that could strengthen them and suggested that the effects of the various forces involved will be different in different countries and for different parties: there will be no convergence toward one "modern" form of party organization (Ware, 1987a, pp. 215-242). In any case, it is safe to assume that Western European parties will continue to be fundamentally different from American ones for as long as they retain control over the selection of their candidates, and there is no prospect of their relinquishing that prerogative.

Elections in Western Europe, then, will continue to center on parties rather than candidates. Electors will continue to vote for parties; seats in parliaments will continue to be divided among parties. The link between votes and seats is forged by electoral systems, and it is to this subject that we now turn.

References

Alexander, Herbert E. (ed.): *Comparative Political Finance*, Cambridge University Press, Cambridge, England, 1989.

Bochel, John, and David Denver: "Candidate Selection in the Labour Party: What the Selectors Seek," *British Journal of Political Science*, vol. 13, no. 1, 1983, pp. 45-69.

Brechon, Pierre, Jacques Derville, and Patrick Lecomte: "RPR Officials: A Report on an Inquiry into the Neo-Gaullist Party Elite," *European Journal of Political Research*, vol. 15, no. 6, 1987, pp. 593-607.

Bruneau, Thomas C., and Alex MacLeod: *Politics in Contemporary Portugal*, Lynne Riener, Boulder, Colo., 1986.

Burnham, Walter Dean: "Foreword," in Martin P. Wattenberg, *The Decline of American Political Parties, 1952-1988*, Harvard University Press, Cambridge, Mass., 1990, pp. ix-xiv.

Byrd, Peter: "Great Britain: Parties in a Changing Party System," in Ware, 1987b, pp. 205–224.

Clark, Peter B., and James Q. Wilson: "Incentive Systems: A Theory of Organisations," *Administrative Science Quarterly*, vol. 6, 1961, pp. 129–166.

Cole, A. M.: "Factionalism, the French Socialist Party and the Fifth Republic: An Explanation of Intra-Party Divisions," *European Journal of Political Research*, vol. 17, no. 1, 1989, pp. 77–94.

Courtois, Stephane, and Denis Peschanski: "From Decline to Marginalisation: The PCF Breaks with French Society," in Waller and Fennema, 1988, pp. 47–68.

Criddle, Byron: "France: Parties in a Presidential System," in Ware, 1987b, pp. 136–157.

Daalder, Hans (ed.): *Party Systems in Denmark, Austria, Switzerland, the Netherlands and Belgium*, Frances Pinter, London, 1987a.

_____: "The Dutch Party System: From Segmentation to Polarisation—and Then?" in Daalder, 1987a, pp. 193–284.

de Esteban, Jorge, and Luis López Guerra: "Electoral Rules and Candidate Selection," in Penniman and Mujal-León, pp. 48–72.

del Castillo, Pilar: "Financing of Spanish Political Parties," in Alexander, pp. 172–199.

Denver, David: "Britain: Centralised Parties with Decentralised Selection," in Gallagher and Marsh, pp. 47–71.

Dewachter, Wilfried: "Changes in a Particratie: The Belgian Party System from 1944 to 1986," in Daalder, 1987a, pp. 285–363.

Duverger, Maurice: *Political Parties*, 3d ed., Methuen, London, 1964.

Epstein, Leon D.: *Political Parties in Western Democracies*, rev. ed., Transaction Books, New Brunswick, N.J., 1980.

Featherstone, Kevin, and Dimitrios K. Katsoudas (eds.): *Political Change in Greece*, Croom Helm, London, 1987.

Gallagher, Michael: "Ireland: The Increasing Role of the Centre," in Gallagher and Marsh, pp. 119–144.

_____ and Michael Marsh (eds.): *Candidate Selection in Comparative Perspective: The Secret Garden of Politics*, Sage, London, 1988.

Gallagher, Tom: "The Portuguese Socialist Party: The Pitfalls of Being First," in Gallagher and Williams, pp. 12–32.

_____ and Allan M. Williams (eds.): *Southern European Socialism: Parties, Elections and the Challenge of Govern-ment*, Manchester University Press, Manchester, 1989.

Gerlich, Peter: "Consociationalism to Competition: The Austrian Party System since 1945," in Daalder, 1987a, pp. 61–106.

Gillespie, Richard: *The Spanish Socialist Party: A History of Factionalism*, Clarendon Press, Oxford, 1989.

_____ and Tom Gallagher: "Democracy and Authority in the Socialist Parties of Southern Europe," in Gallagher and Williams, pp. 163–187.

Hine, David: "Leaders and Followers: Democracy and Manageability in the Social Democratic Parties of Western Europe," in Paterson and Thomas, pp. 261–290.

_____: "Italy: Parties and Party Government under Pressure," in Ware, 1987b, pp. 72–95.

Jacobs, Francis (ed.): *Western European Political Parties: A Comprehensive Guide*, Longman, Harlow, 1989.

Kirchheimer, Otto: "The Transformation of the Western European Party System," in Joseph La Palombara and Myron Weiner (eds.), *Political Parties and Political Development*, Princeton University Press, Princeton, 1966, pp. 177–200.

Luther, K. R.: "Austria's Future and Waldheim's Past: The Significance of the 1986 Elections," *West European Politics*, vol. 10, no. 3, 1987, pp. 376–399.

Mair, Peter: *The Changing Irish Party System*, Frances Pinter, London, 1987.

May, John D.: "Opinion Structure of Political Parties: The Special Law of Curvilinear Disparity," *Political Studies*, vol. 21, no. 2, 1973, pp. 135–151.

McKenzie, Robert: "Power in the Labour Party: The Issue of 'Intra-Party Democracy,'" in Dennis Kavanagh (ed.), *The Politics of the Labour Party*, George Allen and Unwin, London, 1982, pp. 191–201.

Newman, Michael: "Conflict and Cohesion in the British Labour Party and French Communist Party," *West European Politics*, vol. 10, no. 2, 1987, pp. 176–192.

Noelle-Neumann, Elisabeth: *The Spiral of Silence: Public Opinion—Our Social Skin*, University of Chicago Press, Chicago, 1986.

Paltiel, Khayyam Zev: "Campaign Finance: Contrasting Practices and Reforms," in David Butler, Howard R. Penniman, and Austin Ranney (eds.), *Democracy at the Polls: A Comparative Study of Competitive National Elections*, American Enterprise Institute, Washington, 1981, pp. 138–172.

Paterson, William E.: "West Germany: Between Party Apparatus and Basis Democracy," in Ware, 1987b, pp. 158–182.

———— and Alistair H. Thomas (eds.), *The Future of Social Democracy*, Clarendon Press, Oxford, 1986,

Pedersen, Mogens N.: "The Danish 'Working Multiparty System': Breakdown or Adaptation?" in Daalder, 1987a, pp. 1-60.

Penniman, Howard R., and Eusebio M. Mujal-León (eds.): *Spain at the Polls 1977, 1979 and 1982*, Duke University Press, Durham, N.C., 1985.

Pridham, Geoffrey: "Southern European Socialists and the State: Consolidation of Party Rule or Consolidation of Democracy?" in Gallagher and Williams, pp. 132-162.

————: "Southern European Democracies on the Road to Consolidation: A Comparative Assessment of the Role of Political Parties," in Geoffrey Pridham (ed.), *Securing Democracy: Political Parties and Democratic Consolidation in Southern Europe*, Routledge, London and New York, 1990, pp. 1-41.

Ranney, Austin: *Curing the Mischiefs of Faction: Party Reform in America*, University of California Press, Berkeley and London, 1975.

Sjöblom, Gunnar: "Political Change and Political Accountability: A Propositional Inventory of Causes and Effects," in Hans Daalder and Peter Mair (eds.), *Western Europe Party Systems*, Sage, London, 1983, pp. 369-403.

Sully, Melanie Ann: "Austrian Social Democracy," in Paterson and Thomas, pp. 153-171.

Sundberg, Jan: "Exploring the Case of Declining Party Membership in Denmark: A Scandinavian Comparison," *Scandinavian Political Studies*, vol. 10, no. 1, 1987, pp. 17-38.

Tusell Gómez, Javier: "The Democratic Center and Christian Democracy in the Elections of 1977 and 1979," in Penniman and Mujal-León, pp. 88-128.

Urwin, Derek W.: "Norway: Parties between Mass Membership and Consumer-Oriented Professionalism," in Ware, 1987b, pp. 183-204.

Valen, Henry: "Norway: Decentralisation and Group Representation," in Gallagher and Marsh, pp. 210-235.

Von Beyme, Klaus: *Political Parties in Western Democracies*, Gower, Aldershot, 1985.

Waller, Michael, and Meindert Fennema (eds.): *Communist Parties in Western Europe: Decline or Adaptation?* Basil Blackwell, Oxford, 1988.

Ware, Alan: *Citizens, Parties and the State*, Polity Press, Cambridge, England, 1987a.

———— (ed.): *Political Parties: Electoral Change and Structural Response*, Basil Blackwell, Oxford, 1987b.

————: "United States: Disappearing Parties?" in Ware, 1987b, pp. 117-136.

Wertman, Douglas A.: "Italy: Local Involvement, Central Control," in Gallagher and Marsh, pp. 145-168.

CHAPTER 6
ELECTIONS AND ELECTORAL SYSTEMS

Elections have become a central part of the democratic process in all Western European countries. Their significance is both practical and symbolic. Practically, they produce parliaments; they therefore play a large role in determining who becomes part of the political elite. In addition, they have a bearing on the formation of governments, although, given the frequency of coalition governments in Western Europe, their impact in this respect is often indirect (see Chapter 7). They have become the focal point of activity for most European parties.

Elections are also important symbolically, legitimizing a country's political system in the eyes of its citizens. They offer a means of participating in politics at relatively low cost to the individual, in terms of time, money, and mental effort. For most people, indeed, voting in elections is their only active participation in the political process. Elections also give citizens the feeling that they are exercising choices on who should represent them in the national parliament and on who should form the next government, even though the vote of any individual elector is unlikely to have much impact on either matter.

While elections in each Western European country consist of citizens casting votes for candidates and/or political parties, there is considerable variation in the precise set of electoral laws that determines how the votes that are cast are transformed into seats in the legislature in each country. In this chapter, we consider the variations in electoral systems in some detail, since some of the major differences in electoral law have a significant bearing on some of the major differences between party politics in different European countries. Before we consider the nitty-gritty of electoral laws, however, we look at a number of general matters that relate to all electoral systems. These concern the nature of the electorate and the timing of elections.

ELECTIONS IN WESTERN EUROPE

Who Votes?

Elections in all Western European states are now held under a universal adult franchise. In most countries, universal male suffrage had been won by the time of the First World War and female suffrage by the second, although women did not receive the vote until immediately after the Second World War in Belgium, France, Greece, and Italy and not until the 1970s in Portugal, Spain, and Switzerland. Changing legal definitions of adulthood have brought down the voting age in many countries, characteristically from 21 to 18, although in some countries it remains at 20. Most countries restrict voting rights to their own citizens, but the United Kingdom and Ireland allow each other's resident citizens to vote in their general elections. Certain categories of citizens are disenfranchised in many countries, including people serving prison sentences and those confined to mental institutions (for details, see Crewe, pp. 220–222; Mackie and Rose, p. 509). Generally speaking, the qualifications needed to be an election candidate are the same as those for being a voter.

The practice in European countries is that the task of compiling the electoral register—the list of eligible voters—is the responsibility of the state. This means that the register is far more accurate than in the U.S.A., for example, where it is up to individuals to register themselves as voters. Also, the actual electoral turnout of voters tends to be higher in Europe than in the U.S.A., on the average between 70 and 85 percent for most countries. The exceptions are Switzerland, where turnout has fallen steadily since the war to below 50 percent, and, at the other end of the scale, Italy plus some countries where voting is or has been compulsory (Belgium, the Netherlands, Luxembourg, and Austria), in all of which turnout approaches or even exceeds 90 percent.

When Do People Vote?

The timing of parliamentary elections is usually at the discretion of the government of the day, with the head of state (the monarch or the president) involved only to the extent of giving formal consent (see Table 7.1 for full details). The government—sometimes the prime minister alone has this power—is typically free to call an election at whatever moment it believes will give it maximum partisan advantage. One exception is France, where it is the president who has the right to call parliamentary elections at any time, even against the wishes of the government, which may be of a different political complexion. This happened when, immediately after being reelected in 1988, the Socialist President Mitterrand dissolved the parliament without the approval of the right-wing government. French presidential elections are held at fixed seven-year intervals. Other exceptions to the general rule are Norway and Switzerland, where parliaments have a fixed life span of four years. In other countries, the law or constitution prescribes a maximum period between elections, but not a minimum. The period stipulated is four years in most Western European countries and five years in the rest (see Table 7.1).

Parliamentary elections are merely one of a number of opportunities people have to vote in Western Europe. In all countries there are also elections for local councils (these are quite important in Scandinavia), and in several there are regional or provincial elections (for example, in France, Germany, Italy, and Spain). The twelve member states of the European Community (EC) hold elections to choose members of the European Parliament; these elections, which we discuss in more detail in Chapter 10, take place across the Community every five years. In a few countries, as we noted in Chapter 1, the president is directly elected by the people: besides France, these include Austria, Finland, Iceland, Ireland, and Portugal.

In addition, the referendum is increasingly used in a number of European countries. Referendums are far more frequent in Switzerland than anywhere else— between 1978 and 1986 there were nearly as many referendums in Switzerland (58 of them) as in the rest of the world combined (60 of them). It has been suggested that this leads to "voter fatigue" among the Swiss, which would account for both the low turnout at parliamentary elections and the low referendum turnout, just 37 percent in the 1978–1986 period (Austen et al., p. 139). In Italy, since the mid-1970s the people have had, on the average, about one issue a year put before them; here, too, referendum turnout has steadily declined, as voters apparently lose enthusiasm for repeated visits to the polls. In all other countries, referendums are infrequent, fewer than one every two years, and in several countries (Germany and the Netherlands, among others), none has been held since the war. The absence of the referendum from German postwar politics, which is partly due to the way referendums were discredited in the eyes of many Germans by their use by Adolf Hitler in the 1930s to confer a purported legitimacy on his dictatorship, meant that even the reunification of Germany in 1990 took place without the people being consulted directly. The holding of a referendum is typically at the discretion of parliament, except in Switzerland and Italy, where a sufficient number of citizens may initiate one, and in France, where in practice the president plays the decisive role. This does not mean, however, that referendums are mere devices used by ruling parties to get public approval for their policies. This was demonstrated dramatically in 1969 when President de Gaulle resigned after the French electorate defeated a proposed amendment to the constitution to which he had tied his future in politics. Moreover, in Ireland the ruling Fianna Fáil party twice saw its proposal to change the electoral system rejected by the people. (On referendums, see Lijphart, 1984a, pp. 201–206; Lane and Ersson, pp. 217–220; Smith, pp. 145–150.)

Where referendums are held, they tend to be linked to constitutional issues. In Denmark, Ireland, and Switzerland, a constitutional amendment requires the consent of the people, expressed in a referendum, and in France and Italy such referendums are optional. Certain other issues have come to be seen in several countries as appropriate referendum issues—these include major and fundamental changes to the nation's place in the world, moral questions, and issues that cut across party lines. In the first category is membership in the European Community; this issue precipitated referendums in Britain, Denmark (twice), Ireland (twice), and Norway (where the proposal to join the EC was defeated in 1972). Questions on divorce and abortion have been put to a referendum in both Ireland and Italy;

the future of the monarchy in Belgium, Greece, and Italy; nuclear power in Austria, Italy, and Sweden.

TYPES OF ELECTORAL SYSTEMS

In the rest of this chapter we shall be concentrating on parliamentary elections, the most important political contests in every Western European country except France. In particular, we will concentrate on electoral systems, the mechanisms that turn the votes cast by people on election day into seats to be occupied by deputies in the parliament. The electoral system is what converts the choices of the voters into a legislature.

A wide variety of electoral systems is in use across Western Europe, and there is an equally wide selection of literature describing and tracing the history of these systems (see Carstairs; Hand et al.; Lakeman; Mackie and Rose). This variety reflects, in part, the different weights attached to different criteria in different countries. It also reflects the fact that the electoral law a country adopts is usually determined by the political elite of the day, some of whose motivations may be partisan, as we observed in an earlier chapter. In addition, electoral reformers have devised a plethora of systems and formulas, some of which have captured the imagination of politicians in various countries at various times. Having said this, we should note that it is not true that ruling parties constantly tinker with electoral systems for their own advantage; there have been very few major changes in electoral systems in Western Europe since 1945, and only in France and Greece can the electoral system be seen as a political football (Cole and Campbell, 1989; Featherstone, pp. 189, 200).

For all this diversity, there are several systematic patterns in the profusion of electoral systems to be found in Western Europe. One vital distinction is between *proportional representation* (PR) systems, on the one hand, and *plurality* or *majority* systems, on the other. The former put more stress on the concept of proportionality, the numerical accuracy with which the votes cast for parties are translated into seats won in parliament. Under a PR system, if a party receives, say, 25 percent of the votes, it can expect to win close to 25 percent of the seats. If every party participating in an election was guaranteed exactly the same share of seats as it won of the votes, we would describe that system as perfectly proportional, although this would not necessarily mean that the system was "perfect" in an evaluative sense. In practice, no electoral system can guarantee perfect proportionality, but PR systems make a greater effort to get somewhere close to it. An overview of Western European electoral systems in these terms is shown in Table 6.1.

Plurality and PR electoral systems are not polar opposites in the methods they use to allocate seats. After all, even plurality systems are "proportional" in their own way, in that they award the seat(s) within each constituency to the party with the largest number of votes. The real opposite of proportional representation would be a "perverse" system that awarded all the seats to the party with the fewest votes. All the electoral systems currently in use differ fundamentally from such a system and so could be said to have at least something in common with each other. Even so, PR and plurality systems do have significant differences, mainly in regard to the representation of minorities, so it does make sense to distinguish between them.

TABLE 6.1
Electoral Systems in Western Europe, 1991

	Basic Category	Members of Lower House	Number of Constituencies (Districts)	Significant Changes since 1945*
Austria	PR (list)	183	9†	None
Belgium	PR (list)	212	30†	None
Denmark	PR (list)	175	18†	Change of formula from DH to MSL, 1953
Finland	PR (list)	200	15	None
France	Non-PR (2-ballot)	555	555	Many (see p. 152)
Germany	PR (list)‡	656	329†	Minor changes in 1953 and 1956, 1984 and 1990
Greece	PR (list)	300	56†	Many minor changes; abolition of discriminatory thresholds before June 1989 election
Iceland	PR (list)	63	9†	Minor change in 1987
Ireland	PR (STV)	166	41	None
Italy	PR (list)	630	32†	None since 1956
Luxembourg	PR (list)	60	4	None
Malta	PR (STV)	65	13	Winners guaranteed majority since 1987
Netherlands	PR (list)	150	1	None
Norway	PR (list)	165	20†	Change of formula from DH to MSL, 1953; addition of 8 national seats before 1989 election
Portugal	PR (list)	246	20	First democratic election in 1975
Spain	PR (list)	350	52	First democratic postwar election in 1977
Sweden	PR (list)	349	29†	Change of formula from DH to MSL, 1952; introduction of higher-tier seats, 1970
Switzerland	PR (list)	200	26	None
United Kingdom	Non-PR (plurality)	650	650	None

*Abbreviations for electoral formulas: DH—d'Hondt; MSL—modified Sainte-Laguë; STV—single transferable vote.
†Indicates that the country has "complex districting," i.e., higher-tier constituencies to iron out discrepancies arising from lower-level constituencies.
‡328 members are elected from single-member constituencies, while the remaining 328 seats are filled from lists and are awarded so as to make the overall result proportional.
Source: Mackie and Rose.

PLURALITY SYSTEMS

Throughout the nineteenth century, elections in most countries were held under plurality systems, but the shortcomings of these led almost all countries to adopt some form of PR in the twentieth century. At the moment, only two Western European countries do not use an electoral system based on PR: these are the United Kingdom and France.

The electoral system used in the U.K. is the least complicated of all systems. It is the same as that employed for most elections in the U.S.A. and Canada. The country is divided into 650 districts, called "constituencies," each of which returns one Member of Parliament (MP) to the House of Commons. Within each constituency, the candidate with the most votes, whether or not this is a majority over all others combined, wins the seat. The system is best named the single-member plurality (SMP) system, though it is often called "first past the post," in a rather forced analogy with horse racing, or simply "the British system." Voters, on entering the polling station, are given a ballot paper listing all the candidates, and they write an "X" next to the name of the candidate they wish to vote for. The British system predates mass literacy and the secret ballot—the "X" was originally the voter's mark. An example of the operation of the system in an English constituency in the 1987 election is given below.

Colne Valley Constituency, United Kingdom General Election of 1987

	Votes
G. Riddick (Conservative)	20,457
N. Priestley (Liberal)	18,780
J. Harman (Labour)	16,353
M. Mullany (Green)	614

Riddick, having won more votes than any other candidate, was elected.

Source: Wood, p. 83.

This system has the merit of simplicity, both for voters and for those who count the votes. It is also defended on the ground that as Riddick is the only representative for the constituency, he is solely responsible for its interests. This, it is claimed, helps to forge a bond between the MP and the constituents that would be lost if several MPs shared responsibility for the same constituency.

But the plurality system has its critics (many of their arguments can be found in Finer and in Lakeman). Three of the main points made against it are illustrated by the Colne Valley result. Riddick was elected despite winning only about 36 percent of the total votes; 64 percent of the voters are not represented by a candidate of their favored party. It is probable that many Labour voters would have preferred the election of the Liberal candidate to the actual outcome, and so in a straight fight between the Conservative and the Liberal, the latter would have won. Therefore, the British system is criticized for not necessarily producing the MP who would be most representative of the voters' wishes and, worse, for producing results that are in some sense arbitrarily determined by the nomination of "vote-splitting" losing candidates.

In addition, the Colne Valley contest presented Labour voters in particular with a tactical choice: Should they vote for the Labour candidate, or should they vote for the Liberal in order to keep the Conservative out? The second criticism, then, is that the plurality system compels voters to think, and perhaps to vote, tactically. If they vote sincerely, in accordance with their true wishes, then this might help in the election of the candidate they like least. While no electoral system is completely "strategy-proof," the plurality system is almost guaranteed to force at least some voters to think strategically if there are more than two serious candidates.

Third, if the pattern of the Colne Valley result, with **64** percent of the votes wasted on losing candidates, were repeated over the entire country, the House of Commons could be very unrepresentative of public opinion. In practice, the lack of "fairness" in individual constituencies tends to even itself out to some extent across the country. Consequently, between 1945 and the 1970s, when nearly all the votes were won by the two main parties, Labour and the Conservatives, the national outcome in terms of seats was not grossly unrepresentative. But when a third party (the Liberals in 1974 and 1979, the alliance between the Liberal and the Social Democratic party in 1983 and 1987) began winning significant support, the national outcome fell much further short of perfect proportionality, with the third party the main victim. This is illustrated by the result of the 1987 election (see Table 6.2).

In this election, what appeared to be a Conservative landslide in the parliament was in fact "manufactured" by the electoral system, since nearly three out of every five voters voted against the Conservatives. Another dramatic example of the disproportionality of the plurality electoral method can be seen in the results of the 1989 European Parliament elections. Outside observers could be forgiven for not knowing that the Green party won a higher share of the votes in Britain (15 percent) than in any other European country. Although the Greens won seats in seven of the other EC countries, they won no seats at all in Britain.

One modification suggested by some British electoral reformers is the introduction of "preferential" voting rather than "X" voting. Voters would rank the candidates in order of preference by placing a number ("1," "2," etc.) next to each name. The counting process would no longer finish with the counting of the first preferences; instead, if no candidate had a majority, the lowest-placed candidate would be eliminated and his or her votes transferred to the other candidates, in accordance with the second preferences marked on them. So, in Colne Valley, the Green party candidate, and then the Labour candidate, would be eliminated. Assuming that a majority of Labour voters gave their second preference to the Liberal candidate rather than to the Conservative, the Liberal would probably be carried above the Conservative and would therefore win the seat. This electoral system is known as the Alternative Vote, or the single transferable vote in single-member constituencies. It is a *majority* system, as opposed to the British and

TABLE 6.2

Votes and Seats in the United Kingdom General Election of 1987

	% of Votes	% of Seats
Conservative	42.3	57.8
Labour	30.8	35.2
Liberal-SDP alliance	22.6	3.4
Others	4.3	3.5
Total	100.0	100.0

Source: Mackie and Rose, pp. 452–455

French *plurality* systems, since the counting process continues until one candidate has a majority (50 percent plus 1) over all other remaining candidates.

No European country uses the Alternative Vote (though it is employed in Australian elections), but a rather similar system is used in France. There, as in Britain, deputies are returned from single-member constituencies, but there is provision for two rounds of voting, on successive Sundays. If a candidate wins a *majority* of votes in the first round, he or she is elected. Otherwise, it is followed by the second round of voting—from which candidates who received the votes of fewer than 12.5 percent of those registered to vote in the first round are excluded. The candidate with the most votes (a simple *plurality*) in the second round wins the seat, even if he or she fails to achieve an overall majority. For this reason the French system is ultimately a plurality rather than a majority system, since a majority of votes, though of course sufficient, is not always necessary for election. (Presidential elections are held under the same system, except that only the top two candidates from the first round are allowed to proceed to the second.)

The French system has some advantages over the British, as it gives supporters of losing first-round candidates a chance to switch their second-round vote to one of the serious contenders. The second-ballot system could also be used by the two main blocs as quasi-primaries, but in practice only the left uses it this way. The two main left-wing parties, the Socialists and the Communists, both nominate a candidate in every constituency for the first ballot, and the one with fewer votes then stands aside for the stronger on the second ballot. Over the years this has increasingly benefited the Socialists more than the Communists; the latter's first-ballot votes have steadily fallen, to the extent that many more Communist candidates stand aside for Socialists than vice versa, and, in addition, Communist voters switch to Socialist candidates on the second ballot more solidly than Socialist voters switch to Communist candidates. The established right-wing parties, the RPR and the UDF, in contrast, generally agree on a single right-wing candidate in each constituency before the first round, sharing the constituencies out between them. Thus, in 1988 there was just one candidate from the established right on the first ballot in 536 of the 555 mainland French constituencies (Cole and Campbell, 1989, p. 161). But even if it does have the potential to give a slightly greater choice to the voters, the French system, like the British, does not overcome the problem of disproportional overall results. In 1968, for example, the Gaullists (now the RPR) won only 44 percent of the votes but 60 percent of the seats, while in 1981 the Socialists won 56 percent of the seats with just 38 percent of the votes. Like the British system, the French two-ballot system benefits the largest party and penalizes smaller ones.

In France, more than in any other country, the electoral system has been manipulated by ruling parties for their own benefit (for details, see Cole and Campbell, 1989). The second-ballot system was used for most of the period between 1831 and 1939, though other systems were often tried for short periods. After the Second World War, a PR system was briefly used, but in the early 1950s a new system was introduced, with the clear aim of discriminating against the Communist party. The second ballot was brought back under de Gaulle in the late 1950s. The Socialists replaced it with PR for the 1986 election, partly to minimize their electoral losses, but the incoming right-wing administration promptly reintroduced the second ballot, under which the 1988 election was held.

PROPORTIONAL REPRESENTATION

Discontent with the anomalies produced by plurality or majority systems led to discussion of electoral reform throughout Europe in the second half of the nineteenth century. By the time the First World War was over, there was a consensus over most of the continent in favor of PR, and most countries based their electoral systems on it. The key element in any PR electoral system is the *multimember constituency*. Seats are allocated to parties within each constituency in broad proportion to the votes each receives. PR systems cannot be based on single-member constituencies, because a single seat cannot be divided up proportionately, no matter what method is used to allocate it. As a general rule, indeed, the larger the district magnitude (i.e., the number of members returned from each constituency), the more proportional the national election result is likely to be. This, it should be stressed, applies only when a PR formula is used. If a plurality or majority formula is employed in multimember constituencies, as when American public representatives are elected from "at-large" districts, the result is highly disproportional, being even less considerate to minorities than a series of single-seat constituencies.

There are important variations between PR systems, but they can be categorized basically into list systems, on the one hand, and the single transferable vote (STV), on the other. STV systems tend to be confined to the English-speaking world, and systems based on lists are far more common in Europe as a whole.

BOX 6.1
Electoral Systems

FRANCE
France does not use proportional representation to elect deputies to the National Assembly. Metropolitan France is divided into 555 single-member constituencies (the overseas territories and departments return an additional 22 deputies to Paris). Within each constituency there can be two rounds of voting on successive Sundays. A candidate winning an overall majority in the first round is elected as the deputy for the constituency. In constituencies where no candidate wins a first-round majority, the second round takes place a week later; this time, the candidate with the most votes, whether or not this amounts to a majority, wins the seat.

GERMANY
The German electoral system is unique, embodying two routes to parliament, the Bundestag. When voters enter the polling booth, they are faced with two ballot papers. One gives them a vote in the election of a member of parliament (MdB) for the local single-member constituency; half of the 656 members of parliament are elected from single-member constituencies in exactly the same way as in the United Kingdom. The second ballot paper enables them to cast a list vote; the other half of the parliament is elected from party lists. The overall allocation of seats in the Bundestag is decided by these list votes. Each party is awarded as many list seats as it needs to ensure that its total number of seats (constituency seats and list seats combined) is proportional to the share of list votes it received. However, parties receiving fewer than 5 percent of the list votes do not receive any list seats, except in the improbable event that they have won three constituency seats. This requirement was eased slightly for just one election, the first postwar all-German elections in December 1990, which employed separate 5 percent thresholds for the areas covered by the two previous states, West Germany and East Germany, thereby making it

(Continued on next page)

easier for small parties to gain representation than if it had been necessary to attain 5 percent of the total number of national list votes. If a party wins more constituency seats within any Land (province) than it is entitled to on the basis of its list votes, it is allowed to keep these extra seats, and the size of the Bundestag is expanded accordingly. In the December 1990 election there were six of these extra seats (known as Überhangmandate), and the Bundestag therefore contained 662 members.

ITALY

Italy has a PR system with two tiers of seat allocation. At the lower tier, the country is divided into 32 constituencies based on groups of the 95 Italian provinces. Within each constituency, seats are awarded to parties according to a method based on a variant of the largest remainders method. This procedure leaves some of the 630 seats in the Chamber of Deputies unallocated to parties, and it also leaves some parties with votes that they have not "used up" to earn seats. Consequently, each party's unused votes are pooled at the second, higher, tier, a national-level constituency where the seats not allocated in the local constituencies are awarded to parties in proportion to the size of their pool of unused votes. The Italian electoral system is a preferential form of PR—that is, voters for a party are able to express preferences for specific candidates on the party's list. Voters in the southern part of Italy and on the islands (Sicily and Sardinia) are much more likely to use this opportunity than are those in the northern part of the country.

NETHERLANDS

The Tweede Kamer (Second Chamber) contains 150 deputies, and when it comes to awarding seats to parties, the whole country is treated as one 150-member constituency. Each party presents a list of candidates, and the parties receive seats in proportion to the votes they receive nationally; the seat allocation formula used is the d'Hondt highest averages method. Parties receiving fewer than two-thirds of 1 percent of the total votes cast do not qualify for any seats—this is the lowest threshold, as a share of the national vote, imposed by any country in Western Europe.

Voters can cast a preference vote for a candidate on a party list, but the great majority of those who use this opportunity vote for the candidate placed at the head of the list, and in practice the casting of preference votes in the Netherlands has very little impact on the composition of the parliament.

SPAIN

The Congress of Deputies is elected from 52 constituencies, each of which, on the average, returns only 7 deputies, a relatively small figure for a PR electoral system. Within each constituency, the d'Hondt highest averages formula is employed; this tends to favor the large parties rather than the small ones. There is no higher-tier allocation to compensate parties for any under-representation in the constituencies. Voters have no choice of candidate; they simply cast a vote for one of the party lists that are offered.

SWEDEN

The Riksdag has 349 members and is elected by proportional representation based on two tiers. The lower tier consists of 28 constituencies covering the country, which between them return 310 deputies. The remaining 39 seats are held back for allocation at the second tier—they are distributed among the parties in such a way as to ensure that the total number of seats received by each party comes as close to its proportional share as possible. However, a threshold discriminates against small parties: those receiving fewer than 4 percent of the national votes are not awarded any of the 39 higher-tier seats. There is provision for voters to indicate a preference for an individual candidate on a party list, but in practice the initial ranking order of the candidates on each party's list is almost immune to alteration by the voters.

UNITED KINGDOM

Britain employs the single-member plurality system. The country is divided into 650 constituencies, each returning one Member of Parliament to the House of Commons. Within each constituency, the candidate winning the most votes, whether or not this amounts to a majority, becomes the MP.

List Systems

The basic principle of a list system is that each party presents a list of candidates in each constituency. Each list usually contains as many candidates as there are seats to be filled in the constituency. The seats are then shared out among the parties in proportion to the votes they win, in accordance with a predetermined formula. Although PR is scarcely used at any level of elections in the U.S.A., Americans were the first to think about ways of achieving proportional representation. They were interested not in the proportional allocation of seats to parties in accordance with the votes they receive but in the proportional allocation to states of seats in the House of Representatives in accordance with the population of each state. Most of the PR methods used in Western Europe today were either used or discussed in the U.S.A. long before Europeans thought of them.

List systems differ from one another in a number of respects. These include the formulas used to award seats to parties within each constituency; the matter of whether or not there is a second, higher tier at which seats are awarded to override any imbalances that may arise at the constituency level; the degree of choice, if any, given to voters to express a preference for a particular candidate (or particular candidates) on the party list; and the existence of other special features like thresholds. The picture is summarized in Table 6.3 on the following page.

Three different methods are used to decide how seats are shared out among parties. These are known as largest remainders, highest averages using the d'Hondt method, and highest averages using the modified Sainte-Laguë method. In the U.S.A., largest remainders is known as the Hamilton method and d'Hondt as the Jefferson method, used for apportioning seats in the House of Representatives from 1790 to 1830. The "pure" Sainte-Laguë method is known in the U.S.A. as the Webster method, used on seven occasions from 1840 to 1930 to apportion House seats; the modified version used in some Scandinavian countries has the effect of making it more difficult for small parties to win seats. We shall not elaborate the differences between these formulas in any detail (the mechanics are explained in Carstairs; Mackie and Rose), because these differences are less important than the similarities between the methods. However, it should be noted that of these three methods, largest remainders is the most generous in its treatment of small parties, while modified Sainte-Laguë tilts the balance slightly toward larger parties, and the d'Hondt method favors large parties even more. All variants of PR are essentially similar in that they set out to award seats "fairly" to each party according to how many votes it won, while being based on slightly different ideas as to exactly what is meant by the concept of "fairness" (Gallagher, 1991). They share a common attachment to the idea of proportionality, and in this they differ fundamentally from the plurality method, where other criteria take priority.

The seat allocation method is just one factor determining how proportional the distribution of seats will be in relation to the way votes were cast. A second and often more important factor is district magnitude. If the average district magnitude is small, an election outcome is unlikely to be highly proportional, no matter what allocation formula is used. When France introduced PR for the 1986 election, the d'Hondt formula was used in constituencies that returned only six deputies on the average. The resultant bias in favor of the large parties was so pronounced that the

TABLE 6.3
Features of Western European Electoral Systems, 1991

	Constituency-Level Seat Allocation Formula*	Higher-Tier Seat Allocation? (Formula)	Threshold for Participation in Higher-Tier Seat Allocation?	Choice of Candidate within Party?
PR list systems:				
Austria	LR	Yes (DH)	1 constituency seat	Yes, but ineffective
Belgium	LR	Yes (DH)	No	Yes, but ineffective
Denmark	MSL	Yes (LR)	2% of votes nationally needed for parliamentary representation	Yes
Finland	DH	No	—	Yes
Germany	Plurality	Yes (LR)	5% of votes or 3 constituency seats	No
Greece	LR	Yes (LR)	1% of votes	Yes
Iceland	LR	Yes (DH)	5% of votes nationally	Yes, but ineffective
Italy	LR	Yes (LR)	No	Yes
Luxembourg	DH	No	—	Yes
Netherlands	DH	No†	0.67% of votes nationally needed to qualify for seats	Yes, but ineffective
Norway	MSL	Yes (MSL)	4% of votes nationally	Yes, but ineffective
Portugal	DH	No	—	No
Spain	DH	No	—	No
Sweden	MSL	Yes (MSL)	4% of votes nationally or 12% in one constituency needed for parliamentary representation	Yes, but ineffective
Switzerland	DH	No	—	Yes
Other PR systems:				
Ireland	STV	No	—	Yes
Malta	STV	Yes ‡	See ‡	Yes
Non-PR systems:				
France	2-ballot	No	—	No
United Kingdom	Plurality	No	—	No

*Formulas: DH—d'Hondt; LR—largest remainders; MSL—modified Sainte-Laguë; STV—single transferable vote.
†There is only one (national) constituency.
‡In Malta, a party winning an overall majority of first-preference votes is awarded extra seats to give it a bare overall majority of seats, if it has not won an overall majority from the constituencies. This is the only situation in which there is any higher-tier allocation.

system has been described as "one of disproportional representation" (Cole and Campbell, 1989, p. 135). In certain other Western European countries, too, particularly Spain, this is a problem: Spain employs relatively small constituencies (district magnitude averages seven seats), and election results are liable to deviate as much from perfect proportionality as do those in countries using the British plurality system.

One way of overcoming the problem is to use larger constituencies, averaging around twelve seats or more, as in Finland, Portugal, and Luxembourg. This is sometimes criticized on the grounds that the constituencies are made so large that voters might feel remote from their deputies. Another method is to have a second level of allocation at which disproportionalities arising at the constituency level can be ironed out. In some countries, a certain proportion of seats is set aside at the start for this purpose: about 20 percent in Denmark, 20 percent in Iceland, 5 percent in Norway, 11 percent in Sweden, and 50 percent in Germany. These "higher-tier" seats are then awarded to the parties in the appropriate numbers to compensate them for any shortfall in the seats they won in the constituencies and thereby bring the overall distribution of seats as close to perfect proportionality as possible. In other countries (Austria, Belgium, Greece, Italy), the number of higher-tier seats is not fixed in advance, but the effect is just the same. What happens here is that each party's "wasted" votes from the constituencies—that is, the votes it has not used to earn seats—are pooled on a national or regional basis, and a distribution of the unallocated seats takes place in accordance with each party's unused vote totals. This ensures that very few of a party's votes are wasted.

The high number of national-level seats in Germany is needed because the formula used to allocate constituency seats is not a PR one at all: the country is divided into 328 single-member constituencies, where the seat is given to the candidate with the most votes, just as in Britain. A curious and unique feature of this system is that each voter has two votes, one for the single-member constituency and a "second vote" for the national seats. The sharing out of the national seats is then carried out in such a way as to ensure that each party's *total* number of seats (constituency seats plus national seats) is proportional to its share of the second votes. This does not make the German system a "mixed" system, as it is sometimes described; it is, of course, still a PR system. The "second vote" is perhaps an unnecessary complication and could potentially be manipulated by a majority coalition of parties so that the coalition gains a grossly disproportional majority of seats (Roberts, p. 218).

Even PR electoral systems, despite their name, sometimes have features that give an inbuilt advantage to larger parties. This is due either to self-interest on the part of the larger parties or to concern that perfect proportionality could lead to a proliferation of small parties in parliament and thus to difficulty in forming a stable government, or it may be due to a combination of both. To this end, it is common for electoral systems to employ a *threshold* that a party must overcome before it qualifies for seats. The best-known is the German system, which allows only those parties that have won at least 5 percent of the second votes to share in the national list allocation. At the behest of the constitutional court, whose role we discussed in Chapter 1, this provision had to be replaced in 1990 for the first postwar all-German elections by a threshold that allowed parliamentary representation to parties that won 5 percent of the votes cast in the area covered by the former East German state, a significantly easier hurdle to overcome than 5 percent of the national votes. (A party can also qualify by winning three constituency seats, but after 1957 no party other than the big two, the CDU/CSU and the SPD, won even one constituency seat in a West German election.) In Sweden, parties must win 4 percent of the national vote to qualify for a share of the national allocation. In Austria, the threshold is low: a party need win only at least one constituency seat somewhere to be awarded its share of higher-tier seats—not too onerous a requirement, since there are 20 seats at stake in the average constituency. The lowest barrier is in the Netherlands, where a party needs to reach a national vote threshold of a mere 0.67 percent to qualify for seats. It rarely happens that the threshold debars a Dutch party from receiving seats.

Thresholds are usually employed to limit the degree of proportionality achieved and could, if set too high, significantly distort the election outcome. This is precisely what has happened in Greece in most postwar elections. In the 1981 and 1985 elections, for example, participation in the higher-tier seat allocation was restricted to parties that had won at least 17 percent of the national vote. The consequence was to give a large benefit to big parties and to discriminate against smaller ones, and the outcome was thus liable to be as disproportional as that of a British election. In 1985, the largest party, PASOK, won 53.7 percent of the seats with 45.8 percent of the votes, while the minor parties, with 13.4 percent of the votes between them, won only 4.3 percent of the seats. The system was officially, and flatteringly, termed "reinforced PR" but would be more accurately called "loaded PR"—indeed, it is doubtful whether it should be considered a PR system at all. These discriminatory features were dropped before the first election of 1989, and the ensuing three elections (two in 1989 and one in 1990) were held under a more conventional PR system, though the New Democracy government elected in April 1990 soon announced plans to reinstate the high threshold.

Which Candidates Get the Seats under List Systems?

So far, we have been discussing the ways in which the seats are divided up among the parties. Once this has been decided, a second question arises: Which candidates on the party's list are awarded the seats that the party has won? This is dealt with in different ways. In some countries, the ranking order of candidates drawn up by the party organization is a fixed order of priority that the voters cannot alter. In others, in contrast, there is no default order—the voters alone decide which candidates are elected. In others again, the party's ranking stands as a default ordering but can be overturned if enough voters combine against it. Systems in the first category, where the party organization decides, are termed *nonpreferential*; those in the second, where the voters decide for themselves, are termed *preferential*. Those in the third category, where the party organization draws up an ordering that the voters can amend, are nominally preferential but are often, in practice, closer to being nonpreferential, since it may be hard for voters' preferences to overturn the ordering decided on by the party organization. The systems in operation are listed in Table 6.3 (for a more detailed analysis, see Marsh and also Katz).

There are few examples of completely nonpreferential PR list systems. One is that of France in the 1986 election, when the Socialist government brought in a short-lived PR system to replace the usual two-round plurality system already discussed. As we have mentioned, the country was divided up into fairly small constituencies, within which seats were allocated by the d'Hondt highest averages formula. If a party won, say, two seats within a given constituency, those seats went to the top two names on its list. The order of candidates' names on the list was decided by the parties, and voters could not alter it. Other countries where voters cannot express any degree of choice regarding their party's candidates are Germany, Portugal, and Spain.

Among systems in the second category, that is, the genuinely preferential systems, the most fully studied is that of Italy. Here, voters are allowed a certain number of preference votes (usually three, but four in larger constituencies), which they can cast for candidates on their party's list. They can, if they want, simply cast a "list vote," that is a vote for the list without expressing any candidate preferences. If the party wins, say, five seats in a constituency, these go to the five candidates who won the most preference votes; the "list votes" do not affect the outcome between candidates. Within the Christian Democrats in particular, various factions and affiliated interest groups all try to motivate voters to cast preference votes for their particular candidates. In Finland, too, party voters decide which candidates win the seats; but the Finnish system differs from Italy's in that there is no "list vote"; voters are obliged to express a preference for one specific candidate. In Switzerland and Luxembourg, voters express as many preferences as there are seats in the constituency. They can cast a "list vote" for a party, which has the effect of giving one preference vote to each of the party's candidates, or they can cumulate two preference votes on one candidate. They can give their preferences to candidates on more than one party's list, an option known as *panachage* which is confined to these two countries. The Danish system is highly complex, varying from party to party and between and even within constituencies, as the parties can choose how to present their lists; some forms give considerable choice to the voters, whereas others restrict it.

Turning to the third category, we find some systems that in theory offer the opportunity for preferential voting for candidates but that in practice are such that voters' preferences rarely overturn the ordering set by the parties. An example is the system used in Belgium: voters may cast either one preference vote for a candidate on the list or a "list vote," which is taken as an endorsement of the order in which the candidates appear on the list. The method of allocating a party's seats to its candidates means that concerted action on the part of voters is required to secure the election of a candidate not placed by the party in one of the favored positions, and this rarely happens. Although about half of Belgian voters cast personal rather than list votes, only a tiny proportion of seats (0.6 percent of the total since 1919) go to candidates who would not have been elected had the Belgian electoral system included no provision for preferential voting (De Winter, p. 21). The systems in Austria, the Netherlands, Norway, and Sweden differ from the Belgian one in some of the details, but their essential feature is the same: the party supplies a default order of candidates, and such a high degree of concerted action by voters is needed to overturn it that the party's rank ordering almost always stands. In the Netherlands, even this limited opportunity is resented by the parties, which sometimes demand pledges from their candidates that if they are elected "out of order," owing to preference votes, at the expense of a candidate higher on the list, they will resign their seat in favor of the candidate whom the party organization had placed higher on the list.

The Single Transferable Vote (STV)

The STV electoral system was devised in Britain in the middle of the nineteenth century, and enthusiasm for it has been largely confined to English-speaking countries. It is used to elect the parliaments of Ireland and Malta, while elections to provincial assemblies in Northern Ireland have also employed it since 1972. In Ireland, the largest party, Fianna Fáil, has twice (in 1959 and 1968) attempted to have the system replaced by the British plurality system, mainly because it would fare better under the latter, but on each occasion the electorate rejected the proposed change in a referendum. Like list systems, STV aims to give proportional representation to the shades of opinion within the constituency. Unlike them, it does not presuppose that those opinions are organized in terms of parties.

Voters cast a vote by ranking as many as they wish of the candidates, regardless of party, in order of their preference; they place a "1" next to the name of their favored candidate, a "2" next to the name of their second favorite, and so on. The counting of votes revolves around the Droop quota. This is calculated as the smallest integer greater than $[v/(s+1)]$, where v is the number of valid votes and s the number of seats in the constituency. The Droop quota is therefore one more than a quarter of the votes in a three-seat constituency, one more than a fifth in a four-seater, and so on. Any candidate who achieves the Droop quota is certain of election and does not need votes over and above this number, which are surplus to requirements.

Any candidate whose total of first-preference votes equals or exceeds the Droop quota is declared elected. Unless it should happen that sufficient candidates are elected at this stage, the count then proceeds by distributing the surplus votes of the elected candidate(s), that is, the votes they possess over and above the quota. These votes are transferred to the other candidates, in proportion to the next preferences marked for them. If no candidate has a surplus, the candidate with the fewest votes is eliminated, and his or her votes are transferred to the other candidates, again in accordance with the next preferences marked. This process continues until all the seats have been filled.

What are the pros and cons of STV when compared with other PR systems? Its advocates make several points. First, it gives voters the opportunity to convey a lot of information about their preferences; they may rank all the candidates in order of choice, whereas under almost every other system they are limited to expressing a "Yes" verdict on one (or a few) and "No" on the rest. Second, when ranking candidates, voters are not constrained by party lines. Voters vote for *candidates*, not for parties, and STV works perfectly well—some say better—in nonpartisan elections. Some voters' preferences are not determined primarily by the candidates' party affiliations; these might be voters whose main concern is with an issue that cuts across party lines (such as divorce, abortion, or nuclear power) or voters who want to elect a representative whose home base is in their own area of the constituency. List systems do not offer this opportunity, and the apparent exceptions—those of Switzerland and Luxembourg, which offer *panachage*—are not really comparable.

This is because of the third argument in favor of STV, namely that voters control the way their votes will be used. No vote can help a candidate unless it expresses a preference for him or her. This sets STV apart from all list systems, where a preference given to one candidate of a party might end up helping another candidate of the same party—a candidate whom, perhaps, the voter does not like. Under STV, voters can continue to give preferences after their first, knowing that doing this cannot possibly damage their favored candidate. A lower preference given to a candidate can never help that person against a candidate to whom the voter gave a higher preference. This is not the case under *panachage*; the voter giving a preference to a candidate of one party does not know which candidate of that party it will ultimately help, as it is added to the party's pool and could benefit any of its candidates.

Fourth, STV gives voters the opportunity to express an opinion as to the direction their party should take. If there is more than one tendency or faction within a party, voters can express higher preferences for candidates from the one they favor and affect the composition of the parliamentary group accordingly. STV shares this provision with preferential list systems and American primaries.

Fifth, it ensures that voters can vote sincerely, knowing that even if their first-choice candidate is unpopular, the vote will not be wasted, as it can be transferred to another candidate in accordance with the second preference the voter has marked on the ballot paper.

But STV also has its critics, which explains why it has inspired so little enthusiasm on the European mainland. They make two points. First, they are not impressed with the opportunity it gives voters to cross party lines. On the contrary, they feel that this might weaken the internal unity of parties and make them less cohesive. In elections, candidates of one party, rather than being able to concentrate on propagating party policies, must be alive to the possibility of attracting lower preferences from other parties' supporters. This might make the parties "fuzzy at the edges" as candidates adopt bland positions for fear of alienating any voter who might possibly give them a lower preference. Critics argue that modern democratic politics, certainly in parliamentary systems, need strong, cohesive parties to work properly, a subject we discussed in Chapter 5, and that the idea of voting for candidates rather than parties, while all very well for other kinds of elections, is inappropriate for parliamentary elections. This argument is difficult to evaluate, because STV is used in too few countries for us to be able to tell whether it will tend to weaken parties. It must be said, though, that there is no evidence that parties in either Ireland or Malta are any less cohesive and disciplined than parties anywhere else. And while Irish politics do tend to be relatively consensual, with few clear policy differences between the two main parties, Fianna Fáil and Fine Gael, the opposite is true in Malta, where the bitter rivalry between Labour and the Nationalists often spills over into violence.

The second criticism is that STV can realistically be used only in relatively small constituencies, thus raising the prospect of disproportionality (lack of complete correspondence between parties' shares of the votes and the seats). STV is difficult to operate in constituencies larger than about ten seats, because the ballot paper could then contain 30 to 40 names, and most voters' preferences will become meaningless after the first half-dozen or so. In both Ireland and Malta, the largest constituency size now used is five seats. Because votes are assumed to be cast for candidates rather than parties, it is impossible, without contradicting the principles on which STV is based, to have higher-tier seat allocation (without the use of a second vote as in Germany), although Malta does have such an allocation in reserve, introduced before the 1987 election, to ensure that any party winning an overall majority of votes will also win an overall majority of seats. In practice, though, the possibility of disproportionality does not seem to be a major problem, as election results in Ireland and Malta have been as proportional as those of other PR systems.

ELECTORAL SYSTEMS ASSESSED

The plethora of electoral systems used across Western Europe suggests that there is no simple answer to the question "Which is the best electoral system?" But while there has been no trend toward a uniform electoral system, we have seen that the great majority of countries employ some version of PR. Only Britain and France use systems that do not embody the principle of PR. All the remaining Western European countries employ some type of PR: in fifteen countries, a list system is used, while Ireland and Malta employ the single transferable vote. We have already reviewed the arguments about the relative merits of list systems and STV; we must now look at the wider question of the advantages and disadvantages of PR systems generally compared with plurality systems (for general discussions of electoral systems, see Lijphart, 1984b and 1985; Grofman and Lijphart).

There is a grossly simplistic portrait of the main consequences of these two types of electoral systems. It is said that plurality systems may produce disproportional results, with the largest two parties taking nearly all the seats in parliament, but that they also ensure stable majority governments. In contrast, it is said, PR systems give proportional results, but this inevitably entails multiparty systems with parliamentary seats spread among a sizable number of parties, which in turn produces a succession of unstable coalition governments. If these two pictures were accurate, assessing the merits of the two types of electoral systems would come down to the question in which criterion should have greater priority: "fair" representation of parties in parliament or strong, effective government? Needless to say, the actual situation with regard to these two factors is rather complex. There are other criteria, too, that could be taken into account in an assessment of the merits of electoral systems. Which affords more effective representation of ordinary citizens? Do some systems give a better chance than others to women and minorities to win election to parliament? Is redistricting and gerrymandering a greater problem under some systems than others? The overall picture is summarized in Table 6.4.

Proportionality

The proportionality of election results—the degree to which parties' shares of the seats correspond to their shares of the votes—does indeed tend to be significantly greater under PR than under plurality systems. On a scale running from 0 (total disproportionality) to 100 (perfect proportionality), Mackie and Rose (p. 510) found that the average proportionality figures for the most recent Western European PR and plurality/majority elections were 94 and 80, respectively. Lijphart (1990, p. 485) found essentially the same pattern, with the results of elections held under plurality or majority formulas clearly less proportional than those of elections under PR. Generally speaking, as the first column of Table 6.4 shows, proportionality is lowest in non-PR systems (Britain and France) and in Spain, where a PR formula is combined with small district magnitudes. It is highest in PR systems that use large district magnitudes (Austria, Germany, the Netherlands, and Sweden), with PR systems employing a mid-range district magnitude falling somewhere in between.

TABLE 6.4

Aspects of Electoral Outcomes in Western Europe

	Level of Proportionality, 1980–1990	Date of Most Recent Election	Effective Number of Parties in Parliament after Most Recent Election	Actual Number of Parties in Parliament after Most Recent Election*	% of Votes Won by Largest Two Parties in Most Recent Election	% of Seats in Parliament Won by Largest Two Parties in Most Recent Election	Frequency of Coalition Governments 1945–1990†	% of Women in Parliament after Most Recent Election
Austria	Very high	Oct. 1990	3.0	4	75.1	77.1	3	15.8
Belgium	Moderate	Dec. 1987	7.1	11	35.2	39.2	4	8.5
Denmark	High	Dec. 1990	4.4	8	53.5	56.6	2	33.7
Finland	Moderate	Mar. 1991	5.2	10	46.9	51.5	4	38.5
France	Low	June 1988	3.0	7	55.7	69.0	4	5.7
Germany	High	Dec. 1990	2.6	5	77.3	84.3	5	20.5
Greece	Moderate	Apr. 1990	2.4	6	86.4	91.0	2	4.7
Iceland	High	Apr. 1987	5.3	7	46.1	49.2	5	20.6
Ireland	High	June 1989	3.0	7	73.4	79.5	2	7.8
Italy	High	June 1987	4.1	14	60.9	65.2	5	12.9
Luxembourg	Moderate	June 1989	3.7	7	58.6	66.7	4	11.7
Malta	High	May 1987	2.0	2	99.8	100.0	0	2.9
Netherlands	Very high	Sept. 1989	3.7	9	67.2	68.7	5	24.0
Norway	Moderate	Sept. 1989	4.2	6	56.7	60.6	1	35.8
Portugal	Moderate	July 1987	2.4	7	74.1	83.2	2	7.6
Spain	Low	Oct. 1989	2.9	7	66.4	80.3	1	12.6
Sweden	Very high	Sept. 1988	3.7	6	61.5	63.6	2	37.8
Switzerland	Moderate	Oct. 1987	7.5	14	42.9	46.0	5	14.5
United Kingdom	Low	June 1987	2.2	11	73.1	93.1	0	6.5
Average	—	—	3.8	7.8	63.7	69.7	3	17.0

*The "actual number of parties in parliament" excludes independent deputies.

†Countries are rated on a scale from 0 to 5, 0 denoting that no governments are coalitions and 5 that all or virtually all are coalitions. For Greece, Portugal, and Spain, the figures in this column refer only to the period since the restoration of democracy in the 1970s.

Sources: Election results from Mackie and Rose.

Women in parliaments: Belgium, France, Italy, and United Kingdom: *Women in Graphics,* no. 30, Commission of the European Communities, Brussels, 1989, p. 14. Austria: information supplied by Austrian Embassy, Dublin, January 1991; Denmark: information supplied by library of Folketing, January 1991; Finland: Finnish Embassy, Dublin, March 1991; Germany: information supplied by Bundestag, January 1991; Greece: information supplied by Press Office of Greek Embassy, London, July 1990; Iceland: Arnason, p. 124; Ireland: Gallagher, 1990, p. 86; Luxembourg: *Women in Europe,* no. 62, Commission of the European Communities, Brussels, December 1989, p. 21; Malta: European Committee for Equality between Women and Men, *Distribution of Seats between Men and Women in National Parliaments of the Member States of the Council of Europe as at 30 June 1987,* Council of Europe, Strasbourg, 1987, p. 12; Netherlands: information supplied by Monique Leijenaar, July 1990; Norway: Aardal, p. 151; Portugal: information supplied by Portuguese Embassy Dublin, July 1990; Spain: information supplied by Spanish Embassy, Dublin, August 1990; Sweden: information supplied by Swedish Embassy, Dublin, August 1990; Switzerland: information supplied by Swiss Embassy, Dublin, January 1991.

The Number of Parties

In addition, it is true that there tend to be more parties in parliaments elected by PR than in those elected by a plurality system. Using a measure devised by Laakso and Taagepera that counts the "effective" number of parties by taking into account not only the number of different parties but also the relative size of each, Arend Lijphart was able to show that for the period 1945–1980, parliaments elected under plurality systems contained, on the average, 2.1 parties, while those elected under PR had an average of 3.8 parties (Lijphart, 1984a, pp. 160–161). This pattern remains in force: for the elections covered in Table 6.4, the effective number of parties in the two non-PR parliaments (in Britain and France) averaged 2.6, while for the seventeen parliaments elected under PR, it averaged 4.0.

Of course, it is possible for small parties to win a few seats even when a plurality system is used. For example, the British House of Commons elected in 1987 contained MPs of 11 different parties, well above average for Western Europe. However, two of these parties, Labour and the Conservatives, won 605 of the 650 seats between them, so Britain resembled a 2-party system far more than an 11-party system (in Laakso and Taagepera's terms, it was in fact a "2.2 party system"). In general, small parties can fare quite well under the British electoral system if, like the Ulster Unionists, their strength is concentrated in a few areas, but they tend to do very badly if it is spread quite evenly across the country, as in the case of the Liberal-SDP Alliance in 1987. So, generally speaking, though with exceptions we shall mention later, PR elections are associated with multiparty systems and plurality elections with two-party systems.

Electoral systems are partly responsible for this, but not entirely. Non-PR systems have an impact on the number of parties in two ways. First, the large "bonus" of seats given to the leading party or parties means that the legislature is dominated by the largest two parties to a far greater degree than if a PR system were employed. We see in Table 6.4 that in the United Kingdom, the Conservatives and Labour attracted only 73 percent of the votes between them in the 1987 election but won over 93 percent of the seats. In France, too, the two main parties picked up a sizable bonus from the electoral system. The same happened in Spain, where a low average district magnitude made life hard for the smaller parties. In contrast, under PR systems with a high district magnitude, as in Austria and the Netherlands, the bonus derived by the large parties is minimal. So if Britain and France adopted PR systems and Spain employed larger constituencies, then seats in these countries' parliaments would be much less concentrated in the hands of the two main parties.

The second way in which a non-PR system affects the number of parties we find in any country concerns its impact on the way people vote. If Britain, in particular, moved to a PR system, voting patterns would almost certainly change, for supporters of minority parties would be able to vote sincerely; they would no longer have any reason to vote tactically for one of the two leading parties in order to keep their least liked party out. This would undoubtedly be of most benefit to the smaller parties, especially the Liberal Democrats and the Greens, though the major parties might also pick up some votes in areas where they are currently only the third or even fourth party, such as the Conservatives in Scotland or Labour in much of the southern part of England. The plurality electoral system may be all that keeps

Britain (and, indeed, the U.S.A.) looking like a two-party system, and it is certainly the key to two-party domination of the legislature.

In France, too, the contrast between the 1986 and 1988 elections offers a pointer as to what might happen were PR made permanent. The National Assembly elected under the second ballot in 1988 was dominated by the two main blocs to a far greater extent than its counterpart elected under PR in 1986, because most minor parties lost seats in 1988. In particular, the far-right *Front National* fell back from 35 seats to 1, although its share of the votes dropped only marginally. So the experience of both Britain and France supports the view that a plurality electoral system tends to manufacture a two-party system in parliament.

However, there is counterevidence. Several European countries—Belgium, Denmark, Germany, and Norway—had multiparty systems under plurality voting before PR was introduced. In these countries, PR allowed a multiparty system to persist but did not cause it. The case of Austria directly refutes the idea that PR always leads to a multiparty system. The number of parties declined after PR was introduced in 1919, and it went down further following the last war, since when Austrian politics have been dominated by the two large parties, the ÖVP and the SPÖ. From 1956 to 1983 inclusive these two parties won at least 90 percent of the seats between them at every election. One of the purest two-party systems to be found anywhere in the world is that of Malta, which also uses PR. The conclusion must be that PR systems will give parliamentary expression to a multiparty system if other factors, such as the number of political or social cleavages, cause voters to create one in the first place, but PR does not by itself bring a multiparty system into being.

In addition, PR is not associated with a limitless proliferation of parties. In only four European countries (Denmark, Finland, the Netherlands, and Switzerland) did the effective number of parties average as high as 4 over the period 1945–1980 (Lijphart, 1984a, p. 160), though considering the most recent elections alone, these four countries have been joined by four others (Belgium, Iceland, Italy, and Norway), as Table 6.4 shows (with the Netherlands moving out of this category). Looking at the most recent elections covered in Table 6.4, we see that elections in only five countries produced parliaments that corresponded to the vision conjured up by opponents of PR, with more than four "effective" parties and with the two largest winning fewer than 60 percent of the seats between them: these are Belgium, Denmark, Finland, Iceland, and Switzerland.

A plurality electoral system, with its tendency to produce competition between just two large parties, reflects the view that a majority should prevail over a minority. This in itself is an impeccable democratic principle. But it encounters problems in societies that are divided into a number of segments or interests and on issues where there are more than two positions. When there is no majority to represent, plurality systems tend to produce outcomes that favor inordinately the larger minorities and discriminate against the smaller ones. PR systems, in contrast, seek to reflect in parliaments the divergences that exist in society.

Coalition or Single-Party Government?

One argument against PR systems is that the very accuracy with which they reflect parties' electoral strengths in parliament creates problems when it comes to forming a government. It is extremely rare, under any type of electoral system, for one party to win a majority of the votes cast, so a single-party majority government is likely only if the largest party receives a bonus of seats that takes it over the magic 50 percent mark. Obviously, this is most likely to happen under a plurality system, where proportionality is lower and the largest party often wins a substantial bonus. For example, in Britain's 1987 election, the Conservatives received only 42 percent of the votes, but they won 58 percent of the seats, a bonus of 16 percent. Under a PR system, assuming that disproportionality is not introduced as a result of small district magnitudes, no party's seat bonus is very large. Consequently, a single-party majority government is possible only if one party actually wins a majority of votes (as has happened in Austria, West Germany, Ireland, Malta, Portugal, and Sweden) or comes very close to it so that it needs only a small bonus for a parliamentary majority (as has happened in Austria, Greece, Ireland, Malta, Norway, Spain, and Sweden). A survey of the record in twenty countries found that while single-party majority governments were formed after only 10 percent of elections held under PR, they emerged after 60 percent of those held under plurality or majority electoral systems (Blais and Carty, p. 214).

Having said this, we must add that the relationship between electoral systems and government types is not entirely straightforward, as Table 6.4 shows. It is true that in countries with the most fragmented party systems, such as Finland, Iceland, Italy, Luxembourg, the Netherlands, and Switzerland, all or virtually all governments are coalitions. It is also true that Britain, owing to its non-PR electoral system, has not had a coalition government since 1945. However, the British electoral system has not always produced a stable majority government. Some British elections—the most recent being that of February 1974—produced no overall parliamentary majority for any party, and between 1976 and 1979 the minority Labour government was able to survive in office only because of the support of the Liberals, under the terms of an arrangement known as the "Lib-Lab pact." In France, too, the plurality system did not produce a majority government in the 1988 election, and indeed, if we think of the RPR and UDF as separate parties, the Fifth Republic had only one single-party government (the Gaullist government formed after the 1968 election) until the Socialist victory of 1981.

In countries using PR systems, even though coalitions are far more common, there are still many cases of single-party government. The Austrian Socialist party, Ireland's Fianna Fáil, the Norwegian Labor party, the Swedish Social Democrats, and both Labour and the Nationalists in Malta have all had long spells in office alone, and other countries with PR have experienced single-party government for periods.

Critics of PR also argue that coalition governments make it hard for voters to hold a government responsible for its record, because each of the parties in the coalition will try to take the credit for the government's successes and pass the buck where the failures are concerned. They argue that under plurality systems and single-party government, in contrast, the voters know exactly whom to blame and whom to reward and can deliver a clear verdict. But a problem with this argument is that even if the electorate does deliver an unambiguous verdict, the electoral system may distort the message. For example, in 1983 and again in 1987, the outgoing Conservative government placed its record before the British people and asked for a fresh mandate. On each occasion, a clear majority of voters (58 percent) down its request and voted for other parties, but the electoral system turned these votes into large Conservative parliamentary majorities.

Constituency Representation

Another criterion by which electoral systems can be assessed is constituency representation. Defenders of plurality systems such as those in Britain and France argue that there is more to an electoral system than representing parties. They argue that the interests of territorial constituencies are important too and that because each constituency is represented by only one parliamentary representative, a close link between the constituency and the member of parliament is forged. The elected member must accept sole responsibility for attending to all casework problems arising within the constituency. In contrast, they allege, when PR systems are used, each constituency is represented by several members, so a constituent who wants assistance from a member of parliament may not be able to find one to take up the problem.

Whatever the theoretical appeal of this argument, the problem does not seem to have arisen in practice under PR systems. In some countries, especially the Scandinavian ones, citizens have means of seeking redress for a problem that do not entail using members of parliament as intermediaries. In other countries, especially Ireland and Italy, studies have shown that deputies work very assiduously for their constituents, undertaking more constituency business than their British counterparts.

It may be, indeed, that the multimember constituencies entailed by PR might improve the citizen's representation, at least when STV or a preferential list system is used, because the citizen then has several representatives to choose from. Each representative has an incentive to deal helpfully with casework requests for fear of being ousted by the voters in favor of a party colleague. In preferential variants of PR, a voter can punish a lackluster deputy without voting for a rival party. Under a plurality system, furthermore, many citizens may be reluctant to take a problem to a representative whose political views are diametrically opposed to their own. Under PR, in contrast, there is a much greater chance that everyone will be represented by at least one member of parliament from the party he or she voted for. The case could thus be argued either way, and a study that examined the nature of relationships between citizens and their parliamentary representatives in a number of European countries concluded that electoral systems seemed to have little effect on this, one way or the other (Bogdanor, 1985).

The Backgrounds of Parliamentarians

PR elections produce parliaments that differ from those produced by plurality elections. This is true not just as far as the representation of parties is concerned; it also applies to the profile of the individuals who sit on the parliamentary benches.

This is especially obvious when we look at the proportion of women in legislatures around the world. It has frequently been observed (for example, by Bogdanor, 1983, pp. 249–250, and Randall, pp. 140–142) that there are more women in parliament in countries that use PR than in those where a plurality electoral system operates. Table 6.4 confirms this pattern. The average for Britain and France, the two countries that do not use PR, is a mere 6.1 percent, compared with

18.2 percent for the other seventeen countries. In some countries, notably Norway, Finland, Sweden, and Denmark, about a third of parliamentarians are women. Of course, these Scandinavian countries have a progressive attitude toward female participation in politics and in society generally, but the broad tendency remains true even when we look at less progressive countries. Thus Ireland, Italy, and Portugal, where the relatively traditional, rural nature of society and the strength of Catholicism might suggest that women would find it hard to gain entry to the political elite, and Switzerland, where women were denied the vote until the 1970s, all have more women in their national parliaments than Britain.

The explanation is to be found primarily in the multimember constituencies necessitated by PR. Under a single-member constituency system, the candidate selectors might well be reluctant to pick a woman as the party's sole candidate, using the excuse, genuine or otherwise, that they believe some voters will be less likely to vote for a woman than for a man. But when several candidates are to be chosen, it not only is possible but also is positively advantageous for a ticket to include both men and women, for an all-male list of five or more candidates is likely to alienate some voters. It is noticeable that in Germany the proportion of women among the candidates elected from the lists has generally been several times higher than the proportion among those elected from the single-member constituencies. There is no evidence that within the PR group, either STV, preferential list systems, or nonpreferential list systems give any special advantage to women.

There is less research on other underrepresented groups, but the same argument applies. Those who pick the party's candidate in a single-member constituency may be reluctant to take the risk of selecting a representative of a racial, religious, or linguistic minority, but candidate selectors in a multimember constituency will usually feel it wise to ensure that the ticket includes a cross section of the groups to which the party is hoping to appeal. Legislatures produced by PR elections thus tend to be more representative of the population that elects them, in terms of both the backgrounds of the parliamentarians and the relationship between votes won and seats received by political parties.

Redistricting and Gerrymandering

Elections to state legislatures in certain countries, especially the U.S.A., seem to be inseparable from controversy over redistricting and gerrymandering. Every new set of constituency boundaries drawn by the state legislature triggers a host of claims, and often court cases, arguing that the new districts are designed to reduce the representation of the minority party and/or an ethnic group. Yet European elections are virtually free from this kind of controversy.

The main reason for this is that districting—drawing constituency boundaries and allotting seats to each constituency—offers much less scope for gerrymandering or partisan bias under a PR electoral system. Gerrymandering is based on making sure that the opposition wastes as many votes as possible, but there are fewer wasted votes under a PR electoral system. Moreover, multimember constituencies mean that there are fewer boundaries to be drawn. In the extreme case, when the whole country is one big constituency, as in the Netherlands, there are no boundaries to be drawn and so no possibility of gerrymandering. In countries where district magnitude is large—such as Finland, where 200 members of the Eduskunta are returned from just 15 constituencies—it does not matter much how the country is divided up; the outcome within each constituency is bound to be reasonably proportional. The same applies in those countries that use higher-tier seat allocation (see Table 6.3), where any votes that had no effect (in other words, were wasted) at the constituency level can make themselves felt at the higher level. In any case, in most European countries, no redistricting ever takes place. The constituency boundaries, like the boundaries of American states, are absolutely fixed over time, based usually on clusters of local administrative units such as counties. All that ever changes, in response to changes in population across the country, is the number of seats to be awarded to each constituency.

BOX 6.2
The Impact of Electoral Systems

FRANCE

As in Britain, the non-PR single-member constituency electoral system greatly favors the large parties. However, because the French party system is more fragmented than that of Britain, the effects of the electoral system are not quite so drastic. Single-party majority government is uncommon; only twice in the post-1958 Fifth Republic has one party won a majority of seats (the Gaullists in 1968 and the Socialists in 1981).

GERMANY

Under the Weimar Republic established after the First World War, Germany had highly proportional election results and very unstable governments. The electoral system adopted after the Second World War is often seen as having produced the best of both worlds: election results are still highly proportional, but there is no problem of government instability. The 5 percent threshold that parties need to reach before qualifying for list seats has prevented the development of a situation where a multitude of small parties hold the balance of power. During the 1960s and 1970s only three parties (the SPD, the CDU/CSU, and the FDP) were represented in the West German Bundestag, before the Greens joined them in the 1980s. However, the Greens lost their representation in the 1990 all-German elections by falling below the 5 percent threshold in the area covered by the former West German state.

ITALY

Italy's electoral system guarantees a high degree of proportionality, and a large number of minor parties usually gain representation. Voters' ability to indicate a preference for individual candidates on their chosen party's list generates considerable intraparty competition in and, indeed, between elections; this is especially pronounced within the Christian Democrats and reinforces the highly factionalized nature of that party.

NETHERLANDS

Because the Netherlands returns all its members of parliament in one nationwide constituency, proportionality is high, and the largest parties receive a negligible bonus of seats over and above their share of the votes. The absence of any subnational constituencies has led to some complaints that citizens do not have any local constituency representatives with whom they can identify and to whom they can take casework problems.

SPAIN

Spain's electoral system is a version of PR, but it does not produce very proportional outcomes. The main reason is the low number of members returned from the average constituency. In consequence, the largest parties receive a significant bonus from the electoral system, nearly as great as that received by the major parties in Britain and France. The bonus of the largest party, the

(Continued on next page)

Socialists, is particularly pronounced, and during the 1980s it regularly gave the party an overall majority of seats, even though the party's share of the votes was consistently well below 50 percent.

SWEDEN
The Swedish electoral system gives highly proportional results. Consequently, the largest party, the Social Democrats, rarely wins an overall majority of seats, and on the average in postwar elections, it has won a lower share of the seats than has the British Conservative party, even though its average share of the votes exceeds that of the Conservatives. By international standards, women are strongly represented in the Riksdag, and until the Finnish election of March 1991 Sweden had the highest proportion of women in parliament of any Western European country.

UNITED KINGDOM
The single-member constituency electoral system gives a large bonus of seats to the two largest parties, Labour and the Conservatives, which regularly win nearly all the seats in parliament, even though smaller parties may take up to a third of the votes. An observer sitting in the gallery of the House of Commons would infer from the distribution of seats among the parties that Britain has an almost pure two-party system, but this impression is largely created by the electoral system. If Britain adopted a proportional electoral system, small parties, especially the Liberal Democrats, would win many more seats in the Commons, and the likelihood of single-party majority government, currently the norm, would be greatly reduced.

This leaves very few countries where redistricting can become a source of controversy: Britain and France, with single-member constituencies, and Ireland and Malta, which use PR (STV) in small-sized constituencies regularly redrawn by the parliament. Even in these cases, some steps have been taken to take the subject out of the arena of partisan politics. In Ireland, an attempt in 1977 by the ruling coalition government to boost its chances of reelection by partisan redistricting backfired disastrously, and the government went down in world history as possibly the only one ever to implement a gerrymander that favored the opposition. After this debacle, the task of redistricting was handed over by all-party consensus to an independent commission (though the parliament dictates its terms of reference and so can potentially exercise an indirect influence on its conclusions). In Malta, the 1981 election gave the ruling Labour party a majority of seats, even though the opposition Nationalists had won a majority of votes, mainly because the government had drawn the constituency boundaries to suit itself. To allay public discontent, a change was made to the electoral law so that if in the future a party won a majority of votes but only a minority of seats, it would be awarded as many extra seats as it needed to give it a majority. This provision had to be invoked at the next election, in 1987. The Nationalists, with 50.9 percent of the votes, won only 31 of the 65 seats, while Labour, with 48.9 percent, won 34, so the Nationalists were awarded an extra four seats to give them a one-seat overall majority in an expanded 69-member chamber.

With these few exceptions, redistricting rarely emerges in Europe as a source of controversy, and the widespread adoption of PR electoral systems can take most of the credit for this.

CONCLUSION

Studies of electoral systems have progressed a long way over the past twenty years. Before then, some writers used to argue seriously that the adoption of PR in any country was virtually bound to lead to the collapse of democracy and the establishment of a dictatorship. Others claimed that PR was almost a guaranteed recipe for harmony, enlightened government, and a contented citizenry. We are now much more aware of the need to avoid simplistic conclusions. The impact electoral systems have on the political life of a country is more limited than these wild polemics suggested.

Even so, as we have seen, electoral systems *do* have important political consequences. PR electoral systems lead to a more proportional representation of parties in parliament and are more likely to be associated with a multiparty system than are plurality systems. They make gerrymandering more difficult and facilitate the entry of women and ethnic minorities to parliament. But perhaps the most important single aspect of electoral systems is that PR formulas are much less likely than a plurality or majority system to manufacture single-party governments. Since it is very uncommon for a single party to win a majority of the votes cast, PR systems tend to be characterized by coalition government, the subject to which we now turn.

References

Aardal, Bernt: "The Norwegian Parliamentary Election of 1989," *Electoral Studies*, vol. 9, no. 2, 1990, pp. 151–158.

Arnason, Gudmundur: "Fluidity in Icelandic Politics—The Election of April 1987," *West European Politics*, vol. 11, no. 1, 1988, pp. 122–125.

Arter, David: *Politics and Policy-Making in Finland*, St. Martin's Press, New York, and Wheatsheaf, Brighton, 1987.

Austen, John, David Butler, and Austin Ranney: "Referendums, 1978–1986," *Electoral Studies*, vol. 6, no. 2, 1987, pp. 139–147.

Blais, A., and R. K. Carty: "The Impact of Electoral Formulae on the Creation of Majority Governments," *Electoral Studies*, vol. 6, no. 3, 1987, pp. 209–218.

Bogdanor, Vernon: "Conclusion: Electoral Systems and Party Systems," in Vernon Bogdanor and David Butler (eds.), *Democracy and Elections*, Cambridge University Press, Cambridge, England, 1983, pp. 247–262.

———: "Conclusion," in Vernon Bogdanor (ed.), *Representatives of the People? Parliamentarians and Constituents in Western Democracies*, Gower, Aldershot, 1985, pp. 293–301.

Carstairs, Andrew McLaren: *A Short History of Electoral Systems*, George Allen and Unwin, London, 1980.

Cole, Alistair, and Peter Campbell: *French Electoral Systems and Elections since 1789*, Gower, Aldershot, 1989.

Crewe, Ivor: "Electoral Participation," in David Butler, Howard R. Penniman, and Austin Ranney (eds.), *Democracy at the Polls: A Comparative Study of Competitive National Elections*, American Enterprise Institute, Washington, 1981, pp. 216–263.

De Winter, Lieven: "Belgium: Democracy or Oligarchy?" in Michael Gallagher and Michael Marsh (eds.), *Candidate Selection in Comparative Perspective: The Secret Garden of Politics*, Sage, London, 1988, pp. 20–46.

Featherstone, Kevin: "Political Parties and Democratic Consolidation in Greece," in Geoffrey Pridham (ed.), *Securing Democracy: Political Parties and Democratic Consolidation in Southern Europe*, Routledge, London and New York, 1990, pp. 179–202.

Finer, S. E. (ed.): *Adversary Politics and Electoral Reform*, Anthony Wigram, London, 1975.

Gallagher, Michael: "The Election Results and the New Dáil," in Michael Gallagher and Richard Sinnott (eds.), *How Ireland Voted 1989*, Centre for the Study of Irish Elections, University College Galway, Galway, 1990, pp. 68–93.

———: "Proportionality, Disproportionality and Electoral Systems," *Electoral Studies*, vol. 10, no. 1, 1991, pp. 33–51.

Grofman, Bernard, and Arend Lijphart (eds.): *Electoral Laws and Their Political Consequences*, Agathon Press, New York, 1986.

Hand, Geoffrey, Jacques Georgel, and Christoph Sasse (eds.): *European Electoral Systems Handbook*, Butterworths, London, 1979.

Katz, Richard: "Intraparty Preference Voting," in Grofman and Lijphart, pp. 85–103.

Laakso, Markku, and Rein Taagepera: " 'Effective' Number of Parties: A Measure with Application to West Europe," *Comparative Political Studies*, vol. 12, no. 1, 1979, pp. 3–27.

Lakeman, Enid: *How Democracies Vote*, 4th ed., Faber and Faber, London, 1974.

Lane, Jan-Erik, and Svante O. Ersson: *Politics and Society in Western Europe*, Sage, London, 1987.

Lijphart, Arend: *Democracies: Patterns of Majoritarian and Consensus Government in Twenty-one Countries*, Yale University Press, New Haven and London, 1984a.

———: "Advances in the Comparative Study of Elec-

toral Systems," *World Politics*, vol. 36, no. 3, 1984b, pp. 424–436.

———: "The Field of Electoral Systems Research: A Critical Survey," *Electoral Studies*, vol. 4, no. 1, 1985, pp. 3–14.

———: "The Political Consequences of Electoral Laws 1945–85," *American Political Science Review*, vol. 84, no. 2, 1990, pp. 481–496.

——— and ———: *The International Almanac of Electoral History*, 3d ed., Macmillan, London, 1991.

Mackie, Thomas T., and Richard Rose: *The International Almanac of Electoral History*, 3d ed., Macmillan, London, 1991.

Marsh, Michael: "The Voters Decide? Preferential Voting in European List Systems," *European Journal of Political Research*, vol. 13, no. 4, 1985, pp. 365–378.

Randall, Vicky: *Women and Politics: An International Perspective*, 2d ed., Macmillan Educational, Basingstoke, 1987.

Roberts, Geoffrey: "The Federal Republic of Germany," in Finer, pp. 203–222.

Smith, Gordon: *Politics in Western Europe*, 5th ed., Gower, Aldershot, 1989.

Wood, Alan H. (ed.): *The Times Guide to the House of Commons June 1987*, Times Books, London, 1987.

CHAPTER 7
BUILDING AND MAINTAINING A GOVERNMENT

When the dust has settled and the smoke has blown away after a typical election campaign, some parties will have won seats and votes and some will have lost them. But the real prize that is won or lost on these occasions, for most parties at least, is a place in the government. European voters, as we have already seen, do not have the last word on this important matter. In most countries the membership of the government is decided, some time after the election is over, on the basis of bargaining between party leaders.

This is because it is very unusual for a political party to get a majority of all votes cast—and PR electoral systems create legislatures that reflect this pattern of electoral preference. Very, very few European political parties, therefore, ever win a majority of legislative seats. Almost all single-party "majority" governments are actually creations of an electoral system that gives legislative majorities to parties that win less than 50 percent of the votes. This means that governments formed by a single majority party are rare exceptions on the European scene, found only in a small number of countries.

It is of course true that single parties can win legislative majorities under PR electoral systems—this has happened, for example, in Austria, Germany, Ireland, and Norway. In each of these countries, however, the politics of coalition remain very important. In Germany, "surplus majority" coalitions were formed on those occasions when the Christian Democrats won an overall majority—additional parties were thus added to the government even when one party could in theory have governed alone. In Ireland and Norway, the legislative majority of the dominant party has tended to come and go from election to election, and so single-party majority governments have alternated with coalitions. Austria has a long tradition of coalition government. Even when a single party sometimes wins an overall majority, therefore, coalitions are still a central fact of political life. There can be no doubt, taking all of this into account, that coalition government is the European norm.

In a broader sense, even single-party governments can also be seen as coalitions: coalitions of factions within the ruling party. These intraparty coalitions may be kept together not as a result of any great affinity between those involved but by little more than their mutual fear of electoral disaster. The dramatic increase in the level of public faction fighting within the British Labour party when it is in opposition, compared with when it is in government, illustrates this point quite clearly.

Since the first-past-the-post electoral system typically punishes smaller parties and splinter groups so viciously, explicit party splits can be very damaging—the fate of those who broke away from the British Labour party to form the Social Democratic party is a recent and notorious example. One interpretation of the real political impact of the British electoral system, therefore, is that it forces big parties to stay together, however hair-raising the intraparty politics might be. This in turn means that most of the politics of coalition in Britain, and in other systems in which one-party government is the norm, take place within parties rather than between them.

On this interpretation coalition bargaining is fundamental to all political systems. In Britain (and, indeed, the U.S.A.) coalition bargaining takes place for the most part inside political parties as a result of the distorting effects of the plurality electoral system. In most continental European countries, election results are translated more or less proportionally into legislative seat distributions, and so coalition bargaining takes place both within and between political parties. Most governments are executive coalitions, in which more than one party is represented at the cabinet table. Most European single-party governments do not control legislative majorities—they must thus rely for their continued existence upon legislative coalitions. In this case a group of parties supports the government in the legislature, even if only one party controls seats in the cabinet.

Once a government has formed in a coalition system, this is by no means the end of the story. The ability of a government to keep hold of the reins of power depends crucially upon a continuous process of bargaining and negotiation between party leaders. This is because the deals that were made to build the government in the first place can just as easily be unmade, bringing it tumbling down. At a certain point in time, various political variables may come together to encourage politicians to create a particular government. If these variables change in unforeseen ways, the same politicians may face different incentives and choose to destroy the government that they earlier created.

Thus a coalition government can in theory be brought down at any moment in its existence by the defection of one or more of its original legislative supporters. This is why those who oppose PR electoral systems typically do so, as we saw in the previous chapter, on the grounds that "PR generates multiparty systems, which generate coalition governments, which are unstable." Many old saws have an element of truth in them, and this one is no exception. As we will see below, coalition governments do tend, on balance, not to last as long as single-party majority governments. But at the same time we should not forget that some of the most economically successful and politically stable governments in postwar Europe have been the coalition administrations that have governed Germany, Switzerland, Luxembourg, and Austria for most of the period since 1945.

In the rest of this chapter, therefore, when we explore the building and maintenance of governments in Western Europe, we will be looking mainly at the workings of coalition government. First we will look at the "rules of the game" that structure the business of government formation, since much of the recent work in political science has shown us just how important institutional structures and procedural rules are to real-world political outcomes. Second, we will look at factors that affect the party composition of European cabinets—and more specifically at the allocation of cabinet portfolios among parties. Finally, since the specter of "unstable coalition government" is so often raised by opponents of PR, we will look at the durability of European governments, trying to understand why some governments last as long as is constitutionally possible while others form, fall, and re-form at a much faster pace. By the end of the chapter we shall have seen that while most European states are governed by coalition cabinets for most of the time, one coalition cabinet can be quite different from another.

THE RULES OF THE GAME

The fundamental principle of European parliamentary democracy, as we pointed out in Chapter 1, is that the executive is responsible to the legislature. The key constitutional device by which this requirement is typically guaranteed is the legislative vote of confidence in the government. This allows the legislature to replace the executive whenever a majority of legislators choose to do so. The confidence vote is thus far more important to democracy in Western Europe than might on the face of it seem to be the case. (Switzerland is the only real exception to this; Swiss governments, once formed, do not have to face legislative confidence votes.)

Table 7.1 presents a range of factors that have to do with the birth and death of governments and shows that it is almost always the rule that a government defeated in a confidence vote must resign. Where this is not an explicit constitutional provision—the main exceptions are Britain and Finland—there is nonetheless a very strong presumption that a government will in fact resign if defeated in a confidence vote. (Strictly speaking, British governments could defy many votes of no confidence and remain in office, though this has never happened.) The requirement that governments must resign after losing a confidence vote is thus the most basic rule in building and maintaining a government in Western Europe. If a government cannot win confidence votes, there is no point in its forming. If it cannot keep winning them, it cannot remain in office.

A major consequence of this constitutional arrangement, as we saw in Chapter 1, is that European executives do not have fixed terms of office; they are liable to be replaced at any time by the legislature. Thus, while individual European legislators are not particularly powerful people when it comes to passing laws and influencing specific policies, they do collectively have the power to make and break governments. This power derives solely from the device of the vote of confidence, which provides the means by which European voters can be said to have a say in the business of government.

While the vote of confidence is a standard across nearly every European system, most of the other constitutional rules of the game associated with the birth and

TABLE 7.1
Constitutional Factors in Government Life Cycles

Country	Does Head of State Play Active Role in Government Formation?	Is Formal Investiture Vote Needed?	Must Government Resign if It Loses Confidence Vote?	Can Government Dissolve Legislature?	Can Legislature Dissolve Itself?	Maximum Time Between Elections
Austria	No	No	Yes	Yes*	Yes	4 years
Belgium	No	Yes	Yes	Yes	No	4 years
Denmark	No	No	Yes	Yes	No	4 years
Finland	Yes	No	No†	No	No	4 years
France	Yes	No	Yes‡	Yes§	No	5 years
Germany	No	No	Yes¶	Yes	No	4 years
Greece	No	Yes	Yes	Yes	No	4 years
Iceland	No	No	Yes	Yes	No	4 years
Ireland	No	Yes	Yes	Yes	No	5 years
Italy	Yes	Yes	Yes	Yes	No	5 years
Luxembourg	No	No	Yes	Yes	No	5 years
Malta	No	No	Yes	Yes	No	5 years
Netherlands	Yes	No	Yes	Yes	No	4 years
Norway	No	No	Yes	No	No	4 years
Portugal	Yes	Yes	Yes	Yes	No	4 years
Spain	Yes	Yes	Yes**	Yes	No	4 years
Sweden	No	Yes	Yes‡	Yes	No	3 years
Switzerland	No	Yes	No	No	No	4 years
United Kingdom	No	No	No	Yes	No	5 years

*The president may do so.
†President "may" accept resignation in the event of a no-confidence vote.
‡Absolute majority of legislature required to pass no-confidence vote.
§After 1 year.
¶No-confidence vote must designate new federal chancellor.
**Motion of no confidence in prime minister must specify successor.
Source: Laver and Schofield.

death of governments vary considerably from place to place. These, too, are summarized in Table 7.1, and the overall process of building and maintaining a government is illustrated by the flowchart in Figure 7.1, taken from Laver and Schofield. Figure 7.1 shows clearly that two general factors are important in the process of building and maintaining coalition cabinets in Western Europe. The first is that no matter where you are and no matter how chaotic things might seem to be, there is always an incumbent government. The second is that some mechanism must be found for vesting the government formally with constitutional authority, a task usually performed by some ceremonial officer of state.

It is important to remember that even if there sometimes seem to be periods when a country is "between" governments, after one government has fallen and before a new government has formed, there is always a legal government, every minute of every day. This is because, to put it bluntly, somebody must always be available to sign the checks—somebody must always have a finger on the trigger. Thus, when a government resigns, it does not actually stop being the government.

Figure 7.1
Building and Maintaining a Government

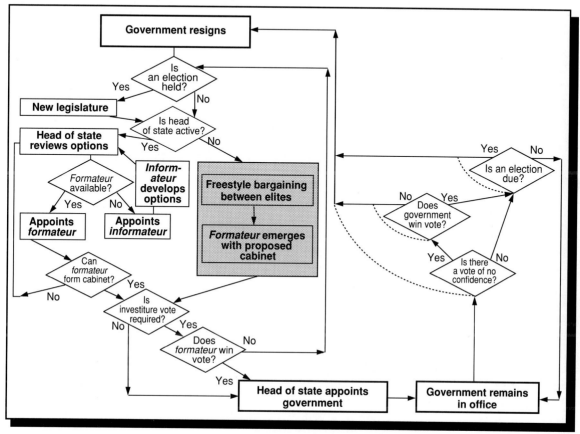

Rather, resignation amounts to a declaration on the part of the incumbent government that it will step down and go quietly the moment an alternative administration takes over the seals of office. In the meantime, the outgoing government remains in office, typically being referred to as a "caretaker" administration. (In Germany, the executive can be defeated only by a "constructive" vote of no confidence. This requirement means that the motion of no confidence must specify an alternative executive.) If putting together an alternative government proves to be a problem, then the caretaker administration can stay in power for quite some time, a situation that is not uncommon in the Netherlands. Conventionally, a caretaker government does not attempt to exploit its position by passing controversial legislation. But it does remain the legal government; its cabinet ministers remain the legal heads of government departments, with the power to set policy, to make patronage appointments, and so on. To be in a caretaker government is not, therefore, to be powerless.

All governments derive their fundamental legitimacy (to put things in a rather grandiose way) and their legal recognition under the constitution (to look at the nuts and bolts of the matter) from somewhere. Thus there is always something "above" a government, typically the constitution. In Europe there is always a person, typically the head of state, with the job of "investing" each new government with its formal constitutional authority. As we saw in Chapter 1, a European head of state may be a relatively powerful figure, as in France, or much more of a purely ceremonial figure, as in Germany. Even if the head of state has very little power, however, one job that must always be done is to transfer the seals of office from one administration to another. This is one of the most important institutional features of the government formation process.

Heads of State and *Formateurs*

Governments do not just emerge; they are formed. Furthermore, while the vote of every legislator may in theory be needed to settle who is entitled to a seat at the cabinet table, in practice the tight discipline of most European political parties means that the actual business of forming a government is conducted by a rather small group of senior politicians, typically comprising the party leaders in consultation with potential cabinet ministers. In general, therefore, we can think of the building of a government as something that is thrashed out between party leaders and presided over by the head of state.

Table 7.1 and Figure 7.1 show that European countries can be divided into those in which the head of state plays an active role in government formation and those in which he or she has a purely formal "swearing in" function, doing little more than passing on the seals of office and shaking the hand of the incoming prime minister. When the head of state does play an active role, this typically involves choosing a particular senior politician to initiate the process of forming a government; in this case, the head of state is effectively designating this person as a potential prime minister. This designated government builder is referred to by political scientists, adopting the usage of a number of European countries, as a *formateur*.

In some countries, for example, it is formally laid down in the event no single party has a legislative majority, that the head of state should first designate the leader of the largest party as the *formateur*. If this person fails to form a government, the head of state must then ask the leader of the second largest party to be the *formateur*, and so on. The interesting consequence of this procedure is that the process of government formation is very sensitive to election results, giving all parties a real incentive to fight elections hard in order to become the largest. This runs counter to the conventional wisdom about coalition government, which is that coalition weakens the link between voters and governments.

An example of this arrangement can be found in Greece. In 1989, a combination of the right-wing New Democracy party (ND) and the left-wing Communists (KKE) made strenuous attempts to unseat a Socialist (PASOK) government led by Papandreou. The two main opposition parties eventually managed to unite against PASOK on a program of rooting out government corruption. The process of government formation was, however, considerably complicated and prolonged by the constitutional requirement that *formateurs* be designated in the order of the legislative strengths of their parties. When this rule is rigidly applied, of course, the role of the head of state in government formation could equally well, though less congenially, be filled by a machine.

In other Western European countries, the head of state plays a far more active role in coalition building, using real discretion in selecting a *formateur*. In the Netherlands, for example, or in Finland, playing a part in the process of forming a government is one of the main jobs of the head of state. And, of course, even in systems in which it is expected that the head of state will behave like a machine, a particularly intractable political stalemate may force her or him to use discretion in order to break the deadlock.

An additional device may be deployed in such circumstances in order to insulate the head of state from partisan politics. This is the nomination of an *informateur*, usually an elder statesperson or senior nonpartisan figure taken to have no personal political ambition. Such a person may arrange formal roundtable meetings between party leaders or move among politicians in an altogether more informal manner. The job of the *informateur* is to find a person for the head of state to designate as the coalition builder, or *formateur*. (A very interesting elaboration of the roles of the *formateur* and the *informateur* for the case of the Netherlands is given by Vis.) Whatever the arrangement, government formation rules are designed to avert the spectacle of the head of state trailing in person from party leader to party leader, trying to make the deal that puts together a government.

Formateurs and Cabinets

Once the *formateur* has been officially chosen, the next item of business is to select a cabinet. As we have argued, the cabinet is the key organ of government in every Western European system. Indeed, the terms "cabinet" and "government" may be used interchangeably. As we saw in Chapter 1, a cabinet is a committee that runs the government; it is a collection of senior politicians, appointed formally by the head of state but in practice selected by the prime minister in consultation with the leaders of the other government parties.

When no single party has a legislative majority, then the system of parliamentary government implies that the cabinet must be acceptable to a majority of the legislature if it is to gain and retain office. Thus the composition of the cabinet must be settled before the government first presents itself to the legislature, and the identity of the particular ministers chosen is one of the major factors that legislators take into account when deciding whether to support the government. The group of cabinet ministers, taken as a whole, must be acceptable to the legislature and hence, indirectly, to the electorate.

In countries such as Britain in which a single party has a legislative majority, this arrangement gives immense power to the prime minister. The prime minister designate is almost invariably the leader of the majority party, who chooses all cabinet ministers and can guarantee a government majority in any vote of confidence. A direct consequence of this situation is that the process of choosing the leaders of major parties is a very important matter.

Conventionally, the prime minister usually takes account of feelings within all sections of the party when selecting a team of ministers, allowing the politics of coalition *within* the governing party to be accommodated. This precedent within the British tradition of government formation was, however, significantly weakened by the manner in which ministerial appointments were made during the series of cabinets led by Margaret Thatcher.

Before Thatcher, it was conventional for a British prime minister to offer cabinet posts to prominent leaders of rival party factions. This was in part a ruse to keep pretenders to the party leadership in the spotlight, where they could be watched. It was in part a ruse to gag them, since rivals were in this way forced to accept collective responsibility for decisions made within the cabinet. However cynical the reasons might have been, the effect was to make the ruling one-party coalition of factions as broadly based as possible, within the confines of a two-party system. One of the innovations of Margaret Thatcher's cabinet style, however, was to replace the system of government by a one-party coalition of factions with a system of one-faction party government. Internal party opponents, no matter how prominent, were banished to the back benches as never before. By 1990, shortly before Thatcher was ousted from the leadership, the British Conservative cabinet was quite remarkable, in European terms, for the number of really senior politicians from the government party who were *not* in the government. It is significant, however, that John Major, who replaced her as Conservative leader, did so on the basis of an explicit promise to be more of a "team player." He did at once reinstate Michael Heseltine, leader of one of the "out" factions, to cabinet office.

While one of the main jobs of the cabinet is collectively to make major policy decisions on behalf of the government, this is only part of the story; most cabinet ministers also serve as the political heads of government departments. This arrangement creates a division of labor within the cabinet, with individual ministers being given effective responsibility for particular policy areas, or "portfolios." Thus the cabinet minister who heads the foreign affairs ministry is typically called the minister for foreign affairs (or some similar title) and is said to hold the foreign affairs portfolio. In this way, every policy arena within which the government must act is assigned to the "jurisdiction" of a particular cabinet minister, who is given responsibility for initiating and implementing policy in the area in question. The system of allocating cabinet portfolios thus gives individual politicians considerable power over public policy in their respective areas of jurisdiction. It is a reason for everyone with an interest in the policy output of government to be concerned with which particular politician gets which particular portfolio.

The head of state scarcely ever refuses to appoint a politician who has been nominated by the prime minister for a particular portfolio and accepted (explicitly or tacitly) by the legislature. Making nominations for cabinet appointments is thus one of the most important practical sources of prime ministerial power in Europe, particularly since European cabinet nominees are almost never subjected to the intense process of individual scrutiny and investigation faced by their U.S. counterparts.

Because of its impact on real policy output, therefore, the overall distribution of cabinet portfolios to senior politicians is a vital part of the process of building a government and is something that is taken very seriously by legislators when deciding whether or not to support a proposed new cabinet. This is because the allocation of cabinet portfolios amounts, when all is said and done, to the only really credible public statement of the specific policies that the new government is likely to enact if it takes office (Laver and Shepsle, 1990a). Once a particular set of cabinet ministers has been installed in office, control over many aspects of public policy passes to those ministers. Control can be reasserted by the legislature only with considerable difficulty, and typically only on the basis of cataclysmic threats to bring the entire government tumbling down.

For those whose main interest in politics has to do with the eventual policy output of the government, the precise political composition of the cabinet is the best available indicator of what is likely to happen once the government is firmly in the saddle. The considerable autonomy of the cabinet to set policy, once it has been installed in office, is why the business of allocating the portfolios in a coalition cabinet is such a vital part of the process of forming a government in most European states.

Replacing an Incumbent Government

Once an agreement to form a new government has been forged between those who are directly involved, attention shifts to the mechanics of installing it. These vary considerably across Western Europe, as Table 7.1 shows. In some countries—Belgium and Italy, for example—it is necessary for a proposed incoming government to submit an *explicit* formal legislative investiture vote before it can take office. In other countries—Denmark and Finland, for example—there is no formal investiture vote, though the incoming government is obviously exposed to the possibility of defeat as soon as it confronts the legislature and motions of no confidence can be proposed by the opposition. In these countries, governments face an *implicit* investiture vote on assuming office.

This distinction is important, as Kaare Strom has demonstrated, since the absence of a strict legislative investiture test makes it easier to form minority governments (Strom, 1990). Once a government is installed, particular issues leave it open to challenge; a particular piece of legislation or a particular policy may rouse the anger of sections of the opposition. As we shall see, however, one strategy for minority governments, if they are not forced to face the test of putting together an overall majority on investiture, is to skip, on an issue-by-issue basis, from one legislative majority to another, with each majority made up of different parties. In such cases—and Denmark is usually cited as the classic example—the government's "majority" may comprise one set of parties for one issue and quite a different set for a different issue. In countries with a formal investiture requirement, however, this is not possible. The incoming government must present the legislature with a general policy program and a set of nominations for all cabinet positions. It must put together majority support in the legislature for the entire package and cannot rely on different majorities on different issues, since a single investiture vote must pass judgment on all of these important matters taken together.

Do the Rules of the Game Make a Difference?

Every European country has a distinctive set of rules that constrains the building and maintenance of governments. Beyond a doubt, these different rules can result in the formation and continuation of different governments in otherwise similar circumstances. The distinctiveness of each country should not be taken to imply, however, that we cannot make general statements about government formation in different countries.

When formation rules are more rigid and the head of state has less discretion, then there is greater scope for election results to influence government formation. Even in this more predictable environment, the composition of the government is not determined in any mechanical fashion, since government formation still involves bargaining between parties. But the fact that the initial *formateur*, at least, is determined by the election results adds a major strategic constraint on what is likely to happen and enables the electorate to have a greater say in the composition of the eventual government.

When the head of state plays a small role and formal investiture criteria are lax, then the "smoke-filled room" bargaining that is the stereotype of government formation in coalition systems is more likely to prevail. Relatively little is settled by the particular election results, since what is important is bargaining power, and, as we shall see, election results and bargaining power are only vaguely related. For this reason, it is much more difficult for voters to estimate the strategic consequences of voting in particular ways.

BOX 7.1
Rules of the Government Formation Game

FRANCE

The powers of the French president are much greater, and more politicized, than those of other Western European heads of state. Executive power is vested jointly in the president and the cabinet (Council of Ministers). Typically, the president asks a senior legislator in his own party to head a cabinet, which may be a single-party administration or a coalition. When a president from a different party comes into office, he can use his power to dissolve the legislature once in any twelve-month period, on the assumption that his party, having just won the presidential election, will win the subsequent legislative election so that he can then nominate a senior party member to form a government. Between 1986 and 1988, however, President Mitterrand, a member of the Socialist party, was forced to "cohabit" with Prime Minister Jacques Chirac, leader of the rightist RPR party. (This was the only time in the history of the French Fifth Republic that this has happened.)

GERMANY

The powers of the German head of state, the federal president, are among the weakest in Western Europe. After a general election the president nominates a prime minister, the federal chancellor, but almost all other actions of the president must be countersigned by the chancellor. As a consequence, the role of president is largely ceremonial, though like the British monarch, the head of state could, in theory, refuse to call elections when asked to do so by the chief executive. This has never actually happened in either country. The ability of the legislature to remove the executive is constrained by the need for a "constructive vote of no confidence," which means that the legislature can bring down a government only if it can also agree on a replacement. Such a vote has been proposed only twice (in 1972 and 1982) and succeeded only once (in 1982).

(Continued on next page)

ITALY

The Italian president is indirectly elected by an electoral college comprising both houses of the legislature and 58 representatives of regional parliaments. He has some practical political power, given the right to dissolve the legislature and the fact that he remains in office for seven years, in a political system where the average duration of an executive is very short (Table 7.8). The president may nominate any legislator as prime minister, takes account of deals between parties when doing this, and does not necessarily nominate a party leader. The prime minister then nominates a cabinet. For most of the postwar era, no-confidence votes in Italy were complicated by the fact that balloting in the legislature was secret. Thus party leaders could not guarantee the support of dissident factions within their own party. The possibility of breakaway voting by "free-lances" in the government parties obviously provided an incentive for governments to form on the basis of more than the bare minimum of legislative votes needed to secure investiture.

NETHERLANDS

The Dutch constitution makes no reference whatsoever to parliamentary government, vesting all executive authority in the monarch, who "appoints ministers and dismisses them at will" (Article 86.2). In practice, the Netherlands has evolved into a parliamentary government system, though the queen still plays quite an active role in government formation. After an election or a government resignation, the queen consults all party leaders and then typically appoints an elder statesperson as *informateur,* the individual who will identify the person best placed politically to lead government formation negotiations. These negotiations can be very lengthy, involving agreement on an extensive, detailed, and technical government program, a process that can take up to six months. Once a prime minister designate has agreed to a coalition deal with other parties, the queen appoints cabinet ministers on his or her advice, though there is a strong tradition that individual parties have control over who fills "their" portfolios.

SPAIN

Under Article 97 of the 1978 constitution, executive authority is vested in a cabinet led by a prime minister. The king proposes a candidate for the office of prime minister, and the candidate is elected by an absolute majority of the legislature. The active role taken by the king in the transition to democracy has given the office high prestige. However, as it happens, Spanish election results have, for the most part, been sufficiently clear-cut to accord the king little effective room for discretion in the government formation process.

SWEDEN

The Swedish monarch has very little real power and, since 1975, has been removed entirely from the government formation process. Instead, the speaker (chair) of the legislature nominates the prime minister, having consulted the leaders of each legislative party. If not more than half of the legislature votes against the proposal, it is approved, a procedure that allows the formation of governments that do not have the publicly expressed support of a majority of the legislature. The procedure in a vote of confidence is similar. A new election must be held after four unsuccessful attempts to approve a prime minister. Once approved, the prime minister appoints other cabinet members, who are not subject to legislative approval.

UNITED KINGDOM

The U.K. is the only state in Western Europe without a written constitution, so government formation is governed by custom and precedent rather than by written rules. The electoral system ensures that one-party government is virtually endemic, and so in practice, the monarch asks the leader of the party with a plurality of seats in the House of Commons to form a government, even when (as in 1951 and February 1974) another party has won more votes. The leader of the largest party typically nominates a cabinet of senior party legislators, which requires no formal investiture vote in the House of Commons. Since the party almost invariably has a legislative majority, the only possibility of defeat arises from splits in the government party.

Students of comparative politics pay far more attention to institutional details than they used to. The business of building a government provides us with some very clear examples of why it is important to do this, of the ways in which details do make a difference. It is equally important not to become lost in a thicket of details, however relevant this may seem. The business of building a government also exhibits some interesting general patterns. These patterns relate to the partisan composition of European governments, to the allocation of cabinet portfolios, and to the duration of coalition cabinets, the matters to which we now turn. Indeed, quite a substantial body of theory has developed concerning the business of building a coalition government in Western Europe. Of course, it is not the theory in itself that should interest us in the present context. What is important is that coalition theorists have analyzed some rather striking regularities in the politics of coalition in Europe, and as a result, we now have a much better idea about the processes that seem to be at work.

THE PARTY COMPOSITION OF GOVERNMENTS

As we have seen, the typical European election does not in any absolute sense settle the matter of who gets into government. Obviously, if members of the incumbent government are reasonably happy with one another, if the election results are not too unfavorable for them, and especially if the government parties between them control a legislative majority, then the incumbent government may well decide to continue in office. No serious consideration may be given to a change of administration. The situation after the 1987 election in West Germany was a case in point. This election involved, on the one hand, an incumbent coalition of the Christian Democrats and the Free Democrats and, on the other hand, two opposition parties, the Social Democrats and the Greens. The coalition as a whole lost a few seats, and within the coalition, a few seats were reallocated from the CDU to the FPD. But there was no serious threat to the government's majority, and to nobody's surprise, the same government continued in office.

Election results may also lead to predictable changes of coalition government. In Ireland in 1973, for example, the two main opposition parties, Fine Gael and Labour, had become extremely frustrated at being unable to dislodge the incumbent Fianna Fáil single-party government that had held office since 1957. The opposition parties decided to bury almost every one of their policy differences and to fight the 1973 election as a coalition, on the basis of a single, very general fourteen-point joint program for government. They won an overall legislative majority between them, and it was taken for granted that they would form a coalition government; this is exactly what happened.

Thus we should not get too bewitched by an image of the political future of most European states being settled not by the electorate but by the wheeling and dealing of party leaders. Even in coalition systems, election results may in practice be politically decisive. They may confirm that an incumbent coalition will remain in office, or they may make it possible for a prearranged coalition in opposition to take over the reins of power. Nonetheless, and this goes to the heart of the matter in most European parliamentary democracies in which one well-disciplined party does not control a majority of legislative seats, the potential always exists for the government to be defeated, both immediately after an election and in the middle of a term of office. Therefore, even when an incumbent government remains in office apparently without incident, this, too, is the result of the politics of coalition. In a coalition system, the bottom line is that the government remains in office for as long as a majority of legislators prefer it to any realistic alternative. Thus how legislators feel about the precise composition of the government, the subject of the rest of this section, is an absolutely vital matter.

Before we can tell a sensible story about how European party leaders set out to bargain their way into government, therefore, and before we can discuss the factors that European legislators take into account when trying to decide which government to support, we must have at least some idea about the motivations of key political actors.

As we have seen, each European government comprises a cabinet led by a prime minister. The prime minister is typically, though not invariably, the leader of one of the main political parties. Thus, in order to become a prime minister, it is almost invariably necessary to become a party leader first, a fact that gives much of the zest to the business of leadership selection in major European political parties. After the prime ministership, cabinet ministries are the most powerful political offices in the land; these jobs represent the pinnacle of a politician's career. Cabinet ministers are typically, though not invariably, senior party legislators, though who is or is not "senior" in a political party is a far less clear-cut matter than who is the party leader. Indeed, a party leader can turn a colleague into a senior politician by successfully imposing him or her as a cabinet minister.

The fact that the positions of prime minister and cabinet minister are such glittering political prizes informs one of the main assumptions that is typically made about the motivations of most politicians. This is that politicians are mainly interested in the "intrinsic" rewards of office. To be a cabinet minister, after all, is to be a famous and powerful person. The desire for such fame and power, though few would admit this openly (or perhaps even to themselves), may well be the most important motivating force for many politicians.

Another important set of reasons for trying to get into government has to do with influencing public policy. If a politician wants to make a difference in the way that the country is run, one of the most effective ways to do this is to get into the cabinet. This, of course, is a far more acceptable motivation, one that politicians are far more inclined to put forward in public. Most European politicians, like their U.S. counterparts, campaign on the basis of promises about all the good that they can do for their country. (Few, whatever their real hopes and fears, solicit votes on the grounds that what they want to do if elected is to make lots of money, get their picture in the newspaper every day, ride around in the backseat of a chauffeur-driven Mercedes, and have a large staff to boss around.)

The desire to consume the intrinsic rewards of office and the desire to have an impact on public policy, therefore, are different plausible motivations for the politicians who are involved in the process of government formation. As we shall now see, however, different interpretations of government formation in Western Europe flow from these alternative assumptions about what drives politicians.

Office-Seeking Politicians and "Minimal Winning" Governments

The best-known approach to the analysis of government formation in Western Europe is based on the assumption that politicians are driven above all else by the desire to enjoy the rewards of office for their own sake. This approach leads to predictions that the coalitions that form will be just big enough to take the prize and no bigger—that "minimal winning" government coalitions are the most likely to be the European norm. Minimal winning governments carry no passengers; they include only parties whose legislative votes are essential for the government's majority.

The logic of this argument is straightforward. If being in government is valued in and of itself, then the set of cabinet positions is like a fixed set of trophies to be shared out by the winners of the government formation game. Any government party whose votes are not essential to the government's legislative majority will be enjoying some of these trophies without having contributed any of the resources essential for their capture. Such "passengers" will therefore be excluded from the government by office-seeking politicians. This logic implies that government coalitions should comprise as few parties as possible, consistent with the need to win confidence votes in the legislature. The "minimal winning" interpretation of coalition formation is most commonly associated with the early work of William Riker on coalitions, though the concept of the minimal winning coalition is by now ubiquitous (see Riker).

Policy-Seeking Politicians and Ideologically Compact Governments

If the politicians who build governments want to leave their mark on public policy rather than merely consume the fruits of office, then a different interpretation of government formation is called for. Public policy, after all, applies to all. It applies to those who are in government and those who are not; it applies, indeed, to the dogs in the street. Above all, public policy cannot in any sense be "used up" at a faster rate if there are more parties in the government. Thus, abolishing the death sentence for convicted murderers is a policy that applies to all, whether they are in the government or outside it, murderers or not. If more people join the government, the policy is in no sense "diluted"; it is no better and no worse than it was before. Those who want no more than to see the death penalty abolished will be delighted when it goes, whether they are in or out of office at the time.

If politicians are driven by nothing but the desire to affect public policy when they set out to bargain their way into coalitions, then the logic of the minimal winning coalition is eroded. If some other politician shares your policies, then there is no reason in the world, if all you are concerned with is policy, to keep this person out of office. In its pure form, this approach suggests that the only criterion that will be used in government formation is the ideological compatibility of the coalition partners. The coalitions that form should contain parties whose policies are as compatible as possible. They will thus be ideologically "compact" in the sense that coalition members will tend to be closer together, rather than farther apart, in their ideological positions.

Obviously, it is rather extreme to assume either that politicians are concerned only with feathering their own nests or that they are concerned only with the good of the country, whatever personal sacrifice is required. The truth is likely to be somewhere in between, and almost all current accounts of the politics of coalition in Western Europe are based on the assumption that politicians are concerned both with getting into office for its own sake and with having an impact on public policy. This leads to predictions that minimal winning coalitions will tend to form, since office motivations are important, but that these will be ideologically compact, since policy is also important. Well-known interpretations of coalition formation based on these assumptions have been put forward by Robert Axelrod—in his "minimal connected winning" (MCW) approach—and by Abram de Swaan—in his "minimum ideological range" approach (see Axelrod and also de Swaan). Minimal connected winning coalitions are coalitions that contain no surplus members and whose members are adjacent, or "connected," to each other on the main left-right policy dimension. A minimum range coalition is the minimal winning coalition with the smallest ideological range on the main left-right dimension.

Minimal Winning Coalitions in West Germany

The various theoretical approaches that we have just outlined have been extensively applied to the interpretation of government formation in Western Europe. This is thus a field of inquiry in which there has been a fruitful and long-standing interaction between theorists, on the one hand, and those whose main concern is the interpretation of European politics, on the other. Obviously, the acid test of the usefulness of a theory, the thing that convinces us that the theory can help us to understand the world a little better, is its ability to predict consistently. Thus we assess the relative usefulness of these approaches to the analysis of government formation in Western Europe by comparing the success rates of the predictions that they make.

The best way to begin this is with a specific example. The top part of Figure 7.2 provides some information about the situation in West Germany after the general election of January 1987, discussed briefly above. Parties are placed on a left-right dimension according to the extent to which they favored, or opposed, public ownership of business and industry (these policy positions are taken from an expert survey of party policy positions in each Western European country, reported by Laver and Hunt). The success of the Greens in this election, eating as they did deep into the Social Democratic vote, made a big potential difference to the politics of coalition in Germany. It resulted in a situation in which, for the first time in many years, the Social Democrats (SPD) did not have enough seats to re-create the coalition with the Free Democrats (FDP) that had allowed them to hold office continuously from 1969 to 1982. The options open to the SPD were thus drastically curtailed by the success of the Greens, which left as possible governments only the range of coalitions outlined in the lower part of Figure 7.2. There were four possible minimal winning coalitions, each of which contained only

Figure 7.2
Coalition Possibilities in Germany: January 1987

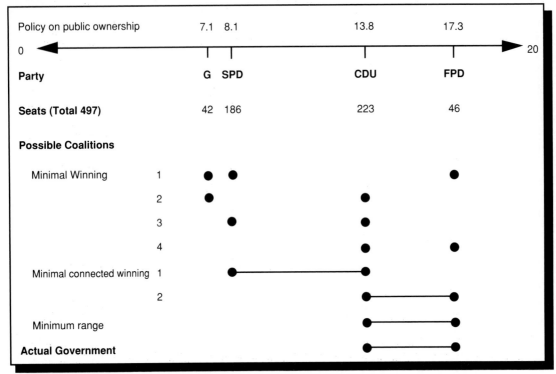

parties that could be disposed of only by depriving the government of its majority. The dominant bargaining position of the Christian Democrats (CDU/CSU) is reflected in the fact that three of these possibilities involved a coalition between the Christian Democrats and one of the other parties; the fourth involved a coalition of all the other parties against the Christian Democrats.

Policy differences between the German parties are now quite large, however, and it does not seem reasonable to assume that each of the arithmetically possible minimal winning coalitions is equally likely to form. As Figure 7.2 also shows, taking policy into account reveals that there were two possible minimal connected winning coalitions in Germany in 1987. One of these linked the FDP to the CDU/CSU, and one linked the SPD and the CDU/CSU. While both of these coalitions are connected, in the sense of comprising parties that are next to each other on the left-right scale, the CDU/CSU was closer on this dimension of policy to the FDP than it was to the SPD, as the more precise estimates of policy positions given in Figure 7.2 show. Thus the coalition between the FDP and the CDU/CSU was the minimal winning coalition with the minimum ideological range, the one with the least ideological diversity. As it happens, this was the coalition that actually formed after the 1987 election in West Germany.

Comparing the Success Rates of Different Coalition Theories

Rather than looking at each approach to the analysis of government formation on a case-by-case basis for each of the hundreds of governments that have formed in postwar Western Europe, we can make more broadly based comparisons of how well each approach predicts the composition of the governments that actually form. The success rates of office-seeking and policy-seeking interpretations of government building Western Europe are compared in Table 7.2, which classifies coalition governments by type for a number of countries.

Looking first at the bottom line, we see that only about 35 percent (77 out of 218) of the European governments analyzed were minimal winning coalitions. Indeed, even if we concentrate only on those situations in which no party won a legislative majority, so that a legislative coalition was essential for the support of a government, only about 40 percent (77 out of 196) of government coalitions were minimal winning. This is not, however, as bad a record for the theory as it might seem at first sight, given the very large number of possible coalitions that could conceivably have formed in the more complicated party systems. The 40 percent success rate of the minimal winning approach is much better than would be achieved by choosing a coalition from the list of possibilities with a pin, but the minimal winning approach is not a method of predicting the party composition of European coalition governments that it would be wise to bet your shirt on.

Of the minimal winning coalitions that did form, about 70 percent (53 out of 77) were also minimal connected winning coalitions between parties that were

TABLE 7.2
Frequency of Coalition Types, by Country: 1945–1987

	One Party Controls Legislative Majority	Situations in Which No One Party Controls a Legislative Majority					
		Minimal Winning (MW)		Non-MW			
		MCW and MW	MW not MCW	MCW not MW	Surplus not MCW	Minority	Total
Austria	6	5	1	—	—	1	13
Belgium	1	7	8	—	4	2	22
Denmark	—	2	—	—	—	18	20
Finland	—	4	1	—	17	10	32
Germany	2	9	1	—	—	—	12
Iceland	—	6	4	—	2	2	14
Ireland	4	—	3	—	—	5	12
Italy	4	—	3	6	8	14	35
Luxembourg	—	8	1	—	1	—	10
Netherlands	—	4	2	3	5	3	17
Norway	4	3	—	—	—	8	15
Sweden	1	5	—	—	—	10	16
Total	22	53	24	9	37	73	218

Source: Laver and Schofield.

adjacent to each other on the left-right dimension. The notion of ideological connectedness, therefore, adds quite a bit to our ability to predict which government is likely to form.

But overwhelmingly the most striking pattern to emerge from the bottom line of Table 7.2 is that the biggest flaw in each of the approaches that we have been discussing so far is that most of the governments that formed were not minimal winning governments. Indeed, nearly 40 percent (73 out of 196) of goverments that formed in minority situations did not have a legislative majority at all; these were "minority" governments. In another quarter of the cases, the government that actually formed would have retained its legislative majority even if one or more of its members had left or been thrown out; these were "surplus" majority governments. Whatever else we can say about European governments, therefore, we cannot say that minimal winning coalitions are the norm. Indeed, on the basis of the numbers in Table 7.2, minority government is as much the norm in Western Europe as anything else.

We can also see from Table 7.2 that different countries tend to have different types of government. While governments in Germany and Luxembourg are nearly always minimal winning coalitions, minority government is the overwhelming norm in Denmark and is very common in Italy, Sweden, and Finland. Most of the surplus majority governments that form are also accounted for by Italy and Finland. It is immediately obvious that before we can hope to understand the business of government formation in Western Europe, we must understand why minority and surplus majority governments are so much more common in some systems than in others.

Minority Governments

At first sight, the idea of minority government might seem to be at best a paradox and at worst downright undemocratic. When there is a minority government, after all, this means that there must also be a majority opposition in the legislature. This opposition could, in theory, throw the government out on its ear but for some reason chooses not to do so. When there is a minority government, furthermore, an executive has taken office with no guarantee that it can stay there for any length of time, since it can be defeated at any moment at the pleasure of the opposition. Yet Kaare Strom has recently argued convincingly that minority government should be seen as a normal outcome of the process of democratic party competition in Europe rather than as some sort of obstacle to it (Strom, 1990).

The main reasons why minority governments are such a common outcome of party competition in Western Europe have to do with the role of party policy. After all, if politicians are motivated solely by the desire to get into office, then it is hard to see why they would choose to go into opposition when they have the legislative muscle to go into government. If politicians are concerned about policy, however, then there may well be circumstances in which policy objectives are better served from a place on the opposition benches than from a seat at the cabinet table. Parties may *choose* to stay in opposition, the better to fulfill their policy objectives.

Strom therefore looked at the influence over policy that can be wielded by the opposition, concentrating mainly on formal influence exercised through the legislative committee system (Strom, 1984 and 1990). The influence of the opposition arises because it is actually rather rare for bottom-line decisions on important policy matters to be slugged out on the floor of the legislature. Most of the real political fights are played out in committees. Different European countries differ considerably, furthermore, in terms of the effectiveness of their committee systems and the policy influence that committees give the opposition. The more powerful the committee system and the greater the influence of the opposition, so the story goes, the less the incentive for opposition parties to get into the government, since they can be just as effective outside it. And the less the incentive to get into government, obviously, the greater the likelihood of finding minority governments.

Strom tested this argument by looking at the size, scope, specialization, and power of the committee system in a number of European democracies. He found that the Norwegian committee system is the one that gives the opposition the most influence over policy. This is followed, according to Strom, by the committee systems of Iceland, Italy, Portugal, Sweden, and France. Strom suggested that the committee systems that afford the opposition the least influence over policy are in Britain and Ireland, followed by the Netherlands. While some of these individual categorizations might be quibbled with, the general pattern is quite clear. The relatively high frequency of minority government in Scandinavia and Italy is consistent, in these terms, with the relatively high formal policy influence of the opposition, exercised through the committee system.

Another way of looking at the impact of opposition parties on the policies of governments in Western Europe is to consider more informal channels of influence. Gregory Luebbert, in a wide-ranging discussion of European coalition government, explained the frequency of minority governments in terms of the role played by interest groups. Looking mainly at the "corporatist" democracies in which interest groups have a powerful institutionalized position (see Chapter 9), Luebbert concluded that the opposition often does not need to get into government in these systems in order to have an effect on policy. When opposition parties have strong links with interest groups, the interest groups can bargain directly with government, backing up the positions that they take with an artillery of threats and promises that have nothing to do with the legislature (see Luebbert). Thus social democratic parties, according to Luebbert, can use trade unions; bourgeois parties can use employers' federations; agrarian parties can use farmers' organizations; and so on. This account seems to be a promising and complementary interpretation of the frequency of minority governments in Scandinavia, where interest groups have both a relatively high influence on the political process and strong links to political parties. In the Scandinavian systems, opposition parties are never fully out in the cold. They can affect government policies using both formal legislative machinery and less formal avenues of political pressure, exploiting the power of the interest groups with which they are associated. The main empirical flaw in this argument is that it is not consistent with the almost complete absense of minority government in Germany and especially in Austria, where interest groups are, by most accounts, very closely integrated into the political process.

A third interpretation of why minority governments are able to stay in power—one that may be more appropriate outside Scandinavia—is based on policy divisions within the opposition (Laver and Schofield). On this account, a minority government can survive and can even be quite stable simply because the opposition parties cannot agree on a replacement. Thus governments can be politically "viable" with far less than a legislative majority. While control over a legislative majority guarantees victory, this does not mean that failure to control a majority spells inevitable defeat.

This logic may well underwrite a number of the minority governments formed by the Christian Democrats in Italy or by the Social Democrats in Denmark. In each case, a substantial party with an ideological position toward the center of the range of positions offered wins less than a majority of seats but faces a divided opposition. Some of the opposing parties are to the left of it; some to the right. As a result of this ideological positioning of the parties, a coalition of opponents formed to evict the center party is not a very plausible possibility. (An added factor in this context is the existence of a large Communist party, whose ideological positions and general "pariah" status can make it even more difficult for the opposition to unite, a factor that has been important in Italy and Finland.) Since it is very difficult to evict the center party from office, that party is in a very strong bargaining position and may well decide to go it alone. Even without a majority, it can't be beaten. Indeed, the ability of a particular party to go it alone as a minority government, in the face of a divided opposition, is one of the acid tests of real bargaining power in the government formation process.

Minority Government in Ireland

An example of the bargaining power that a party can wield as a result of facing a divided opposition can be seen in the outcome of the February 1987 election in Ireland, described in Table 7.3. Fianna Fáil was opposed from the right by Fine Gael and the Progressive Democrats and from the left by Labour and the Workers' party. The underlying bargaining structure of the government formation game was such that there was almost no issue that united all four opposition parties against Fianna Fáil. Thus, while Fianna Fáil could have formed a majority coalition with any one of the opposition parties, it did not need to do so. Since there was little

TABLE 7.3
Distribution of Seats in Dáil Éireann:
March 10, 1987

Party	Seats
Fianna Fáil	81
Fine Gael	51
Progressive Democrats	14
Labour party	12
Workers' party	4
Democratic Socialist party	1
Independent Fianna Fáil	1
Tony Gregory (left-wing independent)	1
Seán Treacy (ex-Labour centrist independent)	1
Total	166

prospect of a rival coalition that could evict Fianna Fáil from office, a Fianna Fáil minority government was relatively secure. There was no reason for the party to take anyone else on board.

The Fianna Fáil leader, Charles Haughey, sensed this bargaining power very clearly and put himself forward as the head of a minority government. While the actual investiture vote was close, as most of the opposition ganged up in an attempt to deny him the prize, the subsequent Fianna Fáil administration was well able to govern, even though it lacked a legislative majority. The opposition often threatened to bring down the government on specific issues. On most of these occasions the government stood firm. Despite much huffing and puffing from the leaders of the opposition parties in the heightened activity before each showdown, one or another of them usually backed down on some pretext just before the critical moment and let the government survive. While this minority government did suffer several minor legislative defeats, it never lost a confidence vote or, indeed, any other vote on a really critical issue. (And even apparently secure single-party majority governments, it should be noted, can suffer minor legislative defeats as a result of wildcat defections on particular issues by disgruntled backbenchers.) The end of this particular minority government came absolutely voluntarily, after Haughey called an election in the hope of winning an overall majority.

Minority Government as a Rule Rather Than an Exception

It should be quite clear from the foregoing discussion that minority government is very much a part of the political scenery in Western Europe. Any model of European politics that cannot give a convincing account of minority government, therefore, is seriously deficient. We should also note that each of the more plausible interpretations of minority government depends upon taking policy seriously. This may be because the opposition to a minority government can be so divided over policy that it can provide no alternative. It may be because parties accept minority governments, anticipating that they can fulfill policy objectives from a position on the opposition benches—by exploiting the committee system or by deploying allied interest groups. If voters are motivated by policy considerations, indeed, then a party may even *prefer* to stay on the opposition benches. By doing this, it can pick and choose the issues on which it makes a policy intervention. In government, in contrast, the same party would be forced to make heavily constrained policy decisions on many issues not of its own choosing and thereby risk alienating its supporters.

Either way, policy figures prominently in accounts of minority government. We might conclude from this that in those countries in which minority government is common, policy is an important factor in party competition. Policy also figures prominently in accounts of "surplus" majority government, the matter to which we now turn.

Surplus Majority Governments in Italy

If politicians are concerned only with getting into office and do not care at all about policy, then governments that include "surplus" parties are as hard to explain as minority governments. Why, after all, would office-seeking politicians agree to

The Making of a Coalition
June 30, 1989: Irish Prime Minister Charles Haughey resigns after his Fianna Fáil minority government was defeated in Parliament, having just lost an election. (© The Irish Times)

July 1, 1989: Fianna Fáil's Joe Walsh delivers a note opening coalition negotiations with election rivals, the Progressive Democrats. (© The Irish Times)

July 7, 1989: PD negotiators Pat Cox and Bobby Molloy whisper to each other during a break in coalition talks with Fianna Fáil. (© The Irish Times)

July 13, 1989: PD leader Desmond O'Malley being appointed by President Hillery to the new coalition government. (© The Irish Times)

July 13, 1989: Fianna Fáil leader Charles Haughey being reappointed as prime minister after the successful conclusion of coalition talks with the PDs. (© The Irish Times)

give some of the scarce rewards of office to a party that contributes nothing to the securing of these rewards in the first place? Yet, as Table 7.2 shows, surplus majority governments are rather common in Western Europe, especially in Finland and, to a lesser extent, in Italy and the Netherlands.

Recent Italian governments, for example, have been based upon the five-party, or *pentapartito*, formula. Almost all of these *pentapartito* coalitions have included some parties whose legislative votes were not needed for the government's majority. Yet those parties were taken into the government and given portfolios anyway. A typical example arose in the wake of the 1981 election, the results of which are listed in Table 7.4.

In this case the Christian Democrats (DC) and the Socialists (PSI) between them controlled a legislative majority. Yet three other parties were included in the government: the Social Democrats (PSDI), the Republicans (PRI), and the Liberals (PLI). The same coalition formed and reformed over and over during the 1980s, and in each case, the same "surplus" parties were included. Only if policy is important in party competition in Italy can this be explained easily; taking "surplus" parties into the government costs little, provided that their policies don't conflict with those of more pivotal government members. Two of the three surplus members in the Italian *pentapartito* coalition—the PSDI and the PRI—did, indeed, have policy positions, at least on the left-right scale, between those of the Socialists and the Christian Democrats. They might have been passengers as far as the government's legislative majority was concerned, but in policy terms, it didn't cost much to carry them along.

Surplus Parties Protect Powerful Players

Luebbert, in his discussion of surplus majority governments in Western Europe, takes a more positive view of surplus majority governments than this. He argues

TABLE 7.4
**Pentapartito Coalition in Italy:
June 1981**

	Seats
Government parties:	
DC	262
PSDI	20
PRI	16
PSI	62
PLI	9
Total	369
Majority threshold	315
Opposition parties:	
PCI	201
MSI	30
Others	30
Total	261

that clear benefits, especially for a dominant party, can arise from carrying passengers in cabinet coalitions. Once a government takes office, after all, any party that is crucial to the government's majority can bring the entire executive tumbling down by withdrawing its support. Even very small parties have a potent threat with which to attempt to extract concessions from their cabinet colleagues, provided, that is, that their votes are critical to the government majority. In anticipation of this, a strong party may choose to surround itself with a protective screen of weaker passengers so that no other single party is critical to the government majority. In this event, none of the weaker passengers can make serious demands once the government has formed, since every one of them is expendable (Luebbert, p. 79). To put it rather crudely, powerful parties might actually choose to carry passengers so that one or two can be tossed overboard without too much fuss if they start to get greedy.

Conclusion: Which Parties *Do* Get into Government?

The matter of which parties get into Western European governments has excited political scientists for a number of years. We have seen from the preceding discussions that there is nothing magical about a majority when it comes to forming a government. Stable governments can form with less than a majority of the legislative seats. And there may be incentives for governments to keep adding members even after they have passed the majority threshold. In theory, the most plausible interpretations of these minority and surplus majority governments assume that policy is a major factor in government formation. In practice, the two countries—Italy and Finland—in which surplus majority governments are most frequent are also countries in which minority governments are common, suggesting that the same factors are at work.

Above all, it is important to note that when a minority or surplus majority government is formed in Western Europe, it must not be treated as some sort of failure in the political process. It is by now widely appreciated that single-party majority government is the exception rather than the rule in Western Europe. What is less commonly understood is that "bare majority," or minimal winning, government is far from being the normal outcome of the government formation process in most European systems.

All of this has important consequences for those who seek to understand the party composition of European governments. It means that it is not at all unusual to find dominant parties forming single-party administrations even when they fall quite a long way short of a legislative majority. In the same way it is quite common to find apparently weak parties being taken into government, despite the fact that their votes could be lost without danger to the government majority. Such parties can make a contribution to the stability of a government, even when their votes are not artithmetically necessary. These conclusions, however, depend on taking policy seriously. If we assume that politicians set out to bargain their way into cabinets with no other objective than to enjoy the perks of office, then the pattern of government formation in Western Europe leaves a number of unsolved puzzles. Thus, the frequency of minority and surplus majority governments is a clear indication that policy *is* important for those people who bargain over the formation of Western European governments.

BOX 7.2
Cabinet Types

FRANCE

Between 1958 and 1981, France was governed by a right-wing coalition. This was sometimes just short of a parliamentary majority but was able to govern, partly owing to divisions on the left. Sometimes the government was a minimal winning coalition, and sometimes it controlled a surplus majority (notably after a Gaullist electoral landslide in 1968). Since 1981, governments have alternated between right-wing coalitions and left-wing socialist administrations, the latter sometimes being minority cabinets needing support from either Communists or centrists.

GERMANY

For most of the postwar period, German politics revolved around three parties, which have at some stage formed every possible two-party minimal winning coalition. In the early postwar period, the Christian Democrats (CDU/CSU) took other parties into surplus majority governments, despite controlling a legislative majority on their own. Coalitions between the large CDU/CSU and the much smaller Liberals (FDP) formed between 1957 and 1966, when a "grand coalition" of the two big parties—CDU/CSU and Social Democrats (SPD)—formed. These were followed by an SPD-FDP coalition from 1969 to 1982, when a coalition between the FDP and the CDU/CSU replaced the government as a result of a constructive vote of no confidence. This coalition remained in place until 1990. The small FDP have thus been in one government or another in Germany for most of the postwar period.

ITALY

The most striking feature of postwar Italian politics is that the Christian Democrats (DC) have never been out of office. Sometimes they have been in a coalition, and sometimes they have formed a single-party minority government. For most of this period, furthermore, the DC have controlled the prime ministership, though this has occasionally been ceded to other parties. Coalition cabinets have often controlled surplus majorities, notably the more stable center-left coalitions that held of-fice from 1980 to 1990. In most of these, only the votes of the DC and the Socialists (PSI) were necessary to control the legislature, but other minor parties (Liberals, Social Democrats, and Republicans) where also included in the cabinet.

NETHERLANDS

Superficially, government formation in the Netherlands appears to involve an immense number of possibilities, given the large number of parties in the Dutch legislature. In practice, only a few of these have any real bargaining power, and government formation has revolved around three key players: the Labor party (PvdA) the Liberals (VVD), and the Christian Democrats (CDA—this pivotal role was formerly filled by the Catholic Peoples party, KVP). The Christian Democrats have been a member of every single postwar Dutch government, in alternating partnerships with either the left or the right. Minority governments are rare, but surplus majority governments were formed in the early postwar era, when the Christian parties brought secular parties into government, even though they did not need their seats for a majority.

SPAIN

Spain since Franco has been characterized by one-party governments. The first five of these were rather short-lived one-party minority administrations controlled by the right-wing Union of the Democratic Center (UCD), which was just short of a parliamentary majority and held office from 1976 to 1982. Since 1982, when the Socialist party (PSOE) won an overall legislative majority, Spain has been governed by one-party Socialist cabinets led by Felipe González.

SWEDEN

For most of the postwar era, Swedish politics have been dominated by the Social Democrats, who typically have not won an electoral majority but have been able to form reasonably stable minority cabinets with the support of either the more left-wing Communists or the more centrist Center

(Continued on next page)

party. Since 1976, there has been some alternation in office, as the Center party usually was the swing voter in the legislature. Thus center or center-right coalitions formed during the period 1976 to 1982, sometimes very far short of a parliamentary majority (the smallest controlled only 11 percent of the seats but nonetheless lasted for one year). A series of single-party minority Social Democratic governments has been in office since 1982.

UNITED KINGDOM
The first-past-the-post electoral system typically ensures one-party legislative majorities—and hence one-party governments, which have alternated between Labour and the Conservatives since World War II. After the February 1974 election, the only one in the postwar era in which no party won an overall majority, a Labour minority government formed with Liberal support and lasted until October of the same year. The 1976–1979 Labour cabinet under James Callaghan lost its majority as a result of by-election defeats and continued in office as a minority government with support first from the Liberals and then from assorted nationalists before being defeated in 1979.

THE ALLOCATION OF CABINET PORTFOLIOS

The cabinet is the key organ of government in most Western European states, acting both as a committee for making decisions in the name of the entire government and as a collection of individuals with responsibility for making and implementing policy in particular areas. Most important policy decisions do not require the direct assent of the legislature, in the sense of requiring legislation or some other form of legislative motion. In theory, the mechanism of the confidence vote gives the legislature control over the executive in all of these matters—legislators can instruct the government to act in a particular way, on pain of defeat in a confidence motion. In practice, however, the threat of such a dire sanction is a constraint on executive action only if the issue is one that a majority of legislators feel very strongly about, strongly enough to be prepared to bring down the government. When legislators do not feel this strongly, then having at their disposal a threat to bring down the government gives them a sledgehammer with which to crack a nut. As a result, cabinet ministers have considerable de facto autonomy regarding most aspects of policy that fall within the jurisdiction of their portfolio.

We have just seen that the motivations of the politicians who bargain over coalition formation are the key to understanding the party composition of governments in most Western European states. The politicians who do the bargaining, of course, are the very same people who consume the spoils if they are successful, whatever their motivations might be. If they succeed in getting their party into government, then most of them will get their feet under the cabinet table, enjoying considerable control over government policy as well as the life-style of an important public figure.

Notwithstanding the control over public policy that can be wielded by cabinet ministers, therefore, we should not ignore the perks. To win a seat at the cabinet table is, after all, the pinnacle of a career in politics for most Western European legislators. The job brings public recognition, power, patronage, and many other pleasant trappings of success. We should not be surprised to find that many politicians dedicate their political lives single-mindedly to the pursuit of these coveted positions.

Thus, following from the two basic drives that we might assume motivate politicians—the desire to consume the benefits of office and the desire to influence public policy—there are two basic ways of interpreting the political value of cabinet portfolios. On the one hand, they may be seen as booties to be distributed among members of the winning side. On the other hand, they may be seen as vital levers with which to control the direction of government policy.

Cabinet Spoils in West Germany

If a cabinet portfolio is seen as booty, then we can easily observe how the booties are divided up in different Western European countries. The patterns that we see are quite striking. Cabinet portfolios tend to be distributed among government parties in strict proportion to the number of seats that each party contributes to the government's legislative majority. As an example, consider the coalition cabinet that formed in Germany in 1980, comprising Free Democrats (FDP) and Social Democrats (SPD). The FDP contributed about 20 percent of the government's seat total and the SPD about 80 percent. Table 7.5 shows the allocation of cabinet seats between the two parties, together with their precise legislative seat totals.

TABLE 7.5

Allocation of Cabinet Portfolios in West Germany: November 5, 1980

Portfolio	Party
Chancellor	SPD
Foreign affairs	FDP
Interior	FDP
Finance	SPD
Economics	FDP
Labor and social policy	SPD
Defense	SPD
Food and agriculture	FDP
Justice	SPD
Transportation	SPD
Postal service	SPD
Housing and urban affairs	SPD
Intra-German relations	SPD
Research and technology	SPD
Education and science	SPD
Economic cooperation	SPD
Health	SPD

Party	Legislative seats
CDU/CSU	226
SPD	218
FDP	53

In crude numerical terms, the FDP got rather more than its "fair" share of the cabinet. It won about 20 percent of the government's legislative seat total but took about 25 percent of all cabinet seats. In terms of naked bargaining power, on the other hand, the legislative seats held by the FDP were every bit as crucial to the government's majority as those held by the SPD, and so the power of the FDP was the same as that of the SPD. If the FDP had pushed its bargaining power to the limit, then it could have demanded the same number of cabinet seats as the SPD. It clearly did not do this; the outcome in this case was quite close to what would be predicted by a "norm" under which cabinet seats are allocated in proportion to legislative seats. It was quite different from the allocation that would be predicted on the basis of the unbridled exercise of bargaining power.

Cabinet Seats and Proportional Payoffs

This example is very typical of the pattern to be found elsewhere. A well-known piece of work by Browne and Franklin demonstrated that a "proportionality norm" such as this is a very good predictor of the allocation of cabinet portfolios, a result confirmed with more recent data by Schofield and Laver (Browne and Franklin; Schofield and Laver). Of course, unbridled bargaining power and legislative seat share, while not strictly related to one another, do tend to go hand in hand—a party that has more seats tends as often as not to have more bargaining power. Schofield and Laver found, controlling for this interaction between the seat share and bargaining power, that countries could be sorted into those where cabinet portfolios seem to be allocated according to a norm of proportionality and those in which bargaining power seems to be more important. These classifications can be found in Table 7.6.

What stands out in Table 7.6 is that different methods of allocating cabinet portfolios seem to be used in different types of party systems. In particular, more complex party systems such as those in Denmark, Belgium, Finland, and Italy show the effects of bargaining power. In contrast, in simpler party systems such as those

TABLE 7.6

Relative Performance of "Proportionality" and "Bargaining" Norms in the Allocation of Portfolio Payoffs

Country	Norm That Better Predicts Actual Payoffs
Luxembourg	Proportionality
Ireland	Proportionality
Austria	Proportionality
Germany	Proportionality
Norway	Proportionality
Iceland	Bargaining
Sweden	Bargaining
Denmark	Bargaining
Belgium	Bargaining
Finland	Bargaining
Italy	Bargaining

in Luxembourg, Ireland, Austria, and Germany, we see the effects of a proportionality norm in the allocation of cabinet seats among parties. The more complex systems have more parties than the others, and anyone with an ounce of arithmetic will know that the number of possible ways to combine parties into coalitions escalates very rapidly as the size of the party system increases. (There are many more ways to build a government in a ten-party system than there are in a nine-party system, for example.)

Schofield and Laver speculated that the proportionality norm operates in the simpler party systems because in these systems, changes in election results tend not to affect the range of possible governments and the balance of power between parties. For much of the postwar period in Germany, for example, it has been a simple arithmetical fact that any two of the three main parties could have formed a majority government—even quite large changes in the distribution of seats among parties made no real difference to the logic of this situation, to its "decisive structure." The fact that the bargaining logic of the simpler party system may well not change over a series of elections may allow for the emergence of norms that govern the allocation of payoffs. In particular, it may encourage politicians to use a proportionality norm when distributing cabinet seats, since in this way the party system can respond to election results, even when "raw" bargaining power is unchanged by these. The counterexample, once more, is Switzerland. Here, a series of "Magic Formula" coalitions has formed, following election after election, on the basis of a fixed allocation of seats among the main establishment parties. Election results make no effective difference to this arrangement, which amounts to a cartel between the government parties.

One thing is quite clear from all of this: the arithmetical allocation of cabinet portfolios among parties is very predictable indeed. Browne and Franklin's findings are based on empirical analyses that explain about 90 percent of the variation in the allocation of cabinet seats in the real world, and as such they have gone down in the annals of political science as some of the most dramatic nontrivial empirical relationships thus far encountered. The facts suggest strongly that European politicians treat the allocation of cabinet portfolios very seriously indeed. This is hardly surprising, since, as we have already argued, a cabinet portfolio represents the ultimate ambition of most of them.

Qualitative Features of Cabinet Payoffs in West Germany

While the quantitative proportionality of portfolio payoffs is quite striking, these findings do not undermine the assumption that many European politicians participate in politics in order to have an impact on public policy—the interpretation that fits squarely with the facts on the frequency of minority and surplus majority governments. Controlling a cabinet portfolio, after all, is the best means for a European politician to have an impact on public policy. This means that we need to do much more than count portfolios when we analyze coalition outcomes. The allocation of particular portfolios to particular parties is a vitally important matter.

Consider the German example described in Table 7.7. Two coalitions between the Social Democrats (SPD) and the Free Democrats (FDP) were headed by SPD leader Willy Brandt. The first formed in 1969, the second in 1972. Despite the fact

TABLE 7.7
**Changing Allocations of Cabinet Portfolios
in Germany, 1969–1972**

Portfolio	Party, 1969	Party, 1972
Chancellor	SPD	SPD
Foreign affairs	FDP	FDP
Interior	FDP	FDP
Economics	SPD	FDP
Labor and social policy	SPD	SPD
Defense	SPD	SPD
Food and agriculture	FDP	FDP
Justice	SPD	SPD
Transportation	SPD	SPD
Housing and urban affairs	SPD	SPD
Intra-German relations	SPD	SPD
Research and technology	*	SPD
Education and science	Nonparty	SPD
Economic cooperation	SPD	SPD
Health	SPD	SPD
Special assignments	SPD	SPD, FDP

*Combined with education and science.
Source: Norpoth, p. 25.

that the two coalitions look "the same" in the sense that they have the same chancellor (prime minister) and the same parties in the cabinet, the detailed allocation of cabinet portfolios reveals a significant shift in policy profile between the two governments. While nearly all the portfolio allocations were the same, a very important change was that the FDP increased its say in economic policy by taking over the economics ministry from the SPD. Since we can expect this switch to have an impact on the economic policy of the government, we might well choose to regard the 1972 government as quite a different type of government, notwithstanding the fact that the party composition of the cabinet remains unchanged. In contrast, the first two coalitions led by Schmidt, which formed in 1974 and 1976, were based upon absolutely identical allocations of cabinet portfolios between the two government parties and may be thought of in terms as being essentially the same government (Norpoth, p. 25).

Cabinet Portfolios and Government Policy

Looking in more general empirical terms at the qualitative allocation of cabinet portfolios, Budge and Keman have found that there is a tendency for parties to be rewarded with the ministries that are crucial in the policy areas of special interest to them (Budge and Keman). There is a very strong tendency for agrarian parties to get the agriculture portfolio, for example, and there are weaker but still distinct trends in relation to other portfolios.

This means that the allocation of cabinet portfolios is not just the handing out of a set of spoils to senior politicians who have managed to take control of the government; it is also a very important way in which the policy profile of any new government is defined. This is because allocating a cabinet portfolio to one senior politician rather than another makes a big difference to the expected policy output of the government in question (Budge and Keman; Laver and Shepsle, 1990a). And it means that cabinet "reshuffles," or changes in the precise allocation of cabinet portfolios, are far more fundamental than many commentators have realized (Laver and Shepsle, 1990a).

Recent work on government formation by Laver and Shepsle and by Austen-Smith and Banks (Austen-Smith and Banks; Laver and Shepsle, 1990a) has extended this approach, seeing the allocation of cabinet portfolios as the fundamental defining characteristic of a government. Indeed, this extended approach sees a cabinet minister not just as a *member* of the government but as *being* the government, more or less as a policy dictator in the particular policy area over which she or he has jurisdiction. Thus a minister of health, for example, has tremendous power to affect the flow of public policy in the area of health; a minister of education has tremendous power over education policy; and so on. This implies that if you want to know a government's policy position on any issue, you do not look at official policy statements (which are regarded as unreliable "cheap talk" by these authors); you look at the policy preferences of the person who has been given the relevant portfolio. These, when all is said and done, constitute the only credible statement about the policy position of the government.

This approach allows us to look inside parties at the role played by senior politicians in government formation (Laver and Shepsle, 1990b). A particular government may be made possible by a particular cabinet appointment—that of a hard-line defense minister, for example. If this person leaves the scene for some reason or another—such as illness or scandal—then no other person may be able to fulfill this role, and the government may be destabilized. This means that shifts in the balance of power *within* parties can have a fundamental bearing upon the politics *between* parties that underpins any particular government.

Practical examples of this abound in Italy, where the lively internal politics can quickly shift the balance of power within the Christian Democrats (DC)—never out of office during the postwar era. This can have a major bearing on the composition of governments. For example, the opening of the DC to a coalition with the Socialists, rather than with the Communists, was made much more likely by the assassination of Aldo Moro, the leader of a DC faction that favored an alliance with the Communists (Pridham, pp. 222–223). Thus the politics of coalition in Italy was affected by a shift in the balance of power within the DC brought about by the assassination of a senior party politician, a process that we can only begin to understand by taking seriously the policy preferences of potential cabinet ministers.

Overall, there can be no doubt that the cabinet is a vital institution in European parliamentary democracy. In theory it is permanently beholden to the legislature, which can evict it at any stage by a vote of no confidence in the executive. In practice, however, the considerable autonomy of cabinet ministers is set public policy in their respective areas of jurisdiction means that the cabinet is much more independent than theory might suggest. And this means that the question of who gets into the cabinet, whether motivated by the desire to change the course of public policy or by nothing more elevated than the desire to be a big shot, should be seen as the fundamental political question with which each European system is concerned. In the last analysis, voters choose between alternative sets of politicians; these politicians bargain over who gets what in the cabinet. The ideological complexion of the cabinet that they form represents the most important single way in which party politics in general and the voters in particular can be said to have an impact on what the government actually sets out to do.

THE STABILITY OF EUROPEAN GOVERNMENTS

Some European countries have much more stable governments than others. Taking the average life expectancy of a cabinet as a measure of government stability, we can see this quite clearly in Table 7.8. (We will return in a moment to discuss the implication of the two different estimates of cabinet stability.) At the "stable" end of the spectrum we find Luxembourg, Ireland, Austria, Germany, and Britain. At the more "unstable" end of the spectrum, with the shortest average cabinet durations, we find Belgium, Finland, Portugal, and Italy. The stability of governments is obviously an important matter for all who are interested in politics, and considerable intellectual energy has been devoted to interpreting the patterns highlighted in Table 7.8. Before we move on to explore these trends in the durability of governments, it is worth commenting on one unexpectedly tricky matter: that of deciding

TABLE 7.8
Average Duration of Postwar Cabinets in Western Europe

Country	Laver and Schofield Estimate, Months	King et al. Estimate, Months
Luxembourg	45	—
Ireland	39	31
Austria	38	—
Germany	37	—
United Kingdom	—	30
Spain	—	29
Iceland	34	28
Norway	32	24
Sweden	28	24
Netherlands	27	24
Denmark	26	21
Belgium	22	15
Finland	15	14
Portugal	—	11
Italy	13	10

Note: Laver and Schofield (1990), using a data set collected by Schofield (1987), define a government termination whenever there is an election or a change in the party composition of the cabinet. King et al., using a data set collected by Strom (1990), define a government termination in these cases, as well as when there is a formal government resignation or change of prime minister (even if the same cabinet forms once again afterward). The latter definition thus identifies more terminations and generates smaller estimates of mean government durations.

when a government has actually come to an end. Unfortunately, different researchers have looked at this in different ways.

To begin with the easy part, all researchers agree that one government ends and a new one takes office when the party membership of the cabinet changes. If a party leaves, or if new parties join, then there is effectively a new government. Some commentators—Lijphart and Dodd, for example—take this as being the only definitive sign that a government has changed (see Dodd and also Lijphart). Others regard a new government as having formed after every election, even if the same parties and the same prime minister resume control. They do this on the grounds that every new legislature represents a completely new bargaining environment, and so explaining what might appear on the face of it to be the "same" government presents a new problem (Schofield). Schofield does not, however, regard a new government as having formed when a cabinet resigns and re-forms under the same prime minister and with the same party composition. In contrast, both Strom and Browne, in their separate studies of cabinet duration, do consider a resignation and re-forming of the same cabinet to imply a new government (Browne, Frendreis, and Gleiber, 1986; Strom, 1990).

All of this shows that the question "How long does a government last?" is more complicated than appears at first sight. Clearly, there is no "right" answer; different researchers have used different definitions for different purposes. But it is important to bear these different definitions in mind when looking at the research on cabinet durability. The two definitions used in Table 7.8, for example, give a different picture of the actual average duration of governments, though they both give the same rank ordering of countries in terms of cabinet durability. In this case, the different definitions do not make a difference to judgments about the *relative* stability of governments.

Most studies of the duration of European cabinets concentrate on two things. First, cabinets themselves may possess certain features that lead some to be more durable than others. It is widely believed, for example, that coalition governments are more unstable than single-party governments and that majority governments are more stable than minority governments. Second, there are features of the bargaining environment in which a government must survive. Some of these may tend to encourage, or discourage, stability. A fragmented party system with many small parties, for example, or a party system with a powerful antiregime party may lead to greater cabinet instability.

Cabinet Attributes and Cabinet Stability

As Table 7.9 shows, the expectation that single-party governments last longer than coalitions and the expectation that majority governments last longer than minority governments are borne out by the figures for actual government durations in Western Europe. On the average, single-party majority governments last about a year longer than minimal winning coalitions and more than twice as long as minority governments. Minimal winning governments, in turn, last much longer than minority governments. These patterns hold when we compare different types of government within individual countries, as well as when we compare different countries that tend to have different types of government.

TABLE 7.9

Average Duration, in Months, of European Cabinets by Type, 1945–1987

Country	Type of Government				
	Single-Party Majority	Minimal Winning	Surplus Majority	Minority	Total
Luxembourg	NA	47	5	NA	45
Ireland	49	42	NA	30	39
Austria	46	40	24	20	38
Germany	NA	33	49	NA	37
Iceland	NA	39	40	8	34
Norway	48	37	NA	24	32
Sweden	24	24	NA	30	28
Netherlands	NA	31	34	4	27
Denmark	NA	43	NA	22	26
Belgium	46	25	12	7	22
Finland	NA	19	15	10	15
Italy	NA	17	17	9	13
Average	45	33	21	19	26

Source: Laver and Schofield.

Table 7.9 also shows, however, that there are large differences between countries in government durability, even when we take account of the different types of cabinet that form. Minority governments are much more stable in Ireland, Sweden, and Norway, for example, than in Italy, Belgium, and the Netherlands. Minimal winning coalitions are more stable in Luxembourg, Ireland, and Austria and much less stable in Finland and Italy. Thus the party system in which a government is set, as well as the type of government itself, appears to have a major impact upon government stability.

System Attributes and Cabinet Duration

As Tables 7.8 and 7.9 show quite clearly, the stability of European governments is closely related to the distinctions between different types of bargaining systems that we drew earlier, when looking at the distribution of cabinet portfolios. The tables show very clearly that governments are more short-lived in the larger and more complex, multipolar bargaining systems, a pattern also found by Grofman (1989). This should not surprise us, since it is precisely in these more complex systems that small changes in the bargaining environment within which a government must exist may destabilize an existing equilibrium and bring the government tumbling down. (Such changes may relate to the distribution of seats between parties, to the expectations of the actors, or to the personalities involved. For example, an unexpected turnaround in opinion poll ratings may change the expectations of politicians about the outcome of the next election. This change might easily destabilize a sensitive bargaining equilibrium.) Obviously, a government is likely to be more vulnerable and thus more short-lived the smaller the change in its overall political environment that is necessary to destabilize it.

In Finland, to take just one example, it is often the case that the set of potential governments that can form depends upon details of the precise distribution of legislative seats between parties. Small changes in this seat distribution can have big effects on the balance of power. This means that even minor political shocks, causing unanticipated small movements in opinion polls, for example, may have important consequences for bargaining. This is because even small opinion shifts may give some parties an incentive to pull the plug on the government and hope for an election, since the election, if called, is likely to shift bargaining power in their direction.

In Luxembourg, in contrast, almost no election result that can realistically be forecast is likely to change the power structure in the legislature. After any election, the situation that is likely to prevail is that any two of the three main parties will be needed to form a government and that the large centrist party, the Christian Social party, is going to be very difficult to keep out of office. Since no election result is likely to change this fact of political life, the incentives to try to bring down the government and force an election are minimal.

Differences between countries in terms of the complexity of their bargaining systems, in short, seem to have a major bearing on government stability. These conclusions are reinforced by an extensive systematic analysis of factors affecting the stability of cabinets that was conducted by King, Alt, Burns, and Laver (1990). This shows that government duration is significantly affected by two factors that contribute directly to bargaining complexity: the fragmentation and ideological polarization of the party system.

Government Stability and Political Shocks

The "political science" approaches to the stability of European governments that we have just discussed appear to stand in stark contrast to the approaches typically adopted by political journalists and practicing politicians. Those who are deeply involved in the rough-and-tumble of day-to-day politics are apt to see the fall (defeat or resignation) of any government as the direct product of a particular sequence of events. When a government falls, therefore, the newspapers are typically full of chronologies that set out the "critical events" that led to its demise. Even governments that seem very durable can sometimes, it seems, be ambushed by events that are largely beyond their control. The tables presented above show very clearly that whatever the superficial plausibility of this view in respect of any individual government, there are also clear general patterns in the stability of European governments that transcend individual cases. Even so, we should not ignore the clear possibility that many governments might have lasted longer had circumstances been more propitious. A government that seems, on the face of it, to be rather durable can slip on a political banana skin (a scandal, perhaps, or the death of a key political figure) and be destroyed quite unexpectedly.

Obviously, when we set out to predict the durability of any particular government, we are talking only about the *probability* that it will last for a specified period of time. A government has a certain durability, arising from the factors that we have discussed above, but it must also exist in an uncertain political world, bombarded by a stream of potentially destabilizing events. Any one of these events may be a bullet with the government's name on it. The mathematics of this type of environment is by now rather well known, and one group of scholars, in particular, has set out with some success to describe the stability of European governments as a result of the impact of a stream of random political shocks (Browne, Frendreis, and Gleiber, 1984, 1986, and 1988).

A complete account of the life cycle of governments must take account both of the key attributes of governments and of the stream of potentially destructive events in which they must exist. Some governments are clearly more durable than others; but even a durable government can be shot down out of a clear blue sky by an unexpected event. Using appropriate statistical assumptions to model the impact of random events, it is possible to combine both approaches into a single account of government duration in Western Europe. A recent analysis by King et al. that did this suggests, as we mentioned earlier, that the complexity of the bargaining environment has an important impact on government stability. In the more complex and sensitive bargaining environments that are found in the "larger" party systems, "smaller" (and more frequent) critical events seem more likely to be fatal. In the less complex environments of the "smaller" party systems, it takes a "larger" (and less frequent) critical event to destabilize the government (King, Alt, Burns, and Laver).

The statistical techniques used by King et al. also allowed them to "remove" the effect of holding scheduled elections on the life span of governments. This allowed them to estimate what the durations of governments would have been, had they not been brought to an end by the constitutional requirement that elections be held every specified period. They found that scheduled elections have little effect on the durations of governments in high-turnover systems such as Finland and Italy. In contrast, if it weren't for scheduled elections, governments in Britain would last even longer, on the average, than they do at present. In other words, there is evidence, for the more stable cabinet systems, that such turnover in governments as does exist is more a product of the constitutional requirement that elections be held at regular intervals than it is of forces at work within the party system. In more complex party systems, a high turnover of governments seems guaranteed as a result of instabilities in the bargaining environment, even without a constitutional limitation on their tenure.

CONCLUSION

The formation of governments in Western Europe has been more extensively studied than many other aspects of the political process. While there is always more work to be done, our conclusions on this important subject can nonetheless be rather more conclusive than those on other important matters that we deal with.

First and foremost, we must reemphasize that the normal situation in Western Europe is for no party to have a legislative majority and for legislative coalitions to be needed in order to keep any government in power, given the system of parliamentary government. While *legislative* coalitions will always be needed in such cases if the government is to gain and retain office, it is by no means always necessary that there be an *executive* coalition of parties. If a single-party "minority" cabinet can find favor with a majority of legislators, then it can form and maintain a

BOX 7.3
Government Stability

FRANCE

The extreme government instability of the Fourth Republic, with an average government duration of well under one year, was one of the main reasons why the constitution was revised to create the Fifth Republic in 1958. Since then, French cabinets have tended to be rather stable, though when a president was elected who belonged to a different party from that of the prime minister, this was followed by an immediate dissolution of the legislature, as the president hoped to get a prime minister of the same political complexion.

GERMANY

German coalition cabinets are very stable, tending to endure for the full interelectoral period. Only once in recent times, in 1982, has a government been brought down between elections. As a result, the average duration of German cabinets, at around three years, is on a par with that to be found in countries with mainly one-party majority cabinets, such as Britain.

ITALY

Italy is often taken as the classic example of a European coalition system with very unstable cabinets; indeed, the average cabinet duration in Italy is the lowest in Europe, at around one year. Minority governments in particular are very short-lived, though often these are seen by the parties themselves as temporary expedients, sometimes formed with the intention of pushing through a series of patronage appointments and implementing other partisan decisions, in the knowledge that the government cannot last. Quite often, however, the same key people fill the same key portfolios across a series of cabinets, and this implies that Italian politics are more stable than cabinet durations alone might suggest.

NETHERLANDS

The average duration of Dutch cabinets is between thirty months and three years, which is very much the norm for continental European coalition systems. Actually, the average figure rather understates the effective durability of Dutch cabinets, which tend to fall into one of two types. There are very short-lived, clearly transitional caretaker governments that hold office during the negotiation of more permanent governments; and there are those governments themselves, which tend to be much more stable. Considering the complexity of the party system, many governments in the Netherlands are quite durable.

SPAIN

A number of rather unstable right-wing minority cabinets formed and fell in the immediate post-Franco period. Since the Socialists gained a single-party legislative majority in 1982, however, Spanish governments have been very durable, typically running for the full interelectoral period.

SWEDEN

Although Sweden has had a large number of minority governments, the average cabinet duration is very typical of that in continental European coalition systems. Indeed, minority governments in Sweden, particularly minority governments in which the Social Democrats have received legislative support from the Communists, have been more stable than other government types. The Swedish case thus suggests strongly that minority governments need be no more unstable than others, provided that they are solidly based.

UNITED KINGDOM

Governments in the U.K. are among the most durable in Western Europe. Single-party majority governments tend to last for more or less the full legal period allowed between elections, though there is a very strong tendency toward the end of this period for governments to watch opinion polls closely and call an election when they hope to maximize their vote. Minority governments tend to be short-lived and viewed very much as temporary expedients.

viable government. Such minority cabinets are very much part of the mainstream experience in Western Europe. Minimum winning coalitions, while common, do not account for the majority of governments that form, notwithstanding the preconceptions of many of those who write about the government formation process.

Second, the details of the composition of the cabinet are a matter of vital political interest. In this regard, political scientists have only just caught up with politicians and journalists, who never doubted the matter. The proportional allocation of cabinet portfolios among parties is clearly a very firmly established norm in most Western European systems. This does not mean, however, that the allocation of portfolios is a minor political matter. What it means is that the real political action is concerned with which particular politician gets which particular portfolio. The end product of this process determines the fundamental character of the government.

Third, certain types of coalition systems do, indeed, generate rather unstable cabinets, with Italy, Finland, and Belgium being the obvious examples. However, other coalition systems—those of Austria, Germany, and Luxembourg, for example—seem to be pretty much as stable as the atypical one-party government system found in Britain (where government stability is often put forward as the main advantage of maintaining a non-PR electoral system).

Finally, putting all of this together, we should remember that the politics of coalition in Western Europe are the vital link between legislative politics, on which the voting population has at least a small impact, and executive politics, which have by far the biggest effect on what actually happens to voters but over which they have no direct control. To put it in a nutshell, it is only as a result of the workings of the politics of coalition that the typical Western European country can be said to be a democracy.

References

Austen-Smith, D., and J. Banks: "Stable Portfolio Allocations," *American Political Science Review*, vol. 84, 1990, pp. 891–906.

Axelrod, R.: *Conflict of Interest*, Markham, Chicago, 1970.

Browne, E., and M. Franklin: "Aspects of Coalition Payoffs in European Parliamentary Democracies," *American Political Science Review*, vol. 67, 1973, pp. 453–469.

———, J. Frendreis, and D. Gleiber: "An Events Approach to the Problem of Cabinet Stability," *Comparative Political Studies*, vol. 17, 1984, pp. 167–197.

———, ———, and ———: "The Process of Cabinet Dissolution: An Exponential Model of Duration and Stability in Western Democracies," *American Journal of Political Science*, vol. 30, 1986, pp. 625–650.

———, ———, and ———: "Contending Models of Cabinet Stability: Rejoinder," *American Political Science Review*, vol. 82, 1988, pp. 930–941.

Budge, I., and H. Keman: *How Party Government Works: Testing a Theory of Formation, Functioning and Termination in 20 Democracies*, Oxford University Press, Oxford, 1990.

de Swaan, A.: *Coalition Theories and Cabinet Formation*, Elsevier, Amsterdam, 1973.

Dodd, L. C.: *Coalitions in Parliamentary Government*, Princeton University Press, Princeton, 1976.

Grofman, B.: "The Comparative Analysis of Coalition Formation and Duration; Distinguishing Between-Country and Within-Country Effects," *British Journal of Political Science*, vol. 19, 1989, pp. 291–302.

King. G., J. Alt, N. Burns, and M. Laver: "A Unified

Model of Cabinet Dissolution in Parliamentary Democracies," *American Journal of Political Science*, vol. 34, no. 3, 1990, pp. 846-871.

Laver, M., and W. B. Hunt: *Policy and Party Competition*, Routledge, New York, 1992.

_____ and N. Schofield: *Multiparty Government: The Politics of Coalition in Western Europe*, Oxford University Press, Oxford, 1990.

_____ and K. Shepsle: "Coalitions and Cabinet Government," *American Political Science Review*, vol. 84, 1990a, pp. 873-890.

_____ and _____: "Government Coalitions and Intraparty Politics," *British Journal of Political Research*, vol. 20, 1990b, pp. 489-507.

Lijphart, A: "Measures of Cabinet Durability: A Conceptual and Empirical Evaluation," *Comparative Political Studies*, vol. 17, no. 2, 1984, pp. 265-279.

Luebbert, G.: *Comparative Democracy: Policy Making and Governing Coalitions in Europe and Israel*, Columbia University Press, New York, 1986.

Norpoth, H.: "The German Federal Republic: Coalition Government on the Brink of Majority Rule," in E. Browne and J. Frendreis (eds.), *Government Coalitions in Western Europe*, Longmans, New York, 1982.

Pridham, G.: "Italy's Party Democracy and Coalitional Behaviour," in G. Pridham (ed.), *Coalitional Behaviour in Theory and Practice: An Inductive Model for Western Europe*, Cambridge University Press, Cambridge, England, 1986.

Riker, W.: *The Theory of Political Coalitions*, Yale University Press, New Haven, 1962.

Schofield, N.: "Stability of Coalition Governments in Western Europe: 1945-86," *European Journal of Political Economy*, vol. 3, 1987, pp. 555-591.

_____ and M. Laver: "Bargaining Theory and Portfolio Payoffs in European Coalition Governments 1945-83," *British Journal of Political Science*, vol. 15, 1985, pp. 143-164.

Strom, K: "Minority Governments in Parliamentary Democracies: The Rationality on Non-winning Cabinet Solutions," *Comparative Political Studies*, vol. 17, 1984, pp. 199-227.

_____: "Contending Models of Cabinet Stability," *American Political Science Review*, vol. 82, 1988.

_____: *Minority Government and Majority Rule*, Cambridge University Press, Cambridge, England, 1990.

Vis, J.: "Coalition Government in a Constitutional Monarchy: The Dutch Experience," in V. Bogdanor (ed.), *Coalition Government in Western Europe*, Heinemann Educational Books, London, 1983.

CHAPTER 8
FROM GOVERNMENTS TO PUBLIC POLICY

Assessing the practical impact of party politics on public policy is, of course, an impossible task. In order to assess the impact of any given government, we need to know what would have happened if a different government had been there in its place. The need to face up to this task, however, is common to all policy evaluations, in both the public and the private sector, and the fact that the task seems impossible should not be taken as an excuse for doing nothing. Indeed, while it can be a tricky enough job to decide whether a particular government made a difference in a particular policy area on a particular occasion, an accumulating body of comparative analyses of the policy impact of a wide range of European governments has begun to throw some considerable light on the matter of whether governments, in general, do make a difference to the real world of public policy. Those who have tackled this problem have approached it from several different directions.

Perhaps the most traditional approach has been based on case studies of major government policy interventions, such as the comprehensive program of privatizing state assets implemented by British Conservative governments during the 1980s. The logic of such studies is quite straightforward. A dramatic policy initiative is launched with the intention of bringing about a major change in the state of the world. *If this change occurs, then we conclude that the policy initiative was the cause of this* (that is, we assume that the world would not have changed in this way without the policy initiative). Where changes of direction really are dramatic, as with the British and French privatization programs we consider below, then this logic is quite plausible.

Such dramatic changes, of course, are rather rare in European politics. We must look beyond these if we wish to find evidence that politics in general makes a difference to the real world of public policy. A second approach has been to compare what government parties promised voters during the previous election campaign with what they set out to do once installed in office. During election campaigns, of course, parties are trying to get as many votes as possible and may well pitch their policy promises in such a way as to do so. If politics makes a difference, however, *policy promises made during election campaigns should have an impact on the policies of the governments that follow.* We can study this by comparing the election pledges of the winning party or coalition with what the government says it will do during its term of office, once it has succeeded in getting into power (Budge, Robertson, and Hearl; Laver and Budge).

A third strategy for determining whether politics makes a difference is to look at the actual fulfillment of campaign pledges and programs by government. The theory of representative government is, after all, based on the premise that *at least some of the pledges made to voters at election time are actually redeemed.* Evidence on this matter is far skimpier, for a number of reasons. Often a campaign pledge is so vague that it is almost impossible to decide whether it has been fulfilled or not. Some pledges, furthermore, are not fulfilled for reasons that are quite beyond the control of the government. An oil crisis may blow up out of the clear blue sky, for example, or there may be a stock market crash in New York, or some other critical event may fundamentally change the universe of feasible alternatives. While it is no easy task to define the universe of campaign pledges that could have been redeemed but weren't, some progress has been made on this in recent years (Rallings; Rose).

A fourth strategy is to look at patterns of public spending. Of course, some of the most important policy decisions to face postwar Europe have been only vaguely related to public spending. These have included matters of social policy such as AIDS, capital punishment, and race relations; matters of economic management such as deregulation and free trade; and matters of foreign policy such as sanctions against South Africa and nuclear disarmament. On top of this, patterns of public spending are very "sticky" in the sense that much of the public money that is spent (on education, pensions, and welfare, for example) is committed over a very long term.

Furthermore, many of the changes in spending patterns that we do observe are the result of changes in the size of various "client" groups (the young, the old, and the unemployed, for example) and are certainly not the result of conscious spending decisions by the government. There is considerable variation in the proportion of the population in each country that is of school age, for example, with Ireland having by far the highest proportion in Western Europe and Germany one of the lowest. It is hardly surprising, therefore, that public spending on education, as a proportion of national income, is much higher in Ireland than it is in Germany. The age structure of the population, rather than anything to do with public policy, may well explain this difference. A more striking example concerns public spending on unemployment assistance. Governments that set out to cut public spending, as the Conservatives did in Britain after 1979, for example, often increase unemployment in the process, at least in the short run. They certainly do not set out to increase public spending on unemployment assistance, but such an increase is the unsought consequence of policy changes in other areas.

Notwithstanding these important complications, governments often promise voters that if elected, they will make dramatic policy changes that have a significant impact on the direction and flow of public spending. Furthermore, the allocation of public spending among different policy areas is a very visible indicator of government policy, one that can reflect an explicit set of priorities argued and decided on at the cabinet table. This allows us to argue that *if politics does make a difference, then different types of government should be associated with different patterns of public spending*. In particular, changes in government should be associated with changes in public spending flows.

A fifth strategy for determining whether politics makes a difference involves looking over a long time period at large-scale socioeconomic variables such as the overall size of the public sector and the operation of the welfare system. The argument that tends to be made in this context is that *if politics makes a difference, then different types of party systems should be associated with major differences in key macrolevel variables*.

In the rest of this chapter we look in more detail at these five general hypotheses about the ways in which politics might make a difference. At the end of it all we still cannot get around the fact that we have no way of knowing what would have happened in a particular country if the particular government in a particular period had been different. But the accumulated weight of the evidence that we will have assembled by the end of this chapter, on the basis of the five different approaches that we explore, will leave us in little doubt that politics does make at least some difference to what goes on in the real world.

TWO CLEAR-CUT CASES OF POLICY IMPACT: PRIVATIZATION IN BRITAIN AND FRANCE

British and French conservative governments during the 1980s introduced comprehensive programs of selling public assets to the private sector, programs designed to "roll back the state" in major and readily observable ways. In each country, there were subsequently large-scale sales of public assets to the private sector. Few would argue with the conclusion that politics made a difference in these dramatic cases.

To get a feel for the magnitude of such policy initiatives, consider Michel Bauer's description of the political impetus toward privatization in France during the period 1986–1988, following the defeat of the outgoing Socialist administration and its replacement by a right-wing coalition government.

The government, which had fought its electoral campaign on privatization, took office on 20 March 1986. On 6 August a law initiating the privatization program was passed. By 24 October the implementing decrees were in the Journal Officiel. *It took only seven months to move from the program of an opposition party to a set of legal rules specifying the aims and methods of privatization. . . . These legal texts envisaged and facilitated the biggest redrawing of the boundary between the public and the private sector yet seen in the West. They applied to 66 firms . . . with a workforce of about 900,000. This involved capital estimated at the time at 300 billion francs, a figure to be compared with the total capitalization of the Paris Bourse* [stock exchange] *at the same date: 1200 billion francs. In seven months the government thus provided for the privatization of the equivalent of a quarter of the firms quoted on the Paris Bourse.* (Bauer, p. 49)

This is a clear-cut example of how politics can make a difference, in the right circumstances. The incoming government had fought an election on the basis of a clear-cut policy of privatization, won the election, gone into office, and immediately set about implementing the policy in a most comprehensive fashion. (As an aside, it is worth noting that several of the firms scheduled for privatization had originally been nationalized by de Gaulle himself—the policy represented quite a considerable *volte-face* for the Gaullists, traditionally committed to a strong state.) What is more, the policy of privatization in France was not just retained as a piece of enabling legislation—it was actually put into practice. Within a year, one-third of the five-year privatization program had been enacted, and the result was a series of stock market flotations valued at a total of 100 billion francs. The number of small shareholders in France rose from 1.5 million in 1985 to 8 million in 1987 (Bauer, pp. 51–54). This explosion in "popular capitalism" was so dramatic that the Bourse was simply not able to cope with the increase in business, much of which was siphoned off by the London Stock Exchange (Cerny, pp. 184–185).

Helped by the steadily rising stock markets of the mid-1980s, many small investors bought and sold shares in formerly public companies and made healthy profits. The end of the era came equally quickly in France, however. The world stock market crash of October 1987, sparked off on Wall Street, badly burned many French small investors. These, coming to share ownership during a bull market, had made a lot of what seemed like easy money—they learned the hard way that what cynics had described as "casino capitalism" involves losing as well as winning. Against this backdrop, the right lost both the presidential elections of May 1988 and the subsequent parliamentary elections, and the privatization program was "stopped in its tracks" (Vickers and Wright, p. 21). Thus the intense flurry of privatization in France began and ended with an election and a change of the party in government. The result was a major realignment of the public sector in France, and the whole episode is one of the more convincing pieces of evidence that in the right circumstances, politics clearly does make a difference.

The program of privatization in Britain ran for much longer than that in France, was even more radical in its effects, and can also be traced directly to the policies promoted by a particular political party. The program provides an example of a very clear-cut discontinuity between the actions of an incoming government and those of its predecessor, one of the most dramatic such examples in postwar British politics. The Conservative government that took office in 1979 had not fought the preceding election on the basis of a comprehensive set of manifesto commitments on privatization, which had been only a "minor theme" in the campaign (Heald, p. 32). The process started more slowly than in France, with the denationalization of a series of profitable companies, such as British Aerospace and Britoil, easy to sell at discounted flotation prices in a robust bull market. Once the program of privatization began, however, it rapidly acquired momentum and probably went further than the Conservatives themselves had initially envisaged (Kavanagh, p. 221).

The success of early privatizations fed back into Conservative policy and encouraged the party to boost the role given to privatization in the party manifesto. Thus the 1983 election was fought and won by the Conservatives on the basis of a much more ambitious privatization program, extending not only to massive public companies such as British Telecom and British Airways but also to enterprises that had previously been thought of as "untouchable" basic services and natural monopolies—electricity, gas, and water services, for example. Virtually all of these ambitious plans had been successfully consummated by 1990. About fifty state corporations—that is, about half of the total state sector—had been sold to private investors since the program began. The shareholding population in Britain had increased threefold to almost 10 million people. Well over 600,000 jobs had been shifted from the public to the private sector, and even by 1988, 24 billion pounds sterling had been raised for the government by asset sales. (Kavanagh provides a comprehensive recent commentary on the policy record of this particular government.)

Britain and France are not, of course, the only European states that have implemented programs of privatizing the public sector in recent years. Privatization has taken place on a more limited scale in Germany (Esser), Italy (Bianchi, Cassese, and Della Sala), the Netherlands (Andeweg), and Belgium (Drumaux), and even in Sweden (Pontusson) and Austria (Müller), to take just a few examples. But in each case, the program has not been associated with unequivocal doctrinaire commitments on the part of the incoming government and has been much less radical in its extent. There is undoubtedly a secular trend in Europe toward some privatization of the public sector, regardless of the parties in power. By any account, however, the privatization programs in Britain and France have involved a massive partisan redirection of public policy that would not have taken place under most conceivable alternative governments. Politics, without any doubt at all, has made a big difference in these cases.

PARTY MANIFESTOS AND GOVERNMENT POLICY PROGRAMS

The prospect that what governments do is affected by which parties get into office is what makes sense of the notion of representative democracy. If government policy does not respond to the intentions of elected government members, then why have elections in the first place? We have just seen two dramatic examples of cases in which almost everyone would agree that politics made a big difference. The important question, of course, has to do with the extent to which we can generalize from this experience.

The first step along the rocky road from what is promised at election time to what is actually done by governments in office is to compare parties' election manifestos with the policy positions of the governments they join. The latter are recorded in the official policy programs typically published by newly formed governments as part of the investiture process and in the formal statements of official government policy that they typically issue at the beginning of each new session of parliament. The analysis of these has recently been undertaken and is reported in Laver and Budge.

In order to compare election manifestos with published government policy declarations, it is necessary to have a systematic way of describing both of these. This is achieved by using the technique of content analysis, which involves coding the entire content of each relevant policy document, sentence by sentence, and placing each sentence into one of a set of categories that captures important features of party and government policy. A key area of party policy in modern Europe, for example, is the running of the economy. This, of course, generates many policy problems relating to unemployment, inflation, exchange rates, investment, government spending, and so on. One general set of policy prescriptions for these matters can be characterized as the promotion of "free market economics." This is associated with the encouragement of private enterprise, private incentive structures, free trade, balanced budgets, and general economic orthodoxy, together with opposition to the expansion of the welfare state. A European Consortium for Political Research (ECPR) research group has analyzed party manifestos and government declarations to assess the relative emphasis that each policy document gives to these and many other themes. (For a detailed description of the basic method used in this study, see Budge, Robertson, and Hearl.)

Table 8.1 describes the different policy emphases on the promotion of free market economics found in the various Norwegian party manifestos issued between 1949 and 1983, to take an example of a single policy area in a single country, selected because there is a very clear-cut alternation in power between single-party Labor governments and "bourgeois" coalitions involving the right-wing parties. The table reports in a systematic manner the obvious difference between the economic policy emphases of the Communist and Labor parties, on the one hand, and those of the Conservative party, on the other. The other parties are to be found somewhere in between.

The interesting question is whether the alternation in party control is reflected in the government's economic policies—whether we can somehow tell which party was in government by looking only at government policy. Table 8.2 answers this question. The first row compares the average emphasis on free market economics in government policy declarations issued when Labor was in power with the average emphasis when it was out of office. The second row performs a similar analysis for the Norwegian Conservative party.

The results are quite striking. There is a large and statistically significant difference between the emphasis on free market economics given by Labor governments, on the one hand, and the emphasis given by governments of which the

TABLE 8.1
Party Policy Emphases on Free Market Economics: Norway, 1949–1983

Party	Average Percentage of Party Manifesto Advocating Free Market Economics
Communist party	0.7
Labor party	0.9
Christian People's party	3.2
Liberal party	3.6
Center party	5.6
Conservatives	15.5

Source: Calculated directly from data used in Strom (1991).

TABLE 8.2
Party and Government Policy on Free Market Economics:
Norway, 1949–1983

Party	Average Government Policy Emphasis: Party in Government, %	Average Government Policy Emphasis: Party out of Government, %
Labor party	3.8	13.5
Conservative party	14.2	4.3

Note: An analysis of variance shows a statistically significant difference in economic policy between "party in" and "party out" for each party (F-ratio significant at $p = .001$).
Source: Calculated directly from data used in Strom (1991).

Conservative party is a member, on the other. What is more, the policy emphasis of Labor governments in Norway is quite close to that in Labor manifestos, while coalitions including the Conservatives have a policy emphasis quite close to that in Conservative manifestos. The evidence from Norway, for this particular policy area, is consistent with the proposition that there is, indeed, a link between party manifestos and government declarations. Parties do make a difference, at least in regard to what Norwegian governments announce that they will do—the first hurdle that policies must clear on the route toward eventual implementation.

Table 8.3 reviews the evidence on this in a more comprehensive manner, for all countries analyzed in this way. As might be expected, not all the results are as neat as those reported for Norway. The six countries analyzed can be divided into three groups. In Denmark and Norway, the parties differ a lot in the emphasis they give to free market economics. There are left-wing parties that hardly emphasize free market economics at all; and there are right-wing parties that give this a heavy emphasis. When party policies diverge, Table 8.3 shows that party platforms do make a difference to published government policy programs. In Denmark, for example, there is a big different between governments involving the Social Democrats and those involving the Conservatives. It would be very easy to infer the party composition of any government just by looking at its published policies, something that we might regard as the acid test of policy impact in this particular context. In the first group of countries, if we generalize from the Norwegian case discussed above, parties clearly make a difference.

In contrast to the large differences in party policy emphases in the Scandinavian systems, policy debates do not figure much in party manifestos in Italy and Germany; in these countries it would be impossible to tell governments apart in terms of the emphasis on free market economics in their policy declarations. The entry or exit of the main socialist party into or from governments in Italy and Germany, for example, has no noticeable impact on government policy in relation to free market economics. In these countries, at least as far as this important policy area is concerned, parties don't seem to make much of a difference at all.

The other two countries described in Table 8.3, Luxembourg and the Netherlands, fall between these extremes. In the Netherlands, Christian Demo-

TABLE 8.3

The Impact of Party Participation on the Economic Policy of Governments: Circa 1945–1982

Party	Percentage of Policy Document Giving Emphasis to Free Market Economics		
	Average Manifesto Emphasis	Average Government Emphasis: Party in Government	Average Government Emphasis: Party out of Government
Denmark:			
Social Democrats*	1.6	5.5	16.6
Social Liberals	7.3	5.9	10.1
Liberals*	19.4	16.6	5.5
Conservatives*	25.2	18.6	6.6
Germany:			
Social Democrats*	7.2	10.1	9.1
Free Democrats	5.7	9.3	10.3
Christian Democrats	3.9	10.1	8.3
Italy:			
Socialists	1.0	3.2	2.5
Social Democrats	0.5	3.2	2.4
Republicans	1.1	3.1	2.5
Liberals	3.0	2.8	2.6
Christian Democrats	1.9	2.7	†
Luxembourg:			
Socialists	1.8	8.6	10.8
Democratic party	5.8	12.0	6.2
Christian Social party	5.7	8.2	†
Netherlands:			
Labor party (PvdA)	3.2	9.8	15.5
Liberals	20.8	14.3	11.2
CHU	10.2	13.5	13.0
ARP	13.2	14.2	11.1
KVP/CDA	10.3	12.8	†
Norway:			
Labor*	0.9	3.8	13.5
Liberals	3.6	11.5	5.9
Center party*	5.6	12.4	5.1
Conservatives*	15.5	14.2	4.3
Christian Peoples party*	3.2	12.4	5.1

*Analysis of variance between "party in" and "party out" yields F-ratio significant at $p = .05$ or better.
†Party always, or almost always, in government; statistics meaningless. Parties never, or almost never, in government have also been omitted.
Source: Computed directly from data used by authors in Laver, Budge, and Byrne (1991).

cratic parties have been in government for more or less the entire postwar period. The alternation of government parties in the Netherlands has thus always been partial, confined to an alternation of the coalition partners of the Christian Democrats. We can classify Dutch governments as those of the center-left, where the Christian parties have taken Labor as a partner, and those of the center-right, where they have taken the Liberals. Concentrating just on Labor and the Liberals in the Netherlands, we see a big difference in policy emphases between the parties. Government policy emphases do not change as much as they do in Denmark and Norway, but they do respond in noticeable ways to changes in coalition membership. Governments that include Labor put the least emphasis on free market economics; governments that exclude Labor put the most emphasis on this. But government emphasis on free market economics, taken over the entire period, is much closer to that of the Christian Democrats, the permanent fixture in government, than it is to that of either of the other main government parties.

A similar pattern can be found in Luxembourg, where both parties and governments put less emphasis on free market economics in their policy statements. Once more, the Christian party is a more or less permanent fixture in office, dampening any policy shifts. Once more, coalitions that include the right-wing Liberals are noticeably more likely to stress free market economics than those that do not.

Overall, the evidence, reviewed more extensively by Laver, Budge, and Byrne, suggests that parties do make a difference to the published policy programs of European governments in those more competitive party systems where the entire party membership of the cabinet is likely to change from one government to another (Laver, Budge, and Byrne). In those European systems in which there is a more or less permanent member of the government coalition, this party exercises a more or less permanent influence on policy. Parties may well still make a difference in such systems, but the effect of the alternation of parties seems to be attenuated, as we might expect. Instead, the party that makes the most difference is the one that is nearly always in power.

REDEEMING CAMPAIGN PLEDGES

It's one thing for a party to say, when it has just formed a government, that it is going to redeem a particular election pledge. It's quite another thing to do so. The second major step on the path that takes us from the promises made by politicians in the heat of an election campaign to what actually happens in the real world is the fulfillment of campaign pledges. Before we can get down to the systematic analysis of the fulfillment of campaign pledges, however, we must deal with a number of tricky methodological problems.

First, we must find a way of deciding in a systematic fashion what is a genuine pledge to the electorate and what is a piece of common, or garden-variety, campaign rhetoric. This, of course, is a highly subjective matter. It has to do with how specific the promise is, with how literally it is intended to be taken by those who hear it, and with whether it concerns real actions or merely expresses pious hopes. Thus a promise to "make this great country of ours a better place to live in" or to "banish nuclear weapons from the face of the earth" ought not perhaps to be seen as a campaign pledge in any real sense of the word, on the grounds that it is too vague to be taken seriously or is no more than a general aspiration.

Second, a pledge may be such that it simply cannot be carried out by the person who makes it. A pledge to "double the rate of economic growth," for example, is beyond the scope of any individual politician who might make it. Such pledges have a status quite distinct from that of a promise by the same politician to "increase old-age pensions by 5 percent," which could be entirely within the jurisdiction of that politician should he or she go into government.

The third problem is deciding who is to blame when campaign pledges are not redeemed. Has the politician who promised to double the rate of economic growth broken that pledge to voters if he or she tries as hard as possible but fails to do this? Has that politician broken the pledge if he or she doesn't try at all? Has the pledge been broken if the politician doesn't try very hard? If we are going to excuse pledges that are thwarted for reasons beyond the control of the pledger, someone will have to call the score, pledge by pledge, on who was to blame for the breaking of each.

Finally, there is the problem that most campaign pledges tend to be carried out a little bit; few are enacted in their full splendor. Political truth, alas, is relative. So much of what is said is slightly true—so many pledges slightly redeemed. A little progress may be made on cutting public spending or reforming the tax system, for example. Unemployment may be reduced somewhat—quite possibly no thanks to the government of the day. Once more, to classify these as pledges broken or as pledges fulfilled is a matter of highly subjective judgment.

There are no easy answers to these problems. The solution adopted by those who have done empirical research on pledge fulfillment in Europe has been to recite the preceding litany of health warnings and then roll up their sleeves and get on with the business of making those subjective judgments. It is difficult to see what else can be done. Campaign pledges are central to representative democracy, and they will remain central even if people just ignore them and go off to study something else.

Much of the work on the fulfillment of campaign pledges has related to Britain. The most detailed analysis forms part of Richard Rose's study *Do Parties Make a Difference?* Rose deals with Britain in the 1970s, comparing the record of redeemed pledges for the 1970-1974 Conservative government with that for the 1974-1979 Labour government (Rose, pp. 52-73). He analyzed specific manifesto pledges by subject area and assessed the extent to which each government acted on its pledges in an unambiguous manner, took no action, or did the opposite of what it said it would do. The results of this analysis are in Table 8.4.

Rose concludes, confounding the skeptics, that manifesto pledges do make a difference, that "Conservative and Labour governments act consistently with the Manifesto model of governing; in office they do the majority of things to which they pledge themselves . . ." (Rose, p. 65). The skeptics might retort that this conclusion is a product of an exclusive concentration on manifesto pledges that Rose deems "doable." This problem is compounded by the fact that one of the real reasons that the arithmetical record of these parties is so good is that they promise to do many things that are really rather straightforward and uncontroversial. Rose finds that about half of all pledges are nonpartisan, in the sense that they represent

TABLE 8.4
How British Parties Acted on Their Manifestos, 1970–1979

Policy Area	Conservatives, 1970–1974				Labour, 1974–1979			
	Acted on	Ambiguous	No Action	Opposite	Acted on	Ambiguous	No Action	Opposite
Economy	22	2	5	1	26	4	9	0
Environment	13	1	1	0	8	4	5	1
Home affairs	11	3	1	0	5	2	5	0
Health, social security	17	2	1	0	10	4	1	0
Education, science	7	0	0	0	2	3	5	0
Foreign affairs, defense	5	1	0	0	3	3	2	0
Agriculture	2	1	0	0	3	0	0	0
Total, N	77	10	8	1	57	20	27	1
Total, %	80	10	8	1	54	19	26	1

Source: Rose (1980, p. 65).

a consensus between the parties (Rose, p. 69). Such pledges are easy to make and are much easier to carry out than others. Whether we should set much store by them when trying to decide whether politicians keep their promises is another matter.

Rallings has extended the general features of Rose's analysis to the period 1945–1979 in Britain and come up with similar conclusions. He finds that about 70 percent of all manifesto pledges are implemented, though some are much more likely to be implemented than others. "Clear promises to increase pensions and other benefits (often by a named amount) and to repeal ideologically unacceptable legislation passed by the previous administration, are almost invariably kept. . . . The pledges least likely to be fulfilled are the small minority where the government cannot ensure their passage or which involve the expenditure of large amounts of public money on electorally unappealing and/or low priority projects" (Rallings, p. 13). The approach has also been extended to analyze the record of the 1981–1985 PASOK (Socialist) government in Greece, and once more a pledge fulfillment rate of about 70 percent was found (Kalogeropoulou, p. 293).

Both Britain and Greece are countries in which one-party government is the norm. This means that we do not have much systematic information about pledge fulfillment in the coalition systems that are far more typical of Western Europe. On the face of things we would expect a lower proportion of pledges to be honored in coalition systems, since different coalition partners may well make conflicting pledges on the same theme; thus one is inevitably bound to be broken. There is no hard evidence on this matter, however.

These results suggest that parties tend to honor more of their pledges than skeptics, rivals, and journalists typically give them credit for. This may, in part, be an artifact of the data, arising because researchers regard as firm pledges only proposals that can be carried out. It may also be a product of real-world party competition, if parties tend to promise a lot of easy and uncontroversial things, precisely so that they can go back to the voters and boast about how they fulfilled most of their promises. Parties may anticipate all the easy things that they can actually deliver and make a great song and dance at election time about promising to deliver them. Notwithstanding these reservations, however, the work that has been done to date suggests that parties do fulfill campaign pledges to a greater degree than many cynics had previously thought—that politics does make a difference in this particular sense.

PARTY GOVERNMENT AND PUBLIC SPENDING

When policy output has a bearing on public spending, there is at least one concrete indicator of what the government is actually doing. If a promise is made to do something that involves public spending—to build more schools, for example—we can see whether or not spending on school construction increases.

Patterns in the flow of public expenditure to various policy areas have been the subject of a growing body of academic research. The problem has been approached from two basic perspectives. The first is to look at different countries in the same time period in order to establish whether countries with particular types of government have particular types of public spending patterns (Castles, 1982 and 1989; Hicks, Swank, and Ambuhl; Keman, 1982). The second is to look at the same country in different time periods in order to establish whether changes in spending patterns can be traced to changes in government (Bergman and Strom; Budge and Hofferbert; Keman, 1989; Hofferbert and Klingemann; Laver and Mitchell).

Differences between Countries

The basic patterns of public spending in European states can be seen in Table 8.5. This shows total public spending, total welfare spending, and total defense spending, each expressed as a percentage of the overall gross domestic product (GDP). It also shows the balance between welfare and defense spending, which we might think of as the butter/guns ratio. Countries are ranked on the basis of the proportion of the GDP devoted to public spending. In addition, Table 8.5 gives two indicators of partisan control of the government during the ten years before these measures of public spending. The first is the number of months during the ten-year period for which the main party of the right, as defined by Castles, was in government, either on its own or in a coalition with others.[1] The second is the number of months for which the main party of the right had sole control of the government.

The patterns that can be seen in Table 8.5 are by no means dramatic. While the degree of right-wing participation in government does tend to be lower in the countries which have a larger public sector, there are several striking exceptions. The Netherlands, with the largest public sector and the highest level of welfare spending, had considerable right-wing participation in government during the preceding period. In contrast, Finland, with a relatively low level of right-wing participation in government, has a relatively small public sector.

It might well be argued, and this is one of the central points made by Castles, that governments cannot really have much impact on the general order of magnitude of public spending. Much of this is determined either by very long-term commitments or by the need to provide for "supply-driven" welfare transfers, such as unemployment benefits or old-age pensions. It is usually argued, rather, that governments can have an impact on spending patterns at the margin, controlling year-to-year *changes* in spending flows much more than the overall scale of spending. The actual level of welfare or defense spending, for example, might be much higher in one country than in another not because of the current political situation but as a result of the interplay of a complex set of historical and structural factors. What an incoming government can do in the short and medium run is to cut or boost welfare or defense spending. But even savage cuts and generous boosts do

---

[1] These other parties, by country, are as follows: Austria (ÖVP); Belgium (PLP/PVV); Britain (Conservatives); Denmark (KF); Finland (KOK); France (Gaullist); Germany (CDU/CSU); Ireland (Fine Gael); Italy (DC); Netherlands (VVD); Norway (H); Sweden (M); Switzerland (Christian Democrats). Note that Castles uses a different measure of the degree of right-wing control: the share of all cabinet seats going to the main right-wing party over the period. We regard the participation, or lack of it, of the main right-wing party as the key factor, however, regardless of the precise number of seats that it controls, and take this as a more appropriate indicator of the degree of right-wing control.

TABLE 8.5
Patterns of Public Spending in European States

Country	Total Public Spending in Policy Area as Percentage of GDP			Ratio of Welfare Spending to Defense Spending	Months Right-Wing Party in Office, 1965–1974	Months Only Right-Wing Party in Office, 1965–1974
	Total Public Spending, (Average, 1974–1976)	Welfare Spending, 1974	Defense Spending, 1975			
Switzerland	33.5	NA	2.0	NA	120	0
Finland	37.3	21.0	1.5	14.0	16	0
Austria	39.9	23.0	1.2	19.2	64	48
France	41.6	20.9	3.9	5.4	120	120
Belgium	43.0	23.2	3.1	7.4	44	0
Italy	43.1	19.6	2.8	7.0	120	11
Germany	44.0	20.6	3.6	5.7	58	0
United Kingdom	44.5	16.7	5.0	3.3	44	44
Denmark	46.4	23.4	2.6	9.0	44	0
Norway	46.6	20.0	3.2	6.3	65	0
Ireland	49.4	16.7	1.7	9.8	22	0
Sweden	51.7	21.9	3.4	6.4	0	0
Netherlands	53.9	29.1	3.5	8.3	66	0

Sources: Castles (1982, pp. 49–51); Keman (1982, p. 179); authors' calculations.

not, unless they are repeated year after year, have a huge impact on the overall level of spending in these areas. This suggests that parties might not be able to affect the broad differences in spending patterns between countries; what they can affect are changes in spending patterns at the margin.

Table 8.6 presents some evidence on this, ranking countries in terms of the increase in overall public spending over the period in question. The patterns in public expenditure *changes* are much more obvious. In countries such as Austria, Britain, Finland, and France, where the growth in welfare spending was slowest, there was noticeably more right-wing government during the period in question. In particular, when a country has a right-wing party in sole control for the period, this seems to be quite clearly associated with a lower level of growth in public spending.

The main features of Tables 8.5 and 8.6 are summarized in Table 8.7, which shows correlations between right-wing participation in government and both the levels of and changes in welfare spending and overall public spending. Note that in each case right-wing participation in government is more highly correlated with changes in public spending than it is with general levels of spending, bearing out Castles' conclusion, based on alternative indicators, that right-wing participation in government does have an impact on changes in policy output. We can extend Castles' conclusion by noting that a right-wing party in sole control of the government is more strongly associated with spending changes than mere right-wing participation in coalitions.

TABLE 8.6
Changes in Patterns of Public Spending in European States

Country	Change in Total Public Spending in Policy Area as Percentage of GDP			Months Right-Wing Party in Office, 1965–1974	Months Only Right-Wing Party in Office, 1965–1974
	Change in Total Public Spending, 1967–1976	Change in Welfare Spending, 1962–1974	Change in Defense Spending, 1955–1975		
France	2.2	3.9	−2.5	120	120
Finland	3.9	7.0	−0.1	16	0
United Kingdom	6.0	4.1	−3.2	44	44
Austria	6.4	3.4	+1.0	64	48
Belgium	7.4	4.6	−0.7	44	0
Italy	7.6	6.0	−0.9	120	11
Norway	8.7	8.3	−0.7	65	0
Sweden	10.4	8.3	−1.4	0	0
Denmark	10.9	9.2	−0.6	44	0
Germany	10.9	4.1	−0.5	58	0
Netherlands	11.3	14.9	−2.2	66	0
Switzerland	12.5	NA	−0.8	120	0
Ireland	15.7	5.6	+0.1	22	0

Sources: Castles (1982, pp. 49–51); Keman (1982, p. 179); authors' calculations.

Recently there has been another wave of research in the same general tradition, dealing not with public spending in general but with the correlates of spending patterns in particular policy areas (Castles, 1989; Hicks et al.). Hicks, Swank, and Ambuhl (p. 423) find that "welfare effort"—the proportion of national income devoted to welfare spending—is "constrained by policy-making inertia and driven by relatively 'automatic' responses to unemployment as well as by (relatively routine) counter-cyclical demand management policy." They also find that welfare effort is significantly related to the relative size of the population of the elderly, who, of course, generate demands for pensions.

Each of these factors has little to do with the ideology of the government. However, the same authors also find significant differences between left- and right-

TABLE 8.7
Correlations between Right-Wing Participation and Public Spending Patterns

	Welfare Spending, 1974	Change in Welfare Spending, 1962–1974	Total Public Spending, 1974–1976	Change in Total Public Spending, 1967–1976
Right wing in sole control	−.15	−.46	−.38	−.66
Right wing in office	+.07	−.15	−.25	−.40

Sources: Authors' calculations from Tables 8.5 and 8.6.

wing governments, as well as between countries with strong trade union movements and those with weak ones. These two factors interact, and so "in nations where labour unions are organisationally strong . . . political actions of left parties evidently can still affect welfare policy fairly directly" (Hicks et al., p. 424). Conversely, in systems where unions are weak, the impact of left parties on welfare effort is much less noticeable.

Francis Castles has performed a similar analysis of cross-national patterns in education expenditure (Castles, 1989). Table 8.8 shows the proportion of national income devoted to spending on education in a range of European countries; it shows figures for both 1960 and 1981, as well as changes in spending levels between the two years. Ranking countries by "education effort" in 1981, we see something very similar to the patterns in welfare effort that we have just discussed. It is not surprising, therefore, that Castles finds strong evidence of "the negative educational impact of right-wing political strength" (Castles, 1989, p. 441). Even when we control for a wide range of other factors, there is a strong link between education effort and partisan control of government.

Overall, therefore, recent cross-national studies have done quite a lot to bolster the argument that "governments do make a difference." Working with comparisons of spending patterns in different systems, we see that it does seem to be the case that those systems with higher levels of education and welfare spending are those in which left-wing governments have been more common. With cross-national data such as these, however, it is dangerous to draw too many firm conclusions about cause and effect in patterns of public policy. Stronger indications of what is going on can be gleaned from analyses of changing spending patterns within given systems, the matter to which we now turn.

TABLE 8.8
Public Spending on Education, 1960–1981

	Percentage of GDP		
	1960	1981	Change, 1960–1981
Germany	2.4	5.2	2.8
Switzerland	3.1	5.5	2.4
France	2.1	5.7	3.6
United Kingdom	3.6	5.7	2.1
Austria	2.8	5.8	3.0
Norway	3.8	6.1	2.3
Finland	6.6	6.2	− 0.4
Italy	3.7	6.4	2.7
Sweden	4.6	6.6	2.0
Netherlands	4.5	6.7	2.2
Ireland	3.0	6.9	3.9
Denmark	4.0	7.7	3.7
Belgium	4.4	8.3	3.9

Source: Castles (1989, p. 433).

Differences within Countries

A more direct test of whether governments make a difference is to look at whether changes in government within a particular political system tend to be associated with changing patterns of public spending. Most writing to date has dealt with broad trends in spending patterns over the entire postwar period, relating these changes to major trends in the party systems of particular countries. Särlvik (1983) has looked at the impact of coalition politics on policy output in Scandinavia; Gladdish (1983) has done the same for the Netherlands. Only very recently has there been an attempt to chart the impact of specific changes in government membership on specific expenditure flows (Bergman and Strom; Budge and Hofferbert; Keman, 1989; Hofferbert and Klingemann; Laver and Mitchell).

The types of patterns that we are looking for are illustrated in Figures 8.1 and 8.2, which show the percentage of all public spending in Ireland devoted to two policy areas, the arts and social welfare, for each year between 1958 and 1987. (Data for this example are taken from Laver and Mitchell.)

The pattern for spending on the arts is particularly striking. For the entire period between 1957 and 1973, Ireland had a single-party Fianna Fáil government (sometimes with an overall majority, sometimes without one). Government spending on the arts was very stable throughout this period, at about 0.03 percent of the total budget. During the 1973 election campaign, the Fianna Fáil manifesto made no mention of arts spending; the joint policy declaration issued by Fine Gael and

Figure 8.1
Arts Spending in Ireland, 1958–1987

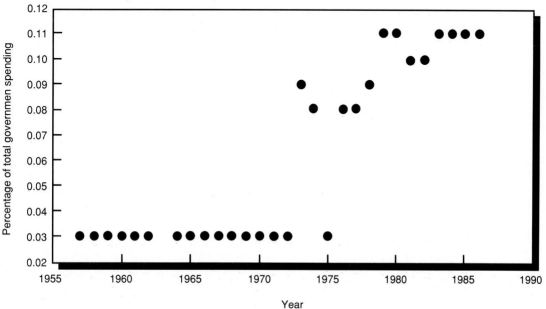

Figure 8.2
Welfare Spending in Ireland, 1958–1987

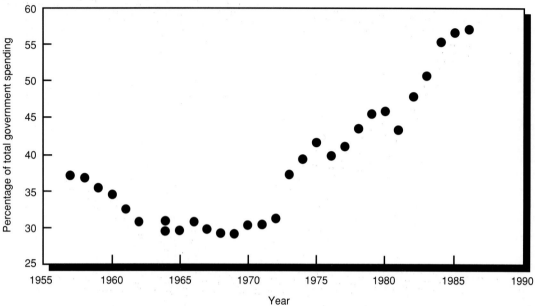

Labour, though very brief, made specific mention of the need to increase spending on the arts. The Fine Gael–Labour coalition won the election; almost immediately, arts spending tripled as a proportion of total public spending. It has maintained this share, or slightly increased it, almost every year since then.

Spending on social welfare policy, a much bigger component of the overall public budget, also showed a sudden shift in 1973; its share of total public spending was increased from 31 to 37 percent after a period of relative stability. The policy declaration of the coalition that took office in 1973 laid considerable stress on the need to increase social welfare spending. The manifesto of the Fianna Fáil party that it replaced made no mention of this.

These examples illustrate a number of points rather neatly. First, government clearly can make a difference to the flow of public spending in certain circumstances. This is by far the most plausible explanation of the fact that major shifts in spending patterns accompanied a major change of government, following sixteen years with the same party in power.

Second, major changes in policy direction over the short term are rather rare. The 1973 shift from long-term Fianna Fáil hegemony to a Fine Gael–Labour coalition was a very important change in the Irish political scene. The patterns identified around 1973 cannot be seen, to anything like the same degree, at other junctures. In other words, the impact of parties on public spending flows is obvious in extreme cases but is not always easy to discern in more normal circumstances.

Third, public spending flows are "sticky"; they clearly require a major effort of political will if they are to be changed to any perceptible degree. Thus the boost

BOX 8.1
Patterns in Public Finances

FRANCE

The dramatic program of sales of public corporations between 1986 and 1988, carried out by a conservative coalition, marked a break in the continuity of public finances. This raised considerable though short-lived nonrecurrent income for the state. Governed for most of the 1980s by a Socialist president in tandem with a Socialist prime minister, France had public expenditures, especially for social welfare, that were higher as a proportion of national income than in Britain, for example, or Germany or Italy. Although nominal income tax rates are low (and thus have in the past attracted rich residents from other European countries), other payroll taxes tend to be high in France. France thus remains very much in the European mainstream in terms of the share of national income (43 percent) absorbed by taxes.

GERMANY

The coalition of the center-right that governed for most of the 1980s pursued financial policies very similar to those of earlier center-left coalitions, since the power of German cabinets in the area of financial policy making is constrained by the operation of a relatively autonomous and very conservative central bank. (In 1990, however, the bank found that it was not as independent as it had liked to think, for it was forced to back down in the face of government pressure on the issue of setting an exchange rate for the conversion of East German marks.) The financial policy pursued by most German governments, of whatever hue, has sought to maintain the value of the currency and keep inflation low. This tight monetary policy has imposed major constraints on public policy making. As a consequence, German budgets have been more or less balanced in recent years, and public debt as a proportion of national income is low in Germany, in comparison with public debt in other European countries. Thus, while the level of taxation is very much in the European mainstream, the level of public spending is rather lower than average. The great unanswered question in German public finances concerns the

eventual impact of German reunification, a matter for which there are few convincing financial predictions, save that the short-term costs will be high.

ITALY

The center-right Christian Democrats have been in every Italian government of the postwar era, and changes in their coalition partners have produced little discernible effect on patterns in public finances. Taxation has traditionally taken a relatively low proportion of national income in Italy, in part because of a very large "informal" economy in which taxes do not figure at all. Public spending, in contrast, is very much in the European mainstream—lower than in France, but higher than in Britain and Germany. It is not surprising to find, therefore, that budgets tend to be well out of balance (the 1989 deficit amounted to 10 percent of national income, a figure surpassed in Europe only by the deficit in Greece) and that public indebtedness is quite high (95 percent of national income, compared with 45 percent in Germany). As a consequence, inflation has traditionally been high relative to the rate found in European neighbors.

NETHERLANDS

The exploitation of offshore natural gas fields produced short-term windfall gains to the public purse in the Netherlands, and the gains were used during the 1970s to increase welfare benefits and certain other public spending programs. As gas revenues began to decline, however, public spending faced a squeeze. Despite the alternation of center-left and center-right coalitions and the relatively large part of the postwar period for which right-wing parties have been in office, the share of national income taken by taxes in the Netherlands is now one of the highest in Western Europe (46 percent in 1989, equivalent to that in Norway and less only than that in Sweden and Denmark), while public spending remains higher than in almost all other European countries outside Scandinavia.

(Continued on next page)

SPAIN

Spain developed a modern industrial economy only after the death of Franco in 1975. Before then, its public finances had been characterized by very low taxes, low or nonexistent welfare benefits, and very low government spending. Since democratization, and particularly since entry into the EC, both taxes and spending have risen rapidly as the welfare system has been extended. These are still, however, at the low end of the European mainstream, though high levels of unemployment are making heavy demands on welfare spending. The share of national income absorbed by public spending as a whole is less than that in Germany and the U.K., while taxation runs at around 34 percent of national income in 1989, barely more than the low levels to be found in Switzerland.

SWEDEN

Sweden, run by the Social Democrats for much of the postwar period, is known, along with most other Scandinavian countries, for having very high levels of taxation relative to taxation in other Western European states. Taxation in 1989 amounted to about 57 percent of national income, with particularly heavy and steeply progressive personal income taxes. Public spending also amounts to a very high share of national income, though very low unemployment rates mean that resources devoted to unemployment assistance are minimal. State spending applies to a wide range of areas of activity, contributing to a high "social wage" that is delivered in terms of services provided either free or at subsidized rates

by the public sector. Sweden was one of the few countries in Europe to return a budget surplus in 1989; however, inflation was high and growth low relative to the rates calculated for European trading partners.

UNITED KINGDOM

Right-wing Conservative governments led by Margaret Thatcher from 1979 until almost the end of 1990 initiated deep cuts in the social welfare element of spending that were offset by increases in public order and defense spending and by increases in the level of unemployment and hence in spending on unemployment benefits. These policies were in sharp contrast with the policies of previous governments, both Labour and Conservative. By the end of the 1980s, the rate of growth (though not the level) of public spending was lower in Britain than in many other European countries. A program of cuts in nominal rates of income tax, particularly for higher-income earners, was offset to a significant extent by increases in indirect taxation. Nonetheless, Britain is at the low end of the mainstream of European countries in terms of the proportion of national income paid in taxes (37 percent in 1989, compared with 32 percent in Switzerland and 51 percent in Denmark). Revenue from taxes on North Sea oil and from the sale of public corporations represented very significant but "nonrenewable" sources of government income during the 1980s. As these run down, there will be a need either for an increase in tax revenue or for further cuts in public spending.

given to arts spending in 1973 persevered throughout the 1980s, regardless of changes in party control. Welfare spending continued to rise, showing no relationship whatsoever to changes in party control, despite the fact that party policies on welfare matters continued to differ significantly.

This is further evidence, if we look at changes over time within a given country, of the political "inertia" of expenditure flows that figured in our discussion of differences between countries in patterns of public spending. It suggests that the political effort needed to reverse broad trends in public spending in particular policy areas is truly Herculean; it may be expended at times of major political change, but not as a matter of routine, day-to-day politics.

All of this means that a picture of the impact of parties on patterns of public spending will not emerge from any simplistic crunching of numbers—a comprehensive analysis of these patterns for each European system is a daunting task. A start has been made, however. Preliminary analyses of the impact of government membership on spending flows in Germany (Hofferbert and Klingemann), Ireland (Laver and Mitchell), the Netherlands (Keman, 1989), Sweden (Bergman and Strom), and the U.S.A. (Budge and Hofferbert) suggest that there are some very strong relationships between government spending and the promises of government parties in particular policy areas. The general patterns that these authors have been able to detect are pretty much what we might expect from the specific examples that we have just looked at. No dramatic trends emerge, but the policies of government parties do tend to be associated with particular patterns of public spending.

While not overwhelming, the evidence is at least consistent with the existence of this particular link in the politics of representative government in Western Europe. It is certainly not the case, however, that government spending patterns follow the policies of government parties in any slavish fashion. While it is very likely that such an effort of will comes only with a change in government, it is certainly not the case that every change in government generates such an effort of will. If we looked only at public expenditure flows, it would be very easy to identify certain changes of government. Many changes of government, however, could take place without anyone who looked only at the flow of public spending realizing that anything at all had happened.

It seems, in short, that parties *can* make a difference to patterns of public spending. Equally it seems, more often than not, that they don't.

BEYOND PUBLIC SPENDING

There is, of course, much more to public policy than public spending. Even in the economic sphere, key elements of policy have to do with matters such as the level of inflation, unemployment, interest rates, and exchange rates. While these are related indirectly to public spending, they are not in themselves things that governments spend money on. We cannot use the direction of expenditure flows to infer things about public policy in these areas. Many other aspects of public policy are even further removed from public spending—foreign policy, for example, or policy on social and moral issues.

Since shifting the deadweight of public finances is not involved, we might expect policy in these areas to be more responsive to politics. Thus, if a government gets into power on the platform of bringing back hanging, it is hardly plausible for that government to claim that it can't afford to build a new gallows. This example also highlights the fact that a number of aspects of social policy, particularly those involving the reform of existing social legislation, are such that either action is taken or it is not. Thus either the law on abortion, on divorce, on the status of women, or on capital punishment is reformed—or it is not. Public policy is easy to see in these areas. Assessing the partisan composition of governments that enact changes in these important aspects of social policy is not difficult and would add greatly to our understanding of whether politics makes a difference. To the best of our knowledge, however, this is a task that has yet to be undertaken in a large-scale, systematic manner.

Foreign relations is another vital policy area that has rather little to do with public spending. Foreign policy output, however, is rarely as cut-and-dried as social policy output. Since foreign policy has a lot to do with attitudes and postures, we are dealing with something that is much more difficult to pin down and evaluate. (Obviously, the fact that the data are far less clear-cut does not mean that foreign policy is not important; it is just more difficult to measure.) Once more, we are aware of no large-scale, systematic study relating foreign policy performance to the partisan composition of governments.

Thus it is only in the economic sphere that nonspending policy output has been systematically related to party control of the cabinet. Views on this matter diverge. On one hand, Richard Rose—writing about Britain in *Do Parties Make a Difference?*—concludes firmly that parties make very little difference to most of what is important about the economy. Most key economic variables, according to Rose, are determined by long-term secular trends. Even changes that can plausibly be traced to political action are likely to arise from changes of policy within a given governing party rather than from changes of the party in government. "The progress of the economy is not completely determined. There is an element of choice open to every government . . . short term changes do occur in the economy, notwithstanding long term trends. The changes do not, however, conform to the normal Adversary model of party government. Instead, there are cycles of *change within* the life of a party in office" (Rose, p. 139, emphasis in original). Rose bases these conclusions on an analysis of trends in interest rates, public-sector borrowing, public spending, growth rates, take-home pay, the distribution of both income and wealth, unemployment, and inflation over the period 1957–1979. British governments alternated between Conservative and Labour single-party control during this period, but, Rose argues, the effects of this alternation cannot be seen in any of these key economic indicators.

On the other hand, a number of other authors, writing about the broad patterns of economic policy making across a range of European states, suggest that politics plays a greater role than Rose suggests in the running of the economy (Armingeon; Cusack, Notermans, and Rein; Muller; Schmidt; van Arnhem and Schotsman). Schmidt provides an overview of the problem. He finds, not surprisingly, that no European government has been able to exercise what he calls "comprehensive political control" over the economy. This is probably a product of his ambitious definition of political control, which he takes to be "simultaneously organizing a potent tax state and controlling both inflation and unemployment" (Schmidt, p. 156). He does, however, find quite a bit of evidence of "partial" political control of European economies, reflecting the apparent ability of governments to control either inflation or unemployment and, in particular, to exert a "pronounced" control over labor market policy. Schmidt finds that the strongest political control over the economy is exercised in Austria, Germany, Luxembourg, the Netherlands, Norway, Sweden, and Switzerland. He finds the lowest levels of political control in Finland, France, and Ireland (Schmidt, p. 157).

A number of more specific aspects of economic policy have been analyzed in terms of the extent to which changes in political control of the cabinet seem to make a difference. These include income policies (Armingeon), income inequality (Muller; van Arnhem and Schotsman), and the level of public-sector employment (Cusack et al.). The extent of political control over specific European labor markets is elaborated by Armingeon, who anticipated the conclusion of Hicks, Swank, and Ambuhl on welfare effort, discussed above. The key precondition for political control of labor markets, argues Armingeon, is the combination of a strong labor movement with a powerful social democratic party; one or the other of these elements, acting alone, does not seem to be enough to make a real difference (Armingeon, p. 234). A union-party nexus, on the other hand, allows for the development of a set of policies on wage restraint, employment, the "social wage," and the role of trade unions. At one end of the scale, Armingeon places Austria, Belgium, Denmark, Finland, and Germany. In these countries, there is a strong social democratic–trade union nexus; in each, changes in the government are associated with changes in effective political control of wages. In Sweden, where the social democratic–trade union nexus is also strong, political control of wages is high relative to such control in other countries; but there is not enough alternation in government to allow the impact of changes in party control of government to be estimated. At the other end of the scale can be found Britain, France, Ireland, and Italy, where the social democratic–union nexus is weaker and political control of wages is less obvious. Armingeon's conclusions on this matter are firmly stated: "It is the relationship between party and union that is the prior condition for effective wage restraint, rather than the institutional and legislative mechanisms of incomes policy" (Armingeon, p. 268).

Given that governments can attempt to modify the distribution of both wealth and income if they choose to do so, using the welfare and tax systems, it is interesting to explore the impact of parties on income redistribution. This can take place in two quite distinct stages. The first concerns gross income, the aspect of inequality on which trade unions can have the greatest impact. The second concerns net income, which reflects how actual take-home pay is affected by taxes and by transfer payments in the social welfare system. This is the aspect of inequality on which governments can have the greatest impact. The bigger the change in inequality between gross and net income, the greater the impact of public policy.

An extensive comparative analysis of the impact of politics on income distribution has recently been completed by Muller (1989). Controlling for a wide range of factors and analyzing data from a long list of countries, Muller concludes confidently that politics makes a considerable difference to income redistribution. According to Muller's empirical findings, socialist governmental strength does depress the income share going to the richest 20 percent of the population and does narrow the income gap between the richest and the poorest 20 percent. Conservative governmental strength does increase the income share going to the richest 20 percent and does widen the income gap between the richest and the middle income groups (Muller, p. 394). He finds that the negative impact of conservative parties on income equality is greater than the positive impact of socialist parties and concludes, quite unequivocally, that "most of the cross national variation [in income inequality] is explained by the inegalitarian influence of strong conservative parties" (Muller, p. 396).

Finally, Cusack, Notermans, and Rein (1989) have shown that changes in the

TABLE 8.9

**Government Employment as a Percentage
of Total Employment: 1980 and 1987**

	1987	1980	Increase
Switzerland	11.2	10.7	0.5
United Kingdom	21.6	21.1	0.5
Italy	15.2	14.5	0.7
Netherlands	15.7	14.9	0.8
Denmark	29.4	28.3	1.1
Germany	16.1	14.9	1.2
Luxembourg	12.0	10.8	1.2
Ireland	16.0	14.5	1.5
Belgium	20.2	18.6	1.6
Sweden	33.0	30.7	2.3
Spain	14.6	11.9	2.7
France	23.1	20.0	3.1

Source: OECD.

level of public-sector employment are significantly related to the partisan composition of governments. Table 8.9 shows the level of public-sector employment in a number of European states, in both 1980 and 1987. The broad patterns in these data are quite clear. There is a general tendency for public-sector employment to increase everywhere as national income increases. However, there are quite large national differences in the rate of increase. In Britain, for example, governed throughout the period in question by a Conservative party absolutely dedicated to reducing the size of the public sector, the proportion of the work force who were government employees did rise very slowly. Low levels of increase can be seen in other countries with conservative governments during this period, including Germany, the Netherlands, and Switzerland. Countries with mainly social democratic governments during this period, such as France, Spain, and Sweden, are characterized by higher levels of increase in public-sector employment.

Overall, then, this range of empirical studies quite clearly confounds the cynics. Every author concludes that the partisan composition of governments does indeed affect economic policy output, at least in those policy areas for which systematic evidence on the matter has been gathered.

DOES POLITICS MAKE A DIFFERENCE?

It used to be fashionable to denigrate the impact of politicians on public policy, to argue that politics does not make much of a difference. Now the reverse is true. In part this is because of the self-evident impact made by particular parties on the ambitious privatization programs of the 1980s. It is very hard to deny that politics made a difference in these cases. If we look at the problem more generally, however, we see that almost all recently published studies conclude that party politics has a major impact on policy output in the real world.

It does seem to be the case that government programs tend to reflect the published policies of government members. At least in those countries in which there is a clear-cut alternation in the party composition of governments, promises made to the voters in the heat of an election campaign do seem to filter through to government policy. It does seem to be the case that parties enact their promises more often than the cynics would have us believe. In part this may be because many of the promises that politicians make are noncontroversial, but at least for one-party governments, pledge fulfillment rates of around 70 percent have consistently been found. It does seem to be the case that changes in government spending flows can be partially predicted by changes in government policies and, in particular, by major changes in the partisan composition of the government. Spending flows are very sticky, but the evidence suggests that they can, from time to time, be shifted as a result of a major effort of political will. It does seem to be the case that nonexpenditure aspects of economic policy vary according to the partisan composition of the government—relative dominance by right-wing governments, in particular, is associated with significant variations in key socioeconomic variables.

Does all of this mean that politics makes a difference? The weight of the evidence that is accumulating suggests that it does—which gives us all one respectable reason to get excited about the results of elections.

References

Andeweg, R. B.: "Less Than Nothing? Hidden Privatization of the Pseudo-Private Sector: The Dutch Case," *Western European Politics*, vol. 11, no. 4, 1988, pp. 117-128.

Armingeon, K.: "Determining the Level of Wages: The Role of Parties and Trade Unions," in F. Castles (ed.), *The Impact of Parties*, Sage, London, 1982.

Bauer, M.: "The Politics of State-Directed Privatization: The Case of France 1986-89," *West European Politics*, vol. 11, no. 4, 1988, pp. 49-60.

Bergman, T., and K. Strom: *Electoral Commitments and Budget Priorities in Sweden*, ECPR Manifesto Research Group Conference on Party Programs and Government Expenditures, Berlin, 1989.

Bianchi, P., S. Cassese, and V. Della Sala: "Privatization in Italy: Aims and Constraints," *West European Politics*, vol. 11, no. 4, 1988, pp. 87-100.

Budge, I., and R. Hofferbert: "Mandates and Policy Outputs: US Party Platforms and Federal Expenditures, 1948-1985," *American Political Science Review*, vol. 84, no. 1, 1990, pp. 111-132.

————, D. Robertson, and D. Hearl: (eds.) *Ideology, Strategy and Party Change*, Cambridge University Press, Cambridge, England, 1987.

Castles, F.: "The Impact of Parties on Public Expenditure," in F. Castles (ed.), *The Impact of Parties*, Sage, London, 1982.

————: "Explaining Public Education Expenditure in OECD Nations," *European Journal of Political Research*, vol. 17, 1989, pp. 431-448.

Cerny, P. G.: "The 'Little Big Bang' in Paris: Financial Market Deregulation in a Dirigiste System," *European Journal of Political Research*, vol. 17, no. 2, 1989, pp. 169-192.

Cusack, T. R., T. Notermans, and M. Rein: "Political-Economic Aspects of Public Employment," *European Journal of Political Research*, vol. 17, 1989, pp. 471-500.

Drumaux, A.: "Privatization in Belgium: The National and International Context," *West European Politics*, vol. 11, no. 4, 1988, pp. 74-86.

Esser, J.: "Symbolic Privatization: The Politics of Privatization in West Germany," *West European Politics*, vol. 11, no. 4, 1988, pp. 61-73.

Gladdish, K.: "Coalition Governments and Policy Outputs in the Netherlands," in V. Bogdanor (ed.), *Coalition Government in Western Europe*, Heinemann Educational Books, London, 1983.

Heald, D.: "The United Kingdom: Privatization and Its Political Context," *West European Politics*, vol. 11, no. 4, 1988, pp. 31-48.

Hicks, A., D. H. Swank, and M. Ambuhl: "Welfare Expansion Revisited: Policy Routines and Their Mediation by Party, Class and Crisis, 1957-1982," *Euro-*

pean Journal of Political Research, vol. 17, 1989, pp. 401–430.

Hofferbert, R., and H.-D. Klingemann: "The Policy Impact of Party Programs and Government Declarations in the Federal Republic of Germany," *European Journal of Political Research*, vol. 18, no. 3, 1990, pp. 277–304.

Kalogeropoulou, E.: "Election Promises and Government Performance in Greece: PASOK's Fulfillment of Its 1981 Election Pledges," *European Journal of Political Research*, vol. 17, 1989, pp. 289–311.

Kavanagh, D.: *Thatcherism and British Politics: The End of Consensus?* 2d ed., Oxford University Press, Oxford, 1990.

Keman, H.: "Securing the Safety of the Nation State," in F. Castles (ed.), *The Impact of Parties*, Sage, London, 1982.

———: *Party Programs and Policy Making in the Netherlands: The Paradox of Coalescence and Confrontation (1948–1986)*, ECPR Manifesto Research Group Conference on Party Programs and Government Expenditures, Berlin, 1989.

Klingemann, H.-D.: "Electoral Programs in West Germany, 1949–1980," in Budge, Robertson, and Hearl.

Laver, M., and I. Budge (eds.): *Party Policy and Government Coalitions*, Macmillan, London, 1991.

———, ———, and A. Byrne: "The Relationship between Party and Coalition Policy in Europe: An Empirical Analysis," in Laver and Budge.

——— and P. Mitchell: *Party Policy and Government Spending in Ireland, 1957–87*, University College Galway, 1989.

Muller, E. N.: "Distribution of Income in Advanced Capitalist States: Political Parties, Labour Unions, and the International Economy," *European Journal of Political Research*, vol. 17, 1989, pp. 367–400.

Müller, W.: "Privatizing in a Corporatist Economy: The Politics of Privatization in Austria," *West European Politics*, vol. 11, no. 4, 1988, pp. 101–116.

Pontusson, J.: "The Triumph of Pragmatism: Nationalisation and Privatization in Sweden," *West European Politics*, vol. 11, no. 4, 1988, pp. 129–140.

Rallings, C.: "The Influence of Election Programs: Britain and Canada 1945–79," in Budge, Robertson, and Hearl.

Rose, R.: *Do Parties Make a Difference?* Chatham House, Chatham, N.J., 1980.

Särlvik, B.: "Coalition Politics and Policy Output in Scandinavia," in V. Bogdanor (ed.), *Coalition Government in Western Europe*, Heinemann Educational Books, London, 1983.

Schmidt, M.: "The Role of Parties in Shaping Macroeconomic Policy," in F. Castles (ed.), *The Impact of Parties*, Sage, London, 1982.

Strom, K.: "Norway: Policy Pursuit and Coalition Avoidance," in M. Laver and I. Budge (eds.), *Party Policy and Government Coalitions*, Macmillan, London, 1991.

Van Arnhem, J. C. M., and G. J. Schotsman: "Do Parties Affect the Distribution of Incomes? The Case of Advanced Capitalist Democracies," in F. Castles (ed.), *The Impact of Parties*, Sage, London, 1982.

Vickers, J., and V. Wright, "The Politics of Industrial Privatization in Western Europe: An Overview," *West European Politics*, vol. 11, no. 4, 1988, pp. 1–30.

CHAPTER 9
POLITICS OUTSIDE PARLIAMENT

Most of this book deals with the "official" politics of representation in countries with a system of parliamentary government. Up until now, we have been dealing with the national politics of selecting a legislature and an executive. While these vital matters are central to politics in any Western European state, they are only part of the story. In the rest of the book, therefore, we look at aspects of the politics of representation that operate outside the parliamentary framework. In the next chapter we deal with the supranational politics of European institutions. In this chapter we concern ourselves with the role of interest and pressure groups in the decision-making process.

While a large part of the political representation of social and economic interests inevitably takes place outside formal parliamentary processes, there are big differences between Western European countries in the extent to which the most important interest groups enjoy a formal role within the political system. Over the past twenty years or so, political scientists have spent a lot of time thinking about these differences and have developed a substantial body of analysis to deal with them. On the one hand, there is a type of interest group politics known as "corporatism," in which interest groups are closely integrated into the formal political process. On the other hand, there is a type of interest group politics known as "pluralism," in which groups compete with each other in a political marketplace outside formal political institutions in an attempt to put pressure on political elites to make decisions in their favor.

A considerable body of theory on these themes has evolved, and as a result, it is sometimes difficult to disentangle the explosive growth in theorization about corporatism and pluralism from suggestions that the involvement of interest groups in decision making is becoming a more important feature of the real world of European politics. (Good introductions to modern corporatist theory can be found in Cawson, 1986, and in Grant. Good introductions to modern pluralist theory can be found in Jordan, 1990a and b, and in Smith.)

In the rest of this chapter, we concentrate on variations in the blend of corporatist and pluralist decision making that sets the tone of interest group politics in Western Europe. We explore how well each of these approaches seems to describe the politics of economic policy making, as well as the politics of decision making in important noneconomic spheres of activity. Before doing this, however, we take time to describe the essential differences between pluralism and corporatism and to illustrate these with brief discussions of the patterns of interest group politics in Austria and in Britain, the former typically seen as the archetypal corporatist system, the latter as essentially pluralist.

CORPORATISM

Unfortunately, more redundant jargon clogs up articles and books on corporatism than in many other areas of political science. A semantic problem has even concerned the very name of the concept. In order to distinguish the notion of corporatism being advanced by western political scientists from the corporatism practiced by discredited prewar fascist regimes, corporatist theorists of the 1960s and 1970s often talked of "neocorporatism" or "liberal corporatism." In recent years, once these ideological points have been made, the cumbersome terms have tended to be dropped in favor of "corporatism," the term we use in this book. Cawson (1986, p. 38) provides a clear-cut definition of the concept:

> *Corporatism is a* . . . process *in which organisations representing* monopolistic *functional interests engage in political exchange with state agencies over public policy* . . . *which involves those organisations in a role which* combines interest representation and policy implementation through delegated self-enforcement. [Emphasis added.]

The essential features of corporatist decision making are thus as follows:

- Large and powerful interest groups monopolize the representation of the interests of a particular functional sector of the population, such as "labor," "farmers," or "employers."
- Interest groups are organized in a hierarchical manner, typically with a powerful "peak organization" (for example, a national trade union or employers' federation) that coordinates strategy at the apex of a pyramid of organizations.
- Groups are integrated in a rather formal way into the political system and play an important role in both the formulation and the implementation of major political decisions.

This basic pattern is emphasized by Phillipe Schmitter and by Gerhard Lehmbruch, two of the most influential figures associated with the resurgence of political science interest in corporatism:

> *Corporatism is more than a particular pattern of articulation of interests. Rather, it is an* institutionalised *pattern of* policy-formation *in which large interest organizations* cooperate with each other and with public authorities *not only in the articulation of interests, but* . . . *in the* "authoritative allocation of values" *and in the* implementation *of such policies.* [Lehmbruch, p. 150, emphasis added.]

The stress in the latter half of this definition on policy implementation is what sets corporatism fundamentally apart from other systems for involving interest groups in political decision making. The implications of this are far-reaching. For any particular decision-making regime to be properly termed "corporatist," interest groups must be comprehensive in their representation of particular sectors of society and must be able to police their membership as well as represent their interests.

Since most important political decisions in postwar Europe have had to do one way or another with economic strategy, the practical impact of corporatism is most easily seen in the interaction between the state and key economic interest groups, especially trade union and employers' federations. Thus, for a trade union federation to be involved effectively in corporatist policy making in the areas of prices and incomes, it must represent a large proportion of the industrial work force; it must be able to negotiate authoritatively on behalf of this constituency; and it must be able to deliver the compliance of its constituency in relation to the agreements that it makes on behalf of that group. If it cannot do this, then it simply cannot act as a true corporatist "social partner." This full-blooded involvement in the implementation, not just in the making, of social and economic policy is often omitted from casual applications of the idea of corporatism. This omission can lead, as we shall see, to misleading conclusions about whether particular political systems are becoming more, or less, corporatist.

Thus corporatism is much more than a system of formalized three-way collaboration between government, unions, and industry, however comprehensive this might be, over the making of economic policy. Such arrangements are more properly described as "tripartite." Rather, true corporatism runs much deeper into the political system. It involves a comprehensive role for the social partners in the implementation of policy, and it is applicable in policy domains well beyond the economy. As Cawson (1986, p. 37) puts it: "The corporatist relationship between state agencies and organised interests is two-way. . . . Under a corporatist arrangement interest organisations are an *integral part of the administration*; they are not merely consulted over the implementation of policy" (emphasis added).

Groups that are important in a corporatist decision-making system, therefore, must have a clientele and an organizational structure that enable them to participate in the process of policy implementation. Thus corporatist economic policy making involves trade unions and employers' federations, but not federations of sports clubs or churches, even if these have strong views on economic policy. Concentrating our attention on functionally important interest groups highlights the fact that corporatist arrangements operate on a sector-by-sector basis. This has been increasingly emphasized by those writing in the corporatist tradition; they have concentrated more and more on sectoral (or "meso-") corporatism.

In general, therefore, the theory of corporatism has proved much more useful as a way to organize discussions of policy-making styles in particular sectors than as an all-encompassing theory of the state. [A typical collection of accounts of corporatist arrangements in particular policy sectors can be found in Cawson (1985)]. Nonetheless, since the making of economic policy, especially on prices and incomes, has been so central to postwar politics in many Western European states, the operation of corporatist arrangements in economic policy making is the phenomenon that attracts the most widespread interest among political scientists. In practice, furthermore, the existence of strong tripartite institutions in a particular country is usually taken as convincing evidence of a tendency toward corporatism. Views about the likely spread of corporatism were modified by the end of the 1980s, however, as the institutions of corporatism appeared to decline in a number of countries during the preceding years of recession. This led to an increasing tendency to categorize corporatism as a "fair-weather" phenomenon—a form of concerted action that tends to fall apart when resources become scarcer and interest groups must bargain more competitively to divide up a pie that is fixed rather than one that is continually expanding (Keman and Whiteley).

Corporatism as we know it today has diverse sources in the political thought of the past one hundred years or so. One important current that fed into modern theories of corporatist policy making was the fascism of the 1920s and 1930s. Fascist corporatism was a system of totalitarian state control of society based on an intimate interpenetration of interest groups and the state. Domination of the major interest groups by the state was one of the main mechanisms of social control by the fascist one-party government, exemplified by Hitler's Germany, Mussolini's Italy, and Salazar's Portugal. Obviously, any form of thought even vaguely linked with fascism was totally discredited in Western Europe after World War II. This is why, as we have seen, postwar theories of corporatism severed any association with fascism before being initially relaunched as "neocorporatist" or "liberal corporatist" approaches.

A second intellectual source that flowed into modern corporatism was "Catholic Social Thought," which was especially influential during the early decades of the twentieth century. Roman Catholic church leaders became concerned that the role of the church was being undermined, on the one hand by the growth of trade unionism and on the other hand by what they saw as the relentless encroachment of the state into many aspects of social life. They regretted the passing of the medieval craft guilds and proposed a much enhanced role for self-governing interest groups that comprised what they described as the "voluntary" sector. These groups would be intimately involved not only in the planning but also in the provision of major social services such as health care and education. What lay behind this was that in a predominantly Roman Catholic society, these groups would be made up primarily of Roman Catholics, and so public policy would be sensitive to the teachings of the church, despite a formal separation of church and state. These ideas were taken up in the early postwar years by Christian democratic parties (see Chapter 3). The electoral success of these parties gave corporatism a further political impetus (Grant).

A third factor that contributed to the rise of neocorporatism was the impulse for "national unity" that followed the destruction and trauma caused by World War II in so many European countries. As we saw in Chapter 7, a number of states went through the immediate postwar period governed by coalitions of national unity encompassing both the right and the left. The sense that industry and labor had to work together in order to rebuild war-torn economies fostered tripartite cooperation in places such as Austria and Germany.

A fourth factor was the close relationship between the trade union movement

Corporatist industrial relations: The heads of Swedish trade union and employers' federations conclude a national wage agreement in 1981. (Sven-Erik Sjöberg/ Pressens Bild AB)

and social democratic parties in several Western European countries (see Chapter 3). Many of these parties had grown out of the trade union movement and were still intimately interconnected with it. When social democratic parties were in power over long periods, notably in postwar Sweden and Norway and to a lesser extent elsewhere in Scandinavia, the relationship between trade unions and political parties became a relationship between trade unions and government. Even in "pluralist" Britain, as we shall see, economic policy making came closest to being corporatist during the "Social Contract" between government and unions executed during the life of the 1974–1979 Labour administration.

For a variety of reasons, therefore, corporatist decision making in the area of economic policy became an important feature of postwar politics in a number of Western European countries. By the early 1970s, those countries with strong corporatist institutions (such as Austria, Germany, and Sweden) seemed to be prospering, while those with weak ones (such as Britain) seemed to be in decline. This prompted widespread interest in neocorporatism among political scientists, crystallized by the influential early writings of Schmitter and Lehmbruch. Since then, debate on the subject has raged intensively. Marxists such as Westergaard have criticized the approach for failing to take account of the fact that a corporatist state is also a capitalist state, which will faithfully serve the interests of capital (see Jessop and also Westergaard). Pluralists (see below) have criticized the neocorporatists for offering nothing new, for doing no more than dressing up some of the insights of pluralist theory in a new terminology while misrepresenting the rest of it (Jordan, 1981; Martin, 1983; Rhodes).

What is absolutely certain about all of this is that for the past couple of decades, it has been impossible to write about the role of interest groups in the policy-making process without considering the implications of the corporatist account of decision making. Most authors agree that of all Western European countries, Austria exhibits the strongest form of corporatism. By looking in greater detail at the situation in Austria, therefore, we can gain some additional insight into what is involved in corporatist policy making.

"CORPORATISM" IN AUSTRIA

Austria is usually taken as the classic case of a political system characterized by a very high degree of neocorporatist policy making. Indeed, Marin (1987) goes as far as to argue that Austria is a "model-generator," one of a very few countries that theorists have in mind when they develop accounts of corporatism. Perhaps the most striking and distinctive feature of Austrian politics in this regard is the important role of the "chambers." These are institutions that provide formal representation for the interests, respectively, of labor, commerce, and agriculture. While chambers (especially chambers of commerce) can be found elsewhere, the Austrian chambers are much more important, given their statutory position and the vital role that they play in decision making. All working citizens in Austria are obliged by law to belong to the appropriate chamber (Marin, 1985). This formal status requires the chambers to run their affairs in a manner that would withstand legal scrutiny—to make internal decisions and hold internal elections in a representative manner, for example. It also confers the formal right to advise on, as well as to be consulted on and/or represented in, a wide range of matters. The chambers nominate members to many other public bodies.

In addition to the statutory chambers, Austria has an extensive system of "voluntary" interest groups. These include a trade union movement organized under the auspices of the "peak" trade union organization, the ÖGB, and the League of Austrian Industrialists, the VÖI. The ÖGB, in particular, is a powerful independent actor in Austria, for a number of reasons. First, it is the main agency engaged in particularlistic collective bargaining on behalf of its members. The Chamber of Labour, by virtue of its statutory status, must also consider the "public interest" in its dealings. Second, the ÖGB is highly centralized. While fifteen unions are affiliated with the ÖGB, individual members do not join the unions themselves; instead, they join the ÖGB, which transfers membership and funds to specific unions. Third, the member unions, legally speaking, are subdivisions of the ÖGB, rather than the peak organization being a federation of autonomous unions. All of these reasons together create a situation in which "organisational authority is where the money is: at the top . . ." (Marin, 1985, p. 99). In addition, the level of trade union affiliation in Austria is relatively high, and unions tend to be organized on an industry-by-industry (rather than a craft-by-craft) basis.

Almost all observers agree that the three main chambers—the Chamber of Labour, of Commerce, and of Agriculture—and the ÖGB interact with each other as the four key players in the process of making and implementing economic policy in Austria, a system known as *Sozialpartnerschaft*, or "social partnership." This system operates in parallel with, rather than in opposition to, the formal parliamentary system. While the key interest associations are quite distinct from the political parties, the obvious political affiliations of their respective memberships mean that each association tends to be dominated by supporters of one or another of the main parties. This gives interest group leaders a very strong position. As might be expected, the Chamber of Labour and the ÖGB are dominated by the Social Democrats (SPÖ), and the Chamber of Commerce and Chamber of Agriculture are dominated by the conservative Austrian People's party (ÖVP) (Gerlich, p. 88).

It is important, however, not to present relations between parties and interest groups in Austria as if these were in some sense exclusive entities. On the contrary, there is an intimate interpenetration of interest groups and parliament, and this symbiosis is identified by many as one of the strengths of Austrian corporatism. The president of the Trade Union Federation was also for a long time the president of the Austrian lower parliamentary chamber, and a steadily growing proportion of parliamentarians are also interest group representatives (Gerlich, Grande, and Müller, p. 216). These interest groups also play an important role in the selection of parliamentary candidates for the major Austrian parties.

The social partners in Austria are concerned first and foremost with economic policy making and, in particular, with prices and incomes. The social partnership that underpins Austrian corporatism thus involves both the negotiation and the implementation of policies on both prices and incomes. This cooperation is formalized in a powerful institution, the Joint Commission on Prices and Wages. Representation on the commission is governed by the principle of parity, and so the representation of the Chamber of Labour and the ÖGB equals that of the Chamber of Commerce and Chamber of Agriculture, and the commission is often referred to as the "Parity Commission." The concept of parity is vital to the operation of Austrian corporatism, implying strictly equal membership for representatives of business and labor in all important economic policy-making bodies. The effect is to force groups that might otherwise be antagonistic to cooperate with one another, since no effective decisions can be made unless they do.

The commission actually operates on a very informal basis "to an extent hardly credible to outside observers: the Parity Commission has no address or fixed meeting place, no telephone number, no independent finance, no statutes, procedural rules, membership, written agreements or even registered existence" (Marin, 1985, p. 110). The Austrian government has no representation on the commission, though it is far from aloof from its activities. Meetings of the commission may be chaired and attended by senior government ministers and often take place in government offices (Lehmbruch, p. 159).

As might be expected in political interactions between sophisticated actors, there is considerable negotiation and coordination between key Austrian interest groups outside the structure of formal meetings of the commission. Thus many important decisions will be "bargained out" by the interest groups before the government becomes involved. While key actors can anticipate the impact of corporatist institutions, however, this is certainly not to say that these institutions are unimportant. The consultative procedures enshrined in the formal decision-making system provide the institutional environment in which all bargaining takes place. Principles such as parity define the game being played, the power relations between the players, and the institutional factors that they must all take account of. Without these procedures in the background, even if they were never to be invoked in earnest, eventual policy outcomes would be quite different.

As a system of economic planning, Austrian corporatism has been judged, especially during the relatively affluent 1960s and 1970s, to be an outstanding success. The Austrian economy enjoyed steady growth and a record on inflation and unemployment that was much better than the European norm. More remarkable than this, however, was Austria's record during the recessionary 1980s, when corporatist forms of decision making seemed to be in decline almost everywhere else. As Gerlich, Grande, and Müller (p. 214) argue, "in spite of predictions to the contrary by domestic as well as foreign observers, the present economic crisis has not led to a breakdown of the consensual climate of negotiation between corporatist elites in Austria. Likewise, these elites still enjoy considerable legitimacy among the members of their respective organizations. Workers as well as businessmen still remain loyal to the *Sozialpartnerschaft* institutions and accept their decisions." The same authors go on to argue that while other countries came to exhibit some of the more visible institutional features of corporatist decision making during the 1960s and 1970s, an effective corporatist system involves far more than mere institutions. It rests upon a history and culture of collective accommodation that cannot simply be invented as the need arises. "Austrians have internalized attitudes and values of social partnership and apply them even when they appear to or do actually contradict their individual and immediate interests. Austrians even consider that, in the long term and overall, social partnership optimally realizes their individual preferences by collective regulation" (Gerlich, Grande, and Müller, p. 218). Full-fledged corporatism based on the Austrian model, therefore, is a comprehensive and deep-rooted decision-making culture rather than a complex of superficial institutions. This explains why key institutions such as the Parity Commission can be run in such an informal way. And it explains why Austrian corporatism is both durable and adaptive.

PLURALISM

Like corporatism, pluralism has tended to occupy an uneasy no-man's-land between being a "normative" theory of how politics *ought* to be conducted and being a "positive" theory of how groups *actually do* operate. As a normative theory, pluralism is one of the underpinnings of Madisonian liberal democracy, perhaps best summarized in recent times by Dahl (pp. 4–33). But this is not our main concern here. As a descriptive scheme, pluralism has typically been used to characterize interest group activity in systems such as Britain (and, for that matter, the United States) where groups put pressure on political elites in a relatively disorganized and competitive manner, in contrast to the well-ordered and collusive interaction between groups and elites under corporatism.

While pluralism has been criticized for being a vague and incomplete theory of politics (Jordan, 1990b), it does, nonetheless, have a set of identifiable features that allows us to regard it as a distinctive approach to the description of political decision making. In particular, pluralism differs from corporatism in a number of respects, the most important of which is that pluralist interest groups have no *formal* institutional role in the allocation of resources and the implementation of policy. A second fundamental difference is that interest groups in a pluralist system are assumed to be self-generating and voluntary. This implies the existence of a range of different groups, typically competing with each other to represent the interests of the same classes of people in a given sphere of economic or social activity. A further assumption that is explicit or implicit in much of pluralist theory is that while it is clear that not all groups have equal levels of power or resources, it is nonetheless relatively easy for people to form an interest group and thereby gain at least some access to the levers of political power (Smith, p. 309). This suggests that a range of salient social interests in a pluralist system will be represented by the set of existing interest groups. New interests that might emerge, for one reason or another, can be covered by the capacity of existing groups to adapt to changes in "market forces" or by the possibility of the relatively unhindered formation of new groups.

The basic process by which pluralist theorists assume that interests are represented in decision making involves groups influencing the output of the executive branch of government by applying "pressure" on political elites. Different groups compete with one another to put pressure on decision makers, who are pressed in many different directions at the same time. Those groups which apply pressure most effectively (possibly because they have the most public support, but quite possibly also because they have the most resources or the most privileged access to elites) have the greatest impact in bringing public policy closer to their own preferred positions.

Despite the allegations made by some naive critics, few pluralists assume that the resources available to different groups are in any sense equal or that different groups have equivalent access to key political decision makers. Most pluralists accept that the market in political influence is far from perfect, containing actors with very different capacities to affect important political decisions. In particular, many pluralists accept that business interests are often in a highly privileged position and that the state is far from neutral, favoring business interests or, indeed, favoring the particular interests of the bureaucracy. A clear statement of this "neopluralist" position can be found in Charles Lindblom's influential book *Politics and Markets*. For Lindblom, there are some "grand" issues that are effectively removed from public debate by the combined power of business interests and the state. In addition, there are "secondary" issues in which conventional pluralist politics takes place (Lindblom, p. 142).

When certain interest groups develop a particularly close long-term relationship with the state, sharing key values and objectives while keeping firm control over the agenda of public debate, then what has become known as a "policy community" is said to emerge (Jordan, 1990a; Rhodes; Smith). As with all other communities, the key to the development of a policy community is the long-term interaction of certain groups with policy makers, along with a set of shared values; together they create a situation in which those groups involved in the policy community tend to be the first to be consulted when a new policy problem arises. This in turn means that policy communities, like other types of communities, tend to exclude certain groups from access to decision makers and to manipulate the political agenda so as to ensure that certain issues are never discussed. It is important to be aware of the possibility of this "hidden face" of power when looking at the relative effectiveness of different groups in the decision-making process.

All pluralists, however, are distinguished by their assumption that there is at least something important left to be contested in the accessible political arena and that such contests take the form of applying political pressure to decision-making elites. Political pressure can be applied in a number of ways, though these are not always very clearly specified by those who write about pluralism. In the sphere of prices and income policy, however, the process is relatively clear-cut. Policy is set on the basis of bargaining between groups, backed up by the threat of the economic sanctions that each group has at its disposal. In the last analysis, trade unions get their way in a pluralistic system, not because they are in some sense integrated into the political process but because they can go on strike and thereby inflict damage on the employers or the government with which they are dealing. Similarly, employers have power because they control the means of production and can inflict pain by engaging in sackings, lockouts, and plant closures if they choose to do so.

Perhaps the single most distinctive feature of the pluralist account of decision making, therefore, is that this is characterized by conflict rather than consensus. The essential pluralist motif is that of a political market, albeit an imperfect one, clearing a competing set of only partially compatible demands. Of course, conflict will not always manifest itself in strikes, lockouts, and so on—rather, it is the threat of such sanctions, whether explicit or implicit, that underpins pluralist bargaining. Indeed, if the various market actors are rational and equipped with perfect information, they will anticipate the outcome of any potential conflict and settle their differences before overt hostilities can begin. Actual observed conflicts—real-world strikes and lockouts—are, according to this view, the product of imperfect information. They are what happens when competing groups test each other's strengths and weaknesses. For all this, however, the outcome of political activity in a pluralist system is assumed to be the product of the balance of forces between the various groups involved. And this balance of forces is determined by the anticipated outcome of head-to-head confrontations over essential conflicts of interest. The politics of economic policy in Britain is often cited as a good example of this style of decision making.

"PLURALISM" IN BRITAIN

During the 1970s, when the interest of political scientists in corporatism was at its zenith, even strike-torn Britain was diagnosed as a system moving toward the corporatist model. This diagnosis had much to do with the emergence of a "Social Contract" between the Labour government of the day; the main British trade union federation, the Trades Union Congress (TUC); and the main employers' federation, the Confederation of British Industry (CBI).

The Social Contract, originally executed in 1975, involved an agreement by unions to accept strictly controlled pay raises in exchange for improvements in social security benefits, a system of price control, and a consultative role in the making of economic policy. For two years, the Social Contract was seen as a reasonable success—wage increases more or less conformed to plan, and the number of strikes fell dramatically. Having failed to get union agreement in a worsening economic situation in 1977, however, the government imposed a unilateral policy that fixed wage increases at 10 percent. The following year, a further policy of wage restraint was introduced unilaterally by the government, and the Social Contract was effectively a dead duck. What followed was the famous

Relations between the state and the labor movement turn violent in Britain as police in full riot gear confront striking miners, October 1984. (Alain Nogues/Sygma)

"Winter of Discontent" of 1978–1979 (a long winter of serious public-sector strikes), a Conservative victory in the 1979 election, and a decisive end to the era of incipient social partnership in Britain.

If we take the setting of prices and incomes as the key arena in which interest groups interact over the making of economic policy, then for most of the postwar era in Britain, competition rather than cooperation has been the order of the day. Trade unions themselves have set great store by their right to "free collective bargaining," backed up by a frequently exercised right to strike. It is significant that several important disputes have involved conflict between unions—such "demarcation" disputes over the right to bargain in particular areas are, of course, almost unheard of in corporatist systems. Even more than the unions, British employers have also been willing for the most part to take their chances in the rough-and-tumble of the labor market.

This mode of economic policy making conforms to the model of a pluralist system based on a political market in which self-generating interest groups compete freely with each other to influence the flow of public policy. Thus, notwithstanding the Social Contract and other periods of trade union involvement in national economic policy making, the argument that Britain is decidedly not a corporatist system rests on two important phenomena. The first is the general lack of integration of both unions and management into the policy-making process. The second is the apparent preference of both sides for confrontational methods of settling their differences.

The fragility of what appeared to be moves toward corporatist decision making in Britain in the mid-1970s can be seen clearly from the speed with which

The bitter end of the British miners' strike, March 1985. (Stuart Franklin/Sygma)

confrontational bargaining was restored after the introduction of government-imposed wage ceilings in 1977. Equally striking is the success of the Conservative attack on trade union rights and privileges after Margaret Thatcher's election victory in May 1979. As early as July 1979, the Conservative secretary for employment issued a consultative document that recommended a series of restrictions on trade union power, including the banning of "secondary" picketing (that is, picketing away from the main scene of an industrial dispute), the restriction of closed shops (which oblige all who work in a particular employment to join a particular union), and the requirement that unions hold secret ballots of those involved before calling strikes (Pelling, p. 282). An attempt to negotiate with the Trade Union Congress over a bill along the same lines understandably failed, and the bill, which became the Employment Act, 1980, was imposed by the government in the face of trade union opposition. This was followed by further antiunion legislation in the shape of the Employment Act, 1982, and the Employment Act, 1984, each designed to undermine union power and eradicate special union privileges.

Confrontation between government and unions came to a head in a long and very bruising miners' strike that began in March 1984. Almost as soon as the strike started, the main miners' union, the National Union of Mineworkers (NUM), refused to abide by various court orders arising from the Employment Acts, thereby putting itself in direct confrontation with the new trade union laws. The NUM was regularly found to be in contempt of court, yet it refused to pay fines, and so court officials eventually moved in to seize large chunks of union funds. The union successfully shifted much of this money out of the country, but the government sought to freeze NUM bank accounts wherever these could be tracked down. The strike became violent and dragged on for fifty-one weeks. The NUM suffered an acrimonious and damaging split before the miners went back to work, embittered because they had won nothing for their pains.

The Thatcherite approach to economic policy making in Britain, then, was to use legislation to weaken the power of trade unions and then relegate the unions to the roles of "mere" economic actors, with no explicit political function. These attacks on the trade unions were defended on the grounds that trade union power hinders the free play of market forces (Kavanagh). A strong belief in the effectiveness of the market left no room for tripartite economic planning, involving agreements between government, employers, and unions. This was replaced by a policy style that kept economic policy making firmly in the hands of the government and depended heavily on the unilateral manipulation of broad-brush macroeconomic instruments such as control over the money supply, the level of public spending, and the size of the budget deficit. British economic policy making under Margaret Thatcher depended not at all on multilateral agreements with the social partners.

PLURALISM, CORPORATISM, AND ECONOMIC POLICY MAKING

Of course, both pluralism and corporatism are ideal types of decision-making regimes, unlikely to be found in their pure form in any European country. In recognition of this, increasing importance is being given, as we have seen, to the operation of corporatist or pluralist decision-making styles in particular policy sectors rather than in the political system as a whole. Nonetheless, in concentrating on the key area of economic policy, it is usual to classify certain European countries as being predominantly corporatist in their decision-making ethos and others as predominantly pluralist.

Two of the key variables that affect such a classification are the level of trade union membership within the working population and the centralization of wage bargaining, or the extent to which the national peak organization for labor is involved in negotiations over wage levels. Information on these matters for some European countries for which figures are available is reported in Table 9.1. Trade union membership is "densest" in Scandinavia, with membership rates of around 90 percent or more in Sweden, Denmark, and Finland (and also in Norway). It is lowest in France (26 percent), Switzerland, and the Netherlands. The level of union membership is also estimated as being very low in Spain (Pérez-Díaz, p. 231). The centralization of wage bargaining is highest in Austria and Scandinavia and lowest in France, Switzerland, Britain, and Italy.

There have been many classifications of European political systems in these terms—we will borrow from one of these, put forward by Franz Lehner (p. 58). At one end of the spectrum are pluralist and "weakly corporatist" systems. These are characterized by a fragmented system of interest groups, a narrow scope for collective bargaining, and, in weakly corporatist systems, limited participation by

TABLE 9.1
**Trade Union Membership and the Centralization
of Wage Bargaining**

	Union Members as % of Nonagricultural Employees, 1989	Centralization of Wage Bargaining
Austria	61	High
Belgium	78	Medium
Denmark	94	High
Finland	86	High
France	26	Low
Germany	44	Medium
Ireland	54	Medium
Italy	46	Low
Netherlands	38	Medium
Sweden	95	High
Switzerland	35	Low
United Kingdom	50	Low

Sources: OECD; *Economist*, Mar. 3, 1990.

organized labor in national economic policy making. Countries classified by Lehner in this way include France, Britain, and Italy (as well as Canada and the U.S.A.). To this group we should add post-Franco Spain, in which there have been several "social pacts" but in which the social partners are not closely integrated into the process of policy implementation (Pérez-Díaz). At the other end of the spectrum are strong corporatist systems. These are characterized by broadly based tripartite cooperation between labor, capital, and government, as well as wide-ranging and comprehensive income policies. Countries classified by Lehner in this way include Austria, Sweden, Norway, and the Netherlands (the latter despite a rather low level of unionization). We could add Luxembourg to the list of strong corporatist systems (Hirsch). There is an intermediate category of "medium" corporatist states, in which there is some explicit cooperation between social partners, though this is not enshrined in a powerful set of multilateral decision-making institutions. Countries classified in this way include Ireland, Belgium, Germany, Denmark, and Finland (as well as Australia). To these we could add Switzerland (Pappi, p. 84).

The differences between these systems are well illustrated by comparing levels of strike activity, which Lehner takes as an indicator of "distributional" conflict. In the more corporatist systems, there is significantly less strike activity than in the less corporatist systems (Lehner, pp. 58–59). In the early 1980s the average number of workdays lost each year per 1000 workers was 968 in Italy, for example, and 531 in Britain. Both political systems were classified as weakly corporatist, in contrast to Germany, where the average number of days lost per 1000 workers was 29 (Dalton, p. 218). The greater the extent to which interest groups are integrated into the process of economic policy making, the greater the possibility that potential conflicts can be resolved within existing structures. The scope for overt conflict, which, as we argued above, is the product of imperfect information available to the protagonists, is greater in pluralist systems, where interest groups do not regularly sit side by side in policy-making forums and where bargaining is fundamentally based on an ethos of confrontation.

Contrary to certain preconceptions, however, a highly unionized work force combined with a centralized trade union movement does not guarantee an effective system of corporatist decision making. Thus, while it is true that the Austrian trade union movement is highly centralized (virtually all trade unionists are members of the main trade union federation, the ÖGB), the level of trade union membership in the work force (around 60 percent) is high but not especially high (Armingeon). Belgium, for example, has a much higher level of trade union membership and a moderately centralized trade union movement, but most people agree that it has a much lower level of corporatist decision making than Austria (Van den Brande). The Netherlands, in contrast, which is generally held to be more corporatist than Britain or Ireland, has a much lower level of trade union membership than either (Hardiman; Armingeon, p. 119).

However, as we have already seen, corporatism cannot operate if the main interest groups cannot bargain authoritatively on behalf of their members and deliver the compliance of their constituencies with the agreements that are made. Thus, the example of Western European corporatism cited most frequently, after Austria, is Sweden, a country with a highly unionized work force, a centralized union federation, and powerful peak organizations (Czada, p. 24). Similar patterns can be seen in Norway, Luxembourg, and Germany.

In Germany, for example, the peak organization for the trade union movement is the German Federation of Trade Unions (DGB), which represents over 80 percent of all unionized workers (Dalton, p. 215). On the side of business and industry, there are three different peak organizations, but these do not compete with one another. The Federation of German Industries (BDI) concentrates on the political representation of business. The Confederation of German Employers' Associations (BDA) deals with social policy and the labor market, including collective bargaining. The Association of German Chambers of Industry and Commerce (DIHT), representing nearly three million companies, all of which are obliged by law to affiliate, deals with trade and commerce. Thus the three peak organizations representing the interests of capital coordinate their activities and often function as one—though attempts to fuse them into a single organization have up until now been unsuccessful (Dalton, pp. 215–217).

This division of the employers' peak organizations, as well as the fact that the DGB can negotiate on general prices and income strategy but cannot bind individual member unions in its negotiations, means that Germany is typically cited as an example of a "moderate" corporatist system. There have been periods of much tighter cooperation between social partners in Germany, notably the period of the "Concerted Action" (*Konzertierte Aktion*) process set up in response to the economic crises of the 1970s. During this period, the peak organizations bargained far more explicitly over prices and incomes, the government implemented their agreements, and the social partners undertook to deliver the consent of their members. Overall, however, the German system of interest group representation lacks the continuous and comprehensive integration of peak organizations into the formal decision-making process that is the hallmark of a full-fledged corporatist system.

BOX 9.1
Economic Policy Making

FRANCE

The low level of unionization, divisions in the French labor movement, and the fact that the left did not come to power in France until 1981 have led most people to characterize economic policy making in France as confrontational and pluralist rather than corporatist. A small number of big labor unions have been important, each traditionally associated with a political party rather than with a trade or an industry. Thus political divisions have been reproduced in the union movement, which has rarely been a united, monolithic bloc working against either government or employers. When there have been income policies—for example, in the early 1980s—these have not been based on tripartite agreements between the social partners; instead, they have been imposed by the government. Both unions and employers are unwilling to sacrifice their autonomy, and even during the period of socialist government during the 1980s, relations between unions and government did not become particularly close.

GERMANY

Germany is usually referred to as a "medium corporatist" system. While the level of unionization is not high, unions are organized on an industry rather than a craft basis, and so all employees at a particular facility belong to the same union. The German Federation of Trade Unions (DGB) represents the vast majority of unionized workers; it deals with union-government relations, while individual unions take care of collective bargaining over wages and conditions. Different employers' federations coordinate their actions rather than compete with one another. There have been periods of explicit "Concerted Action" when the social partners negotiated an economic program of prices and incomes that was implemented by the government. In general, the social partners in Germany have proved to be oriented toward negotiation rather than confrontation in economic policy making, though some sections of the union movement became more radical and confrontational during the 1980s.

ITALY

Italy is characterized by a set of labor unions divided on political lines rather than in terms of crafts or industries. Despite the relatively low level of unionization, there are three competing union federations—the CGIL, the CISL, and the UIL—confronting a single employers' federation, the *Confindustria*. Despite this, there have been periods during which the social partners attempted to emulate the concerted action arrrangements found in northern Europe, notably the period of "national solidarity," 1977–1979, when wage restraint was traded for a program of legislation on matters ranging from youth employment to pension reform; also notable was the Tripartite Agreement of 1983, which traded wage restraint for an improvement in the conditions of service for employed workers. Deals such as these have not expanded into more broadly based tripartite arrangements, however, and relations between the social partners have remained essentially market-oriented and pluralistic.

NETHERLANDS

Economic policy making in the Netherlands has proved hard for political scientists to classify. The level of unionization is low by European standards, and the major trade union federation does not have a high share of trade union membership. Yet economic policy making has a broadly cooperative style. Unions have engaged in centralized bargaining with the government, though a strong bureaucratic tradition in the Netherlands has tended to mean that such negotiations are usually dominated by the state. Dutch unions, compared with unions in most other European states, have placed a heavier emphasis in their dealings with government on the development of an extensive system of welfare benefits. In this regard, they have been quite successful, and levels of welfare benefits in the Netherlands are among the highest in Europe. The economy of the Netherlands is one of the most open in Europe, with very high levels of foreign investment. This tends to restrict

(Continued on next page)

the impact of indigenous employers on the economy and hence their role as social partners.

SPAIN

Spain under Franco was a totalitarian state, with government domination of all aspects of economic life over a very long period. The traumas associated with the liberalization of the economy have very much conditioned economic policy making. In post-Franco Spain, as in France and Italy, unions are organized along political lines, and the level of unionization is relatively low. Nonetheless, there has been a series of pacts between government, the two key peak organizations of unions (the CCOO and the UGT), and a single peak employers' federation (the CEOE), beginning with the Moncloa Pact of 1977. These pacts dealt with wage restraint, on the one hand, and a restrained approach to the problem of rectifying public finances, on the other. Although unions and employers were involved in the negotiation of the pacts, which continued under both bourgeois and socialist governments, they had little formal role in their implementation.

SWEDEN

After Austria, Sweden is typically regarded as one of Europe's classic cases of corporatist policy making. The level of trade union membership is the highest in Europe, and unions are incorporated in an executive role in the administration of labor market policies. Swedish industry tends to be export-oriented, concentrated, and strong, and there is a traditionally powerful state. For most of the postwar period, Swedish politics has been dominated by the Social Democratic party, giving the Swedish unions much more sustained access to political elites than other unions were able to enjoy in most other European countries. All of this

has contributed to a situation in which each of the social partners has felt able to negotiate with the others from a tradition of strength. The unions have accepted relatively lower wage increases in exchange for stable, full employment and a high level of welfare benefits. The employers have conceded high levels of job security for wage restraint. There were some signs, however, that the "Swedish model" was beginning to break down by the end of the 1980s, as inflation in Sweden rose well above inflation in Sweden's European trading partners and employers' groups, and conservative politicians increasingly promoted more liberal free market policies.

UNITED KINGDOM

Often cited as one of the classic examples of a pluralist rather than corporatist system, the United Kingdom has a relatively decentralized system of wage bargaining. Wage negotiations are conducted by a large number of trade unions, organized on a craft basis rather than on an industry basis, and so many unions may well be involved in negotiations with a single employer—a car manufacturer, for example. Most but not all unions are affiliated with a relatively weak national federation, the Trades Union Congress (TUC), and the proportion of the work force belonging to trade unions is about average by European standards. For a brief period during the mid-1970s, there was a "Social Contract" between unions, employers [represented by the Confederation of British Industry (CBI)], and a Labour government. This collapsed after unilateral action by the government, however, and has not since been renewed. Relations between unions and government have been essentially confrontational since then.

This is in contrast to the situation that obtained during a brief but intense experiment in strong corporatism in Luxembourg. Faced in the early 1970s with the acute problem of an overstaffed and declining traditional steel industry (involving 15 percent of the GNP, 12 percent of the work force, and over 50 percent of the country's industrial production), the Luxembourg government became part of a Tripartite Conference involving the peak organizations of capital and labor (Hirsch, p. 54). Tripartitism was formalized by law in 1977 with the establishment of a Tripartite Coordination Committee, comprising four government nominees, four employers' representatives, and four from the trade union movement. This committee was given a wide-ranging formal role in economic policy making for a brief period of time, and the most striking aspect of this role was that the social partners had a formal right of veto over certain features of government policy (Hirsch). This initiative prompted heated discussion, both within Luxembourg and outside, on the constitutional basis of such an arrangement, as well as its place in a democratic system. The period 1977–1980, however, can be seen as a time when an attempt was made to impose strong corporatism according to a formula that became known as the "Luxembourg Model," the key feature of which was the veto power of the social partners. However, the Luxembourg Model was heavily watered down by a new law in 1980, and the current Tripartite Coordination Committee in Luxembourg has an advisory role only, without a formal veto right.

The decline of the Luxembourg Model supports one of the main conclusions of a recent study of the perseverance of corporatism in Austria, namely that a full-blooded implementation of corporatist decision making requires a political culture that nourishes strongly held values in favor of social cooperation. Without this, formal corporatist institutions cannot put down deep roots (Gerlich et al.). Most of the evidence that we have reviewed, indeed, supports the contention that corporatist decision making cannot simply be imposed from above as a set of rules, regulations, and institutions; rather, it must be based in a political culture that places a high value on social coordination rather than social conflict.

BEYOND THE SOCIAL PARTNERS: ENTRENCHED INTEREST GROUPS

The tripartite institutions that are the most visible signs of corporatist decision-making regimes, as we have seen, involve government, employers, and trade unions. There are, however, many more interest groups than these. Even in corporatist systems, most interest groups are not formally incorporated into the decision-making process, though some groups are more incorporated than others. We have picked three types of entrenched interest groups—churches, farmers, and doctors—to illustrate the basic political patterns that are encountered in different European countries. We by no means imply that these are the only entrenched interest groups, but it is clear that we cannot provide a comprehensive catalog of all the political interests represented in Western European politics. Such a catalog would be a book in its own right. Most of the other important entrenched groups, however, are represented in a manner rather similar to those we discuss below.

Churches

There is immense diversity, within individual European countries, in the political role of churches. At one extreme, there are countries in which there is an "established" religion, where the state is officially identified with a particular religious denomination. The best-known example is England, where the monarch is the head of the Church of England. While in theory there can be no more powerful position for a religious denomination than that of the official religion of the state, the fact that England is one of Europe's more secular societies means that the established position of the Church of England has relatively few practical political consequences. In Ireland, a clause in the 1937 constitution gave a special position to the Roman Catholic church, but this was removed by referendum in 1972.

In many other European countries, one particular religious denomination is dominant in the sense of claiming the vast majority of inhabitants as adherents. Typically, this is Roman Catholicism, since, on the Protestant side, religious affiliation tends to be organized on the basis of a range of different denominations. In predominantly Roman Catholic countries—such as Austria, Belgium, Ireland, Italy, Luxembourg, Spain, and Portugal—the monolithic hierarchical structure of the Roman Catholic church makes it potentially very powerful.

Interventions by the Roman Catholic hierarchy into public debates on matters such as abortion, divorce, and contraception have not always been successful, however. Divorce was introduced, and defended, in Italy in the face of active clerical opposition, for example. Nonetheless, the church can function as a most effective entrenched interest group, bringing about a situation in which much social and moral legislation conforms to the beliefs of one particular denomination, even when this legislation conflicts directly with the beliefs of others. Perhaps the most pointed recent example of this involves the reaction of the Roman Catholic hierarchy in a number of countries to the AIDS epidemic. Public health authorities have argued that the practice of "safe" sex, especially the use of condoms, is one of the most effective methods of preventing the spread of AIDS. The Roman Catholic church has objected to health education campaigns based on this premise for two reasons. The first is that campaigns to promote safe sex might be seen as encouraging sex outside marriage, and the Roman Catholic church strongly disapproves of this. The second is that safe sex involves the use of a device, the condom, that is prohibited by the Roman Catholic church on moral grounds for use by anyone (including monogamous, heterosexual married couples). Such objections have aroused the bitter antagonism of groups concerned more with preventing deaths arising from the spread of AIDS than with promoting Roman Catholic morality. Notwithstanding this, the Roman Catholic church has been successful in bringing about the modification of AIDS education campaigns in several European countries, so as to downplay the emphasis given to the use of condoms.

Protestant Christian denominations, with the exception of the Church of England, are much less hierarchical than the Roman Catholic church, and, as we have observed, several Protestant denominations typically coexist in a predominantly Protestant society. The result is that the Protestant Christian churches in Europe have typically been much less effective politically as entrenched interest groups. This is not, of course, to say that the attitudes of Protestant religious groups have had no impact on the societies in which these groups exist. In overwhelmingly Protestant Scandinavia, for example, or in parts of Scotland and Wales, legal constraints on the use of alcohol or on Sunday observance show the clear impact of Protestant attitudes. In Northern Ireland and the Netherlands, fundamentalist Protestant denominations have been strident participants in the political process. There are also, however, strong traditions within certain strands of Protestantism that regard all forms of political activity as ungodly, and, all in all, there are few if any examples in Protestantism of the potential for mass political mobilization based on religious affiliation that exists in predominantly Roman Catholic societies.

Overall, there has been a clear tendency throughout the twentieth century for the mainstream Christian churches to withdraw, as far as possible, from explicit political interventions in Europe. Rather, they rely where they can on Christian democratic parties (see Chapter 3) or on their ability as entrenched pressure groups to influence the political agenda. Minor religious denominations in Europe, furthermore, tend, with one or two exceptions, to adopt a very low political profile, moving into open confrontation with political elites only when fundamental values are attacked, something which happens only rarely.

Farmers

There is a strong tradition in Europe for farmers' groups to be very well integrated into the political system, wielding disproportionately more influence over policy makers than many other types of economic actor–consumers, for example, or the unemployed. A succession of wars in Europe has led governments to cultivate indigenous food producers very carefully. As a result, there is a long tradition of farm support programs, typically involving government intervention in agricultural markets at guaranteed prices, to protect the interests of farmers. For those countries in the European Community (EC), this tradition became regularized in the Common Agricultural Policy (CAP), with its system of intervention prices and consequent "mountains" of stored butter or grain and "lakes" of surplus wine or milk. Payoffs for farmers have been immense (see Chapter 10). The very generous terms of the CAP, for a long time the most important and expensive feature of EC economic policy, are a testimony to the power of the farmers' lobby in each of the member states.

This power is usually exercised, even in pluralist systems such as Britain, in a very institutionalized way. Farmers' organizations, such as the British National Farmers' Union (NFU), have traditionally had consultative status with ministries of agriculture on many matters, a relationship that is one of the classic examples of a "policy community" (see above). Farmers and civil servants have tended to settle matters between themselves and to exclude other interest groups if at all possible (Smith, p. 313). It has been quite common, furthermore, for farmers' groups to be involved in policy implementation, especially in relation to the distribution among individual farmers of the official national and regional production quotas for particular agricultural commodities. (Such quotas tend to go hand in hand with above-market intervention prices, which would otherwise lead to massive overproduction.) In many European systems—Norway and Sweden are good examples—the access of farmers' groups to civil service policy makers is very good indeed (Steen). This close cooperation between the farmers and the civil service might on the face of it look almost corporatist. However, the lack of any formal role in the political equation for any other "social partner," together with the fact that bureaucrats rather than politicians are involved on behalf of the executive, identifies this type of decision-making arrangement as a closed policy community rather than an example of corporatism.

Doctors

Physicians are typically organized as members of a self-governing profession. This provides a rather different model for the exercise of political power on behalf of sectional interests. The key powers associated with the professional status of physicians derive from the fact that health care is an expert service, one that cannot properly be evaluated by its consumers or even by nonspecialist political elites. This gives doctors the more or less unchallenged ability to define and defend professional standards of medical practice and therefore to control medical training and licensing—and hence access to the profession. This control is typically exercised by a powerful guildlike medical association to which all licensed physicians must belong. The medical association typically also plays a vital policy implementation role, besides controlling professional ethics and standards (and thus practice) via a system of peer review. While politicians can make all the policies they want on health and medicine, they cannot implement such policies effectively without the cooperation of the medical profession, organized by the medical association. This gives the medical lobby a very powerful position in the policy process.

European medical associations are incorporated into political decision making in ways that vary somewhat from country to country. In Germany, for example, the process of making health policy has taken on a decidedly corporatist flavor since the establishment of a Concerted Action organization in 1977. This has a sixty-member council, with representatives of medical associations, hospitals, insurers, and government, that makes annual recommendations on health-care spending and doctors' pay (Altenstetter; Döhler). Despite some attempts by governments to clip doctors' wings,

> the autonomy of German physicians remains unchallenged. . . . On the macroeconomic level, their participation in a corporatist negotiating institution serves as a buffer against possible threats to professional autonomy . . . [facilitating] package deals between government and physicians, such as moderate fee increases in return for restricted access to medical schools. On the regional and local level the extensive self-governing authority, which is legally as well as structurally established . . . makes changes in the power structure extremely difficult to implement.
> (Döhler, pp. 186–188)

The situation in Sweden is rather different, despite the existence of the centralized Swedish Medical Association (SLF), which represents about 90 percent of all Swedish physicians (Döhler, p. 193). The SLF has monopoly bargaining rights in negotiations over pay and conditions, but the effectiveness of such an apparently powerful position has been undermined by the recent dramatic decentralization of the responsibility for health-care provision to Swedish local councils (Lane and Arvidson). What the Swedish example teaches us is that a powerful and hierarchical medical association can have a major impact on national policy making at an elite level, but its ability to influence a much larger set of local policy makers may be much weaker. At the local level of politics, the electoral concerns of politicians are more likely to prevail over sectional interests, and policy makers seem less likely to be co-opted into the received wisdom of what is good and bad about medical policy.

Overall, however, the Swedish case seems to be the exception to the European norm. When health policy is made at the national level, medical associations in Europe appear to be able to exploit with potent effect their ability to monopolize the market in expertise [a situation also found in the United States, given the political role of the American Medical Association (Björkman)]. And the exercise of this monopoly inevitably gives them a key role in the implementation, as well as the making, of health-care policy.

BEYOND THE SOCIAL PARTNERS: "OUTSIDER" INTEREST GROUPS

Of course, major entrenched interest groups are but a tiny fraction of the vast range of groups to be found in every European country. Any decent-sized European city, after all, has literally thousands of groups that are active at any particular time, from white witches to wine buffs, though a few key groups are obviously far more salient politically than the rest. Once more, we concentrate our attention on some of the most striking and suggestive examples of such groups, often associated with what is rather vaguely referred to as the "new politics." These are the women's movement and the environmental movement.

Women, as we saw in Table 6.4, are systematically underrepresented at virtually every level of politics in virtually every European country. This underrepresentation arises not only in political parties and bureaucracies but also in the peak organizations of the social partners (there are relatively few senior women among trade unionists or business leaders) and in entrenched economic and professional interest groups such as churches, farmers, and doctors. And the political underrepresentation of women arises even in Scandinavia, where the women's movement has made more progress than anywhere else (Hernes). With the exception of the recently formed and successful Women's Alliance in Iceland (Arnason), there is no legislative party primarily devoted to the advancement of the interests of women. All of this places women's groups in the position of being on the outside of the political system, looking in—very much in the mold of an archetypal pluralist pressure group rather than of a corporatist social partner.

What has tended to happen in recent years, though there has been no particular grand scheme about this, is that those who have been active in furthering policy proposals of particular interest to women have tended to operate not as a monolithic "women's movement" but in one of two alternative and more diffuse ways. In the first place, women's issues have been pursued within existing organizations, be they trade unions or political parties. Activists promoting women's issues have rarely had complete success in persuading such organizations to adopt their suggested program in its entirety. Almost invariably, therefore, women's activists have been placed in the role of "ginger group" within a particular organization, where they apply internal pressure for a change of policy with varying degrees of success. One of the best examples of this approach is the way in which many European trade unions have now been convinced—often not without a struggle—to campaign for equal pay and conditions for women doing the same jobs as men.

In the second place, campaigners for women's rights have become prominently involved in single-issue pressure group politics where this is of particular relevance to women. Obvious examples include the politics of abortion (Lovenduski and Outshoorn), divorce, and a range of equal rights causes (Dahlerup). As far as single-issue campaigns are concerned, women's political activism in Europe has been quite similar to the pattern found in the U.S.A. (Mansbridge). In more general terms, the women's movement has been more successful at pluralist pressure politics in the U.S.A., while European women's campaigners, especially those in Scandinavia, have tended to be more successful when they have worked within established channels—in particular, the trade union movement. On both sides of the Atlantic, however, the "outsider" status of women's groups has meant that they have had to fight very hard for every centimeter of ground that they have gained over the past two decades.

The environmental movement in Europe has adopted a very different strategy in its attempt to have an impact on public policy. The effects of this can be seen in the rise of Green parties in many European countries, a phenomenon discussed in Chapter 3. None of these Green parties has been in a position of power at the national level, though the German Greens have been significant forces in certain regional administrations. Few Greens have had any real bargaining power in the formation of national coalition executives. The main impact of the Greens on environmental policy, therefore, has been an indirect one, namely the "greening" of their main political opponents, who adopted more environmentalist policies once it became clear that green politics could attract votes. The 1989 European Parliament elections, in particular, were the occasion of some unexpectedly strong electoral performances from the Greens, even in apparently unpromising countries such as Britain. Many European party programs have become greener in response to this potential challenge.

Notwithstanding the electoral role of the Green parties, there are still many active environmental groups in Europe, most of which employ the classic techniques of pressure politics. The Greenpeace organization, to take just one example, has engaged in a series of effective and headline-grabbing campaigns, blocking an outfall from the British nuclear reprocessing plant at Sellafield and placing Greenpeace members in rubber dinghies between whaling ships and whales in the Antarctic or in the way of ships dumping toxic wastes in the North Sea. Many of these campaigns have generated dramatic newsreel footage, and Greenpeace's membership underwent spectacular growth during the second half of the 1980s.

Environmental groups have almost no institutionalized access to power and are thus forced to rely on traditional pluralist "outsider" politics. When state agencies are established to deal with environmental issues, for example, prominent individuals associated with environmental causes may be selected for some role or another, but there are very few examples in Europe of environmentalist groups being given formal consultative status. In part this may be because the more successful groups, like Greenpeace, have been quite militant and have deliberately distanced themselves from the political establishment. In part it may be because established groups have identified the politics of the environment as something that they can annex for themselves. They are therefore unwilling to allow outsider groups to use green politics to gain any sort of foothold within the established system.

CONCLUSION

Most recent developments in both the corporatist and the pluralist theory of interest representation imply that we are asking the wrong question if we ask whether a particular political system *as a whole* is characterized by corporatist or pluralist policy making. Political scientists these days concentrate much more on policy making within particular sectors. Corporatists see this as "sectoral corporatism," while pluralists make a distinction between sectors dominated by particular "policy communities," which include some groups and exclude others, and those in which more traditionally pluralist competition between groups determines policy output.

Even in a country such as Austria, the "model-generator" that all commentators agree provides the clearest examples of corporatist decision making in Europe, corporatism is concerned mainly with economic policy, especially with prices and income policy. A great many groups that represent important political interests have nothing to do with corporatist decision making. At the other end of the scale—even in Britain, cited by most as having a very clear-cut pluralist decision-making regime—there is an officially established state church, there are self-governing professions in the key areas of law and medicine, there is very close interaction between farmers' groups and the relevant government department, and there has been a major experiment with "contracts" between the social partners over prices and incomes.

The parallel development of the pluralist notion of a policy community and the notion of sectoral corporatism highlights the fact that these two approaches to the study of interest representation have been jousting with each other in the literature for over twenty years now. As each approach has come to terms with the counterargument, it has grown toward the other; there is much less difference between the two ways of looking at the same problem than there used to be.

Nonetheless, given the vital importance of economic policy making and the role of employers and trade unions in this, it does still make some sense to classify countries in terms of the extent to which the economic policy arena, at least, is characterized by corporatist or pluralist institutions. In some countries, the ones that we might think of as being more corporatist, a small number of powerful, authoritative, and centralized "peak" organizations monopolize the legitimate right to participate in the policy-making process on behalf of their clients. These groups are involved in the process of both making and implementing economic policy. In other countries, which we might think of as being more pluralist, trade union and employers' federations may well get their voices heard, but only if they make an explicit and often divisive political effort to do so. And these groups rarely participate in policy implementation.

In all countries, however, the only recourse for groups outside the political establishment—and these are inevitably the vast majority of groups anywhere—is the traditional portfolio of techniques that characterize pressure politics. In this case policy outcomes are determined, as often as not, by the different access of different groups to resources, threats, and contacts in the political elite.

References

Altenstetter, C.: "Hospital Planners and Medical Professionals in the Federal Republic of Germany," in G. Freddi and J. W. Björkman (eds.), *Controlling Medical Professionals: The Comparative Politics of Health Governance*, Sage, London, 1989.

Armingeon, K: "The Compatibility of Economic, Social and Political Goals in Incomes Policies: A Comparative Analysis of Incomes Policy Developments in Ten West European Countries in the 1970s," in H. Keman, H. Paloheimo, and P. Whiteley (eds.), *Coping with the Economic Crisis: Alternative Responses to Economic Recession in Advanced Industrial Societies*, Sage, London, 1987, pp. 111–126.

Arnason, G.: "Fluidity in Icelandic Politics: The Election

of April 1987," *West European Politics*, vol. 11, no. 1, 1988, pp. 122–125.

Björkman, J. W.: "Politicizing Medicine and Medicalizing Politics: Physician Power in the United States," in G. Freddi and J. W. Björkman (eds.), *Controlling Medical Professionals: The Comparative Politics of Health Governance*, Sage, London, 1989.

Cawson, A. (ed.): *Organised Interests and the State: Studies in Meso-corporatism*, Sage, London, 1985.

————: *Corporatism and Political Theory*, Basil Blackwell, Oxford, 1986.

Cox, A.: "The Old and New Testaments of Corporatism: Is It a Political Form or a Method of Policy-Making?" *Political Studies*, vol. XXXVI, no. 2, 1988, pp. 294–308.

Czada, R.: "The Impact of Interest Politics on Flexible Adjustment Policies," in H. Keman, H. Paloheimo, and P. Whiteley (eds.), *Coping with the Economic Crisis: Alternative Responses to Economic Recession in Advanced Industrial Societies*, Sage, London, 1987.

Dahl, R. A.: *A Preface to Democratic Theory*, University of Chicago Press, Chicago, 1956.

Dahlerup, D. (ed.): *The New Women's Movement: Feminism and Political Power in Europe and the USA*, Sage, London, 1986.

Dalton, R. J.: *Politics in West Germany*, Scott, Foresman and Company, Glenview, Ill., 1989.

Döhler, M.: "Physicians' Professional Autonomy in the Welfare State: Endangered or Preserved?" in G. Freddi and J. W. Björkman (eds.), *Controlling Medical Professionals: The Comparative Politics of Health Governance*, Sage, London, 1989.

Gerlich, P.: "Consociationalism to Competition: The Austrian Party System since 1945," in H. Daalder (ed.), *Party Systems in Denmark, Austria, Switzerland, the Netherlands and Belgium*, Frances Pinter, London, 1987.

————, E. Grande, and W. Müller: "Corporatism in Crisis: Stability and Change of Social Partnership in Austria," *Political Studies*, vol. XXXVI, no. 2, 1988, pp. 209–223.

Grant, W. (ed.): *The Political Economy of Corporatism*, Macmillan, London, 1985.

————: "Introduction," in W. Grant (ed.).

Hardiman, N.: "Consensual Politics?" Public Goods and Collective Action in Ireland," in I. Scholten (ed.), *Political Stability and Neo-corporatism: Corporatist Integration and Societal Cleavages in Western Europe*, Sage, London, 1987.

Hernes, H. M.: "The Welfare State Citizenship of Scandinavian Women," in K. Jones and A. G. Jónasdóttir (eds.), *The Political Interests of Gender*, Sage, London, 1988, pp. 187–213.

Hirsch, M.: "Tripartism in Luxembourg: The Limits of Social Concertation," *West European Politics*, vol. 9, no. 1, 1986, pp. 54–66.

Jessop, B.: "Corporatism, Parliamentarians and Social Democracy," in P. Schmitter and G. Lehmbruch (eds.), *Trends towards Corporatist Intermediation*, Sage, London, 1979.

Jordan, G.: "Iron Triangles, Woolly Corporatism and Elastic Nets," *Journal of Public Policy*, vol. 1, 1981, pp. 95–123.

————: "Sub-governments, Policy Communities and Networks: Refilling Old Bottles," *Journal of Theoretical Politics*, vol. 2, no. 3, 1990a, pp. 319–338.

————: "The Pluralism of Pluralism: An Anti-theory?" *Political Studies*, vol. XXXVIII, no. 2, 1990b, pp. 286–301.

Kavanagh, D.: *British Politics: Continuities and Change*, 2d ed., Oxford University Press, Oxford, 1990.

Keman, H., and P. Whiteley: "Coping with Crisis: Divergent Strategies and Outcomes," in H. Keman, H. Paloheimo, and P. Whiteley (eds.), *Coping with the Economic Crisis: Alternative Responses to Economic Recession in Advanced Industrial Societies*, Sage, London, 1987.

Lane, J.-E., and S. Arvidson: "Health Professionals in the Swedish System," in G. Freddi and J. W. Björkman (eds.), *Controlling Medical Professionals: The Comparative Politics of Health Governance*, Sage, London, 1989.

Lehmbruch, G.: "Liberal Corporatism and Party Government," in P. Schmitter and G. Lehmbruch (eds.), *Trends towards Corporatist Intermediation*, Sage, London, 1979.

Lehner, F.: "Interest Intermediation, Institutional Structures and Public Policy," in H. Keman, H. Paloheimo, and P. Whiteley (eds.), *Coping with the Economic Crisis: Alternative Responses to Economic Recession in Advanced Industrial Societies*, Sage, London, 1987, pp. 54–82.

Lindblom, C.: *Politics and Markets*, Basic Books, New York, 1977.

Lovenduski, J., and J. Outshoorn: *The New Politics of Abortion*, Sage, London, 1986.

Mansbridge, J.: *Why We Lost the ERA*, University of Chicago Press, Chicago, 1986.

Marin, B.: "Austria—The Paradigm Case of Liberal Corporatism?" in W. Grant (ed.).

————: "From Consociationalism to Technocorporatism: The Austrian Case as a Model-Generator?"

in I. Scholten (ed.), *Political Stability and Neo-Corporatism: Corporatist Integration and Societal Cleavages in Western Europe*, Sage, London, 1987.

Martin, R. M. "Pluralism and the New Corporatism," *Political Studies*, vol. XXXI, no. 1, 1983, pp. 86–102.

———: *Trade Unionism: Purposes and Forms*, Clarendon, Oxford, 1989.

Pappi, L.: "Neo-corporatist Arrangements, 'Konkordanz' and Direct Democracy: The Swiss Experience," in I. Scholten (ed.), *Political Stability and Neo-Corporatism: Corporatist Integration and Societal Cleavages in Western Europe*, Sage, London, 1987.

Pelling, H.: *A History of British Trade Unionism*, Penguin Books, Harmondsworth, 1987.

Pérez-Díaz, V.: "Economic Politics and Social Patterns in Spain during the Transition," in I. Scholten (ed.), *Political Stability and Neo-corporatism: Corporatist Integration and Societal Cleavages in Western Europe*, Sage, London, 1987.

Rhodes, R. A. W.: "Policy Networks: A British Perspective," *Journal of Theoretical Politics*, vol. 2, no. 3, 1990, pp. 291–318.

Schmitter, P.: "Still the Century of Corporatism?" *Review of Politics*, vol. 36, 1974, pp. 85–131.

Smith, M. J.: "Pluralism, Reformed Pluralism and Neopluralism: The Role of Pressure Groups in Policy-Making," *Political Studies*, vol. XXXVIII, no. 2, 1990, pp. 302–322.

Steen, A.: "The Farmers, the Consumers and the State: Redistribution Conflicts in Norway, Sweden and the United Kingdom," *European Journal of Political Research*, vol. 9, 1981, pp. 1–16.

Van den Brande, A.: "Neo-corporatism and Functional-Integral Power in Belgium," in I. Scholten (ed.), *Political Stability and Neo-Corporatism: Corporatist Integration and Societal Cleavages in Western Europe*, Sage, London, 1987.

Westergaard, J.: "Class, Inequality and Corporatism," in A. Hunt (ed.), *Class and Class Structure*, Lawrence and Wishart, London, 1977.

CHAPTER 10
TOWARD ONE EUROPEAN GOVERNMENT?

In the previous chapters of this book, we focused on the politics of representation in the individual countries of Western Europe. We have seen general patterns and broad trends, as well as interesting variations and idiosyncrasies. Europe has always been a fascinating continent to study for these reasons, but in recent years a new development, quite different from anything that has ever taken place in any part of the world, has made its politics even more intriguing than before. We are referring to the moves toward a pooling of sovereignty among many Western European states, expressed most tangibly in their membership in the European Community (generally known as the EC). While some would like the EC to reach the point where it facilitates close and smooth cooperation between the governments of the member countries and then to stop, others hope that the Community is going down a road that will inevitably end in a federal Europe, with just one central government. Some even talk of a United States of Europe. In this final chapter, therefore, our focus shifts from the purely national level to the supranational level as we assess the significance of the emergence of the European Community as a major factor in the politics of representation in contemporary Western Europe.

First of all, we will outline the evolution of the European Community since the dream of European unity began to be taken seriously in the 1940s. We will then look at how the EC works and consider whether it has made national governments less important political actors. As in the previous chapters of this book, we shall examine the process whereby interests are turned into policies, which entails asking who plays what role in the decision-making process and to whom the various actors are accountable. Finally, we will attempt to assess the direction of the Community and the chances that a United States of Europe will one day parallel the United States of America.

THE DEVELOPMENT
OF EUROPEAN UNITY

Given the record of war between European countries during the first half of the twentieth century and for many centuries before that, the prospect of a united continent might not have seemed bright in the 1940s. However, the very ruthlessness and destructiveness of modern warfare was one of the factors that led to a conviction among the postwar political elites in a number of countries that such a tragedy must never again take place on European soil. The causes of the Second World War were, of course, many and varied, but two of the more obvious were unbridled and sometimes rabid nationalism (manifesting itself both in xenophobia and in the persecution of internal minorities) and the diktat imposed on the vanquished Germany after the First World War. However understandable the latter might have been from the viewpoint of the victorious allies, it served merely to fuel German resentment and was eventually seen to have contained the seeds of the 1939–1945 war. For this reason, once World War II was over, the politicians of the wartime allies looked for ways to integrate Germany into the postwar European framework rather than ostracize it; they also looked for structures that would promote cooperation rather than rivalry between the countries of Western Europe. The emergence of the "iron curtain" dividing Europe, following the imposition on the reluctant populations of Eastern and Central European states of communist regimes in the Stalinist mold, heightened a belief in the West that adherence to common democratic political values was something worth preserving.

Despite all of this, the road toward even a partial undermining of the traditional fetish of absolute national sovereignty was long and rocky (for details, see Pryce and also Urwin). In the late 1940s, a number of international organizations were formed, each with significant—and in some cases exclusively—European membership. Examples are the United Nations, the North Atlantic Treaty Organization (NATO), the Council of Europe, and the Organization for European Economic Cooperation. Whatever their distinctive features, each of these organizations was essentially *intergovernmental* in nature; each provided a forum in which sovereign governments participated without ceding any of their sovereignty to a supranational authority. This refusal to go beyond the traditional form of international organization, which had much to do with the caution of a British government that did not see its country's destiny as lying primarily with Europe, produced a growing impatience among the leaders of several other European countries. Most British politicians of all parties regarded Britain's links with the Commonwealth and its "special relationship" with the U.S.A. as more important than involvement with what was disparagingly referred to as "the continent." Since Britain was the wealthiest and most industrially developed state in Europe, other European countries were reluctant to embark on any major cooperative venture without its participation. Eventually, though, the time came when the more integrationist of European leaders realized that if they waited for Britain to climb aboard, the train would never leave the station, and that if they wanted to build a new kind of Europe that transcended the traditional nation-state, they would have to begin without Britain.

The first tangible step along the road to what some hoped might one day become a federal Europe was taken in April 1951 with the signing of the Treaty of Paris, which established the European Coal and Steel Community (ECSC). The treaty came into effect in July 1952. Many countries were invited to take part in the creation of this new body, but in the end only six did so: France, Germany, Italy, and the three Benelux countries (Belgium, the Netherlands, and Luxembourg). We will not describe the institutions of the ECSC in detail, since they correspond to those of today's European Community. But they incorporated the key constitutional element that is the basis of the EC: member states ceded some of their sovereignty to a supranational body. The ECSC had a quasi-government (known as the High Authority), whose nine members (appointed by the member states) were obliged to make decisions in the interest of the ECSC as a whole, and not in the interest of the member states from which they came. The High Authority made decisions regarding investment and production levels of coal and steel and had the power to impose fines on governments if they disobeyed its decisions. There was also a quasi-parliament called an Assembly, with little real power, whose members were appointed by national parliaments, and there was a Council of Ministers, containing ministers from national governments, which could in some circumstances amend or reject the decisions of the High Authority. In addition, there was a Court of Justice, which could arbitrate between the institutions if there were complaints that the High Authority was exceeding its powers. The presence of these supranational bodies was enough to dissuade Britain from joining, and Britain's economic significance at that time was such that a number of smaller countries who felt that their fortunes depended on the British market (particularly Ireland and the Scandinavian countries) also remained aloof.

The European Coal and Steel Community worked very satisfactorily from the viewpoint of the member states. Over the next few years, production of coal and steel rose greatly in these six countries, and because many trade barriers came down, as the Treaty of Paris envisaged, the volume of trade also increased greatly. Within a few years the ECSC was judged to be an unambiguous success. This led to a discussion of the idea of extending the range of policy areas in which countries might agree to combine in similar organizations. In the summer of 1955, the foreign ministers of the six countries met in Messina, Sicily, and decided to work toward the establishment of a customs union that would involve the creation of a common, or single, market embracing all the countries. They invited Britain to join them, but the invitation was declined. The British, while keen on the idea of turning Western Europe into a free trade area, were still suspicious of any supranational political authority with the right to constrain their own government, and they remained unconvinced that their destiny lay primarily with the rest of Europe. The ideas of the six ECSC countries were fleshed out over the next two years, and in March 1957 two Treaties of Rome were signed.

Each of these two treaties established a new Community. The more important and wide-ranging in scope was the Treaty of the European Economic Community (EEC), which laid down policy aims and guidelines concerning the establishment of a common market and the creation of a common policy in areas such as agriculture and transportation. The other treaty was the Euratom Treaty, which dealt with atomic energy and covered matters such as the pooling of resources and research.

As a result, the six countries involved were now members of three different Communities: the ECSC, the EEC, and Euratom. Each of the two new Communities had a set of institutions based on those of the ECSC: a quasi-government (now termed a Commission rather than a High Authority), a quasi-parliament (the Assembly), a Council of Ministers, and a Court of Justice. Sensibly, it was decided that only one Assembly and one Court of Justice were needed to serve all three Communities. However, the Commission/High Authority and the Council of Ministers continued to exist in triplicate until the mid-1960s, when the 1965 Merger Treaty, which came into effect in 1967, merged the three sets of institutions into one. Technically, there are still three Communities, but since 1967 the body to which the member states belong has been generally known as the "European Community," although some prefer to speak of the "European Communities." The three founding treaties, together with subsequent treaties and acts amending the original treaties, make up what is in effect the Community's written constitution.

Since 1958, the size of the European Community, as we shall henceforth call it, has doubled to twelve countries (see Table 10.1). The first enlargement did not take place until 1973. The British government, having remained aloof from the EC when it was being established, changed its mind dramatically in the early 1960s. Britain now came round to the view that Europe was likely to be far more significant in its future foreign and trade relations than either the U.S.A. or the Commonwealth. It had played a leading role in the creation in 1959 of the European Free Trade Association (EFTA), a body whose aim was to achieve

TABLE 10.1
Member Countries of the European Community

Country	Date of Joining the EEC
Belgium	1958
France	1958
Germany	1958
Italy	1958
Luxembourg	1958
Netherlands	1958
Denmark	1973
Ireland	1973
United Kingdom	1973
Greece	1981
Portugal	1986
Spain	1986

Note: The first six countries were all founding members of the EEC and of Euratom in 1958 and were all already members of the European Coal and Steel Community (ECSC). The remaining six countries joined all three Communities at the same time upon their respective accessions.

complete free trade between its member countries by the end of the 1960s and which was inevitably seen as a rival to the EC. Its seven members (along with Britain, these were Austria, Denmark, Norway, Portugal, Sweden, and Switzerland) were rather a mixed bag; they came to be known as the "outer seven," in contrast to the "inner six" of the EC. Consequently, the Conservative government announced in 1961 that Britain would apply for EC membership, and several of the countries dependent on the British market, such as Denmark and Ireland, followed suit.

However, Britain found that the EC door was no longer open. Although five of the EC countries would have welcomed British membership, the French president, Charles de Gaulle, responded with an emphatic negative. Since each EC member state has a veto over the question of admitting new members, this put an end for the time being to the prospect of Britain joining. The other applicants decided not to press their bids for membership. The same thing happened in 1967: there was a bid by Britain and its economic satellites, followed by a veto of the British application by de Gaulle and a drawing back by the other applicants. De Gaulle's hostility to British membership has been ascribed to a number of motives. These include doubts about the sincerity of Britain's willingness to play a constructive role within the EC, general Anglophobia, concern that Britain would be a Trojan horse within the EC for American influence, and fear that his own position as the dominant political voice within the Community would be challenged if Britain joined. In any event, it was only after de Gaulle's retirement from French politics in 1969 that enlargement could be seriously contemplated. Four countries opened negotiations with the EC in 1970 and signed a Treaty of Accession in 1972. Three of them—Britain, Denmark, and Ireland—joined the EC the following year. The fourth, Norway, did not—the issue generated a deep division in Norwegian society, culminating in a referendum in which the people voted by a narrow majority against EC entry.

Following this, the next three new members all came from southern Europe, and all were countries with a history of authoritarian government. Greece was under military rule from 1967 to 1974, and when civilian rule and democratic elections were restored, the new government was quick to ask to be admitted to the EC, using the argument that EC membership would help consolidate its still fragile democracy. Negotiations took a long time to complete, but Greece eventually became the tenth EC member, in 1981. Portugal and Spain had both experienced long periods of dictatorship, under Salazar and Franco, respectively, before democracy was inaugurated (in Portugal) or restored (in Spain) in the mid-1970s. In these cases, too, the new governments were keen to have their countries incorporated into the EC, both to bolster the political system and to reap economic benefits. Again negotiations were protracted, and it was not until 1986 that Spain and Portugal joined.

Enlargement has undoubtedly affected the nature of the EC very considerably. The original six members were all close to each other geographically and, with the exception of the poor southern part of Italy, had very similar levels of wealth and economic development. Two languages (French and German) were enough for virtually all informal transactions between members of the political elite. Even if it did not always operate entirely harmoniously, the EC in its original form was much more of a cozy club than its expanded version proved to be. With twelve members, the post-1986 EC is a much less homogeneous organization. Geographically, it embraces two offshore islands, Britain and Ireland, as well as one country, Greece, that does not share a border with another member state. The range of languages and cultures is much broader than was the case before 1973, and the new southern European members, in particular Greece and Portugal, are far less wealthy than the original six. The process of making decisions in this twelve-member EC is more complex and often more protracted than was the case when there were only six member states, and if the Community still consisted of only the original six countries, it is likely that the process of European integration would have advanced considerably further during the 1970s and 1980s than it actually did.

HOW THE EC WORKS

The EC, like the ECSC that preceded it, has four main institutions: the Commission, the European Parliament, the Council of Ministers, and the Court of Justice. The *Commission* is the body that initiates proposals for legislation. Its proposals go to the *Council of Ministers*, made up of ministers from the governments of the twelve member states, which immediately forwards them to the *European Parliament*. The Parliament considers them and sends them back to the Council, together with its recommendations. The Council has the power to accept the Commission's proposals (and the Parliament's recommendations) or to reject them. Questions of the applicability or interpretation of EC law are decided by the *Court of Justice*.

We shall now look in more detail at the role played by each of these institutions (for accounts of how the EC works, see Nugent; Lodge, "EC Policymaking"; and Wallace, 1983). We shall follow the flow of policies through the EC's decision-making process, from Commission to Parliament to Council of Ministers. However, it is important to bear in mind that the Council of Ministers, though only third in this sequence, is in reality more important than either the Commission or the Parliament, since it has the power to alter or reject proposals backed by the other two bodies. In addition, the European Council (made up of the heads of government of the member states), a body to which the treaties give no specific powers, has become the most powerful body of all and has emerged as the place where the really important decisions are now made within the Community, and so we shall examine its role in some detail. Finally, we shall look briefly at the provision for interest groups to play a part in Community decision making.

The Commission

The Commission looks, at least at first sight, like the "government" of the EC. In reality, its role is rather less than this because the Council of Ministers is a more powerful institution. The Commission consists of seventeen members, each with a specific policy jurisdiction (or "portfolio"), appointed by the governments of the member states. Each of the largest five countries (Britain, France, Germany, Italy, and Spain) appoints two commissioners, and the remaining seven countries have one nomination apiece. The Commission is headed by a president, who is chosen

The twelve stars of Europe keep off the rain in front of the EC's headquarters at Berlaymont, Brussels. (Jacques Langevin/Sygma)

by consensus among the member states. Each Commission has a four-year term in office and is based in the Berlaymont building in the "European quarter" in the eastern part of Brussels, the capital of Belgium. Most commissioners are former senior politicians in their home countries. For example, in the Commission that came into office on January 1, 1989, the president, Jacques Delors (who had also been president in the 1985–1989 Commission), had in the past been a French government finance minister, and eleven of the other sixteen commissioners had at some stage been members of their domestic governments.

Once the commissioners have been appointed, the president and the other sixteen commissioners together decide which commissioner should be given which portfolio, although member governments often lobby vigorously to get "their" commissioner assigned to a significant position. The portfolios, which correspond to ministries in domestic government, include external relations and trade policy, budget, regional policy, taxation and customs union, Mediterranean policy, agriculture, social affairs, transport, and internal market and industrial affairs, among others. Apart from the president, six of the commissioners are vice-presidents, though the position of vice president is indistinguishable from that of an "ordinary" commissioner, except that it carries a slightly higher salary.

Although commissioners are nominated on national lines, they are emphatically *not* in the Commission to represent national interests—at least in theory. Upon taking office, each commissioner has to take an oath to the effect that he or she will serve the overall interest of the EC and will not take instructions from a national government or from any other body. After all, another Community institution, the

Council of Ministers, exists expressly to safeguard national interests, as we shall see. Despite this, it is tacitly accepted that commissioners do not suddenly slough off their national identities the moment they are appointed and become transformed into Euromen or Eurowomen. A commissioner wishing to make a point at the weekly meeting of all seventeen commissioners may well draw on knowlege of his or her own country to make that point, in a way that sometimes comes close to special pleading for that country. And since every commissioner is ultimately dependent on a government back home for reappointment, he or she is unlikely to want to alienate that government. This is not to say that any commissioner acts as a government puppet, but undoubtedly governments do expect "their" commissioner to give them advance warning of impending developments. In addition, a commissioner from, say, Portugal might well receive representations from Portuguese interest groups, which are likely to see him or her as "the Portuguese commissioner."

Each commissioner has a small political staff, or *cabinet*, of six to ten people, at least one of whom is conventionally of a different nationality from that of the commissioner. The *cabinets* do a certain amount of preparatory work on issues due to come before the weekly meetings of the commissioners (these meetings are known as "Colleges"), in an attempt to iron out potential differences and disagreements. Members of these *cabinets* are selected by the commissioner and are thus in broad sympathy with his or her political outlook. They act in a manner similar to that of political advisers in some domestic governments, which we mentioned in Chapter 1. Given the way the Commission works, they are indispensable: in the 1989–1992 Commission, an Italian commissioner, Filippo Pandolfi, attempted for a while to operate without a *cabinet* but soon found it impossible and reluctantly appointed one. Each *cabinet* is headed by a *chef de cabinet*, and this person may sometimes be a conduit for communication with national governments. For example, in the 1989–1992 Commission, the *chef de cabinet* of the president, Jacques Delors, was known to maintain close contact with the French government in Paris.

The Commission has three main powers. First, it has the sole right, among all the Community's institutions, to initiate legislation, and it sends a steady stream of proposals and recommendations into the EC's policy-making process. This power is not quite as significant as it might appear, however, because other institutions—notably the Council of Ministers, representing the national governments—may reject Commission proposals if they wish. Consequently, there is little point in the Commission, simply coming up with proposals out of thin air, only to have them turned down by the Council. If its proposals are to have a serious chance of being accepted and ultimately becoming legislation, even in modified form, they must be broadly acceptable to the member governments. As a result, the Commission spends a lot of its time consulting the twelve governments and the major interest groups about its ideas, thereby ensuring that the proposals it feeds into the decision-making process are more likely to make headway. In addition, the Council of Ministers may formally ask the Commission to draft a proposal, sometimes giving it such explicit directions that the Commission has little room for initiative. National governments, too, attempt to use the Commission to push matters forward in an area important to them. While it is true that only the Commission can actually initiate legislation, in practice it is often more of a mediator and broker between various interests than a real independent initiator.

The Commission's second power is that it is responsible for trying to ensure that others in the Community are doing what they are supposed to be doing. When EC legislation is passed, this generally imposes obligations on the twelve national governments and/or parliaments to take action, either by introducing domestic legislation or by implementing a policy. If this is to mean anything, then clearly someone has to check that these obligations are being fulfilled, and it is the Commission that has this role. However, the Commission is grossly understaffed and is unable to monitor Community-wide policy implementation in anything like a comprehensive fashion, so it tends to concentrate on potential major breaches such as failure to comply with Community directives concerned with the free movement of goods. If it discovers a case where a national government has apparently failed to meet its EC obligations, it informs the government of its view and waits a reasonable time, usually a couple of months, for a response. If the government in question is uncooperative, the Commission can refer the case to the Court of Justice, though this step has to be taken in only a small minority of cases. Partly because of the Commission's limited resources, implementation of Community law is becoming a significant problem, as we shall see later in the chapter.

The Commission's third power entails issuing laws of various kinds. On a purely numerical basis it issues many more of these every year than the Council of Ministers, but the latter is still the more important lawmaking body, because the Council controls major legislation, whereas the great majority of laws issued by the Commission are of a purely technical and administrative nature. Most Commission legislation is confined to filling in details or making decisions that follow automatically from Council decisions, and much of it concerns regulations dealing with price adjustments and market support measures under the Common Agricultural Policy (Nugent, p. 71; Freestone and Davidson, pp. 112–114).

The Commission, then, plays a vital role in providing an overall Community viewpoint on important matters, however attenuated or diluted this may sometimes appear, and in negotiating with and mediating between the other actors in the decision-making process. The Commission president may not quite be the "Prime Minister of Europe," a phrase used by Walter Hallstein, one of the occupants of the position in the 1960s, but he or she is nonetheless a significant actor and has the right to attend all meetings of the most powerful body in the EC, the European Council, which we discuss below. In addition, the Commission represents the Community externally in important ways: it negotiates trade issues with other international actors, and its president attends the gatherings of the heads of government of the wealthiest seven nations in the world, known as "G7." However, the Commission is a far cry from the engine of European integration that some would like it to be. It contains a mix of both nationalities and political views—a typical Commission containing commissioners from most of the main political tendencies in the EC apart from the extremes of the left and right. Since it is appointed in a piecemeal fashion by twelve different governments of varying political persuasions, it has no overall goal or program of the sort that national governments usually adopt. Consequently, it is not surprising if the Commission sometimes seems to lack a sense of purpose.

The European Parliament

If the Commission is a quasi-government, then the European Parliament (EP) can reasonably be described as a quasi-parliament. Although it has styled itself the "European Parliament" ever since the early 1960s, it was only in 1986 that the Council of Ministers finally agreed to change its formal name from "European Parliamentary Assembly" to "European Parliament." It has three main powers, which concern dismissal of the Commission, legislation, and the budget.

The first of these is dramatic but, in practical terms, not especially useful. If a motion to censure the Commission is passed by a two-thirds majority, and those voting for the motion amount to more than half of the total number of MEPs (Members of the European Parliament), then the Commission is dismissed. If the Commission were the real government of the EC, then this power would have greater significance than it actually does. In practice, the Council of Ministers is considerably more powerful than the Commission, and the EP has no real weapons to use against the Council. Moreover, even if the EP did dismiss a Commission, it would have no say in the appointment of a new one, which would remain the prerogative of the national governments. Only twice (in the late 1970s) have censure motions against the Commission been voted on in the EP, and neither came anywhere near succeeding. This is partly because most fundamental conflicts within the EC tend to see the EP and the Commission ranged on the same side, in favor of greater European integration, with the Council on the other, defending the position of the national governments, and so the EP is unlikely to reach a

The European Parliament in session. (EC Office of Press and Public Affairs)

position of complete disgruntlement with the Commission. However, MEPs would like to have powers over the Commission that are more useful and practical than the drastic option of complete dismissal. They would like to have the power to censure one specific commissioner rather than having to censure the entire Commission, and they are keen to be given some say in the initial appointment of the Commission. This could, for example, involve being able to choose the president from a shortlist drawn up by the Council, having a veto over the choice of president by being able to vote for or against a single name put forward by the Council, or being given the power to accept or reject the entire Commission at the start of its term.

The EP's role in the legislative process, the second area where it plays a part, is essentially advisory. Its precise position in the legislative process varies according to the type of legislation under discussion. Most legislation comes to the EP just once. When Commission proposals reach the Parliament, it refers them to one of its specialist committees—thus, a proposal dealing with railways would go to the Transport Committee. The specialist committee examines the proposal carefully and makes a recommendation to the full Parliament. On the basis of the committee's report, the EP usually calls for a number of amendments to the proposal. The Commission then signals its acceptance or rejection of the amendments (known collectively as the EP's "Opinion"), which are passed on to the Council of Ministers. The Council has to wait a reasonable time for the EP to make its views known, but it is not obliged to heed them when they arrive. It may overrule them or simply make no decision at all, thereby consigning the proposal to a kind of administrative limbo, which is inhabited at any one time by a sizable number of proposals. Moreover, it sometimes happens that the Council has already made up its mind by the time it receives the EP's Opinion, in which case the chances of it altering its position are very slim.

More recently, a second legislative procedure was introduced as a result of the 1986 Single European Act, which came into operation in 1987. The effect of this is to give the EP a "second reading" of pieces of legislation based on certain articles of the EEC Treaty, particularly those dealing with completion of the internal market. In these cases, proposals go from the Commission to the EP, as before, and then on to the Council. However, the Council cannot make a final decision at this stage; instead, it adopts a "common position" and communicates this to the EP. The EP considers this and then makes its views known to the Council for a second time. The Council still has the final say, but experience with the operation of this "cooperation procedure," as the new procedure is termed, suggests that the Council does take on board more of the EP's amendments in these cases than where only one reading is involved.

The EP's third role concerns the EC's budget, which is the one area of EC activity where the Parliament can be considered a major player and the only one where it could plausibly claim to be more important than the Commission, though not more important than the Council (for the budgetary procedure see Nugent, pp. 258–278, and Shackleton). The budget is one of those pieces of legislation to which the EP gives both a first and a second reading. The draft budget is drawn up by the Commission and then goes to the Council. The Council tends to make cuts in the overall package and may shift the allocation of spending between different areas. It passes the budget on to the EP, which generally undoes most of the Council's changes and then sends the budget back to the Council. The Council now has a formal "conciliation meeting" with a delegation from the EP to try to reach an agreement between the two institutions, and then it makes more amendments. From here, the budget goes back once again to the EP, but in contrast to the position where ordinary legislation is concerned, this is the end of the road; the Council does not have the final say. At its second reading, the EP is entitled to make some changes in certain areas of spending; its powers enable it to increase or trim the budget by about 10 percent (Budd and Jones, p. 133). If these changes satisfy it, the president of the Parliament signs the budget into law. If the EP is still not satisfied—in other words, if it would like to make changes greater than those it is allowed to make under the terms of the treaties—then it can reject the entire budget. In order to do this, it needs a two-thirds majority, provided that those voting for rejection constitute a majority of all MEPs. If the budget is rejected, as happened several times during the 1980s, the EC does not grind to a halt. Funding continues on a month-by-month basis according to the previous year's budget until the Council and the Parliament, with the Commission playing a mediating role, are able to come to an agreement, as they invariably do in the end.

Having outlined the Parliament's powers, we turn now to its composition and operation. The Parliament contains 518 members, who come from the member states in approximate proportion to their population, although the smaller states are generously overrepresented in per capita terms (see Table 10.2). The Assembly (as it then was) decided as early as 1960 that it should be directly elected by the people of the EC member countries. However, it took many years for the Council of Ministers to agree, during which time MEPs were appointed by the national parliaments and thus carried little credibility when they claimed to represent the will of the European public. Eventually, the Council gave in on the issue, and the first direct elections to the European Parliament took place in June 1979. This date marked the first occasion on which people from different countries went to the polls to elect members to the same body, and in a sense the EP, as a genuine representative body, really came to life only with the first direct election. Elections have taken place at five-year intervals since then. The elections take place in all countries within a few days of each other; the different dates reflect different national traditions as to which day of the week (usually Thursday or Sunday) is the best on which to hold elections. For example, in 1989 voting took place on Thursday, June 15, in Denmark, Ireland, the Netherlands, Spain, and the United Kingdom and on Sunday, June 18, in the other seven countries. No results were released from the five early-voting countries until voting was completed in every country.

Although the EEC Treaty speaks of a uniform electoral system being used for European Parliament elections, this can happen only when all twelve member governments, acting in the Council of Ministers, agree on one. At the moment, eleven of the twelve countries use some variant of PR (proportional representation) to elect their MEPs, though not necessarily the same one that they use in domestic elections. The exception is the United Kingdom, where the single-member constituency system is used to elect 78 of its 81 MEPs, with the other three being elected by the single transferable vote version of PR (which we discussed in Chapter 6) in Northern Ireland.

TABLE 10.2
**Seats in the European Parliament
at the 1989 Election**

Country	Population	Seats	Population per MEP
Germany (West)	61,451,000	81	758,654
Italy	57,441,000	81	709,148
United Kingdom	57,065,000	81	704,506
France	55,873,000	81	689,790
Spain	38,996,000	60	649,933
Netherlands	14,765,000	25	590,600
Greece	10,010,000	24	417,083
Belgium	9,879,000	24	411,625
Portugal	9,819,000	24	409,125
Denmark	5,130,000	16	320,625
Ireland	3,538,000	15	235,867
Luxembourg	375,000	6	62,500
Total	324,342,000	518	626,143

Note: After the merger of West and East Germany in October 1990, which created an all-German state with a population of almost 77 million, 18 "observers" without voting rights from the area of the former East German state were allowed to attend the Parliament, but there was no formal increase in German representation.

Elections to the European Parliament are, in some senses, rather curious affairs. They are impressive in their own way, as the people of twelve countries, with a total electorate of over 240 million, turn out at about the same time to elect a genuinely transnational body, the only one of its kind in the world. But they are a far cry from being the EC equivalent of general elections at the national level. In general elections, the question of the composition of the next government is uppermost in voters' minds, even if, as we saw in Chapter 7, government formation is sometimes a complex process not directly related to the preferences expressed by voters. But in European Parliament elections, it is often hard to say exactly what is at stake. No government is accountable to the EP, and, as we have seen, the EP has rather limited powers. Many voters undoubtedly conclude that in fact nothing much is at stake, and so they don't bother to vote. Turnout is lowest in Britain, where in 1989 only just over a third of voters turned out (though even this was more than in 1984), and the turnout in 1989 was also below 50 percent in Denmark, the Netherlands, France, and Portugal (see Table 10.3). Overall turnout (valid votes divided by electorate) across the EC in both 1984 and 1989 (57.3 percent and 56.7 percent, respectively) was well below the comparable figure for domestic general elections (for an analysis of the turnout pattern in 1989, see Niedermayer and also Lodge, 1990, pp. 218–221).

This lack of clarity about the real purpose of European Parliament elections arises partly because, despite the theory, they are not fought on the basis of European issues. Indeed, few could say if pressed just what "European issues" really are. It is true that there are pan-EC political groups that correspond quite closely to the party families we discussed in Chapter 3, the most important of

TABLE 10.3
Results of European Parliament Elections, June 1989

	Belgium	Denmark	France	Germany	Greece	Ireland	Italy	Luxembourg	Netherlands	Portugal	Spain	U.K.	Total
Seats	24	16	81	81	24	15	81	6	25	24	60	81	518
Electorate, millions	7.1	3.9	38.3	45.8	8.4	2.5	45.7	0.2	11.1	8.1	29.3	42.1	242.4
Valid votes, millions	5.9	1.8	18.2	28.2	6.6	1.6	34.6	0.2	5.2	4.0	15.7	15.4	137.4
Turnout, %	83.1	46.2	47.4	61.6	78.5	66.5	75.7	87.4	47.2	49.5	53.5	36.5	56.7
MEPs in each Group:													
Socialist	8	4	22	31	9	1	14	2	8	8	27	46	180
EPP	7	2	6	32	10	4	27	3	10	3	16	1	121
Liberals	4	3	13	4	—	2	3	1	4	9	6	—	49
European Democrats	—	2	—	—	—	—	—	—	—	—	—	32	34
Greens	3	—	8	8	—	—	7	—	2	1	1	—	30
Unitary Left	—	1	—	—	1	—	22	—	—	—	4	—	28
EDA	—	—	13	—	1	6	—	—	—	—	—	—	20
European Right	1	—	10	6	3	1	—	—	—	—	—	—	17
Left Unity	—	—	7	—	—	1	3	—	—	3	—	—	14
Rainbow	1	4	1	—	—	—	3	—	—	—	2	1	13
Others	—	—	1	—	—	1	5	—	1	—	4	1	12

Notes: "EPP" is the European People's party (Christian Democrats). The European Democrats consist of the British Conservatives and the Conservative party from Denmark. "EDA" is the European Democratic Alliance, composed of the RPR (the Gaullists) from France, Fianna Fáil from Ireland, and DIANA from Greece. Unitary Left and Left Unity are both communist groups. The turnout figures refer to valid votes only.
Source: Mackie, pp. 17, 40, 49, 86, 116, 139, 150, 191, 199, 209, 226, 300, 321.

which are the Socialists and the European People's party (representing Christian Democratic parties), but these are little more than very loose umbrella bodies linking national parties. EP elections are fought on the ground in each country by national parties rather than by these transnational groups, and the parties stress national issues when campaigning. Although they may be criticized for this "parochial" behavior, the parties argue that there is no other way of generating any interest at all among the electorate. The consequence is that the performance of the current national government tends to become the main EP election issue in each individual state. When the EP election falls midway in the domestic electoral cycle, as is usually the case, it is seen by voters, the media, and the political parties alike as a midterm test of the national government's popularity. Sometimes a general election takes place on the same day as an EP election. This happened in Luxembourg in 1979, 1984, and 1989, as well as in Greece in 1981 (when its first batch of MEPs was elected) and in 1989, and in Ireland in 1989. On most of these occasions, voting patterns in the two elections were very similar, suggesting strongly that voters do not make much of a distinction between them.

Once the elections have been held, the MEPs sit in the Parliament's chambers in Strasbourg and Brussels according to their political group, not according to the country they represent. The EP operates very much along party lines, like national parliaments throughout Western Europe. Table 10.3 shows that in the Parliament elected in 1989, the Socialists were the largest group, with 180 seats out of 518, followed by the European People's party (Christian Democratic) group with 121, with the Liberals a good way behind. In fourth place were the European Democrats (mainly the British Conservatives), with the Greens fifth. The Socialists thus became the most influential group in this Parliament. There was a narrow left-wing majority in the EP, and so if the Socialists could mobilize the support of the two Communist groups (Unitary Left and Left Unity), plus the Greens and the "Rainbow" group of regionalist parties, they could secure the passage of a motion. However, they tended to do this only for declaratory motions or statements, since a partisan left-wing line from the EP would have stood little chance of being accepted by the Council of Ministers. So when the Socialists wanted to make a real impact on legislation, they linked up not with the rest of the left but with the Christian Democrats, and since these two groups controlled 301 seats, they effectively controlled the EP between them. Voting within each of the political groups is fairly solid, even if less so than in most European national parliaments. The MEPs from each national party maintain a separate existence within the EP groups (thus, for example, there is a British Labour group, a French Socialist group, and so on, within the Socialist group, each with its own internal structure), but the MEPs within each EP group generally vote together, even though there is no real sanction the group can employ against a maverick.

The EP does most of its work through committees, of which there are approximately twenty at any one time, corresponding to the main areas of EC activity. Seats on the committees are shared out among the political groups in proportion to their size; within each political group, posts are shared out among the various countries represented within the group. Besides holding committee meetings, the Parliament meets in week-long plenary sessions twelve times a year, at which it considers reports from the committees and votes on declarations or proposed amendments to legislation. The plenary sessions are chaired by the president of the Parliament, who is elected by the MEPs at the start of each Parliament and at the halfway mark (after two and a half years). The president of the Parliament from January 1987 to June 1989 was Sir Henry Plumb, a British Conservative; he was succeeded by Enrique Barón Crespo, a Spanish Socialist.

The European Parliament, as we have seen, does not have most of the powers that belong, at least in theory, to domestic parliaments in Western Europe. It cannot dismiss or appoint the EC's government, and it cannot initiate or promulgate legislation. An apparently trivial but nonetheless telling measure of the EP's weakness is its lack of control over its location. With both the Commission and the Council offices based in Brussels, it would seem natural for the Parliament also to be there. Instead, its operations are scattered around three countries. It holds its plenary sessions in Strasbourg, in northeastern France. Most of its administrative staff are based in Luxembourg. However, it holds its committee meetings in Brussels, the seat of most of the real action in the Community. Most MEPs would like the Parliament to move permanently to Brussels, but this decision is in the hands of the Council, representing the national governments. Neither the French nor the Luxembourg government has been willing to give up the prestige and the highly localized financial benefits arising from having the Parliament meet in its territory. Consequently, truckloads of documents are constantly on the road between Brussels, Luxembourg, and Strasbourg, at a considerable cost in terms of time and money.

There are other reasons for the EP's relative powerlessness. It may well be that the Parliament stands fairly low in public esteem, given the low turnout at EP elections and the way they are dominated by domestic rather than European political issues. This weakens any claim by the EP to represent the views of the European public on European issues. The regular proceedings of the EP receive little media coverage in the member states, and when the EP does get into the news, it is quite likely to be for all the wrong reasons. Allegations about MEPs engaging in "creative accountancy" over their expenses surface from time to time, and the Parliament attracted some cynical comments in January 1989 for choosing Barbados as a venue for a conference on third world poverty. MEPs are often exasperated by this kind of approach by the media, complaining that the serious work they do in EP committees goes virtually unreported, while the most minor misdemeanors, real or alleged, are blown up out of all proportion. But although they have a fair point, it remains a fact that the EP has been unable to mobilize European public opinion in its campaign to gain greater powers.

This being the case, the EP is faced with an uphill struggle to become a strong and effective legislative body. The Council of Ministers has generally been hostile to this idea, as shown by its protracted delay in agreeing to allow direct elections and in permitting the change of name to "European Parliament," and no change can take place without the Council's consent. The Council believes that the second-reading procedure introduced in 1987 has slowed down the decision-making process and that to extend the Parliament's powers would slow things down even further. MEPs would respond that the main reason for the logjam in EC decision making is the insistence of the Council on keeping the reins of power in its own hands. While the Council is not dogmatically opposed to the idea of the Parliament being given more power at the expense of the Commission—for example, by being allowed to initiate a proposal if the Commission fails to act or by being granted extended powers of inquiry and scrutiny—it is not keen to see the Parliament whittle away specific Council prerogatives. Moreover, in an era of the "decline of parliaments," the EP is trying to reverse what seems to be a worldwide trend, which suggests that its prospects are not good.

But the EP would not entirely accept this gloomy analysis. Its tireless pleas during the 1980s to be given more teeth did not bring it more than a fraction of what it wanted, but they did bring some rewards, in the form of greater budgetary powers and the second-reading procedure. Thus, unlike other parliaments in Western Europe, the EP does actually seem to be growing in strength rather than declining. Moreover, since it became a "real" assembly only in 1979, when its members were at last directly elected, it is still too early to evaluate its likely eventual role. MEPs are still learning how to use their existing responsibilities to maximum advantage, and it is possible that they will in the future be able to use the powers they have, especially those in the areas of the budget or the dismissal of the Commission, in such a manner as to get their way in other matters. If the EP ever does gain significant formal powers, it is likely to become a major actor in the Community's decision-making process, precisely because of the separation of its role from that of the executive. While parliaments in Western European countries are generally dominated and controlled by the government, as we saw in Chapter 1, the EP, like the American Congress, can vote against individual items of legislation without thereby bringing down a government. Moreover, its members see the job of an MEP as a worthwhile one in itself, and this attitude would apply even more if the EP were given extended powers. In contrast to national parliaments, the EP is not, and is unlikely to become, a mere stepping-stone on the way to a position in a European government. It is thus likely that MEPs in a more powerful EP will take their parliamentary role more seriously than do many deputies in national parliaments in Western Europe.

The Council of Ministers

So far, the Council of Ministers has been mentioned quite frequently in this chapter, and we have said that it is more powerful than either the Commission or the Parliament, but its precise nature has not been spelled out. This is rather appropriate, because there is something shadowy, if not even Kafkaesque, about the Council, and especially about its supreme manifestation, the European Council.

The Council of Ministers represents the governments of the twelve member states of the EC. Although there is in principle only one Council, in practice there are many, or at least the Council meets in many guises. This is because each national seat on the Council is filled not by the same person every time but by the national minister with responsibility for the policy area that is to be discussed. Thus, if a forthcoming meeting of the Council is going to discuss EC transport policy, then each government sends its transport minister to the meeting; if farm prices are to be discussed, it sends its agriculture minister; and so on. The Council meets in one form or another about 80 to 100 times a year, with the foreign and agriculture ministers meeting most often, perhaps once a month, and the other ministers meeting less frequently.

At any given time, one of the member states holds what is termed the Council presidency, and meetings of the Council are chaired by the minister from this country. The presidency rotates among the member states in alphabetic order of their names, with each country having the office for six months. The first four presidencies of the 1990s were thus held by Ireland (January to June 1990), Italy (July to December 1990), Luxembourg (January to June 1991), and the Netherlands (July to December 1991). The period of each country's presidency is too short to make this a very significant role. Since it is generally reckoned that the "lead-in" period for a new policy is about eighteen months, it is clear that the country holding the presidency cannot bring any new initiatives to fruition; the most it can do is speed up or leave to one side some of those projects already on the books. In recent years, there has been more coordination between adjacent presidencies in an attempt to avoid the situation where a new presidency might try to reserve the priorities of the previous one.

The Council is (on everything except the budget) the last and most important step in the decision-making process. It has the power to reject or amend a proposal from the Commission, even if both the Commission and the Parliament are against it doing so. A proposal that has been discussed by the Commission and its advisers for years and examined line by line by the Parliament for months can be decisively altered or simply rejected by the Council in twenty minutes. Every important piece of legislation (as opposed to the more technical instruments that the Commission is empowered to issue, which mainly involve filling in details that follow from Council decisions) must be approved by the Council. Moreover, although the Council does not have the power to initiate a proposal for legislation, it can lean so heavily on the Commission that it comes close to achieving this power in practice. Consequently, the Council could be seen as both the real government *and* the real legislature of the Community.

When the Commission sends a proposal over to the Council, the Council forwards a copy to the Parliament and also begins extensive scrutiny of the proposal itself. The Council has a large network of specialist committees, staffed mainly by senior national civil servants. This is the first stage at which the acceptability or otherwise of the proposal to the twelve national governments is assessed. One writer has spoken of "the aura of xenophobia" that can characterize the work of these committees (Wallace, 1985, p. 264). Not surprisingly, quite a few proposals are killed off at this stage, if the committee finds it impossible to reach an agreement and explicitly rejects or simply shelves the proposal. The best the Commission can hope for is not unanimous approval from the committee, which is unrealistic to expect, but an agreement to pass the proposal on to the next stage of the decision-making process, subject to some or all of the member states entering specific reservations about it.

From the specialist committee, the proposal goes to a body called COREPER, the Committee of Permanent Representatives. Each country maintains a fairly small permanent delegation based in Brussels, in effect an embassy, and the heads of these twelve delegations collectively make up COREPER. For a diplomat in any of the member states, the posting to the position of permanent representative in

Brussels is regarded as one of the three or four most important postings in the entire diplomatic service, and in some cases it is considered the most important. Given their seniority and political authority, the permanent representatives can iron out some of the problems identified by the specialist committee. A certain amount of horse trading takes place at this level; a permanent representative will agree to drop an objection to one part of the proposal provided that his or her objection to another part is accommodated fully. COREPER aims to reach as much agreement as it can, especially on details, so that when the twelve ministers meet, they can deal with the proposal as quickly as possible. It meets every week and exercises very considerable power. Because the ministers who attend the Council meetings and make the ultimate decisions simply do not have the time to familiarize themselves with every detail, they must allow their permanent representative a fair amount of discretion. In addition, ministers are heavily dependent on the briefing they get from their permanent representative as to the best negotiating strategy in the Council meeting—on matters such as where another country might lift an objection if the terms are right and where there seems to be an absolute deadlock. Despite its considerable effective political power, COREPER was not even mentioned in the original treaties of the Community, though it received brief mention in the 1965 Merger Treaty, which states that it has the role of preparing the work of the Council of Ministers. No one who merely reads the formal constitutional framework of the Community would come close to realizing the real significance of COREPER.

All proposals pass from COREPER to a meeting of the Council of Ministers itself. The Council, unlike the Commission, has no permanent presence in Brussels; indeed, it has no permanent physical existence at all. When a Council meeting is to take place, the relevant ministers fly in from the respective national capitals, and they usually go home again a day or two later. While both the Commission and the European Parliament maintain information offices for the public in many cities across the Community (and, indeed, outside it), the Council has none. Those who want to learn what the Council is thinking cannot find a door to knock on. Its secretariat—based in the Charlemagne building, adjacent to the Berlaymont in Brussels—does not welcome lobbying by interest groups, in contrast to the Commission's secretariat. To add to the impression that the Council is a somewhat shadowy and nebulous body, all its meetings take place behind closed doors. Moreover, unlike the Commission the Council has no fixed and permanent membership. The membership even of particular Councils is constantly changing, as elections, changes of government, or cabinet reshuffles mean that the twelve trade ministers who attend one Council meeting may well not be the same twelve who attend the next meeting of trade ministers.

When the ministers do gather in Brussels, they are likely to be faced with a number of proposals that have come through the Community's policy-making process, and perhaps with other decisions as well. In areas where COREPER has reached an agreement, the Council needs merely to give formal ratification to the proposal or decision. If COREPER has proved unable to sort out the problems, the ministers themselves will try to break the deadlock. Horse trading here can cross policy areas. The French transport minister might agree to support a point being made by his or her Spanish counterpart on the understanding that later in the year, when the Fisheries Council is meeting, Spain will back France's case for a larger quota. The kind of wheeling and dealing that goes on at Council meetings makes it easy to understand the relatively peripheral position of the European Parliament. If the Council manages to put together a package (which does not always happen), it is not keen to unravel it merely because the Parliament has a different suggestion on some particular point. While, as we saw earlier, the Council is obliged to wait a reasonable time for Parliament's Opinion before it makes its formal decision, it may in practice have already made up its mind, at either the Council or the COREPER level, before it receives the EP's Opinion. In such cases it is rather obvious how little interest the Council is likely to take in the EP's views when they arrive.

The manner of Council decision making is important in bolstering its power. The treaties provide several ways for the Council to make decisions: by unanimity, by qualified majority, and by simple majority (the last of these is hardly ever used). *Unanimity* is needed when a new policy is to be initiated or when the Council wants to amend a Commission proposal against the wishes of the Commission. *Qualified majority* voting applies when the Council is making decisions on less fundamental changes in Community policy. When a decision is reached by qualified majority, each minister wields a number of votes corresponding approximately to his or her country's population, though, as with the allocation of European Parliament seats, the small countries are overrepresented (see Table 10.4). The total number of votes among the twelve ministers is 76, and 54 are needed for a majority. It can be seen from the table that at least seven countries are needed to produce a qualified majority and at least three to produce the 23 votes that make up a blocking minority.

If the Council were to use qualified majority voting on all occasions where the treaties permit, then the speed of decision making would increase greatly, as

TABLE 10.4

Votes per Country in the Council of Ministers When Decisions Are Made by Qualified Majority

Country	Population	Council Votes	Population per Council Vote
Germany	76,750,000	10	7,675,000
Italy	57,441,000	10	5,744,100
United Kingdom	57,065,000	10	5,706,500
France	55,873,000	10	5,587,300
Spain	38,996,000	8	4,874,500
Netherlands	14,765,000	5	2,953,000
Greece	10,010,000	5	2,002,000
Belgium	9,879,000	5	1,975,800
Portugal	9,819,000	5	1,963,800
Denmark	5,130,000	3	1,710,000
Ireland	3,538,000	3	1,179,333
Luxembourg	375,000	2	187,500
Total	339,641,000	76	4,468,960

Note: A majority requires 54 votes.

progress would no longer be at the pace of the last country to be persuaded. This would also increase the power of the Commission relative to that of the Council. Since Commission proposals can be accepted by a majority vote of the Council but can be rejected or amended only by unanimous agreement, a wider use of qualified majority voting would see more Commission proposals getting through the Council without amendment. It would also, at a stroke, make the European Community a much more supranational body, since nations would be powerless to resist proposals, however strongly they opposed them, if they found themselves in a minority.

Precisely for this reason, the Council operates mostly on the basis of unanimity. The mold was set back in the mid-1960s, when the prospect of a move toward more majority voting was in the air. Although five of the six member states favored this, the sixth, France, was adamantly opposed; President de Gaulle, in particular, felt that it would lead to an unacceptable overriding of French sovereignty. The French representatives withdrew entirely from Council meetings from the summer of 1965 until January 1966, when the so-called Luxembourg Agreement was reached. Although this was little more than an agreement to disagree, it has been interpreted ever since by the Council as giving every minister the right to veto proposals when his or her country's vital national interests are at stake. Moreover, it is each country, rather than the rest of the Council, that decides when its vital national interests really are at stake. In practice, the veto is very rarely used; if one state indicates that it cannot accept a proposal, a vote is simply deferred indefinitely. To the frustration of the Commission, the Parliament, and proponents of European integration, the Council has operated this way ever since. This ensures that progress is made only on the basis of consensus and also, incidentally, that the Council remains the most powerful EC institution.

It is possible, however, that majority voting will become rather more common in the future. It is already the mode for reaching decisions on the budget, because the tight schedule means that decisions cannot be put off until unanimous agreement is reached. In addition, the Single European Act of 1986 provided for a wider use of qualified majority voting, especially in areas related to the creation of the single European market, and this has been reflected in the Council's decision-making procedures.

We have pointed out that there is, in effect, not just one Council but rather a series of parallel Councils, each dealing with its own particular policy area. If one of these Councils cannot reach an agreement but does not want to let the matter rest, it will refer the issue to the Council of Foreign Ministers. Although not legally superior to any other brand of Council, this Council (which is termed the "General Council") is expected to try to iron out problems that no other set of ministers has managed to solve. When the foreign ministers meet, of course, they also discuss foreign policy issues and the question of a common EC foreign policy, an area known as European Political Cooperation (or EPC). Foreign (especially defense) policy tends to be a sensitive area, one over which states are reluctant to lose control to a supranational body, and so decisions here always require consensus—majority voting is not used. When a state wants to go its own way on foreign policy, there is nothing to stop it. This was demonstrated in the second half of 1990, when the twelve governments made their own widely varying decisions as to how to react to the Iraqi invasion of Kuwait. The lack of a common foreign policy has been one factor leading to the frequent description of the EC as "an economic giant and a political pygmy." Nevertheless, the EC has been able to reach common positions on some important matters, notably the Israeli-Palestinian conflict. Indeed, there can be advantages for the member states in being able to take shelter behind a common foreign policy position.

The foreign ministers do not usually prove very successful at resolving problems that the agriculture or environment ministers, say, were unable to sort out, since they generally have only a little, if any, more political clout than the set of ministers who referred the problems to them in the first place. With no other institution to turn to, the EC would be in danger of drifting into deadlock or simply into irrelevance, with the member states deciding that they had to find their own national solutions to problems. This danger was perceived in the early 1970s and led to the creation of a new institution, the European Council, which came out of the skies, as it were, to become the single most important body in the entire Community.

The European Council

The European Council was created in 1974, and its first meeting was held in Dublin in March 1975. It is composed primarily of the heads of government of the twelve member states (the twelve foreign ministers, the president of the Commission, and another commissioner also attend European Council meetings). It meets at least twice every year, that is, at least once in each of the two countries that hold the presidency of the Council of Ministers during each year, and these summit meetings attract extensive press coverage. The European Council has emerged as the only body in the EC capable of giving direction to the Community, so much so that it has been said that "it is not unreasonable to argue that the Community's history since 1975 is the history of summit meetings" (Bulmer and Wessels, p. 2). Virtually all the major steps forward taken by the EC since then have been initiated by the European Council or, at the very least, have needed the backing of the European Council to get going. Examples include establishing the European Monetary System (which ties together the currencies of several member states) in the late 1970s, issuing the Venice Declaration on the Middle East in 1980, finally solving a long-running dispute over Britain's contribution to EC finances in the mid-1980s, deciding in 1976 how many seats each country should have in the directly elected European Parliament and in 1978 when to hold the first direct elections, agreeing on a common fisheries policy at a number of summits in the early 1980s, agreeing on all enlargements of the Community, commissioning heavyweight reports on the future institutional development of the Community, clearing the Single European Act for progress in Luxembourg in 1985, and agreeing on the principle of "political union" in Dublin in 1990.

This list, which is far from exhaustive, shows the broad scope of the European Council's deliberations. The European Council has also become, among other things, a kind of final decision-making level when no other set of ministers can reach an agreement on, say, fisheries or agriculture policy. This was contrary to intentions when the European Council was first set up—the idea then was that the

European summit, Brussels, 1988. (Jacques Langevin/Sygma)

Council would, at all costs, avoid getting embroiled in the details of specific policies and would confine itself to the broad and important issues. The above list shows that it has managed to achieve this aim, and once a number of protracted financial disputes were sorted out in the second half of the 1980s, it was able to concentrate on the loftier areas that it was established to contemplate.

Given the centrality of the European Council in the Community's decision-making process, one might expect to find its role and functions prominently defined in the treaties. Instead, it is not mentioned there at all. The first mention of the European Council in any official document came in 1986, after it had been shaping the EC for over a decade. Even in 1986, the mention was cursory in the extreme; the Single European Act contained three sentences on the European Council, and these, unlike other parts of the act, were not incorporated into any of the treaties. These three sentences merely defined the membership of the Council and said that it shall meet at least twice a year. Consequently, the authority of the European Council is entirely political rather than legal. Although it is reasonable to see it as the most important of the many versions of the Council of Ministers (which in political terms it is), in legal terms it is not part of the Council of Ministers hierarchy at all. It could meet under the framework of the Council of Ministers if it wished and in that capacity issue legislation, but it has never done so. Its lack of legal powers is more realistically seen as a lack of constraints; its relationship with the rest of the Community's decision-making structure is that of a free-floating agency, able to intervene in any area at any time.

Advocates of closer European integration regret the dominance of the European Council in the Community. It further confirms the position of the member states

European leaders dine together and discuss Eastern Europe, Paris, 1989. (Patrick Robert/Sygma)

and their governments, rather than the Community institutions (the Commission and the Parliament), as the central actors in the EC. On the other hand, it could be argued that the EC would be far less relevant to the member states were it not for the direct interest and involvement of the heads of government in shaping its affairs and that EC initiatives and policies, if they are to make fundamental progress, need behind them the weight that only the heads of government can supply.

The primacy of the European Council, and of the Council of Ministers generally, raises fundamental questions about democratic accountability within the EC. The Commission is accountable to Parliament (which can dismiss it), and the Parliament is accountable to the European public through the direct elections (every five years). But to whom are the Council of Ministers and the European Council accountable? The short answer is, to no one. It is true that all the heads of government attending a European Council meeting, as well as all the ministers attending a Council of Ministers meeting, are individually accountable to their own parliament for what they have or have not done at the meeting—though how effective parliaments are in enforcing this accountability is another question. But neither the Council of Ministers nor the European Council as an institution is in any way answerable or accountable to anyone at all, either in theory or in practice. This has led to much talk of a "democratic deficit" within the EC, and given that the Community has been willing to admit only democracies to membership, it has been asked ironically whether the EC itself would be eligible for EC membership if it had to apply.

The Court of Justice

The Court of Justice is based in Luxembourg and consists of thirteen judges—one from each member state and a thirteenth agreed on among the governments. It interprets and applies EC law and the Community's constitution (in other words, the treaties). Its decisions are binding on all member states, and this marks one of the main differences between the EC and other international organizations. While a state can refuse to accept a judgment made by another international court (such as the International Court of Justice at The Hague or the European Court of Human Rights at Strasbourg), those states belonging to the EC cannot pick and choose among the judgments of the Court of Justice. Its decisions override those of domestic courts, and it is accepted throughout the Community that EC law overrides domestic law, even though this is not explicitly stated in the treaties (for a discussion of the relationship between the two, see Collins, pp. 9–21). The Court of Justice is in effect the final court of appeal in the EC; there is no higher authority. In giving its judgments, the Court has not confined itself to the treaties (which are concerned mainly with economic matters); it has also looked for inspiration to the constitutions of the member states and to the European Convention of Human Rights. It has taken a creative rather than a positivist approach to its role—that is, it has supplied interpretations to fill gaps in the Community's legislation and has cited its own case law rather than feeling confined strictly to the letter of the treaties.

Domestic courts frequently refer cases to the Court if a question of the interpretation of Community law is involved. In addition, one government or the Commission may take another government before the Court for failing to meet its obligations; such cases (which in practice are almost invariably brought by the Commission rather than by another government) often concern a state's alleged discrimination against imports from other EC countries. The Commission has brought over 500 such cases against a member government over the years. As a result of such cases, the Court has stated, to give a few examples, that it is not permissible for a member state to fund advertising campaigns designed to promote domestic products; to discriminate against workers—with regard to employment, pay, or other conditions of work or employment—on the basis of nationality; or to conduct excessive checking or inspection of imported goods.

Implementation of judgments of the Court has become a cause of some concern. The Court of Justice, unlike domestic courts, has no police force or army to enforce its judgments, and neither does it have other formal sanctions to impose on those who do not obey its decisions. A judgment arising from proceedings under the EEC Treaty "is only declaratory; it has no executory force, no sanctions are provided, nor are any national measures thereby annulled" (Brown and Jacobs, p. 85). The machinery of enforcement is, in short, "far from perfect," and the only sanctions are the informal ones of political pressure from other member states, the Commission, and the European Parliament (Lasok and Bridge, p. 333). The Court must rely on the law enforcement agencies of the member states, and hence ultimately on their governments, to enforce compliance. Generally, it is true, the lack of formal sanction for the breach of a treaty obligation or for noncompliance with a Court judgment does not pose a major problem. It seems that in most cases

The European Court in session. (European Community Delegation, Washington, D.C.)

"the declaratory judgement is its own sanction," and states usually seek to avoid a judgment against them (Freestone and Davidson, p. 152). However, this does not always apply, and in one notorious case the Italian parliament repealed an offending law only after the Court had delivered a judgment on the matter on three separate occasions (Brown and Jacobs, p. 77).

Outright and explicit refusal to comply with a Court judgment, as opposed to procrastination, has occurred only once. This was in the late 1970s, when France refused to obey a Court declaration that it should lift a ban on imports of British lamb and mutton, a problem that was eventually resolved at the political level. Delaying tactics are more common than outright defiance: states receiving an adverse judgment from the Court sometimes respond by saying that they will need time to consider the full implications of the verdict, a process that in some cases has apparently required several years. Moreover, some governments seem to be little put out by receiving judgments against them. Table 10.5, which shows the position in 1989, reveals that this is especially true of the Italian government. Altogether, across the EC, there were 82 cases where member states had not complied with a Court judgment, though in 21 of these the Commission had been informed that the state was taking steps to rectify the situation.

A detailed examination of these 82 cases gives a flavor of the difficulties that can arise in trying to enforce EC law when a member government is uncooperative (the accounts can be found in the source cited for Table 10.5). In several cases in the second column, judgment had been delivered as far back as the early 1980s, but the

TABLE 10.5
**Judgments of the European Court of Justice with Which
Member States Have Not Complied**

Country	Cases Where the Commission Has Been Informed that Measures Are Being Taken	Other Cases
Belgium	1	11
Denmark	1	0
France	2	4
Germany	6	6
Greece	1	7
Ireland	1	0
Italy	7	30
Luxembourg	0	0
Netherlands	1	3
Portugal	0	0
Spain	0	0
United Kingdom	1	0
Total	21	61

Note: The first column of numbers refers to the position as of December 31, 1989; the second column, to the position as of January 31, 1989.
Source: Seventh Annual Report to the European Parliament on Commission Monitoring of the Application of Community Law 1989, Commission of the European Communities, Brussels, 1990, pp. 57–71.

member state at fault had still not come into line. For example, the Italian government was subject to two adverse judgments in November 1981 concerning its refusal to allow specific individuals to practice as a road haulage operator and a road passenger transport operator. After some years, the Commission began fresh proceedings, and the Court issued a second judgment in November 1986. However, over two years later, nothing had happened. Another example concerns a decision of the Court in June 1986 that the French practice of recruiting separately men and women to public service jobs was contrary to EC law. The Commission noted in 1990 that French rules for public service recruitment had not been amended and that in March 1989 two job advertisements for police inspectors in Paris had indicated that the system of separate recruitment was still in existence. Even among the 21 cases in the first column, where there were at least signs of progress, the picture was not always very bright. With regard to a judgment delivered against Germany in 1984 concerning the additives allowed in beer and the labeling of beer bottles, the Commission expressed "reservations" about the steps the German authorities had taken and said it felt that Germany had not fully complied with the Court's judgment. With regard to a judgment given against the French government in 1988, the Commission reported that it had "learned informally" that something was going to be done about it but noted plaintively that "no reply has been received" to a telex communication it had sent some months earlier inquiring about the precise position. It need hardly be said that the respective national governments do not take such an indulgent attitude toward the enforcement of judgments given by their own domestic courts.

The Economic and Social Committee and Interest Groups

The only other significant actors in the EC decision-making process are interest groups, which can work in three different ways: through a committee specifically provided for them, by lobbying the Commission and/or the European Parliament, or by lobbying the member governments.

First, the EC provides formal institutional representation for interest groups through a body called the Economic and Social Committee (also known as the ESC, or Ecosoc). This consists of approximately 200 representatives of interests throughout the EC. Each country has a number of places on the committee, depending on its size, and allocates them among its main interests, and so most members of the ESC represent employers, workers, or farmers. The ESC holds two-day meetings in Brussels about once a month. It has a right to give its views (termed an "Opinion") to the Commission and/or the Council of Ministers on matters directly relevant to any interest group, and it may give its views if it wishes on most other subjects. But unlike the Parliament, it has no teeth whatsoever. It cannot delay a proposal, and the Council is free to make a decision without waiting for its Opinion. The ESC, then, is not an important factor in the policy-making process.

Consequently, when interest groups wish to influence a decision, they usually pursue one or both of the other two routes. The first of these is to lobby the Commission or the Parliament, or both. The Commission is generally quite receptive to being lobbied, since if its proposals are acceptable to the major interest groups, they stand a better chance of getting through the legislative process without being changed too much. Interest groups are keen to make their views known while proposals are being drawn up, because changes are much more difficult to make once a proposal has been formally published. Many major interest groups maintain full-time offices in Brussels; the largest are the farmers' lobbies, but various industrial and manufacturers' groups also maintain a permanent presence. In addition, there are a number of professional lobbyists who will present a case on behalf of a client (usually a group of manufacturers or a specific company) to the appropriate Commission employee. The European Parliament is also willing to listen to interest groups, partly because it makes MEPs feel more relevant. As the EP's power has increased, it has become the focus for increased lobbying activity.

The Council offices in Brussels are much less receptive to lobbying; of course, the Council itself is in session only rarely and has far too full an agenda at its meetings to be prepared to spend time listening to interest groups. Although interest groups do their best to familiarize Council officials with their views, most conclude that the best way to influence the Council is to work through national governments. Given the Council's penchant for sticking to the principle of unanimity, if just one minister can be persuaded to oppose a proposal to the death, then the Council will not approve it. Conversely, an interest group might wish to persuade a government to drop its opposition to a Commission proposal. Consequently, a lot of Eurolobbying actually takes place in Paris, London, Madrid, and the other capitals, as groups put pressure on their country's minister for transport or fisheries, for example, to agree or not to agree to a particular Commission proposal. The prime exponents of this are the farmers' groups, which have a cozy relationship with the Ministry of Agriculture in virtually every country, as we saw in Chapter 9. Overall, interest groups are significant actors in the EC's policy-making process, although the EC should not be seen as a larger version of a corporatist state. The reluctance of the Council of Ministers to encourage direct interest-group involvement in decision making means that the EC exhibits the characteristics of corporatism only in a weak form (Sargent).

WHAT DOES THE EUROPEAN COMMUNITY DO?

As time has passed, the range of policy areas in which the EC shows an interest has steadily increased. The main one has traditionally been agriculture, and in recent years the aim of establishing a "single market" across the Community has grown in importance. In addition, in an attempt to give the EC a human face and to moderate some of the effects of giving market forces fairly free rein, members of the Community have set about creating a "People's Europe" or a "Social Europe."

Agriculture

Agriculture stands head and shoulders above the rest as a concern of the Community. It consumes the bulk of the Community's budget, through the Common Agricultural Policy (CAP), and some cynics have even gone so far as to suggest that the EC is little more than an elaborate camouflage for the CAP. This is not true, but it is easy to see how that impression could arise, given the centrality of agriculture in EC politics. Although the proportion of the Community's labor force working in agriculture has fallen from over 25 percent in the late 1950s to less than 8 percent, the share of Community expenditure going to agriculture has consistently been far in excess of this: since 1973, this proportion has only once (in 1981) fallen below 60 percent, and twice it has exceeded 75 percent (Shackleton, p. 136).

The aim of the CAP is to establish a single, or common, market in agricultural products so that they cost the same anywhere within the EC. The setting of prices is not left to the market. Instead, agricultural prices are very highly regulated, with the Council of Ministers fixing prices for nearly all products—prices that are invariably higher than world market prices. In October 1986, EC prices, compared with estimated representative world prices, were more than twice as high for wheat, more than three times as high for sugar and butter, and more than nine times as high for skimmed-milk powder (Harrop, p. 68). In order to protect EC farmers from competition from lower-cost producers elsewhere, levies are imposed on imports coming into the Community. Since prices are fixed above free market levels, production quotas must be set, and the Commission undertakes to buy up, at a guaranteed and high "intervention" price, what farmers are unable to sell on the open market. The results of the CAP are highly satisfactory for EC farmers (especially large farmers, who have benefited most from its operation) but less so for consumers, who have to pay higher food prices than they otherwise would.

The CAP is a very expensive feature of the EC's operations. In the first half of the 1980s, indeed, it seemed possible that the operation of the CAP was going to

A tiny part of the EC butter mountain. (Topham/The Image Works)

bankrupt the EC and bring the entire edifice crashing down. The quantity of many products was far in excess of what EC consumers were prepared to buy, and their price was so high that they could not be sold on world markets. Because of its undertaking to buy up unsold products, the Commission spent large amounts of money buying the surplus of certain commodities, especially beef and butter, and then spent more money storing the surplus in the notorious beef and butter mountains in refrigerated warehouses all over the EC. Some of this surplus was sold at low prices to the Soviet Union or third world countries, but most remained in the warehouses. After a few years in storage, the beef and butter had, naturally, deteriorated beyond fitness for human consumption and were either fed to animals or simply destroyed.

While the farming interest groups saw nothing wrong with this system, others questioned the sense of giving farmers generous grants to produce ever-increasing quantities of commodities that no one would buy and then paying even more to purchase the produce from them and store it until it rotted. It was realized that it would be better to pay the farmers *not* to produce; that way, at least the cost of storing the commodities would be avoided. With a budget catastrophe looming ever closer, the Community finally took decisive action, in the period 1986 to 1988, of a kind that critics had not believed it capable of: it stood up to the powerful farming lobby. A series of much stricter production limits and quotas was introduced, and farmers who produced more than their quota were heavily fined.

The European Council, meeting in Brussels in February 1988, agreed on a tighter set of controls over, and a reduction in, agricultural spending over the next few years, and this package was later approved by both the Commission and the Parliament. But even at the end of the period covered by the agreement, agriculture was still set to account for about 60 percent of all EC spending.

The sheer size of the agriculture budget and the convoluted nature of the schemes established by the CAP provide plenty of opportunities for fraud. The export refund scheme appears to be particularly open to abuse; it guarantees a refund to those who export agricultural produce to many of the non-EC countries in order to cover the gap between the lower world market price and the higher price that would have been received if the produce had been sold within the EC. The exporter receives this refund from his or her own government, which in turn is paid by the Community. Examples of abuse are numerous. The Court of Auditors, the body charged with checking that EC money is spent as it should be, discovered on one occasion that the area of land in Sardinia declared by farmers as being under olive trees was greater than the entire area of the island (Budd and Jones, p. 45). Another case that came to light involved refunds paid when beef was purportedly exported to Egypt, a transaction earning a high refund; the beef was actually sent to Brazil, and that transaction should not have entitled the exporter to any refund. Some of the goods supposedly exported from the EC are subsequently reimported into the EC, having earned their export refund on the way out, while some refund-earning transactions may exist only on paper. A report by the Court of Auditors in 1990 accused the Commission of gross mismanagement in the way it decides how and how much to pay European farmers to export beef, cereals, and dairy products from the Community. To give an example of the abuses it had discovered, it cited a case where French cereals were off-loaded from the stern of a Soviet ship in the port of Hamburg and then immediately reloaded at the bow so that they could be classified as being of German origin and thus qualify for a special export rebate (*Times*, May 31, 1990).

Needless to say, no one can determine how high a proportion of the agriculture budget goes astray in this way. The Court of Auditors in its annual reports highlights proven or suspected abuses, but it is reluctant to make a specific assessment of the cost of fraud. An estimate from a German specialist in economic crime is that fraud accounts for anywhere from 10 to 20 percent of the money spent on agricultural subsidies (Tutt, pp. 100–132). As things stand, neither the Court of Auditors nor the Commission has the resources to ascertain with confidence the level of fraud, let alone eradicate it.

The Single Market and 1992

A second prominent concern of the Community over the years, particularly in the 1990s, has been the completion of the single internal market. The Community has long been colloquially known in Britain as the "Common Market," and while it is more than this, the aim of creating a common European market certainly features strongly in the EEC Treaty of 1957. A common market would mean that goods and services could be marketed and sold with equal ease all across the Community; there would be no barriers to trade within the Community. The fact that this is still an aim rather than an achievement after more than 30 years of the EEC emphasizes the problems in creating a true single market. While it is easy enough for the Commission to spot and remove formal trade barriers (such as tariffs or quotas) raised by one state against other EC countries, there are many other less obvious devices that thwart the dream of an open market. A state may impose a set of health or safety standards on food or manufactured products, arguing that it is entitled to do this in order to protect its citizens. But it might just happen that the standards it lays down—for example, for beer—are met only by beer of the type traditionally produced in that particular country. Alternatively, a country might require that all video recorders being imported be examined by a safety standards inspectorate, which is situated in an out-of-the-way town and is so understaffed that only a handful of video recorders a week can be processed. The Commission has a responsibility to monitor this kind of informal restriction on trade and to decide whether the measures involved are in any way justified. Another frequent area of complaint concerns state aid to producers of particular commodities, such as shipbuilders, steel manufacturers, and growers of vegetables or flowers. Again, the Commission has to decide whether such aid as it knows about—this is an area where governments are sometimes rather secretive—is within the terms of the treaties or is distorting the market.

With the budget problems finally sorted out in the late 1980s, the Community was finally able to make a priority of trying to complete the single internal market. A report drawn up for the Commission by a committee chaired by Paolo Cecchini attempted to quantify the cost of the existing barriers to trade, which it termed "the cost of non-Europe." It concluded that huge benefits would flow from their elimination. For example, it estimated that customs formalities were costing somewhere between 4.5 and 15 billion Ecus in lost intra-Community trade and that if they were abolished, the member governments could dispense with anywhere from 20 to 40 percent of their customs officials (Cecchini, pp. 13–14). (The Ecu, or European currency unit, was worth $1.22 or £0.67 when the report was completed.) The report also highlighted the problems caused by the lack of Community-wide specifications. For example, a driver wishing to use a car telephone on a trip from Germany via Belgium to the United Kingdom would need to install three different systems; also, in the ten largest areas of the foodstuffs sector, more than 200 nontariff barriers were identified (Cecchini, pp. 53, 58). In 1983, it had been estimated that there might be 100,000 different product specifications altogether throughout the EC (Pinder, p. 96). The Cecchini report suggested that the achievement of a true single market would trigger a major relaunch of economic activity, adding nearly 5 percent to the Community's gross domestic product, reducing consumer prices by an average of 6.1 percent, and creating 1.8 million new jobs, thereby reducing the jobless rate across the Community by 1.5 percentage points (Cecchini, p. 97). The adoption of a common set of standards and specifications would, of course, benefit not only Community producers but also those from non-EC countries, who would then need to manufacture products to only one set of specifications rather than twelve different sets in order to reach a market of 340 million people.

The EC chose the target date of December 31, 1992, for the completion of the single market and sought to publicize it through a Community-wide campaign urging people throughout the EC to make themselves ready for "1992," even though most EC citizens had little idea of what they were supposed to do to prepare for this date or what exactly was going to happen then. The likelihood of there being a true single market by this date was never very realistic. One major barrier is that governments impose different levels of indirect taxes on many goods; for example, the excise duty on cigarettes in Denmark is six times as high as that in France and Greece, while taxation levels on car sales range from 12 percent in Luxembourg to 200 percent in Denmark and Greece (Pinder, p. 101; Budd and Jones, p. 47).

Plans to standardize indirect taxes across the Community have foundered, since some states with generally high rates (such as France and Ireland) are very dependent on the revenue they get from this source, and their governments could not sustain the loss they would suffer if they had to lower their rates, while states with low rates would face public protest if they increased them significantly. However, without such standardization it is hard to see how a true single market can emerge, since if tax rates in neighboring countries diverge to any great extent, there will be an obvious temptation to engage in cross-border smuggling and a consequent need to retain the full complement of customs personnel. Different rates of indirect taxation distort competition, and "fiscal frontiers" will still exist even if border controls disappear (Harrop, pp. 148–153). In addition, producers may set different prices in different countries, as they are entitled to. For both these reasons, it is unlikely that there will be a general convergence of prices by 1992. Moreover, the aim of creating a single labor market will also be difficult to achieve, as several states still have requirements that "foreigners" (i.e., all nonnationals, whether or not from another EC country) must register with the police and go through a sometimes very lengthy bureaucratic process of obtaining a residence permit and a work permit before they are allowed to seek employment or set up a business. However, progress has already been made in this field, and given the political will behind the aim of completing the single market, it is certain that much more will be made during the 1990s, even if a true single market never actually arrives.

A People's Europe

Although agriculture and the single market are the main areas of EC involvement, there are nowadays very few policy spheres in which the EC is not concerned, at least to some degree. The EC has the aim, even if this is not precisely expressed in any of the treaties, of bringing about an equality of civil and social rights, of living and working conditions, of opportunities, and of income across the Community; this is sometimes characterized as building a "Social Europe." To this end it has tended to get involved in virtually all policy areas, whether or not they are explicitly enumerated in the founding treaties. It has issued legal instruments covering such diverse subjects as the size and grading of eggs, the purity of tap water to which citizens are entitled, the length of time truck drivers can drive without a break, the safety and cleanliness of the sea at bathing beaches, the extent to which countries can reserve their coastal waters for the exclusive use of their own fishing fleets, equal pay for men and women, the rights of consumers, and aid for the third world.

In addition, the Community has the aim of ironing out, or at least reducing, the significant disparities in wealth that exist within its boundaries. Regional disparities within the EC are twice as high as within the U.S.A. in the case of gross domestic product (GDP) and three times as high in terms of unemployment (Harrop, p. 108). There are fears that the moves toward a single market could even exacerbate the problem, as the economic growth generated might be concentrated in a "golden triangle" covering the southeastern part of England, parts of France, northern Italy, and most of Germany, with the rest of the Community becoming ever more peripheral. Table 10.6 shows the degree of variation between the member states, with GDP per capita in Denmark nearly five times the corresponding figure for Portugal. The table shows that the budget has some redistributive effect: the poorest four countries receive more from the EC budget than they give to it, while of the wealthiest four countries, three (Denmark being the exception) give more than they receive. The difference between the German inflows and outflows is so great that Germany is sometimes described as the "paymaster" of the Community. To try to even out the fruits of economic growth, the EC has established "structural" funds, the most important of which are known as the Social Fund and the Regional Fund, to be used to promote development in the less wealthy parts of the Community, particularly Greece, Portugal, Spain, Ireland, and southern Italy. Under these headings, the Community funds schemes to give job training to the unemployed throughout the EC and to combat unemployment in the peripheral regions. However, given the fact that the CAP has always taken the lion's share of the budget, these funds have never been large enough to bring about a major redistribution of wealth.

TABLE 10.6

Gross Domestic Product of EC Member States, and Contributions to and Receipts from the 1989 Budget

	Gross Domestic Product in 1989, $ billions	Gross Domestic Product in 1989 per Capita, $	Share of 1989 EC Budget Revenues Contributed, %	Share of 1989 EC Budget Expenditure Received, %
Denmark	105	20,912	2.0	3.1
Germany (West)	1,200	19,581	25.1	13.5
Luxembourg	7	17,592	0.2	0.0
France	948	17,002	19.5	16.7
Netherlands	225	15,461	6.1	11.3
Belgium	151	15,180	4.1	2.0
Italy	864	14,430	17.2	18.2
United Kingdom	832	14,413	14.8	9.5
Ireland	33	9,182	0.8	5.0
Spain	376	8,722	8.1	10.4
Greece	54	5,244	1.3	7.5
Portugal	45	4,265	1.0	2.8
Total	4,840	14,922	100.0	100.0

Note: Countries are ranked in order of per capita gross domestic product.
Sources: Gross Domestic Product 1989 as Table 2 on page 6. EC budget 1989 from Official Journal of the European Communities, C313, vol. 33, Dec. 12, 1990, *Annual Report of the Court of Auditors Concerning the Financial Year 1989,* Office for Official Publications of the European Communities, Luxembourg, pp. 76–77. The analysis of budgetary expenditure received by each member state refers to the payments made under the principal sectors, which in 1989 represented 82.8 percent of all expenditure.

As to the substance of EC policies, it would be difficult to categorize these unequivocally as either basically left-wing or basically right-wing; indeed, the EC comes under attack from both the left and the right. Its decisions tend to promote private enterprise and free trade, but it also adopts a very interventionist approach to agriculture and is active in defending the social rights of sections of society who suffer discrimination of one sort or another, such as women, migrant workers, and workers in general. Some on the left have accused the EC of being a source of centrist policies that make it difficult for any single country within the EC to pursue radical left-wing policies. When the left-wing PASOK government in Greece attempted to nationalize the pharmaceuticals industry in the 1980s, it discovered that the country's membership in the Community "raises impediments to the creation of politico-economic institutions which do not conform to EC models" (Verney, p. 220). In contrast, some on the right are unhappy with the EC's interest in social rights. In a significant and widely reported speech in Bruges, Belgium, in September 1988, British Prime Minister Margaret Thatcher complained that the British people had voted for a government that had rolled back the frontiers of the state, only to be faced with the threat that they would be "reimposed" by the Community institutions in Brussels (Taylor, pp. 22–23). On balance, though, it is hard to resist the impression that much more emphasis has been given to the opening up of markets than to the promotion of social policies.

BOX 10.1
The European Community

FRANCE
France was one of the six original members of the EEC in 1958. Under General de Gaulle, the French president from 1958 to 1969, France opposed the admission of Britain, but de Gaulle's attitude toward the EC was not too different from that displayed by British governments after 1973. De Gaulle was in favor of the economic benefits that the Community brought but was very suspicious of any steps that might dilute the traditional sovereignty of the state. Since his departure from office, France has been more willing to contemplate closer integration among the member states, but despite the rhetoric of some of its leading politicians, it is not generally seen as being at the forefront of the integrationists.

GERMANY
For Germany, one of the six founders, membership in the EC offered the prospect both of economic gains and of political rehabilitation after the Second World War. Even before German reunification in October 1990, West Germany had

the largest economy in Europe. As the wealthiest EC member, Germany has picked up the largest share of the bill for funding the EC. Most Germans see this as a price worth paying, even in pure economic terms, for securing access to the huge EC market for their efficient industries, but in recent years there have been signs that some of them are coming to feel that their country is asked to shoulder an unfairly large proportion of the contributions to the EC's budget. Although West Germany was supportive in the late 1980s of moves toward closer European integration, the need to cope with the problems of assimilating the former communist-run East German state is likely to loom larger in its priorities during the 1990s.

ITALY
Italy was one of the founders of the EC, which has brought significant economic benefits to the country. In the late 1980s Italy's economy overtook that of Britain, in both gross and per capita terms, although its wealth is concentrated heavily

(Continued on next page)

in the northern half of the country. The southern half of the country and the two main islands, Sicily and Sardinia, are among the poorest regions of the EC, and they also tend to feature prominently in accounts of fraud within the EC. Italy has a poor record when it comes to implementing Community law and complying with judgments of the Court of Justice. Despite its size, Italy has generally been content to allow other countries, particularly France and Germany, to take the lead in shaping the future direction of the Community. Among both politicians and the public, enthusiasm for moves toward a federal Europe is high.

NETHERLANDS

The Netherlands was one of the founding members of the EC, but as a small country it has accepted that its impact on decisions will be relatively marginal. Although it is one of the wealthier countries in the Community, the Netherlands receives more from the EC budget than it contributes, and attitudes toward the EC in general, as well as specific attitudes toward closer integration, are broadly favorable.

SPAIN

Soon after the first democratic election in forty years was held in 1977, Spain applied for membership in the EC, and after a protracted period of negotiations, it joined on January 1, 1986. The potential economic benefits of membership were a powerful incentive, but just as important were the political implications. Under the long rule of the dictator Franco, Spain had been isolated from Western European political thought and developments, and joining the EC was an ideal opportunity to join the mainstream rather than remain on the fringe. In addition, it was felt that the risk of a military coup by far-rightists attempting to restore a quasi-Francoist dictatorship would be greatly reduced if the country was part of (and was benefiting economically from its membership in) a community committed to the preservation of liberal democratic values. Spain is one of the more integrationist of the member states and favors an expansion of the role of the European Parliament.

SWEDEN

Sweden has a long-standing policy of neutrality, which kept it out of the Second World War. This led to its refusal for many years to consider joining the European Community. Until the late 1980s, the communist bloc regarded the EC as an antisocialist organization and refused to have any dealings with it. In the context of this perception of the Community, it was felt in Sweden that joining the EC would be incompatible with the country's neutrality. Developments after the accession of Mikhail Gorbachev to power in the U.S.S.R. in 1985 changed the international climate dramatically. The ending of the cold war and of the old bipolar world order led to doubts as to what neutrality meant when there were no longer two blocs to be neutral between. With one neutral country, Ireland, having been an EC member since 1973 and another, Austria, applying for Community membership in the late 1980s, Sweden's attitude underwent reassessment, and the country may well be an EC member by the end of the century.

UNITED KINGDOM

Britain stood aloof from the moves toward European integration in the late 1940s and the 1950s. By the time it had changed its mind, in the early 1960s, the previously welcoming climate had grown chillier, and it had to wait until 1973 to gain admittance. Once Britain was inside the EC, its former ambivalence reasserted itself. Successive governments resisted attempts to promote closer integration of the member states, and Britain was sometimes accused of having, psychologically at least, one foot inside the EC and one still outside it.

In order to make the EC clearly and directly relevant to its citizens and to justify the claim that a "People's Europe" is being constructed, the Community has attempted to create symbols with which Europeans can identify. The EC has its own flag, consisting of twelve gold stars arranged in a circle on a blue background, and this can be seen flying from many public buildings across the Community alongside the appropriate national flag. It also has its own anthem (the prelude to Beethoven's "Ode to Joy") and a Youth Orchestra. The passports of all EC countries are now issued in a uniform size and color, and holders of a passport of any EC country are often waved through immigration at borders between member countries, without even needing to open the passport for inspection. In June 1990, five member states (France, Germany, Belgium, Luxembourg, and the Netherlands) went one step further and signed an agreement whereby all border controls between them were abolished.

THE EUROPEAN COMMUNITY: INTERGOVERNMENTAL OR SUPRANATIONAL ORGANIZATION?

There are two ways of looking at the EC. One is to see it as an organization in which the governments of twelve sovereign member states cooperate, but without giving up the ultimate right to make their own decisions. This view sees the EC as an *intergovernmental* organization, similar in type to other international organizations, though with rather more contact and cooperation between the participants. The second way of looking at the EC is to regard it as a *supranational* body, one in which the ultimate power rests with the Community institutions and in which the twelve national governments have room to maneuver only within the framework of policy decided at the Community level. This view sees the EC as being more like a federal state, such as Germany or the U.S.A., than like a conventional international organization.

As things stand, no one would seriously defend the second of these views. Although it has supranational elements, the EC is still far closer to the intergovernmental end of the spectrum. As we have seen, the two most powerful actors in the EC are the Council of Ministers, which generally operates by a procedure that gives each country a veto over issues especially important to it, and the European Council—both of which explicitly represent the national governments. Nothing really major happens in the EC without the twelve heads of government first agreeing to it. No fundamental shift of power from national to Community institutions can take place in the future without the agreement of the European Council.

It is true that the supranational bodies—the Commission and the Parliament—have some power and influence and that Community law, as interpreted by the Court of Justice, takes precedence over domestic laws and constitutions. These facts are not to be minimized; they distinguish the EC from every other international organization, past or present. Nevertheless, even the supranational bodies find their power checked by the national ones. Commissioners who want to be renominated need to preserve the goodwill of their national government, and decisions of the Court of Justice are not always implemented with alacrity.

Moreover, implementation of EC decisions generally, not just judgments of the Court, is quite a serious problem. There are known cases of states dragging their heels for years over pieces of Community legislation they do not like. Perhaps surprisingly, there is some tendency for the most pro-integration states, such as Italy and Belgium, to have the worst record on implementation, while Denmark and the United Kingdom, usually the least enthusiastic about moves toward supranationalism, have good records, just as tends to be the case when it comes to compliance with Court judgments. The growing volume of EC law and the limited resources of the Commission have raised questions as to whether the impressive volume of legislation emanating from the Community has as much practical effect as intended. There is some evidence that it does not. One cross-national project (Siedentopf and Ziller) concentrated on the two main types of Community legislation, regulations and directives. The distinction between them concerns the role of the member states in turning them into law (see Freestone and Davidson, pp. 38–42). In the case of *regulations*, the member states are not required to take any action, because regulations automatically become part of the national legal systems of all member states as soon as they are adopted by the Council of Ministers. *Directives*, in contrast, bind the member states as to the end to be achieved but leave to the respective national authorities the precise method of achieving this end. Consequently, once a directive has been issued by the Community, each member state is obliged to incorporate it into domestic law within a stipulated period of time.

Examining the fate of a set of sixteen directives, the study found that on the average, for each directive, only four of the (then) ten member states incorporated the directive into domestic legislation within the fixed time limit, another four incorporated it late, and the other two countries had not incorporated it at all. Moreover, some civil servants believed that while the Commission took some interest in whether the directives were incorporated, it seemed to have rather less interest in how and to what effect the directives were actually being applied (Siedentopf and Hauschild, pp. 51–55, 70).

Regarding regulations, the conclusion was similarly pessimistic. A detailed study of the EC regulations on the number of hours that truck drivers are allowed to drive without a break found that the national governments implemented the regulations in the manner that suited them best, "taking advantage of tactical ambiguities or not too intrusive Commission monitoring where possible." Although each government is obliged to send the Commission an annual report on the implementation of the regulations, the information supplied was in practice so late as to be almost useless, and besides, there were gaps and evasions in the information supplied. Moreover, the member states fixed very low penalties for noncompliance with the regulations and in most cases coupled this with weak enforcement, which could be interpreted as "a relatively low level of political commitment to the successful implementation of these rules" (Philip, 1988a, pp. 99–104). The author of the study concluded that "it seems rather strange for the Community to continue to pass regulations which all the parties concerned must know are unlikely to be well enforced" (Philip, 1988b, p. 189). It is clear, then, that Community legislation requires the cooperation and commitment of the member governments at the implementation stage if it is to mean anything and that this is not always forthcoming.

The supremacy of the member states is shown in a number of other ways. When it comes to making policy, governments have some degree of latitude even in the most regulated area, agriculture, and they have great latitude in most other areas. If the ability to pursue an independent foreign policy is an acid test of sovereignty, as some would argue, then each of the member states is sovereign, especially given that decision making by the Council of Foreign Ministers operates on the principle of unanimity, as we noted above. There is no Community army or police force. Besides, even if the member states are in some ways less than completely sovereign, this may be as much a consequence of a growing general interdependence between developed countries as it is of Community membership per se.

Member states retain the right to leave the Community whenever they wish. Although the treaties do not prescribe a right or a method of withdrawal, it is inconceivable that the other members could, or would attempt to, compel one country to remain within the EC against its will. The only state to depart so far has been Greenland, which entered the EC in 1973 as a part of Denmark and subsequently gained autonomy. It voted to leave in a 1982 referendum and did so three years later after negotiations with the EC (Urwin, p. 361). Even if this proves little, given Greenland's tiny population (about 50,000), it remains the case that members of the EC, unlike units in a federal country, are free to leave if they wish. There would, of course, be strong economic arguments against the wisdom of any state pulling out, but whether it would be wise or not, each member country remains in the EC entirely voluntarily.

The extent to which the EC is still an intergovernmental rather than a supranational body is shown also in the manner in which resources are concentrated at the level of the member states. The Community is financed on the basis of what are termed "own resources." This means that it does not receive a block grant from the twelve governments, which would give it an overtly subordinate and dependent position; instead, it has a statutory right to the revenue it derives from the flow of money into and around the Community. It has been pointed out that this distinguishes the EC from other international organizations such as the United Nations, which have no "own resources" and are entirely dependent on direct payments from the governments of member countries (Shackleton, p. 146). The EC has two main sources of revenue: it receives 1.4 percent of whatever each national government collects from the main indirect tax in the Community—the value-added tax (VAT)—and it also keeps the duties collected from trade with countries outside the EC (for details, see Nugent, pp. 259–261). As part of the budgetary reforms of the late 1980s, a five-year plan was put into effect, one element of which entailed putting a ceiling on the size of the EC's budget relative to the total gross national product of the member states for each year. This was set to rise by 1992 to a figure of 1.2 percent, illustrating the way in which the resources available to the EC institutions are dwarfed by those controlled by national governments. This is partly because some responsibilities usually shouldered by the central government in a federal state, such as defense, are handled at the national level within the EC. However, small as the figure of 1.2 percent is, it represents a steady upward trend since 1973, when the EC budget was only 0.5 percent of member states' gross national product. The 1989 EC budget amounted to 3.5 percent of the total of all the member states' budgets for that year (Pracht, chap. 5). The 1990 budget, at almost 44 billion Ecus, represented a cost to Community citizens of about 135 Ecus per person (at prevailing exchange rates in mid-1990, $175 or £95).

Another illustration of the relatively peripheral nature of the Community is the small size of its staff. Altogether, the EC has only about 24,600 employees, of whom 17,200 are employed by the Commission, 3600 by the Parliament, 2200 by the Council of Ministers, and the rest by other bodies such as the Court of Auditors and the Court of Justice (*Official Journal of the European Communities*, L30, vol. 34, Feb. 4, 1991, p. 103). Moreover, a large percentage of the Community's employees are translators. Such figures put into perspective the occasional complaint from critics that Community bureaucrats, or "Eurocrats," are seeking all-embracing powers over the people of the Community. All the institutions, especially the Commission, would need considerably more employees if they were even to be able to carry out their allotted functions thoroughly.

There is therefore no doubt that the European Community in the early 1990s is still basically an intergovernmental organization, not a supranational one. This is not, however, to belittle the achievements made since the EC was founded. Even if the EC were purely an intergovernmental organization, it would still be an impressive and unique one, given the closeness of the contacts between the twelve governments and the high degree of coordination and cooperation between them. But in fact, as we have seen, there are also undeniably supranational elements in the Community, and even though these are less significant than the national ones, they make the EC a type of international organization that is qualitatively different from any other.

Finally, it is worth observing the extent to which the EC has developed to its present position without direct consultation with the people of Europe. The most important decisions have been made by governments and ratified by parliaments, with the people simply not being consulted directly. Only six referendums have been held in the member states, and one of these (the French referendum of 1972 on whether to approve enlargement) was primarily an exercise in a domestic political battle. The other five all took place in the three countries admitted in 1973. Both Denmark and Ireland held referendums in 1972 on entry. In Britain, there was no referendum, but the Labour party, which was in opposition at the time of entry, returned to office in 1974 and the following year, after a somewhat cosmetic "renegotiation" of the terms of British entry, held a referendum on whether Britain should remain in the EC. Most recently, Denmark (in 1986) and Ireland (in 1987) held referendums on the Single European Act. In all five cases, the vote went in favor of the EC.

It cannot be argued that the people of the twelve member states have been dragged thus far along the road to a supranational state against their will; if they were unhappy, this would be reflected in the results of their parliamentary elections. But the devolution of significant powers to Community institutions without a perceived need to consult the people directly, and without protest from the people, demonstrates the extent to which traditional notions of absolute sovereignty are now widely seen as irrelevant within Western Europe. Although opponents of the Community, who exist within each member state, stress the loss of sovereignty that membership entails, defenders of EC membership argue that it no longer makes sense, if it ever did, to think in terms of absolute national sovereignty. The latter argument was concisely expressed by the pro-EC side in Britain's 1975 referendum on whether the country should remain in the Community (Butler and Kitzinger, p. 300):

> *Whether we are in the Market or not, Common Market policies are going to affect the lives of every family in the country. Inside the Market, we can play a major part in deciding these policies. Outside, we are on our own.*

Moreover, whatever diminution in sovereignty is brought about by EC membership is balanced by the acquisition of a voice in the shaping of a much larger political entity. In other words, there has been a pooling of sovereignty among twelve countries rather than a loss of sovereignty by each of them.

THE FUTURE OF THE EUROPEAN COMMUNITY

Ever since the first of the three Communities, the ECSC, was founded in the early 1950s, there have been some who have hoped, and others who have feared, that the existing Community framework would become the vehicle for a process generally termed "European integration," ending in the creation of a federal Western European (or even all-European) state, similar in its political structure to the United States of America. The hopes of integrationists have been dashed many times over the years. France's empty-chair policy in the mid-1960s showed that even with only six member states, closer union would not be easy to achieve. In the 1970s, the oil crisis and the subsequent economic recession brought out a nationalistic response from the members of a Community that was still experiencing difficulty adjusting to its recent enlargement. In the first half of the 1980s, the Community appeared to be in real danger of being buried under a beef or butter mountain or drowned in a milk or wine lake. But in the second half of the 1980s and in the early 1990s, integrationists began to feel more optimistic again. With the multifaceted budget problem seemingly sorted out, at least for a while, and no further enlargement imminent, the auguries for a move in the direction of a federal Europe looked brighter than they had perhaps ever been.

Certainly, the momentum of integration did seem to pick up during the 1980s (see Pryce). In 1981 the German and Italian foreign ministers published the "Genscher-Colombo Plan," which called for a move toward European unity. In 1984 the European Parliament passed a resolution proposing a draft treaty for European union, inspired by the veteran Italian left-wing MEP Altiero Spinelli. The following year, the Dooge Committee, which had been set up by the European Council, came up with a report whose recommendations, though far more cautious than the Parliament's proposals, were seen by integrationists as at least a step in the right direction. And in 1986 the Community passed the Single European Act (SEA). Despite its clear-cut title, the SEA was actually a hodgepodge of different measures, but these included important decisions relating to the achievement of the internal market, such as the extension of majority voting within the Council of Ministers on market-related matters. The volume of Community legislation is steadily increasing, and the president of the Commission from 1985 to the early 1990s, Jacques Delors, predicted in July 1988 that "in ten years, 80 per cent of economic legislation—and perhaps tax and social legislation—will be directed from the Community" (George, p. 193).

In the late 1980s and early 1990s, some of the leaders of the twelve governments began to think in more ambitious terms about the future development of the EC. Two concepts frequently aired at European Council meetings in the early 1990s were economic and monetary union (EMU) and European political union (EPU). The first of these refers to the idea of making the EC one large economy, with one Central Bank, one currency, a common rate of interest, and so on. A first step in this direction had been taken in 1979, when the European Monetary System was established. This fixes, within narrow bands, the exchange rates for the currencies of the participating member states. There is also the EC currency, the Ecu, which is increasingly quoted within the Community, although if there ever is a single EC currency, it is as likely to be the German mark as the Ecu. French President Mitterrand and German Chancellor Helmut Kohl have called for the achievement of EMU by the beginning of 1993, leading some skeptics to recall that as long ago as 1972, the Paris summit of EC heads of government had committed the Community to attaining EMU by 1980. However, even if the 1993 target date is rather optimistic, moves toward this end can be expected during the 1990s.

European political union is a rather different matter. Every state is in favor of it, but each has its own definition of the concept. For some states, it means something close to a federal arrangement, a United States of Europe. For others, it means small and tentative steps in that direction. For others still, it means closer cooperation between the governments and a greater role for the Council of Ministers, but with no drift of power to the Commission or the Parliament. A powerful argument in its favor is that if anything like European monetary union is achieved, it would be illogical, inconsistent, and undemocratic not to have Community-wide political institutions to monitor economic decisions made at the Community level.

There is some variation among the member states on the question of giving more power to the Community institutions (in other words, the Commission and the Parliament) and taking power away from the Council of Ministers. Of course, there are also nuances of opinion within each country, and there may be differences between verbal positions and the action a government takes when it comes to the crunch. Even so, a certain degree of generalization is possible. Some countries are traditionally *communautaire*; in the forefront of the integrationists can be found Belgium, Italy, the Netherlands, Germany, and Spain, while Greece has recently swung to this end of the spectrum. Others are notoriously recalcitrant when it comes to European integration; they prefer former British Prime Minister Margaret Thatcher's vision of a Community of "proud, sovereign states," which echoes Charles de Gaulle's earlier invocation of a "*Europe des Patries.*" In her 1988 Bruges speech, mentioned above, Thatcher declared that *willing and active co-operation between independent sovereign states is the best way to build a successful European Community. . . . Europe will be stronger precisely because it has France as France, Spain as Spain, Britain as Britain, each with its own customs, traditions and identity. It would be folly to fit them into some sort of Identikit European personality.* (Taylor, p. 22)

The countries that generally lead the resistance to moves toward greater unity are Britain and Denmark, but it is likely that several other states—Ireland, Luxembourg, Portugal, and probably France—would not be far behind them, even though they are usually content to let others take the lead.

Surveys conducted in April 1990 across the EC give an insight into the views of the public on closer integration within the EC (see Table 10.7). It shows that a majority in the EC as a whole said that they would be very sorry if the Community were scrapped, and only 9 percent would be glad to hear that this had happened. The Greeks and the Italians were most enthusiastic about the EC, but in Denmark and Britain it is clear that there is still a substantial body of citizens who oppose their country's membership. When asked about the prospect of a European government by 1992, a majority again expressed itself in favor, with 21 percent against and 24 percent (not included in the table) expressing no opinion one way or the other. Once more, the strong opposition of the Danes (and, to a lesser extent, the British) stands out, and some others, notably the Irish and the Germans, were somewhat lukewarm in their enthusiasm. The large transfers that flow from Germany to EC coffers every year (see Table 10.6) have led to a certain cooling among Germans in their attitude toward the Community.

Respondents were also asked whether they thought policies in twelve areas should be decided at the national level or at the Community level. A majority favored decision making at the Community level in six areas (protection of the environment, currency, cooperation with developing countries, scientific and technological research, rates for the value-added tax, and foreign policy toward countries outside the EC) and decision making at the national government level in five areas (health and social welfare, education, basic rules for broadcasting and the press, participation of workers' representatives on company boards, and protection of computer-based information on individuals). Opinion was evenly divided on the twelfth area, security and defense. Table 10.7 shows the breakdown of attitudes on two of these issues. Only in Greece and Italy was there a preference for deciding education policy at the Community level, but when it came to foreign relations with countries outside the EC, even the Danes showed a slight preference for allowing this to be settled at the Community level.

Most integrationists recognize that a quantum leap by the twelve governments toward a federal Europe is unlikely, so they advocate more modest proposals that would tilt the balance more toward the Community institutions. Foremost among these are proposals to extend the Parliament's second-reading procedure to all legislation and to extend majority voting in the Council of Ministers, perhaps to all areas except fundamental matters such as enlargement of the EC or amendment of the treaties. Whether either of these is likely to occur is questionable. The first would slow the decision-making process considerably unless it were accompanied

TABLE 10.7

Attitudes toward the EC and toward a European Government among Citizens of the Member States, 1990, in %

| Country | Reaction if EC Were Dissolved | | | European Government | | Who Should Decide Policy on: | | | |
| | Very Sorry | Indifferent | Relieved | For | Against | Education | | Foreign Relations with non-EC Countries | |
						National Government	EC	National Government	EC
Belgium	46	49	5	61	12	64	29	19	70
Denmark	38	36	27	21	63	75	22	45	47
France	54	39	7	60	17	53	42	23	63
Germany	57	35	8	49	24	64	32	32	60
Greece	72	23	5	60	15	41	49	42	42
Ireland	63	30	7	43	16	68	27	26	62
Italy	68	30	2	73	8	43	53	15	74
Luxembourg	62	33	5	54	10	49	41	23	65
Netherlands	60	37	3	54	25	60	35	24	66
Portugal	47	51	3	53	11	52	31	30	47
Spain	52	42	7	62	18	55	39	21	69
United Kingdom	35	45	20	33	35	68	28	28	64
Whole EC	53	38	9	54	21	57	38	25	64

Notes: The questions asked were as follows:
1. "If you were to be told tomorrow that the European Community had been scrapped, would you be very sorry, indifferent, or relieved?"
2. "Are you for or against the formation by 1992 of a European Government responsible to the European Parliament?"
3. "Some people believe that certain areas of policy should be decided by the (national) government, while other areas of policy should be decided jointly within the European Community. Which of the following areas of policy do you think should be decided by the (national) government? And which do you think should be decided jointly with the European Community?" [The table shows responses for "Education" and "Foreign policies toward countries outside the EC."]
The surveys were carried out across the EC in April 1990.
Source: Eurobarometer, no. 33, June 1990, pp. A10, A23, A31.

by the second, and while more majority voting in the Council of Ministers might seem a good idea, it has its dangers. It would raise the possibility that a state or a group of states (for example, Mediterranean states or less wealthy states) could be consistently outvoted within the Council and thus be compelled to accept decisions it regarded as trampling on its vital national interests. In the short run, more majority voting would make for faster decision making but in the long run, it would be a recipe for conflict within the Community and would raise the prospect of states contemplating pulling out altogether.

A further complication is the question of enlargement. When planning for the single market got under way in the late 1980s, there was agreement that no new members would be admitted until the single market was completed, and perhaps until monetary union was close. The aspiring members, such as Austria, Cyprus, Malta, Turkey, and (rather optimistically) Morocco, would just have to wait for their applications to be given serious consideration until the existing twelve had determined how far they wanted to go down the road toward integration. But the events in Eastern Europe of 1989, when nearly all the postwar communist regimes collapsed, reopened the issue.

For one thing, some of the newly democratic states (most notably Czechoslovakia, Hungary, and Poland) soon made it clear that they were keen to join the EC. East Germany has already joined the EC, not as a separate member but by merging with West Germany in October 1990. The member states have decidedly mixed feelings about the possible admission of the former communist states. On the one hand, their run-down economies and industries and their lack of a sustained tradition of liberal democracy do not make them the most attractive of prospective partners. But on the other hand, the EC has always been sensitive to accusations that it is a "rich man's club," and just as it admitted Greece, Spain, and Portugal, despite their backwardness, when they emerged from periods of dictatorship, so it might feel obliged to listen sympathetically to pleas from Eastern Europe that democracy will not survive there unless the EC allows the countries of the region to join.

A second way in which the collapse of the communist regimes affects the prospect of enlargement is that with the disappearance of the "communist threat," military alliances are becoming less important. Long-standing neutrals such as Sweden, which had felt that neutrality was incompatible with EC membership, are likely to reconsider. If Sweden applies for membership, Norway will probably do the same, the scars created by its bitter 1972 referendum having partly healed by now. Non-EC countries are affected by the EC's decision—for example, on product specifications—but are not able to participate in making them. Enlargement creates its own momentum; the more countries that join, the greater will be the disadvantages for those few still left out, and the greater will be their incentive to get on the bandwagon.

Further enlargement, though, would make the achievement of a federal Europe more difficult, as the range of interests and traditions coming under the Community umbrella would increase. One practical impediment to the achievement of close union between even the existing twelve states is the language difficulty. There are at present nine "official" languages in the EC: Danish, Dutch, English, French, German, Greek, Italian, Portuguese, and Spanish. Any of these can be used in any

Community forum, thus creating the need for a large army of translators to be present whenever Community business takes place. In informal discussions, either English or French tends to be used, as there are few politicians or officials who are not reasonably fluent in at least one of those languages. Nevertheless, attending a meeting of the EP or one of its committees can call to mind the Tower of Babel, and the profusion of working languages does impose a limit on the closeness of identity that can be expected to develop.

In the past, the pace of European integration has been dictated more by national factors than by Community ones. In particular, it has often been noted that a strong Franco-German axis has seemed necessary to act as the engine of advancement. It was agreement between the French and the Germans that got the Community off the ground in the first place, and the close relationship in the 1970s between French President Giscard d'Estaing and German Chancellor Helmut Schmidt—and in the 1980s and early 1990s between their successors, François Mitterrand and Helmut Kohl—played an important part in the creation of initiatives during those periods. Thus, ironically perhaps, future prospects for European integration depend primarily not on the wishes of commissioners or MEPs but on the decisions made by the leaders of the governments of key member countries.

References

Brown, L. Neville, and Francis G. Jacobs: *The Court of Justice of the European Communities*, 2d ed., Sweet and Maxwell, London, 1983.

Budd, Stanley A., and Alun Jones: *The European Community: A Guide to the Maze*, 3d ed., Kogan Page, London, 1989.

Bulmer, Simon, and Wolfgang Wessels: *The European Council: Decision-Making in European Politics*, Macmillan, Basingstoke, 1987.

Butler, David, and Uwe Kitzinger: *The 1975 Referendum*, Macmillan, London, 1976.

Cecchini, Paolo, with Michel Catinat and Alexis Jacquemin: *The European Challenge 1992: The Benefits of a Single Market*, Wildwood House, Aldershot, 1988.

Collins, Lawrence: *European Community Law in the United Kingdom*, 3d ed., Butterworths, London, 1984.

Freestone, D. A. C., and J. S. Davidson: *The Institutional Framework of the European Communities*, Croom Helm, London and New York, 1988.

George, Stephen: *An Awkward Partner: Britain in the European Community*, Oxford University Press, Oxford, 1990.

Harrop, Jeffrey: *The Political Economy of Integration in the European Community*, Edward Elgar, Aldershot, 1989.

Lasok, D., and J. W. Bridge: *Law and Institutions of the European Communities*, 4th ed., Butterworths, London, 1987.

Lodge, Juliet (ed.): *The European Community and the Challenge of the Future*, Pinter, London, 1989.

_____: "EC Policymaking: Institutional Considerations," in Lodge (ed.), pp. 26–57.

_____: "1989: Edging towards 'Genuine' Euro-elections?" in Juliet Lodge (ed.), *The 1989 Election of the European Parliament*, Macmillan, Basingstoke, 1990, pp. 210–235.

Mackie, Thomas T. (ed.): *Europe Votes 3: The European Parliament Elections of 1989*, Dartmouth, Aldershot, 1990.

Niedermayer, Oskar: "Turnout in the European Elections," *Electoral Studies*, vol. 9, no. 1, 1990, pp. 45–50.

Nugent, Neill: *The Government and Politics of the European Community*, Macmillan, Basingstoke, 1989.

Philip, Alan Butt: "The Application of the EEC Regulations on Drivers' Hours and Tachographs," in Siedentopf and Ziller, pp. 88–129 (1988a).

_____: "The Application of the Transport Regulations by the Administration of the Member States," in Siedentopf and Ziller, pp. 181–189 (1988b).

Pinder, John: "The Single Market: A Step Towards European Union," in Lodge (ed.), pp. 94–110.

Pracht, Louis (ed.): *Europe in Figures*, 2d ed., Office for Official Publications of the European Communities, Luxembourg, 1989.

Pryce, Roy (ed.): *The Dynamics of European Union*, Croom Helm, London, 1987.

Sargent, Jane A.: "Corporatism and the European Community," in Wyn Grant (ed.), *The Political Economy of Corporatism*, Macmillan, Basingstoke, 1985, pp. 229–253.

Shackleton, Michael: "The Budget of the European Community," in Lodge (ed.), pp. 129–147.

Siedentopf, Heinrich, and Christoph Hauschild: "The Implementation of Community Legislation by the Member States: A Comparative Analysis," in Siedentopf and Ziller, pp. 1–87.

——— and Jacques Ziller (eds.): *Making European Policies Work: The Implementation of Community Legislation in the Member States*, Sage, London, 1988.

Taylor, Paul: "The New Dynamics of EC Integration in the 1980s," in Lodge (ed.), pp. 3–25.

Tutt, Nigel: *Europe on the Fiddle: The Common Market Scandal*, Christopher Helm, Bromley, 1989.

Urwin, Derek W.: *Western Europe since 1945: A Political History*, 4th ed., Longmans, London and New York, 1989.

Verney, Susannah: "To Be or Not to Be within the European Community: The Party Debate and Democratic Consolidation in Greece," in Geoffrey Pridham (ed.), *Securing Democracy: Political Parties and Democratic Consolidation in Southern Europe*, Routledge, London and New York, 1990, pp. 203–223.

Wallace, Helen: "Negotiation, Conflict and Compromise: The Elusive Pursuit of Common Policies," in Helen Wallace, William Wallace, and Carole Webb (eds.), *Policy-Making in the European Community*, 2d ed., John Wiley, Chichester and New York, 1983, pp. 43–80.

———: "The Presidency of the Council of Ministers of the European Communities: A Comparative Perspective," in Colm O Nuallain (ed.), *The Presidency of the European Council of Ministers*, Croom Helm, London, 1985, pp. 261–279.

INDEX